Jesus: This is the picture I want in My messages. When you read these messages, look at My picture and know I love you. These messages are My words of love for each of you.

Open Anywhere

Love, Jesus

I give my heart to Jesus and Mary with you in love.

GOD'S
BLUE BOOK 15
Life

The Mass is the Sacrifice of Calvary Sacramentally Made Present

Rita Ring

Fr. Edward J. Carter S.J.

Shepherds of Christ Publications

Shepherds of Christ Publications
P.O. Box 627
China, Indiana 47250 USA

Tel: (812) 273-8405
Toll free: (888) 211-3041
Fax: (812) 273-3182
Email: info@sofc.org
http://www.sofc.org

Shepherds of Christ Publishing recognizes and accepts that the final authority regarding private revelation rests with the Holy See of Rome, to whose judgment we willingly submit.

This book is published by Shepherds of Christ Publications, a subsidiary of Shepherds of Christ Ministries, a tax exempt, religious public charitable corporation organized to foster devotion to the Two Hearts, the Sacred Heart of Jesus and the Immaculate Heart of Mary.

ISBN: 978-1-934222-47-8

First Printing: June, 2015.

Scriptural quotations are taken from
The New Jerusalem Bible, Doubleday & Co.
Imprimatur granted by Cardinal Hume.

Prayer for Union With Jesus

Come to me, Lord, and possess my soul. Come into my heart and permeate my soul. Help me to sit in silence with You and let You work in my heart.

I am Yours to possess. I am Yours to use. I want to be selfless and only exist in You. Help me to spoon out all that is me and be an empty vessel ready to be filled by You. Help me to die to myself and live only for You. Use me as You will. Let me never draw my attention back to myself. I only want to operate as You do, dwelling within me.

I am Yours, Lord. I want to have my life in You. I want to do the will of the Father. Give me the strength to put aside the world and let You operate my very being. Help me to act as You desire. Strengthen me against the distractions of the devil to take me from Your work.

When I worry, I have taken my focus off of You and placed it on myself. Help me not to give in to the promptings of others to change what in my heart You are making very clear to me. I worship You, I adore You and I love You. Come and dwell in me now.

January 17, 1994

Dedicated to Pope Francis

Dedication of These Writings

I dedicate this book to my beloved Jesus and to my Mother Mary.

This is a labor of love. I present this book to My loving Father in the Holy Spirit, through the pierced Heart of Jesus with My Mother Mary at my side.

This book was given by Mary and Jesus to help in the renewal of the Church and the world. I dedicate this book to the Sacred Heart and the Immaculate Heart.

Mary appeared as Our Lady of Clearwater in Clearwater, Florida, December 17, 1996.

Introduction

R. To my dear mother, I dedicate this note to my mother, Alice, for all her prayers for me, for guiding me in the greatest way in my life, from heaven.

I dedicate this book to Fr. Carter, my best friend, who has taught me endlessly about our beloved God. I have shared these mystical experiences with Fr. Carter. It is in living in one mind and one heart with each other, united to the Mass, in the Hearts of Jesus and Mary, in the Holy Spirit, that we will light the world with the fire of God's love.

The key message from Fatima is to join in one mind and one heart in the Hearts of Jesus and Mary and be united at every moment to the Mass. We unite all our sacrifices to the Holy Sacrifice of the Mass, all over the world.

We are helping to bring down great grace on the Church and the world when we give our lives as a sacrifice united to the Mass.

The bell tolls at every moment of our lives and graces and mercies are released through the sacrifice of the Mass.

My act of loving at every moment united to the Masses going on around the world is an act of helping souls. I offer my life to the Father in the Holy Spirit, in union with the Holy Sacrifice of the Mass, with all the angels and saints and the souls in purgatory, through the powerful intercession of Mary, our spiritual Mother.

Grace and mercy will be spilled out on the earth. God calls us to dwell in the Hearts of Jesus and Mary and unite to the Holy Sacrifice of the Mass.

I thank my daughter Cathy for her endless hours of service. No one can imagine how generously she has given herself to God's work.

I thank Ellen for her endless hours of typing, manuscript after manuscript, newsletter after newsletter.

4/19/96

We want Adoration Chapels
around the world –
The Mighty Medicine

Table of Contents

Title	Date	pg
A Message from Florida	April 1, 1997	1
History	April 6, 1997	3
Letter to Fr. Carter's Provincial from Ellen	April 8, 1997	9
Thoughts on the Mass by Fr. Carter	March/April 1997	12
Love Gives	April 9, 1997	16
April 10th God the Father	April 10, 1997	22
The 13ths	Concerning April 13	24
Glorious Mysteries At Our Lady of the Holy Spirit Center	April 13, 1997	25
Pray in Crisis	April 14, 1997	46
God the Father: To All Florida Apostles	April 16, 1997	47
A Letter to Tom	April 16, 1997	47
Spread My Love	April 16, 1997	48
To Apostles in Florida	April 17, 1997	49
Directions From Jesus	April 21, 1997	50
To Shepherds of Christ Associates	April 21, 1997	52
Jesus and Mary's Picture on Cover	April 25 6:00 a.m.	54
Will You Help Me	April 25, 1997	57
A Second Letter to Tom	April 25, 1997	57
A Letter to the Provincial from Rita Ring	April 29, 1997	58
The Mass – Fr. Carter/Rita Ring At St. Gertrude Church	May 1, 1997	62
A Leader in the Shepherds of Christ Movement	May 1, 1997	84
Lay Apostles of the Shepherds of Christ Movement	May 3, 1997	86
Mary is Mother	May 3, 1997	88
Joyful Mysteries - Morrow, Ohio	May 4, 1997	89
Mary is the New Eve	May 5, 1997	105
The Litany	May 6, 1997	108
Life is, Not Life If It is Not Rooted in Him	May 7, 1997	108
Satan Wants to Tear Apart - Bloody Friday	May 9, 1997	114

Sorrowful Mysteries - Morrow, Ohio	May 11, 1997	117
Running for Cover	May 13, 1997	136
Glorious Mysteries - Rosary on Tom's Farm	May 13, 1997	137
The Events That Day	May 13, 1997	162
From the Internet - Mary's Head Broke Off	May 13, 1997	163
Glorious Mysteries - Morrow, Ohio	May 18, 1997	167
The Mass	May 22, 1997	181
Mary Loved God's Will	May 22, 1997	188
The Spouse of the Lamb	May 22, 1997	190
This Movement is for the Renewal of the Church and the World	May 27, 1997	191
The Mass - A Journey into the Heart of Jesus	May 27, 1997	194
Sorrowful Mysteries - Morrow, Ohio Feast of the Precious Body and Blood of Jesus	June 1, 1997	195
A Letter from Rita	June 2, 1997	215
Ministries of Shepherds of Christ	June 3, 1997	220
A Letter to a Donor	June 3, 1997	221
Satan Wants You to Focus on Yourselves	June 4, 1997	223
Glorious Mysteries - Morrow, Ohio Rosary with Rita Ring	June 5, 1997	224
Feast of the Immaculate Heart of Mary Sorrowful Mysteries - Toledo, Ohio	June 7, 1997	244
Feast of the Immaculate Heart of Mary	June 7, 1997	261
Glorious Mysteries - Morrow, Ohio	June 8, 1997	263
Two Visions at Falmouth	June 8, 1997	284
Vision of a Flood	June 8, 1997	286
Fr. Carter and My Writings, Antidote for Poison	June 8, 1997	295
Fr. Carter and Rita's Writings as One	June 9, 1997	296
Jesus Says Your Joint Writings, Fr. Carter and Rita, are Important	June 9, 1997	296
All Different Love Relationships	June 9 11:00 p.m.	300
My Mother	June 10, 1997	304
God the Father Wants Us to be One With Him	June 10, 1997	305

35th Anniversary of Fr. Carter's Ordination	June 10, 1997	306
Mary: I Stood Beneath the Cross	June 10, 1997	309
Priestly Newsletter May/June 1997	May/June 1997	312
The Elements	June 14, 1997	331
Priestly Newsletter - Thoughts on the Eucharist	Jan/Feb 1997	337
Priestly Newsletter - Fr. Carter quoted the Mass Book	March/April 1997	338
A Letter to Core Leaders	June 14, 1997	341
Mary: Don't Offend God	June 14, 1997	344
Joyful Mysteries - Morrow, Ohio	June 15, 1997	345
Mother's Day Picture 1995	June 1997	360
Jesus the King of Kings	June 20, 1997	361
One Flock and One Shepherd	June 20, 1997	365
Sorrowful Mysteries - Morrow, Ohio	June 22, 1997	368
Sufferings of the Body	June 25, 1997	389
The Pain - Naples, Florida	June 26, 1995	390
Wolves	June 26, 1997	396
Glorious Mysteries - Morrow, Ohio	June 29, 1997	398
Listen to My Messages	June 30, 1997	417
Introduction to the Shepherds of Christ Prayer Manual		419
Shepherds of Christ Prayers		420
Holy Spirit Novena		431
Song: *A Song From Jesus*		446
Prayer to the Father	May 16, 1998	447
A Prayer before the Holy Sacrifice of the Mass	Dec 27, 1995	448
Prayer for Union with Jesus	Jan 17, 1994	449
Shepherds of Christ Prayer Cards and Books		450
Other Available Books from Shepherds of Christ		451
We Pray for You		456

Introduction to Blue Book 15

Fr. Edward Carter, S.J.

Founder of Shepherds of Christ - Rita's Spiritual Director
Rita Ring, Co-founder of Shepherds of Christ

Excerpt from *Response in Christ* - Chapter 4
by Fr. Edward J. Carter, S.J.

In schematic outline we have discussed the manner in which the baptized Christian extends his Mass to his daily existence. As he so lives out his Mass, he is becoming more Christlike. He becomes a more perfect priest and victim for his next participation in the eucharistic sacrifice.[42] The beautiful cycle which the Mass contains lies exposed before us. As part of this cycle the Christian is intimately involved in the process of continued redemption. The Mass is the center of the Christian life: ". . . the liturgy *is* the summit toward which the activity of the Church is directed; at the same time it is the fount from which all her power flows." [43]

42. For a current treatment of the varied richness of the Eucharist, cf. J. Wicks, "The Movement of Eucharistic Theology" in *Chicago Studies*,Vol. 10 (1971), pp. 267-284.

43. *The Constitution on the Sacred Liturgy*, No. 10.

Given November 21, 2013

Jesus: I call you to live your lives as devout members of the mystical body of Christ. I have given these writings that men will realize that they are to live united deeply to the Mass going on around the world. Your lives, given as an offering, a sacrifice every moment in union with the Mass going on around the world. Your life, a sacrifice, offered to the Father, in union with the Mass in oneness with Me, in the Holy Spirit through the intercession of the Blessed Mother with all the angels and saints and the souls in purgatory.

Your lives given as members of My mystical body can help to bring down great graces for the priest, the Church and the world.

The Mass is the Sacrifice of Calvary sacramentally made present.

The Eucharist

- The death-resurrection of Jesus, which is encountered in a special way through the sacraments, is most especially renewed in the Eucharistic Sacrifice. Consequently, we can see the logical connection between the sacraments and the Mass. Indeed, all of the sacraments point to the Eucharistic Sacrifice.

- *At the Last Supper, on the night He was betrayed, our Saviour instituted the Eucharistic Sacrifice of His Body and Blood. He did this in order to perpetuate the sacrifice of the Cross throughout the centuries until He should come again, and so to entrust to His beloved spouse, the Church, a memorial of His death and resurrection: a sacrament of love, a sign of unity, a bond of charity, a paschal banquet in which Christ is consumed, the mind is filled with grace, and a pledge of future glory is given to us (Vatican II, Constitution on the Sacred Liturgy, No. 17)*[26]

- *The Church, therefore, earnestly desires that Christ's faithful, when present at this mystery of faith, should not be there as strangers or silent spectators. On the contrary, through a proper appreciation of the rites and prayers they should participate knowingly, devoutly, and actively. They should be instructed by God's word and be refreshed at the table of the Lord's body; they should give thanks to God; by offering the Immaculate Victim, not only through the hands of the priest, but also with him, they should learn to offer themselves too. Through Christ the Mediator, they should be drawn day by day into ever closer union with God and with each other, so that finally God may be all in all.* (*Constitution on the Sacred Liturgy, No. 48*) [27]

- *Through the Eucharistic Sacrifice Christ the Lord desired to set before us in a very special way this remarkable union whereby we are united one with another and with our divine Head, a union that no word of praise can ever sufficiently express. For in this sacrifice the sacred ministers act not only as the representative of our Saviour, but as the representative of the whole Mystical Body and of each one of the faithful. Again, in this act of sacrifice, the faithful of Christ, united by the common bond of devotion and prayer, offer to the eternal Father through the hands of the priest, whose prayer alone has made it present on the altar, the Immaculate Lamb, the most acceptable victim of praise and propitiation for the Church's universal need. Moreover, just as the divine Redeemer, while dying on the Cross, offered Himself to the eternal Father as Head of the whole human race, so now, 'in this clean oblation' He not only offers Himself as Head of the Church to His heavenly Father but in Himself His mystical members as well. He embraces them all, yes, even the weaker and more ailing members, with the deepest love of His Heart. (Pope Pius XII, Mystici Corporis AAS, XXXV, 232-233)*[28]

- Pope John Paul II states: "This worship, given therefore to the Trinity of the Father and of the Son and of the Holy Spirit, above all accompanies and permeates the celebration of the Eucharistic Liturgy. But it must fill our churches also outside the timetable of Masses. Indeed, since the Eucharistic Mystery was instituted out of love, and makes Christ sacramentally present, it is worthy of thanksgiving and worship. And this worship must be prominent in all our encounters with the Blessed Sacrament, both when we visit our churches and when the sacred species are taken to the sick and administered to them.

"Adoration of Christ in this sacrament of love must also find expression *in various forms of Eucharistic devotion:* personal prayer before the Blessed Sacrament, Hours of Adoration, periods of exposition — short, prolonged and annual (Forty Hours) - Eucharistic benediction, Eucharistic processions, Eucharistic congresses. A particular mention should be made at this point of the Solemnity of the Body and Blood of Christ as an act of public worship rendered to Christ present in the Eucharist, a feast instituted by my predecessor Urban IV in memory of the institution of this great Mystery.

"All this therefore corresponds to the general principles and particular norms already long in existence, but newly formulated during or after the Second Vatican Council.

"...The Church and the world have a great need of Eucharistic worship. Jesus waits for us in this sacrament of love. Let us be generous with our time in going to meet Him in adoration and in contemplation that is full of faith and ready to make reparation for the great faults and crimes of the world. May our adoration never cease."[29]

• The following words of Fr. M. Raymond, O.C.S.O., emphasize the great importance regarding personal holiness and one's participation in the Mass: "Mass, insomuch as it is Christ's offering, is not only always acceptable to God, but is of infinite value as well.

"But, inasmuch as it is your offering and mine, and that of every other member of the Mystical Body ... we can limit the effectiveness of God's great Act of Love; we finite beings can set bounds to the veritable flood of God-life made possible by the Infinite Son of the Infinite Father."[30]

Yes, the effectiveness of each Mass, which makes the sacrifice of Calvary sacramentally present, depends in part on the holiness of the entire Church offering it with Christ to the Father in the Holy Spirit, including the holiness of the individual priest offering and the holiness of his participating congregation.

- The Sacrifice of Calvary is sacramentally made present in the Mass. When we pray the Morning Offering Prayer, united to the Holy Sacrifice of the Mass, we act as intercessors, pleading to God that great graces be released all day through our prayerful actions as we act in love according to the Father's will. Whether we are eating, taking care of a sick parent, enjoying time spent with a friend, working at our job, we can help bring down great graces for the world.

  When we pray the Morning Offering Prayer we offer our lives to the Father, through Christ, in the Holy Spirit, with the prayerful assistance of Mary, our Mother. Let us pray together united in our hearts in the Holy Sacrifice of the Mass. There follows a Morning Offering Prayer.

"My dear Father, I offer You this day all my prayers, works, joys, and sufferings in union with Jesus in the Holy Sacrifice of the Mass, in the Holy Spirit.

"I unite with our Mother, Mary, all the angels and saints, and all the souls in purgatory to pray to the Father for myself, for each member of my family, for my friends, for all the people throughout the world, for all the souls in purgatory, and for all other intentions of the Sacred Heart.

"I love You, Jesus, and I give You my heart. I love you, Mary, and I give you my heart. Amen."[32]

26. *The Documents of Vatican II*, "Constitution on the Sacred Liturgy", America Press Edition, No. 17.

27. *Ibid*, No. 48.

28. Pope Pius XII, Encyclical Letter, *Mystici Corporis*, AAS XXXV, pp. 232-233.

29. Letter of Pope John Paul II, *The Mystery and Worship of the Eucharist*, Pauline Books and Media, No. 3.

30. M. Raymond, O.C.S.O. *This Is Love*, Bruce, p. 106.

32. Rita Ring, *Rosary Meditations for Parents and Children*, Shepherds of Christ Ministries, p. 189.

Hebrews 10: 11-17

Every priest stands at his duties every day, offering over and over again the same sacrifices which are quite incapable of taking away sins. He, on the other hand, has offered one single sacrifice for sins, and then *taken his seat for ever, at the right hand of God,* where he is now waiting *till his enemies are made his footstool.* By virtue of that one single offering, he has achieved the eternal perfection of all who are sanctified. The Holy Spirit attests this to us, for after saying:

No, this is the covenant I will make with them, when those days have come.

the Lord says:

In their minds I will plant my Laws writing them on their hearts, and I shall never more call their sins to mind, or their offences.

The Theology of Consecration

A. Boussard gives an extremely fine and concise sketch of the theology of consecration:

"By the Incarnation, in and of itself, the Humanity of Jesus is consecrated, so that in becoming Man, Jesus is ipso facto constituted Savior, Prophet, King, Priest, and Victim of the One Sacrifice that was to save the world. He is the 'Anointed', par excellence, the 'Christ' totally belonging to God, His Humanity being that of the Word and indwelled by the Holy Spirit. When, by a free act of His human will, He accepts what He is, doing what He was sent to do, He can say that He consecrates 'Himself'. In Christ, therefore, what might be called His 'subjective' consecration is a perfect response to the 'objective' consecration produced in His Humanity through the Incarnation.

"And what Christ does brings with it is a 'consecration' for His disciples, a very special belonging to God, since He imparts to them His own life precisely by making them participate in His own consecration.

"Through Baptism Christians also are consecrated and 'anointed' by the power of the Spirit. They share, in their measure, in the essential consecration of Christ, in His character of King, Priest, and Prophet (cf. 1 Peter 2:9; 7 Peter 1:3-4; Rev. 5:9, etc.). With Christ and through Christ, they are 'ordered' to the glory of God and the salvation of the world. They do not belong to themselves. They belong to Christ the Lord, who imparts His own life to them…

"The vocation of those who have been baptized is to 'live' this consecration by a voluntary adherence — and one that is as perfect as possible — to what it has made of them. Living as 'children of God', they fulfill subjectively their objective consecration; like Jesus, they consecrate themselves. This is the deeper meaning of vows and baptismal promises, together with the actual way of life corresponding to them. The baptismal consecration is the fundamental one, constitutive of the Christian. All consecrations which come after it presuppose and are rooted in it…"[3]

3. A. Boussard in *Dictionary of Mary*, Catholic Book Publishing Co., pp. 54-55.

St. John Eudes On Union With Jesus

"You belong to the Son of God, but more than that, you ought to be in him as members are in the head. All that is in you must be incorporated into him. You must receive life from him and be ruled by him. There will be no true life for you except in him, for he is the one source of true life. Apart from him you will find only death and destruction. Let him be the only source of your movements, of the actions and the strength of your life. He must be both the source and the purpose of your life, so that you may fulfill these words: *None of us lives as his own master and none of us dies as his own master. While we live, we are responsible to the Lord, and when we die, we die as his servants. Both in life and death we are the Lord's. That is why Christ died and came to life again, that he might be Lord of both the dead and the living.*

"Finally, you are one with Jesus as the body is one with the head. You must, then, have one breath with him, one soul, one life, one will, one mind, one heart. And he must be your breath, heart, love, life, your all. These great gifts in the follower of Christ originate from baptism. They are increased and strengthened through confirmation and by making good use of other graces that are given by God. Through the holy eucharist they are brought to perfection."[4]

4. St. John Eudes, from a treatise on the Admirable Heart of Jesus, as in *The Liturgy of the Hours,* Catholic Book Publishing Co., Vol. IV, pp. 1331-32.

Luke 22: 19-20

Then he took bread, and when he had given thanks, he broke it and gave it to them, saying, 'This is my body given for you; do this in remembrance of me.' He did the same with the cup after supper, and said, 'This cup is the new covenant in my blood poured out for you.

Thoughts on the Eucharist

• The Eucharist is not only a very special contact with God in Christ. In Christ we also relate to the other members of the Church. In receiving the Eucharist we pledge ourselves to deepen our love-union with all members of the Body which is the Church. We pledge to use these means which foster union. We determine to avoid that which causes selfish divisiveness.

The Eucharist also reminds us of our relationship with the entire human family. Jesus died and rose for all. The Eucharistic making-present of this paschal mystery nourishes our determination to assist in the work of ongoing redemption. The light of the Eucharist points to what we should be doing. The strength of the Eucharist assists us to so act in behalf of all.

The Eucharist, then, possesses the richest capacity to help us maintain and develop our personal relationship with God, the members of the Church, and all other members of the human family. And it will do just this if we surrender to its love, its power, its beauty.

• Henri Nouwen observes: "Jesus is God-for-us. Jesus is God giving himself completely, pouring himself out for us without reserve. Jesus doesn't hold back or cling to his own possessions...He gives all this to us...'Eat, drink, this is My body, this is My blood...this is Me for you!'"[5]

5. Henri Nouwen, *With Burning Hearts*, Orbis Books, p. 67.

Thoughts on the Eucharist

The Eucharist is our chief source for growth in the Christ-life. There follow some thoughts on this magnificent Gift of Jesus to us.

- When Jesus speaks of His Blood as the "Blood of the Covenant" (Mt 26:28), we are reminded that blood sealed or ratified the Mosaic covenant at Mount Sinai. Moses sprinkled sacrificial blood upon the altar, which represented God, and upon the Jewish people. Because blood was a distinctive symbol of life for the Jewish people, such an action had a deep significance for them. This action of Moses symbolized the sealing or ratification of the covenant—a new life relationship between Yahweh and the Jewish people.

  The sacrificial Blood of Jesus has also formed a covenant — the New Covenant. In the shedding of His Blood, Jesus has established a new life relationship between His Father and the human race. Forming a core, focal point of the redeemed human race are the members of the Christian community, the Church. The Eucharist, in recalling and making sacramentally present the shedding of Jesus' covenant Blood, is the Church's great covenant act. The Eucharist sustains the life of the covenant, nourishes it, causes it to grow. Through participation in the Eucharistic liturgy we should be growing in our covenant life. We should be developing a greater love-union with the Father, Son and Holy Spirit. We should be growing in a sense of community, in a deep love for the Church, in a desire to contribute our share to the building up of the body of Christ. We should be learning to curb our selfishness, this selfishness which deadens a dynamic concern for the Christian community and the entire human race. Participation in the Eucharist should also be curbing divisive jealousy, forming us more and more as persons who want deeply to love all so that it can be more often said of us, "See those Christians, how they love one another." The Eucharist can more radically shape us according to these covenant attitudes if we allow it to do so. We repent over the times we have resisted. We rejoice regarding the times we have opened ourselves to the Eucharist's transformative power.

Given March 13, 2015

R. We should pray with all of our hearts united as one – as never before –

We pray to the Father – united to Jesus in the Holy Sacrifice of the Mass, (the Sacrifice of Calvary, sacramentally made present)

We pray in the Holy Spirit with all the angels and saints and the souls in purgatory – through the powerful intercession of Mary, Our Lady of Clearwater –

Pray with me, now, with all of your heart –

We pray for the pope, for all cardinals, for all bishops, all priests –

We pray for all of us, all members and donors and all their families, all our families.

We pray for anyone who touches all these people –

We spread the Blood of Jesus on all mentioned – on China and the Florida site and on the whole Church – the whole world –

We cast the devil far, far from this place, from all mentioned – the whole Church and the whole world –

We want to Consecrate to the Hearts of Jesus and Mary in as far as we are able

1) all mentioned people

2) the priests, the Church and the world.

We beg for a special outpouring of the Holy Spirit – on all mentioned – the Church and the world –

We love You God, we love You so much.

We worship You God.
We adore You God.
We give You Our Hearts.

Amen.

In uniting ourselves as one this way – we pray deeply for the Church and for the world. We pray for all who are receiving the Easter mailing –

Dear God – hear our prayer –

We love You – We love You – We love You –

Say the Morning Offering every day at the end –
Say the Holy Spirit Novena at the end.
Pray the Shepherds of Christ Prayers at the end.
Listen to every word deeply in the Mass.
Block out distractions.
Stay focused on the Mass –
Pray for the Church and the world and your intentions.
Beg for grace to be outpoured.
See Jesus before You on the Cross.
Hear Jesus say –
"I love you, I love you, I love you"

Jesus: I am the Sacred Heart – the Heart of pure and tender love – I love You so much –

R. The incarnation goes on in us. We are witnesses in the world.

Every action – Every prayer in our lives is united to the Mass – It is a Font of God's Grace.

The Divine Bridegroom gave His Life on the cross and He rose from the dead victorious on the third day. The sacrifice of Calvary is sacramentally made present in the Mass today. We unite to it pleading as a body for ourselves, the Church and the world. We beg for grace from our Divine Bridegroom. As members of the Church we live as His spouse our bridal union all day.

Christ is Chief Priest and Mediator. We are His flock, the ones He came to save.

Yes, the Good Shepherd laid down His life for us. And it is in this that we must lay down our lives daily in the Morning Offering, offering all we do as a sacrifice united to the Holy Sacrifice of the Mass and great grace will be released for souls. We can identify with Him in this that we offer everything we do in trying to please Him and serve Him as a sacrifice united to the Mass. The more we tell others to pray the Morning Offering, the more people will lay down their lives for souls and the more grace will be released for the troubled hearts.

end of Introduction

A Message from Florida

Message given through Rita Ring

Jesus: You are the leader. There will be no one in line behind you. You may be on the hill and look around and no one will appear to be near, but I am there in the silence of that moment. Know I am with you. The Father and the Holy Spirit are with you. You are one with My Mother and are surrounded by angels and saints.

The world is blind and they do not see. You must see with spiritual vision. See the world beyond. It is real. You are not alone. I am with you at every second, watching you and controlling your breath.

If you cease to believe, who will be the leader? All I have called through you must realize they are the leaders. No one may appear to be near, no one is in line behind you.

You must be constantly motivated by faith. It comes down to this – it is your belief. For, if I call you and you do not hear Me, then My work will not get done. For I am calling you and you can plug up your ears, but souls are being lost at this very moment that you can be helping through your faith. You must have fervor in your prayers.

Satan attacks you all day, in prayer and in work. Will you listen to him or to Me?

I am begging you to see Me alive before you as I came forth from the tomb, glistening and all white. I am here. I have called you by name. You are the apostles I am calling. If you say 'no' the work will not get done.

Read this letter over and over and when you are alone and feel as if you are standing on the hill by yourself see the heavens open up. See Me in celestial light as you saw Me transfigured on the altar. See the great vision of March 26, 1996. Read that message. See Me almost dead on the cross as I was on December 5, 1996 at Immaculata. See My lips move and hear Me speak. No one is listening. They will hear you speak. They will respond to you.

If you give into satan, they will not hear and they will not know for his whole attempt is to silence you.

So you go to the hilltop. You are close to Me. You look

around and you see no one. Below the hill is a throng of people. They have forgotten I exist. The heavens open and I appear and the sky is filled with saints and angels. They continue talking and laughing at the bottom of the hill. The celestial light falls upon them and they continue as in a fog and as blind men to focus on the rocks and the things of this earth.

And you speak. The voice they hear is your voice from the top of the mountain. You appear to be alone by these blind men, but the heavenly court has surrounded you and you see not with earthly vision but with the eyes of faith and you speak in My Name...

"Glory and Praise to God! Hear the words of your Savior. Listen from the mountain top for He has risen and we are His witnesses."

He calls you from the mountain and you say nay for your foolish whims. Come to the mountain top with Me and you will taste of milk sweeter than honey. You will run and not get weary, you will be His faithful witnesses. You will be the children of light shining from the mountain top on the dark world below.

Oh, do not say no, My chosen ones, you are My children of light. I have called and you have responded. Do not be discouraged, but encouraged for (she) appears, the Lady of Light, the Lady of Fatima, the Lady of the Holy Rosary. She appears Our Lady in Clearwater to bring about the completion of the Fatima message there. If you do not believe, who will I send to do the work for I have chosen you!

The Fatima mission will greatly unfold there through the Shepherds of Christ Movement. She appears Our Lady of Light in all the splendor to call her children to her Son, Jesus. She appears as Our Lady of Fatima, 80 years later, to call to the world, to deliver the same message she delivered then. Come to the water and drink and you will not be thirsty for God has visited His people. He has risen. He sends great gifts in the woman clothed as the sun on your building. Some look and they do not see. Some are touched for their hearts are open to the graces that are pouring out there.

Mary: I appear to you, the woman clothed as the sun, Our Lady of Fatima, in splendor and glory to lead a sick race to holiness, to lead them to healing in the Heart of my Son.

For His Heart will reign despite all the actions of men. I appear Our Lady of Fatima on the (former) bank in Florida to you this day. This is my message. This is my little Fatima in the Americas. A permanent sign I give to you this day on the building, a sign for the world and for you.

And you, my chosen one, have faith for it is faith that will save you. The devil wants you stopped. If you listen to him, who will lead the people to my Son? You have been called and chosen by me, Our Lady of Fatima, the woman clothed as the sun and there will be the weeping and gnashing of teeth for many will be lost forever. I send you in the darkness as a beacon light to the world.

I love you. I am your Mother Mary.

4/1/97

From Blue Book 14 - March 31, 1997 (excerpt)

I am Mary, your Mother. I will continue to talk to you, my priest-son, as our Lady of Fatima from my Florida apparition site.

I give you my Son Jesus, born in the town of Bethlehem.

I appear on a former bank to bring about the Reign of His Heart. These are His messages of love given to all.

I love you my son. I am your Mother. I hold you in my arms and press you as a tender child to my breast. You are my priest son and I love you so much.

Love, Mary

History

Message for Fr. Carter

R. My dear priest,

I thank you for everything you have permitted to allow us to do the work of Jesus in the Shepherds of Christ Movement.

At Fatima Mary told us we must give our hearts to her and the Heart of her Son Jesus. She promised peace in the world if we (1) consecrate our hearts to her and her Son; (2) pray the Rosary; (3) observe the First Saturday devotion; and (4) make reparation to Their Hearts. She appeared and told us if we did not respond there would be World War II.

I submit to the teachings of the Church as the final authority for all private revelation.

This was the Plan of the Father as revealed to me through the messages I received from Mary and Jesus, and in January 1997 from the Father.

I was told to go to Our Lady of the Holy Spirit Center in June 1993. Mary appeared here in the Cincinnati area to call her children to consecrate their hearts to her. In so doing, the Holy Spirit would work in them and they would be brought forth children of light. Mary appeared as the Lady of Light. As children of light we would know God and love Him in such a way as never before. We would have the light and in knowing Him in this intense way we will help to spread the devotion to the Two Hearts. Jesus says He was showing us things never shown before. We would receive lights to know God most intimately through the workings of the Holy Spirit.

Mary leads us to Jesus. Mary appeared to lead men deeply into the Heart of her Son. Mary promised at Fatima that in the end the Sacred Heart of Jesus would Reign and the Immaculate Heart of Mary would triumph. And, so, we go from the state of the world today to know there will be an era of great peace and love where men will love God with the most intimate love as never before, where they will be so united with each other in the great love as the Father intends us to be: One holy, happy family, loving God and one another as His holy family with God, as our Father, and Mary as our Mother. God calls us to this spiritual family – to know God as our family. Mary is our Mother.

Mary called and appeared here in Cincinnati - this was the initial stage. Jesus called me to the Holy Spirit Center to deliver His love letters to help bring about the Reign of His Heart.

The books Jesus has asked me to write are the books of love stories. This book has not been written like this by Jesus before. It is written by Jesus to His people. It is centered in the most intimate love affair with God. Jesus outpours His grace to us when we sit in front of the tabernacle and stay after communion and attend daily Mass. God gives us a sharing in His life in baptism and Jesus saturates us with His life and when we read His letters of love, our hearts burn with greater intimacy with Him.

This is the final stage to help bring about this new era in which the Sacred Heart of Jesus will reign in men's hearts.

Jesus loves men with burning love and wants a burning love relationship with men. Jesus calls out, "I am alive, I am alive, I am alive. I am treated by many as a dead object." Jesus wants the souls to come and long for Him and thirst for Him and pour out their love to Him. This takes tremendous grace to be this close to Jesus. Jesus outpours His grace to us in the Holy Eucharist and when we sit in front of the tabernacle. This is what Jesus wants from all souls. Jesus does not want us to come to the Mass with cold hearts. Jesus does not want them to throw heartless words at Him. Jesus wants our hearts to burn for love of Him. Jesus wants us mystically united to God and to one another in great love that we would give our lives for Him and love each other. Jesus wants us to give our hearts to Him and His Mother in consecration. When the people in the Church and the priest do this we are deeply united. We are one in Their Hearts and are united in a deep, holy union and the Church is a powerhouse of His burning love. The Eucharist is the Power. It is Christ Himself. Jesus wants the Mass to be the greatest love affair between God and man when He gives Himself to us and we give ourselves to Him. He wants the Mass and the reception of the Eucharist to be the most intimate union between God and man. Now at Mass most of the people get up and leave right after communion and our Beloved Lord is giving Himself in the greatest love to them. Oh, Jesus wants intimacy and love!

This is the message He delivered in *God's Blue Books* and *Rosaries from the Hearts of Jesus and Mary.* It is a love story to help bring about the Reign of His Most Sacred Heart.

The Fatima message has been greatly blocked for 80 years. The devil does not want the Sacred Heart of Jesus to reign in hearts and the Immaculate Heart of Mary to triumph.

Look how they persecuted Christ. I have been asked to deliver these messages that men will love God with the deepest love. That they will go deeper into the Heart of Christ and know His most intimate love.

Mary appeared over and over and over again to call her children to consecration of their hearts and lead them to the

Heart of her Son. In Cincinnati Mary appeared and appeared as Our Lady of Light and Our Lady of the Holy Rosary to help bring about the completion of the Fatima message. The appearances were to lead men to these messages of most intimate love of Jesus that would take them deeply into His Heart.

Mary appeared to me. Mary gave signs at Cold Springs and the Falmouth Farm and the Holy Spirit Center. Many lives were touched by these appearances. The devil does not want people sitting in front of the tabernacle. Jesus wants all to know His intimate love.

After one month of intense messages (some of these are Blue Book II - March 7, 1994 and March 13, 1994) and after futile attempts to deliver the messages on March 20, 1994 I received a most strong message from Jesus. I cried and cried. The end of the building collapsed on March 22, 1994 – the old Cincinnati Seminary where most Cincinnati priests went.

They ignored Jesus' messages to me. The messages continued to be blocked and on May 4th, 1994 (Blue Book 3) I received a message from Jesus on loving God and loving one another. Jesus wanted the messages out on the Falmouth Farm. They refused to put the message out on the Farm even after you (Fr. Carter) told them they needed to do it.

A person responsible for taking the messages to the printer for June 8th took the message of Jesus off the back of the paper and left the messages from other visionaries on the front.

The first Blue Book went out in May, 1994. Thank you for discerning this and supporting the messages.

From this point on, and the continuing time I was at Our Lady of the Holy Spirit Center, Jesus and Mary's messages, given through me, were blocked. They would go through periods when a few were released, when the books were allowed to be sold and they would be taken off of the shelf.

Mary appeared every day for 14 months at Our Lady of the Holy Spirit Center. Jesus told you in a message, you received, to go every day. You then went for 4 months when Mary appeared to me. Jesus told you, in that message, to lead the rosary. Mary appeared as Our Lady of Light in the back of the chapel to me.

God the Father called, through Mary, to lead them to the burning messages of her Son, Jesus, which would then lead people to the tabernacle and loving Him in the Eucharist with an intimate love.

It was the plan of the Father to lead men to the Shepherds of Christ Movement, centered in consecration, given by Our Lady to help bring about the renewal of the Church and the world.

On January 18, 1997, God the Father gave the following message:

> "Read the accounts of Noah. Nowhere in human history am I so offended as I am today by the sinfulness of men. You will suffer a fate for your deeds."

The Plan of the Father was to give these messages to lead men to the Heart of His Son.

On January 18, 1997, the same day I received the message from God the Father.

On January 18th I received the message that talked about Noah.

On February 10th the Father gave another message.

Our focus as designated by Our Lord, is to spread the Priestly Newsletter to the priests, centered in consecration.

This has been given to us as a major part of the completion of the Fatima message.

Our Lord gives messages on the 13th of the month in the rosary to help send the apostles into the Church to pray for the priests, the Church and the world. Our main focus is in praying for priests.

God has helped us start prayer chapters all over the world, praying for the priests.

Our Lord, through the Shepherds of Christ Movement, has called us as apostles to help bring about the completion of the Fatima message.

Most of our apostles go to daily Mass, Communion, spend one hour before the tabernacle each day, and pray one to three rosaries a day.

Our whole focus is to be one with Jesus. We are called to

begin and attend the prayer chapters, centered in consecration of our hearts to Jesus and Mary.

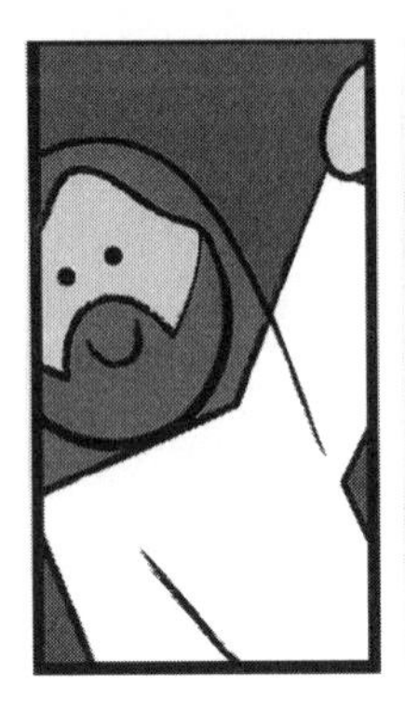

Consecration to Jesus

Dear Sacred Heart of Jesus, I love You so much and I give You my heart. Help me to love God. Help me to love my neighbor as a child of God. Help me to love myself as a child of God.

Amen

Consecration to Mary

Dear Mary, my holy mother, I love you so much and I give you my heart. Help me to love God. Help me to love my neighbor as a child of God. Help me to love myself as a child of God.

Amen

R. We have people all over the United States spreading the consecration to children with little cards that tell Jesus and Mary they love Them and give Them their hearts. We give away thousands, and thousands of rosaries and Ave meditation sheets, with the *Imprimatur,* to school children. We have apostles contacting the priests and telling them about the Priestly Newsletter and asking them to start adoration in their churches.

We have an organization, *Apostles of the Eucharistic Heart of Jesus* in which so many people pray two hours weekly before the tabernacle to pray for:

1) the spread of the devotion to the Hearts of Jesus and Mary culminating in the Reign of the Sacred Heart and the triumph of the Immaculate Heart;

2) for the Pope;

3) for all bishops of the world;

4) for all priests;

5) for all sisters and brothers in the religious life;

6) for all members of the Shepherds of Christ Movement and for the spread of this movement to the world;

7) for all members of the Catholic Church;

8) for all members of the human family;

9) for all souls in purgatory and pray the prayers of the Shepherds of Christ Associates Handbook before the tabernacle during this hour.

The Shepherds of Christ Movement is majorly helping to bring about the completion of the Fatima message.

The Fatima message has been blocked greatly for 80 years.

The fruits of this Movement and these messages are far reaching. We have letters and letters telling about the good that has been accomplished in the lives of so many.

We are reaching children all over the world. We are reaching the priests, the sisters, the brothers – thousands are consecrating their hearts to Jesus and Mary.

I would like to address the issues with you.

We are operating to help bring about the Reign of the Sacred Heart. We want only to do the will of God.

Our Lord has revealed the most hidden secrets of His Heart in the Mass and wants this published for priests and religious, and all.

Jesus wants a love affair with His people. He wants hearts on fire for love of Him.

I love you and I thank you for being His Holy Priest. It is the highest honor God calls a man to be - a holy priest!

With Love in the Hearts of Jesus and Mary,

Rita

4/6/97

Letter to Fr. Carter's Provincial from Ellen

To Fr. Carter's Provincial because of a few noisy people causing complaints against us.

April 8, 1997

Dear Father:

"It was said that a few noisy people got prayer out of the schools and all the good people didn't say anything." The situation is similar here in that you only hear from the bad; you don't hear from the good.

When I first met Rita Ring I had just retired from the U.S. Foreign Service serving in embassies abroad. She asked if I would like to type some letters/meditations that she had been receiving for a few years. I agreed when I had witnessed the inspired word come to her in a moment with such beautiful words from the Lord. Thus Blue Book 1, 2 and 3 were born. From the beginning, as I typed the messages they dwelt deeply in my heart. We began our rosaries at the Holy Spirit Center and many came. I thank God daily for the privilege of being associated with this noble work. There are too many experiences to share. I list only a very few testimonies:

Examples: (1) At my prayer group last evening one of the men witnessed the following: He was in in Chicago and had gone to the Cathedral to Mass. A homeless man came up to him for a handout and he showed him he had about $7 in change and said he wanted to show him something better. He took the man over to the Stations and asked him to look at Jesus at the cross and say the rosary. He used the Ave's Rita Ring had written, and the man was so touched! (2) I have a friend from N.Y. who recently called and said she would be near Cincinnati and asked if I could meet her and bring plenty of books for her friends in the Gospa group. (3) A Puerto Rican friend told her friend about our rosary at Our Lady of the Woods so when she visited her daughter here she came to our rosary and meeting. When she returned she sent a lovely letter telling us that she had just lost her husband and would not have been able to function without the peace she received from the Lord, through the Blue Books. We have many letters in our files that we would be glad to share with you, including a recent letter telling us that the Blue Book someone read saved her from suicide!

Shepherds of Christ is a movement to pray for priests, to send them a Priestly Newsletter from Fr. Carter, S.J. that will build them up in their faith and show them how valued and loved they are! There has never been a movement such as this in our lifetime, and surely Our Lord would choose a special priest to direct such an important mission! This year my sister from Minnesota came to our 13th Chapter meeting. She is completely devoted to her Catholic faith. She reiterated what we hear all the time that she had never experienced anything like the holiness, love and devotion she felt at our rosary and meeting. A priest I knew from India told me how he has used the Blue Books and Rosary meditations in his ministry, especially with the teenagers, drug problems and with tribal groups. He receives the Shepherds of Christ newsletters and wrote that when he visits here this summer he wants to work with Fr. Carter in Shepherds of Christ so he can spread the word in India.

If only you could witness the phone calls we receive requesting material from devout Catholics who are starting Shepherds of Christ prayer chapters. They are opening their hearts to the priests, something that has been neglected for years. We hear from people all over the U.S. and overseas. It makes one wonder who could question that this is indeed God's work, which has to be good, or surely we would have known otherwise by now, BUT satan attacks!

Witness the workers in the Movement: we are all simple people, in love with the Lord and hoping to help lives while we are on this earth. We are spreading the consecrations, the rosaries to the schools, volunteering endless hours knowing this work is the most important thing we can do to help souls, especially in view of what is going on in our world today! There is only love, not dissension, in our hearts for we have learned through the Holy Spirit to love. Mary has become so close to us. Mary is our spiritual Mother. This has come about because of our involvement in the Shepherds of Christ Movement. We are committed to daily Mass and communion, hours spent in front of the tabernacle. It has made us one - and we have time and time again had people come to tell us of the change they see in us, and wish they had it!

I thank our Lord everyday for showing me (at 69) a love for the Father, Son and Holy Spirit, and for my Church, that was started by my loving parents and throughout my life but never would I have known such love had I not been involved with Rita Ring, and Fr. Carter in the Shepherds of Christ Movement.

Sincerely yours, in the love of Christ,
Ellen S.

Jesus said: I want the writings of Fr. Carter and Rita to be as one.

At the same time as this Priestly Newsletter Fr. Carter put the following excerpt from the Mass Book in the Priestly Newsletter that went to 75,000 priests. It was also put in the Spanish Priestly Newsletter.

From the Priestly Newsletter March/April 1997

**From the Priestly Newsletter March/April 1997
and also the Mass Book**

Thoughts on the Mass

- Vatican II tells us: "At the Last Supper, on the night when He was betrayed, our Savior instituted the Eucharistic Sacrifice of His Body and Blood. He did this in order to perpetuate the sacrifice of the Cross throughout the centuries until He should come again, and so to entrust to His beloved spouse, the Church, a memorial of His death and resurrection: a sacrament of love, a sign of unity, a bond of charity, a Paschal banquet in which Christ is consumed, the mind is filled with grace, and a pledge of future glory is given to us.

  "The church, therefore, earnestly desires that Christ's faithful, when present at the mystery of faith, should not be there as strangers or silent spectators. On the contrary, through a proper appreciation of the rites and prayers they should participate knowingly, devoutly, and actively. They should be instructed by God's word and be refreshed at the table of the Lord's body; they should give thanks to God; by offering the Immaculate Victim, not only through the hands of the priest, but also with him, they should learn to offer themselves too. Through Christ the Mediator, they should be drawn day by day into ever closer union with each other, so that finally God may be all in all."[4]

- Here are thoughts from one woman's spiritual journal on the Mass:

"The priest needs to feed the people with the love of God. When people come to the Mass and the sacraments, they are spiritually fed.

"The world cries out to be fed. The Church is the body of Christ. Jesus has chosen each priest and anointed him as Christ alive in this world today. The greatest calling is to be called to be a holy priest by our Lord Himself. How dearly He loves His beloved priests and longs for their love. As He suffered so during His bitter Passion for the lack of love of some of His chosen priests betrothed to Him, He was comforted by His holy priests. Jesus truly loves His sacred priests.

"Jesus must live in the priest. The priest's every action must be one with Jesus. He is a priest forever according to the order of Melchizedek.

"When a priest is filled with the love of Jesus, He will unite more deeply with Christ in the great sacrifice being offered to the Father. In the holy sacrifice of the Mass, the faithful will see Jesus through the priest offering sacrifice to the Father. We will lift our eyes and we will feel, at this great sacrifice, the presence of God, Father, Son and Holy Spirit. We unite in offering sacrifice to the Father. We all unite as one and give ourselves in such oneness with Jesus, in such love to the Father, in the Holy Spirit. We die to all those things that are not of Him and join in this great miracle taking place. The Father looks down and He sees the sacrifice of His beautiful Son through the consecrated hands of His holy priests. Heaven unites to earth. Earth cries out in such jubilation at the great gift given from the Almighty God, and we unite as creatures giving ourselves as a sacrifice to our beloved Creator. Do we experience the presence of God as His power flows through the hands of a man, the priest who takes ordinary bread and wine and changes them into the Body and Blood of our Lord? Do we hear Jesus cry out, as He did at the last supper, with the intensity in His voice reflecting all knowledge of the upcoming events of His passion and death?

"Do we hear the priest say the words of consecration with the emotion of Jesus, about to give His life for His beloved souls? And the earth stands still. There is, at that moment, the sacrifice of Calvary sacramentally made present through the hands of the priest. Oh, that God so loved this world to give His only Son as a sacrifice and that God wants us in this deep oneness with Him. I give You myself, my beautiful God, as You so willingly gave Yourself to me on Calvary. I want to die with You.

"Love between two persons is mutual giving. It is interaction between two people. It is intimacy. It is dependent on how much we give. We receive intimacy, interaction, according to how much we put into it. God gives His all. We see Him hanging, covered with blood, crowned with thorns, hands and feet pierced. We see His precious heart, font of life and love and mercy, pierced. This is freedom. He shows us the way. We give ourselves. We sacrifice and beg to be made holy, beg to be like Him in this holy sacrifice. The most important aspect of our offering sacrifice is how we are in our heart. Are we one with Jesus, giving ourselves to our beloved Father Who is all worthy of our love? Who are we that God loves us creatures so much that He, Almighty God, becomes present, no less present than the day He walked this earth, through the hands of a man, and we take it so lightly. Think of Jesus calling out. Raise the Host high, beloved priests. This is the Son of God and you have been given the greatest honor on this earth.

"God comes to us. He gives Himself to us. Let us see ourselves as one in Him. Let us unite. Let us look at ourselves, all creatures of our beloved God, God, all Holy, all Magnificent, Almighty, all Powerful, and see what He gives us. Let us see ourselves as His creatures and Him as the Creator, and look at ourselves and see how we, and all men, are offending our precious God. As we unite, we beg, beg, with this holy sacrifice of His Son, for mercy. We watch it flow from the Father, in the Holy Spirit, through the font of grace and mercy, the pierced Heart of Jesus, through the heart of Mary, by the hands of the priest, who is one with Jesus, to us. We are so joined in such oneness with the Hearts of Jesus and Mary. We have given ourselves to Them. It is here, united to Christ in such oneness, that my sacrifice is received by the loving hands of the Father. It is in this oneness that He pours out His grace. We unite through Him, with Him, and in Him, in the unity of the Holy Spirit, and we beg for mercy as His creatures who have offended our beloved God. This is our gift to You, our beloved Father. As Vatican II says, in union with the priest, we offer the Son to the Father. We give Him the greatest thanks for this holy and living sacrifice. We unite with the whole Church. We ask to be nourished by His Body and Blood, to be filled with the Holy Spirit, and increasingly become one body in Him. We join with Mary and all the saints and constantly plead for help through this sacrifice. Through this sacrifice may we make peace with You and peace for the salvation of the whole world. We pray in love and faith for your pilgrim Church, for the Pope, our bishop and all bishops, all clergy and all people. We ask the Father to hear the prayers of His family and ask Him in mercy and love to unite all children the world over. We ask the Father to take all our brothers and sisters that have died, that were good, into heaven. And we pray that we will have the vision of Your glory, through Christ, Our Lord, and we pray through Him, with Him and in Him, in the unity of the Holy Spirit. All glory and honor is Yours, Almighty Father, forever and ever.

"We pray to the Father, with all our hearts and all our love, the 'Our Father.' We say every word. We say with such love, 'Our Father,' we pray that Thy kingdom comes on earth as it is in heaven. We want this kingdom here, we are all brothers and sisters and God is our Father and we want all men doing His will. We ask to be fed both spiritually and physically every day. We beg to be free from evil and have peace. We ask Him to keep us free from sin and anxiety and hope for His coming. We pray that the kingdom and power and the glory are God's now and forever. We give to each other peace and we beg for forgiveness and mercy. We are sinful, but we want mercy. We stand. We should shout out to the Father, "Look how sinful we are!" We beg for mercy for our sins and those of all men.

"I experience the action of the Holy Spirit in a special way from the Consecration of the Mass. It fills me with such anticipation to receive Jesus, and I want to be holy. From the Consecration, I give myself to the Father, united in the Holy Spirit, in a special way. Consecrated to the Hearts of Jesus and Mary, I experience God. I love the Mass so much. The rest of this book that follows are my experiences during Mass, after Communion, and other times. Many are experiences at Holy Cross-Immaculata

Catholic Church in Cincinnati, Ohio. For four months straight I experienced special moments with my beloved Jesus there daily."[5]

4. Documents of Vatican II, *Constitution on the Sacred Liturgy,* Nos. 47-48, America Press edition.
5. Rita Ring, *The Mass: A Journey Into His Heart,* to be published by Shepherds of Christ Publications.

Love Gives

Mary: What love a father and mother have for a child. God the Father, the most loving of all Fathers, how He loves His children to send His Son, Jesus, the Savior/Redeemer.

Love gives. Love does not hold back. It fills the heart and wants to pour out endless blessings, endless gifts of love.

R. God is love. We do not comprehend fully the ways of God. Our life is a journey of learning about God, hence it is a journey to learn how to love, love God and love each other.

God loves perfectly. His love is so far beyond our human comprehension. Our life is to learn how to love more perfectly like our Father in heaven.

Mary's heart is pure and sinless. She loves. Mary was conceived sinless.

Adam and Eve were given great gifts.
Adam and Eve sinned.
Adam and Eve disobeyed God.

Jesus is the New Adam.
Mary is the New Eve.

God the Father said Mary was a gift He gave us.

Jesus gave us His Mother on the cross.

R. Mary is the Spouse of the Holy Spirit.

Fr. Carter had a Dream

From *Tell My People* by Fr. Edward J. Carter, S.J.

The Holy Spirit

Jesus: "My beloved friend, tell My people to pray daily to the Holy Spirit. They are to pray for an increase in His gifts. My people must realize that the Holy Spirit comes to transform them. The Spirit desires to transform you more and more according to My image. Those who are docile to His touch become increasingly shaped in My likeness. He performs this marvel within Mary's Immaculate Heart. The more one dwells in My Mother's Heart, the more active are the workings of the Spirit. The Spirit leads Mary to place you within My own Heart. In both Our Hearts, then, your transformation continues. The more you are formed after My own Heart, the more I lead you to the bosom of My Father. Tell My people all this. Tell them to pray daily for a greater appreciation of these wondrous gifts. I am Lord and Master. All who come to My Heart will be on fire to receive the gifts of the Spirit in ever greater measure! I love and bless My people!"

Reflection: The Holy Spirit is given to us to fashion us ever more according to the likeness of Jesus. And the more we are like Jesus, the more Jesus leads us to the Father. Do we, each day, pray to the Holy Spirit to be more open to His transforming influence? Do we strive each day to grow in union with Mary? The greater our union with our Mother, the spouse of the Holy Spirit, the greater is the transforming action of the Holy Spirit within us.

end of excerpt

R. Darkness came to the minds and hearts of men.

The light was dimmed in the minds and hearts of man.

Reference: Romans 6: 1-11

R. Mary stood beneath His cross. The Father's gift to sinful men – His Son, the new Adam. Our Mother, the new Eve. We would be brought forth children of light.

Who could have chosen to ignore the woman clothed with the sun? Who could refuse Mary and ignore Mary and blaspheme Mary? Adam and Eve sinned. Mary is the New Eve, we go to her Immaculate Heart. Jesus is the New Adam, we go to His Sacred Heart.

Reference: Luke 1: 46-55 The Magnificat

R. And so Mary appeared at Fatima and she warned men that they must heed her words. In her Immaculate Heart they can unite deeply in the Heart of Christ. Mary is the gateway to intimacy with the Trinity, and she said: "You must come to my heart. You must make reparation for blasphemies against my Immaculate Heart. You must make reparation to the Heart of my Son, for the offenses against God."

The light shown in the darkness and the star was the brightest star over the bed of Our Savior. No longer would a nation walk in darkness.

Song: *A Song from Jesus*

A Song from Jesus

1 Corinthians 15: 20-28

In fact, however, Christ has been raised from the dead, as the first-fruits of all who have fallen asleep. As it was by one man that death came, so through one man has come the resurrection of the dead. Just as all die in Adam, so in Christ all will be brought to life; but all of them in their proper order: Christ the first-fruits, and next, at his coming, those who belong to him. After that will come the end, when he will hand over the kingdom to God the Father, having abolished every principality, every ruling force and power. For he is to be king *until he has made* his enemies his footstool, and the last of the enemies to be done away with is death, for *he has put all things under his feet.* But when it is said everything is subjected, this obviously cannot include the One who subjected everything to him. When everything has been subjected to him, then the Son himself will be subjected to the One who has subjected everything to him, so that God may be all in all.

R. Mary stood beneath the cross of her Son and she cried –

Mary's Message

- from the Rosary of August 27, 1996

Mary: I stood beneath the cross of my Son, and my Heart was in such pain for I saw Him before my eyes. I saw Him covered with blood. I saw Him die. My Heart, my children, my Heart to watch my Son, but my Heart, my Heart, how I suffered for my little children of the world that give in to this world and give up the love of my Son. O my little children of light, I give you this message. Carry this light into the darkness for your Mother Mary, for I stood beneath the cross and I cried. I cried for the little ones. I cried for the young ones, the ones that do not care and will lose their souls. How do I make you see for you will not listen to me? What can I do? I come. I appear. I beg. I plead. I give you these gifts from my Son, and you reject me. I do not deliver messages very often anymore for I have been ignored. The message is the same. You do not read the messages I have given to you. Please help me. Help the little children. I appear. I appear. I appear, and I am ignored. I stood beneath the cross, and I cried. I cried, and my Heart was in such anguish for my little children, for I am searching for them this day as I searched for the Child Jesus. Please, please help me. I cannot hold back the hand of my Son any longer. I am Mary, your Mother. I ask you to help my children. You are my children of light. *end of excerpt*

R. Mary appeared on a building in Clearwater to give this message.

Mary appeared at Our Lady of the Holy Spirit Center for 14 months as the Lady of Light to me - her mission, to take her children to the Heart of her Son.

In the message from the Father, He speaks of His anger over how we abused the gift He gave us - Our Mother Mary.

Image at Clearwater, FL
December 17, 1996 - March 1, 2004

So, the Father speaks - January 18, 1997.

This was to help in the completion of the Fatima Mission, 80 years later. Mary appeared as Our Lady of Light to lead men to the greatest intimacy with her Son that would bring about the Reign of His Sacred Heart.

This is why the Father speaks in January and He says: You ignore Mary, you ignore Jesus, you think you will ignore Me?

March 22, 1997

God said: Gifts are given and they are abused. Then all that is left is the sufferings to turn you around.

God the Father's Message of January 18, 1997

> "I tell you all to read the accounts concerning Noah. Nowhere in history has God been offended as He is this day by this sinful world. You will suffer a fate for the offenses against God."

(Read the Message of God the Father, January 18, 1997).

February 10, 1997 Message:

God the Father: The completion of the Fatima Mission will greatly come through the Shepherds of Christ Movement. All in opposition to these messages will be weeded out. I am the Father. This is the third time heaven has tried to spread the messages to bring about the Reign of the Sacred Heart of My Son. I will not tolerate any more. You will suffer in the Shepherds of Christ Movement if you do not obey the messages, for this is My Plan.

The 13th is a major part of the completion of the Fatima Mission.

R. God is saying we must start prayer chapters.

God the Father says if we make reparation to Mary's heart and do as He says, what is coming can be averted and be lessened.

The Priestly Newsletter, the prayer chapters and the Apostles of the Eucharistic Heart are crucial to the renewal of the Church and the world. It is His Plan.

The Father gives great lights to Adam and Eve - the light of knowing God. Read in the Apostles Manual.

We are little children of the Father. He has picked Mary, the pure one, the Immaculate Mother. She is the gift to lead men to great intimacy with God.

Go to Mary's Immaculate Heart. 4/9/97

April 10th God the Father

God, the Father:

You must release this information. If you do not, people will continue to test the authenticity of these messages. I am God and I am speaking here. Satan has blocked these messages and I have given great signs of the authenticity. To continue to withhold this information without addressing the issue will cause people to attack you and you will suffer from these attacks. I write to be heard. The Falmouth flood was a sign I have given. I have asked that prayer chapters be started, centered in consecration. Only when you comply with your Mother's requests at Fatima will there be peace. Men do their own will and are offending God. I give to you My plan for peace on this earth. I am asking you to release the information given and to read the messages that address the issues. Those who have turned from you will now support you and you will not suffer this great persecution. Mary appeared and she was ignored. My Son gave messages of His love and they were abused at the Mary apparition site. This is not My plan for peace. Mary appeared and there was hatred in the hearts of the chosen ones. I am speaking to be heard. What will follow will be far worse than any warning. I am asking the faithful to begin prayer chapters centered in consecration and praying the rosary. I am asking you to circulate the Mass Book and that

reparation be made to the Hearts of Jesus and Mary. I am asking that the First Saturday devotion be observed. I am asking that a strong effort be made to spread the consecration to the schools and that children be told to pray the rosary. I am asking you to publish the *Parents & Children's Rosary Book* and spread the Rosary Aves to children in schools.

Lastly, but of major importance to the renewal of the Church and the world, I am asking that the Priestly Newsletters be made available in abundance, that the apostles spread these Newsletters to the priests and encourage them to read them. I am asking the *Priestly Newsletter Book* be published as soon as possible and circulated to all priests and bishops in the United States.

I am the Father. You must pray as never before and join in one mind and one heart.

Fr. Carter is not to worry for I am guarding you. This is My Plan. It will unfold if you obey the messages I give to you.

4/10/97

Concerning April 13, 1997

The 13ths

A Message from Jesus

Jesus: Mary appeared at Fatima May 13, 1917 - October 13, 1917, 6 apparitions.

I called the meetings of October 13, 1996 - March 13, 1997, in which I gave important messages concerning the completion of the Fatima mission (6 rosaries with Father Carter). My Mother appeared on the building in Florida December 17, 1996, after 3 of the 13th rosaries. These rosaries were messages from Me to help in the completion the mission begun by My Mother at Fatima.

I have continued to give special information on the 13th of each month to help bring about the Reign of the Sacred Heart and Triumph of My Mother's Heart and lead men to a deeper intimate union with Me. The Shepherds of Christ is My Movement to help bring about this most holy spousal union between men and God.

R. On April 12-13, 1997, we had a National Conference of Shepherds of Christ as called by Our Lord at Our Lady of the Holy Spirit Center. I had received this direction in a message February 16, 1997. It was called by Our Lord. His request was to meet there on that weekend. God the Father told me to release the story of Falmouth and the flood of March 3, 1997.

God the Father said it must be released on April 13, 1997. It was the hardest thing I felt I ever did. I know what the Father told me to do and I had to do it. I was filled with fire for love of Him and I did as He told me.

R. Every 13th we would get together and pray from about 12:00 until very late in the afternoon. Our Lord said there were great graces given for the world. We prayed with all our hearts and souls united to the Masses going on around the world for the priests and the Church and the world.

April 13, 1997

This rosary was received on Sunday, April the 13th, 1997 at an International Shepherds of Christ Associates Meeting at the Holy Spirit Center, Cincinnati, OH. The meditations and messages were given to Rita Ring during the rosary. This rosary was received live and transcribed from the recording.

Glorious Mysteries

The Resurrection

1. Song: *A Song from Jesus*

2. **R.** Did you see Him come forth from the tomb adorned in the brightest light and splendor? Did you see Him? I saw Him. I saw Him before my eyes transfigured in the brightest light and I cried. He is alive. He is risen. He is alive and He is treated like a dead object in many cases. But He cries out. From this tabernacle, He cried out and He said, "I long for the soul that comes to Me and gives Me their love."

   Song: *He is risen, He is risen, He is risen*

3. **R.** I had a vision. I had 3 great visions. The one was on March the 26th, 1996 and this account is written in the *Apostles Manual*. (Also *Blue Book 10*) The second was on Holy Saturday night and the whole wall was adorned in this light that I cannot describe for it was not a light. It was something supernatural or so it seemed. It kind of looked like a mirror and it looked like the water glistening on the river over at Tom's farm, except it's golden. But that's nothing like what it is because to describe a supernatural thing is impossible it seems to me in human terms. But this was on Holy Saturday and there was a resurrected Jesus statue there and the whole light that went up to St. Joseph, the whole wall was adorned in this light, I don't even know what to call it, because it's brighter than any light. Jesus was transfigured, I saw this light, I can't even describe it. Envision Jesus as He comes forth from the tomb as I saw

Him transfigured, as I saw this light on this night. Jesus the Light of the World. Do we know? Do we understand? Do we comprehend? We have bits and pieces of things in our head about Jesus and it is all so clear to me. This is how it is. Adam and Eve sinned. The light had been dimmed because Adam and Eve sinned. They had this intense knowing of knowing God, all these gifts that God gave to them and it was dimmed from the sin. And Jesus comes and He is born the Light of the World. But we are still a people walking in darkness for we never comprehend or have this understanding that Adam and Eve had. And Jesus comes and He comes into the world and the light shines over the stable, for He is the Light. Jesus teaches us about God. We are children of the light. God gives us the Church. God gives us baptism – Jesus died and rose so we could share in His life. In baptism our knowing and loving capacity is elevated. We share in God's loving activity. WOW. Adam and Eve sin. The light is dimmed. They do not know God as they once did. Jesus comes the Light of the World, but the people do not comprehend.

From *Tell My People*
by Fr. Edward J. Carter, S.J.

The Holy Spirit

Jesus: "My beloved friend, tell My people to pray daily to the Holy Spirit. They are to pray for an increase in His gifts. My people must realize that the Holy Spirit comes to transform them. The Spirit desires to transform you more and more according to My image. Those who are docile to His touch become increasingly shaped in My likeness. He performs this marvel within Mary's Immaculate Heart. The more one dwells in My Mother's Heart, the more active are the workings of the Spirit. The Spirit leads Mary to place you within My own Heart. In both Our Hearts, then, your transformation continues. The more you are formed after My own Heart, the more I lead you to the bosom of My Father. Tell My people all this. Tell them to pray daily for a greater appreciation of these wondrous gifts. I am Lord and Master. All who come to My Heart will be on fire to receive the gifts of the Spirit in ever greater measure! I love and bless My people!"

Reflection: The Holy Spirit is given to us to fashion us ever more according to the likeness of Jesus. And the more we are like Jesus, the more Jesus leads us to the Father. Do we, each day, pray to the Holy Spirit to be more open to His transforming influence? Do we strive each day to grow in union with Mary? The greater our union with our Mother, the spouse of the Holy Spirit, the greater is the transforming action of the Holy Spirit within us. *end of excerpt*

R. Jesus is the Light of the World. We are like people that are walking this earth with a shade down, a veil. We do not comprehend and we do not understand. We do not see Him in His magnificence and His light. We do not know many things. If we did we would all be on our faces right now, flat on the ground giving praise and worship to the Almighty God. Jesus is truly present and in this room in the Eucharist. But there is a shade down; it is as in a room. If the shade is down, there is darkness and the sunlight does not come through from the outside. But if the shade is lifted, the sunlight comes into the room. Jesus is the Light of the world. What we know is veiled. God can lift the veil. We can see more and more if God lets us. We do not need to be focused on so many foolish things. He is risen, the Light of the World, and He gives to us a sharing in His life.

Song: *He is risen, He is risen, He is risen*

4. Song: *City of God*

R. It is all there. The Mass is there. The Sacraments are there. God wants to fill us more and more with His life. This grace is outpoured on this earth. But we do not comprehend. Spread the consecration to the Sacred Heart and Immaculate Heart to priests. We need grace to be outpoured more and more on the world. Pray the prayers Jesus gave Fr. Carter. This is what the Shepherds of Christ Movement is all about. It is the Father's plan from all eternity that the Shepherds of Christ Movement would be major in helping to spread the consecration to the priests, that priest's hearts would be consecrated to the Hearts of Jesus and Mary, that a nation, that a Church, that a people that are walking in darkness will see the light and that grace would be outpoured. Spreading the Consecration will help us to have holy priests. It is now as if the shade is down and the sun is on the other side of the shade but I do not see it. Jesus is giving us immense light, the more we consecrate our hearts to Jesus and Mary. God wants our intimate love. We must reach the priests with the Priestly Newsletter that they will consecrate their hearts to Jesus and Mary, that their hearts will be turned to hearts of love, that they will know God with the greatest intimacy, for the Holy Spirit works within the heart of the Virgin Mary and gives great lights.

5. **R.** Jesus is alive. We are His faithful witnesses. Jesus is in this room, the Almighty God, the same Jesus that came forth from the tomb, truly present in the Eucharist. He will give to us this understanding into Him in this new era, the Reign of the Two Hearts, for we will be the children of light that will know God with such intensity.

6. **R.** And so how did the stone come away from the tomb? When Mary Magdalene got to the tomb, the stone had been rolled back. Jesus had risen. And where were the Apostles? Where were they a lot of the time? They were afraid. They touched Jesus. They talked to Jesus. He taught them. They ate with Jesus and they were afraid. Where were they when the stone was rolled back? Were they in a room? Were they afraid in that room? Were they talking about how they were going to be apprehended because they knew Him? They didn't hear what Jesus said. Jesus kept telling them but they did not hear for they were deaf. They were in the room discussing how someone might get them - being afraid.

7. **R.** Isn't this kind of like us today? Mary appeared over and over and over and over and over again as Our Lady of Light to me every day for 14 months and it was a gift from God. Mary appeared as Our Lady of Light for she was calling out to us to tell us that we must consecrate our hearts to her heart and when we do, the Holy Spirit will fill us with His grace and we will know God more and more from the light that He will give to us. We are blind like the Apostles and you say, "How can they be so blind? They walked with Him. They touched Him. They talked to Him." But they did not comprehend. Is this not how it is today? For we should believe. Some people have not believed in Fatima. It has been approved by the Church. The Almighty God sent Mary

to this earth as a great gift, the pure and Immaculate One, and she tells us what we have to do. We have to consecrate our hearts to her heart and the Heart of her Son. There is no other way. Because, in order to go into this era in which men will know God with this immense light, we have to go to the heart of Mary or the spiritual womb of Mary. Why don't we listen to Mary at Fatima? Why don't we spread the consecration? Because the devil has blocked the Fatima message for 80 years now. This, today, is a major part of the completion of the Fatima message and Jesus is the teacher. He is teaching us about what will bring about this great era in which men will know God, will love God, and the earth will be as the Father intended from the beginning - one happy family in one mind, in one heart, loving God and loving one another. Jesus is risen. Jesus is with us. Let us pray for the light that we will see, that we are not in the darkness, that we will be the leaders, that we will go out and spread the consecration as Mary said at Fatima, that we will help to spread it especially to the priests. For it is when the priests are celebrating the Mass with hearts consecrated to the Hearts of Jesus and Mary, we can be so united in holy love – one body in Him.

8. **R.** Somewhere in the Scriptures Jesus says that they pray to Me only with their lips. This will be the Age of the Two Hearts. We look at the Sacred Heart of Jesus. Jesus has His hands on both sides of His Heart. He's showing us "this is My Heart. You must come to Me with your heart of love!" Not in our head! We must know things in our head. But we must be a people that are filled with heart-felt love for God in our hearts. How is our love for God? Is it in our mouth and in our head? Love is not in our head only. God wants hearts that are loving. That's what Jesus shows us with His hands on each side of His Heart, that love is in the heart. We must lead the priests to the Priestly Newsletter for it is in the Priestly Newsletter that He will write the messages of His love on their hearts. We want the Word to live in us. Jesus is alive! Now many read the Word of God with no emotion, no feeling, no love! God gives Himself to us! He is love! We must have love for God. It isn't conversation. It isn't little prayers that we throw at Him. It is love that He wants. He is alive.

9. Song: *Jesus, Jesus, Jesus, the Light of the World*

10. **R.** Peter, James and John slept in the garden. Christ was in the Garden in such suffering and they slept. And He went to them and said, "Can you not spend one hour with Me?" And so we think back and we think, "How, how could these Apostles sleep when they saw Jesus, Jesus, the Almighty God, Who was always so full of peace? When they saw Jesus and He was asking them for this hour and they slept." Is this kind of like us? There are 24 hours in the day, but in our busy lives, as little ants, we are so busy with all of our work and our paper work and the Almighty God, Who gives us every breath and every heartbeat, Who controls everything, Who is truly present, we don't have time for Him. But in a second He can stop us in our place. We are the apostles that He is calling this day, to go into the new era, to bring the light, to bring His love into this world, a love that will make their hearts burn, for now many hearts are so cold. That's what He said to me. "You come to Me with such a cold heart." And I think, "Oh, Jesus." Jesus is God. Jesus is love. Jesus' Heart is a furnace, a burning furnace of love. We do not even know love. God is love! Jesus is truly present in the tabernacle and in the Eucharist. And if we want to know love, we must go to the source, for it is in going to the source that we will be satisfied and that we will share love with one another. How silly when God is love, but we leave Him out of the picture many times.

    Let us sing this song to the Holy Spirit and let us beg Him to come.

    Song between decades: *Come Holy Spirit*

The Ascension

1. **R.** How is it in this world today? You go out and you see all of the things that we do not like in the world. And we feel so uncomfortable for it just doesn't devi-up with our hearts. And so then we go back to Jesus and it feels really, really good and then we go back out to the world and then the world is, for a large part, not like Jesus. And so we go back and forth between these two worlds, but we know the world that feels so good is the world that's in our heart. We live in Him in the world.

2. **R.** When the world out there feels good, when the world feels good when I leave out Jesus, then we're in big trouble because He is the source of life. He is the source of love. He is the Almighty God.

3. **Jesus:** And so My beloved ones, I have called you, for I am the teacher and I have called you here this day to teach you. But you must open up your heart and listen. For I am the Almighty God with a Divine mind and I am speaking to you and your minds are limited. They are human minds and you do not comprehend My ways; but I teach you and you turn away. My word I give to you, My word written from My Divine mind. My beloved ones, you must pray to the Holy Spirit that you will see, that you will comprehend, for My world is so different from your world. I see you there and I know you are struggling. But each person in this room I have called. I have called you to be My apostle to go out into the darkness and to spread My light. The Apostles slept in the garden. They did not comprehend. They did not believe. They were blind and they were deaf. But, the Church, this day, is built up from the work of the Apostles. You are My apostles that I am sending into the Church, into the school, to the families to help lead them to the love in My Sacred Heart. If you say "no" to Me, who will I send? Do you know that I have called you today? How is your mind? Is it half closed or half open? How is your heart? You just do not know. Is it safe to get into your heart for you may feel pain? Do you see My Heart surrounded with a crown of thorns? My beloved ones, the gifts I give to you are far greater than any suffering that you experience. If you close your heart, you will never be happy, for you were created to know My love. Open your heart now. Open your heart wide. Open your mind and listen as I speak to you, for I will teach you My ways and you will be My soldiers, My soldiers of light. How you respond will make the difference to so many souls. And there was a soul, let us think about the soul, the soul that is on the edge of death at this moment. And what did they do with their life? Did they go to Church? Did they think about God? Did they think about their money? Did they think about their children? Were they always looking for something more? What did they do? But at this moment,

they are being called forever and ever and ever to go somewhere. There is a soul on the edge of death. Where will the soul go? It depends on how they lived their life.

4. **Jesus:** And so I tell you, My sweet one, I tell you how much I love you. Do you hear Me? Do you crave love in your heart but you are not satisfied? You must come to Me for you were created with the desire to know, love and serve God. The Father has a plan for you from the day you were born. You were created to know My Divine love and nothing here will fill that craving in your soul. Was it your money? Was it your car? Was it your business? What was your god? There is a soul on the edge of death. What was his god and where will he go?

5. **R.** Jesus took the Apostles out to a town near Bethany and He raised His arms and He ascended into heaven. And they were awestruck as they looked from the field below and they were filled with fear. And they locked themselves in a room.

6. **R.** Do we see the world? Do we turn on the television and see how it is? Do we realize that we are the apostles that He has called to carry out the Good News? We know what it is like on the television. Does it make sense that God after He gave Himself and died on the cross that He would not send messages this day in order to change men's hearts?

7. **R.** And Mary speaks in the message in the *Mary Message* tape and she says, "I appear, I appear, I appear, I appear, I appear and I am ignored." She appeared, and she appeared, and she appeared so many times since Fatima to tell the children that they must go to her heart, that in order to see the light that we must go to the heart of Mary. It is like this: Adam and Eve sinned; the new Adam and the new Eve, are Jesus and Mary. Jesus comes into the world in the womb of the Virgin Mary and Mary brings forth the Light of the World. He is the first born from the dead. We are the children of Eve. The sin has been passed down. We are tainted in our human natures. In order to be close to God, He gives us the one pure, Immaculate one, the new Eve. We must go to Mary's Immaculate Heart, her spiritual womb, and be brought forth a child of light. The light was dimmed for Adam and Eve. Christ showed us the way. He came in the womb of Mary and was brought forth the Light of the World. If we want to know God, we must go to the heart of

Mary and be brought forth a child of light.

8. **R.** It was on Ascension Thursday, 1995, and Our Lord called out, "I am alive. I am alive. I am alive." And I was in immense suffering, buckled over as if someone was sticking swords inside me and hearing His voice. This is what He calls out to us today, "I am alive. I am alive. I am alive and I am treated in many cases like a dead object." We are His apostles that will carry the light into the darkness and they will know that He is alive in these messages. You read the *Blue Book* messages and you hear Him speak in those letters, "My dear one, I love you so much. I am with you. Do you not know I stand by your bed at night? I am guarding you. I am in your every breath. I am with you." And so from reading His letters of love, the mighty medicine that He sends to this earth, He tells us that He is alive. And from reading the messages, the Scriptures are alive in our hearts.
9. **R.** And the Apostles slept and then they locked themselves in the upper room.
10. Hail Mary

Song between decades: *A Song from Jesus*

The Descent of the Holy Spirit

1. **R.** And there was a gigantic wind and there appeared over their heads parted tongues of fire. The Apostles were in the upper room with the Blessed Virgin Mary and the Holy Spirit came upon them and they were filled with the fire of God's love. And they went out into this world to preach the Good News.
2. **R.** And so Mary says, "The time is nigh for I appeared and I appeared and I appeared and they ignored me." Mary appeared at Fatima and she told them 80 years ago that they must give their heart to her. And they did not listen and He gave them great proof. The sun almost came crashing to the earth (or so it seemed) and they still did not listen. And there was World War II. And she appeared and she appeared and she appeared and we do not listen. But she did say at Fatima that there will be this great era in which the Sacred Heart of Jesus will Reign and the Immaculate Heart of Mary will triumph. So we know that we're going to go from wherever we are, at this present moment, into this era when everybody

is going to live in the Father's will, when everyone is going to be loving and good. So we have to go from where we are to this place in which the Sacred Heart of Jesus will Reign. He sends the gifts to tell us what to do. He sends the warnings. He tells us. Mary told us at Fatima what we had to do. She told us if we didn't do it we would suffer the war. We ignored her. Eighty years later Jesus sends these messages to tell us what we must do. Mary appeared and appeared and appeared to so many visionaries at Medjugorje for 10 years and then look at the town around there. Mary appeared. She appeared here. She appeared at Cold Springs. She appeared at Falmouth. She appeared to me every day and I spoke and I spoke and I spoke and their response to me was, "Are you going to keep listening to Mary when everybody else is ignoring you?"

3. **R.** It is like the apostles. They slept. Peter denied Christ. He went away. He was in his human mind thinking about the things of the earth. He was not thinking of the things as coming from God, even though he walked with God and Jesus was his teacher. We get too caught up in our human mind and we do not look at things from God's perspective. This is the truth that this is God's world, that the Father is with us at this very second, that the Holy Spirit is here, that Jesus is in the tabernacle, truly present, no less present than the day that He walked on the earth, that the Father has the plan, God is the I AM, without a beginning, without an end. God is Supreme, Almighty. We see where we are in our little seat, looking at our little rosary, thinking about what we are going to have for dinner and we are rooted in this moment in time. But He is telling us that we must see beyond, that we must listen to the warnings that He is giving to us, that no longer can He be ignored, and He is calling each one of us. He has brought us to a great level in holiness. Each one of you here are people that are very close to Him and He is forming our hearts to be the apostle of light to go into the darkness.

4. **R.** The same Peter that denied Jesus was made head of the Church. These apostles were people like us, people that were kind of a motley crew, coming together. But the Holy Spirit descended upon them and they were filled with fearlessness because they were in one mind and one heart

with the Almighty God. They were thinking in their human minds in the room after Jesus ascended into heaven. They had locked themselves in the upper room. Then the Holy Spirit descended upon them and the Blessed Mother and they were fearless. And so I would like to read to you from one of the readings of last week.

Reference: Acts 5: 17-26

R. And the apostles were locked up but they got out of prison singing. These were the same men that were afraid, the same men that slept, the same men that ran and hid and locked themselves in the room. But when the Holy Spirit came upon them, they were the Apostles that would do all the work that the Father intended them to do, to help them in the work of building up the Church.

5. **R.** How is your shade? Is it down or is it up? For He gives to us His light. We go to Mary's Immaculate Heart. We must spend this time alone with Jesus every day or we get caught up in this world and we keep our focus on the world. When the world feels good, then there's something wrong with our spirituality, for our hearts were made for God and for Him alone, for His love. We need to spread the Consecration to the Two Hearts as Mary said at Fatima. We need to heed Fr. Carter's message July 31, 1994.

July 31, 1994

Words of Jesus to Members of Shepherds of Christ Associates:

"My beloved priest-companion, I intend to use the priestly newsletter, *Shepherds of Christ*, and the movement, *Shepherds of Christ Associates*, in a powerful way for the renewal of My Church and the world.

"I will use the newsletter and the chapters of *Shepherds of Christ Associates* as a powerful instrument for spreading devotion to My Heart and My Mother's Heart.

"I am calling many to become members of *Shepherds of Christ Associates.* To all of them I will give great blessings. I will use them as instruments to help bring about the triumph of the Immaculate Heart and the reign of My Sacred Heart. I will give great graces to the members of *Shepherds of Christ Associates*. I will call them to be deeply united to My Heart and to Mary's Heart as I lead them ever closer to My Father in the Holy Spirit."

- *Message from Jesus to Father Edward J. Carter, S.J., Founder, as given on July 31, 1994, feast of Saint Ignatius Loyola, Founder of the Society of Jesus (The Jesuits)*

6. **R.** Read:

   Reference: Acts 5: 27-33

7. **R.** And so they hung our beloved Savior on a tree, but the stone was rolled back and our Lord rose victorious on the third day. These men were locked in prison and an angel left them out. We are too bolted to the earth. Our minds are too focused on so many incidental things and we lose sight of the Almighty God. I beg you to read the messages in the *Apostles Manual* for it makes me shudder. I started receiving these messages in 1991 but Mary started to appear in 1994. The intensity was so high already in March of 1994 that God was displeased because they had ignored the messages. I am the messenger, but I cannot sleep at night if I do not deliver the message, for my peace is in doing what He is asking me to do.
8. Hail Mary

9. **R.** Who is our God? Is it man or is it God? Look at this earth. He is calling you as the apostles. How can we ignore our Heavenly Mother 80 years later? Doesn't it send a shudder inside of you to think that the Father sends the Blessed Mother here, tells us what we must do, that there was World War II - where over 60,000,000 were killed — A World At War — such destruction and devastation - that He has the sun almost come crashing down on the people at Fatima or so it looked and they do not listen and they don't think that 80 years later that He is warning us at Clearwater.

10. **R.** And so they said to me, "Are you going to keep listening to Mary when we're ignoring you?"

Message before the Glory Be:

R. When God speaks, the words that I hear are nothing compared to the penetration in my being. The way that He gives me the message is so intense. The words are little things that come out on the paper and out of my mouth. But inside to hear the Father speak as He spoke in those 2 messages, January 11, 1997 and January 18, 1997, and to know God is warning us, was far greater than anything on that paper. You must look at the messages given with an open heart and an open mind as coming from God and as responding to help me spread these prayer chapters and messages in God's Blue Book for the sake of souls, to help to spread the love of God. We must do as God is saying. Why are we not doing what Mary said at Fatima?

Song between decades: *Our Lady of Fatima*

R. What is so interesting is that Mary appeared all that time as Our Lady of Light to lead us to her heart, the spiritual womb, and on March the 20th, 1997 she appeared as Our Lady of Fatima.

The Assumption

1. Hail Mary
2. **R.** And so Mary speaks on December the 19th, 1996, 2 days after she appeared - on the building in Florida she said:

December 19, 1996

Mary: My dear children, I give to you, my Son, Jesus, born in a stable in Bethlehem on Christmas morn. He is the Almighty God, the Light of the World.

I appear to you, my children, on a (former) bank in Florida. You have made money your god! Do you know how cold are your hearts? You turn away from my Son, Jesus, for your money. Your money is your god.

I am Mary, your Mother. I do not appear as I once appeared to you. I am asking you today to circulate my message given on a tape on the feast of Our Lady of Guadalupe, December 12, 1996. Please circulate this

tape now. Give it to as many people as you can. I am Mary, your Mother. Please circulate my *Rosary Book.*
end of excerpt

R. And then I got a very strong message from Jesus and from Mary and she spoke in this message (December 19, 1996) and she said, "Oh, my children, my little children of light, the time is nigh and many will be lost forever. I appeared and warned and told all to mind their ways and come to the Heart of my Son and they said "No, my Lady, not for you or any mother. We are children of darkness and that we remain, for we seek our pleasure by day and feast on sin all night and when you called, mother, we laughed at your Son and ignored Him and His ways." And He called and His call fell on deaf ears.

Please, my children of light, come to my heart now for although you walked next to the children of darkness. I smite the dragon that whirled around you and protected you in my heart and you will now feast on the glories of His Kingdom, my little children of light."

3. **R.** On December 17, 1996 Mary appeared in Clearwater and this book (Red Rosary Book) left the printer.

shipped from the printers December 17, 1996

Mary appeared December 17, 1996

R. And the messages that He gave on the 19th and the 22nd of December 1996, both referred to the moon turning to blood. For this is what will happen. We are a people walking in darkness and He is allowing us to go further and further and further down into this darkness. And then the time will come and there will be whatever it takes in order to turn us into children of light. And in this new era we will see with the light of 7 suns that will blind us and we will fall to the earth for we will know God and we will be so happy in our hearts. For now, we are walking in darkness. We do not know God as we should. If we did, we would all be down on our face in this very room. For Jesus, Lord Jesus is in this room, truly present in the Eucharist. Jesus calls out, "Please I came, I came. I want to be loved." And we treat Him many times as a dead object.

4. **R.** And this is what Jesus said in the first strong message (December 19, 1996) that I received in the *Apostles Manual* pp. 204-205 (also *Blue Book 13* pp. 275-276).

"You will know a great time of trial and darkness. I have written to you of the great sufferings to come. The sinfulness of this world greatly displeases Me. I beg you to pray for forgiveness and turn your hearts to love.

And darkness covered the earth and the light was cast in little corners of the earth. Those who were willful remained in intense darkness, those who were rooted in God, and giving themselves to consecration, were the children of the light.

And the light shown in the darkness and the darkness grasped it not, but to as many as responded, they became the children of the light and from them His life flowed into the hearts that were cold and dark and slowly, very slowly, the light began to steal across the darkened sky and the moon was covered with blood. The blood was the blood of the Lamb. The blood represented the blood He shed to give us life. But the blind just saw ordinary blood and were scared to death. They responded with the greatest fright and lacked peace, but those rooted in God, those whose hearts were consecrated to Mary and Jesus, knew the sign was from God – that the time of reckoning was at hand. Many were punished and suffered a great chastisement. Many were left to death, but the children of light prayed the rosary and trusted in God.

And the night was no more for the light of day came stealing across the sky and myriads of angels filled the sky and the heavens. Sing Alleluia, Praise the Lord, you saints and angels, show yourselves to the survivors for they walked in darkness and could not see, but the light was alive in their hearts and they dwelt within the furnace of His Heart.

Have no fear now, My people, for you are the children of the light and My hand is forever upon you. You may suffer now a little, but it is nothing compared to the splendor to come."

5. **Jesus:** And so the plan of the Father is unfolding in your life, My beloved ones. Do you see, do you see the windows in this chapel? From the Annunciation to the Assumption how the plan of the Father unfolded in the life of My Mother. You have been called and you have been chosen My apostles and My plan is unfolding in your life. You must not turn away for there will be that day when you will be taken into heaven, if you love and serve Me! My beloved ones, I will wrap you in My Divine embrace and you will know joy beyond all joys, love beyond all love, light beyond all lights. You will know and love the Almighty God. You were created for this, but you must withstand this trial. You must be a child of light. You must obey the Father and obey your Mother. You must live according to the commandments and you must carry the Good News out to those that are suffering and in pain.

6. **R.** In the Father's messages there is so much reference to obedience. For the tone of the way the Father talks is different than the tone of how Jesus talks and different than how Mary talks. "...Thy will be done on earth as it is in heaven."

7. **R.** And so the Lady of Light appeared. She appeared in the most brilliant light on March the 20th of this year and she would keep going into Our Lady of Fatima. I know that when Our Lady said on December the 19th, 1996 that "the time is nigh" that it was important that we follow what she is saying.

Mary: Oh, my children, my little children of light, the time is nigh and many will be lost forever. I appeared and warned and told all to mind their ways and come to the Heart of my Son and they said "No, my Lady, not for you or any mother. We are children of darkness and that we remain, for we seek our pleasure by day and feast on sin all night and when you called, mother, we laughed at your Son and ignored Him and

His ways." And He called and His call fell on deaf ears.

Please, my children of light, come to my heart now for although you walked next to the children of darkness. I smite the dragon that whirled around you and protected you in my heart and you will now feast on the glories of His Kingdom, my little children of light.

8. **R.** Mary spoke, she appeared and no one listened, or few listened, or some listened, whatever it is. The response was not there according to what heaven expected when they gave such a great gift, the apparitions of the Blessed Mother. Jesus has given to us all these letters and they have been blocked tremendously. Over and over again this whole story is a story of how the messages have been blocked when Jesus wanted them out. The Father gave me a message in January, 1997 after Mary appeared at Clearwater and He said, "You disobey Mary. You disobey Jesus. Now are you going to disobey Me?"
9. Hail Mary
10.

Revelation 12: 1-2

Now a great sign appeared in heaven: a woman, robed with the sun, standing on the moon, and on her head a crown of twelve stars. She was pregnant, and in labour, crying aloud in the pangs of childbirth.

Message before the Glory Be:

R. Mary Immaculate; Mary, the pure one; Mary, the model that God gave to us; the New Eve; the Mother of Jesus and of us. And it is through Mary's heart that we are taken into the deepest intimacy with God. She appeared Our Lady of Light for 14 months to give this message: we must go to her heart so that we are brought forth children of light. Mary and Jesus' messages are in this book.

Song between decades: *Immaculate Mary*

The Coronation

1. **R.** The Father gives to us this message. (Apostles Manual p. 48 and Blue Book 14 pp. 72-73) **January 18, 1997**

"I am the Father. My plan is unfolding through you, My beloved priest, Fr. Carter, and Rita and the core group in the Shepherds of Christ Movement.

I tell you all to read the accounts concerning Noah. Nowhere in history has God been offended as He is this day by this sinful world. You will suffer a fate for the offenses against God.

Mary appeared at Fatima to warn you, the sinful children, how they were offending God, but you did not listen. The war did not change the hearts of many evil men.

I warn you through My beloved daughter, Mary. You did not heed her warnings. Disobedience against the Mother I gave you displeases Me greatly. Mary is the Mother of all children. Mary is a gift from Me, but you are willful and abuse the gift I send you.

You do not make reparation to her Immaculate Heart; you continue to offend her. I will not tolerate the deeds of evil men any longer."

2. **R.** Mary is a great gift that God gave to us. Jesus, tells us from the cross, He tells us that this is our Mother. But Mary appeared at Fatima and all these other times when God sends great gifts to the earth, when He gives warnings, they are to be heeded. We are disobedient children. We do not pay attention to what our Mother has told us at Fatima. Do we think that the Father is going to go away? When He sends the Queen of Heaven and Earth to the earth and gives us these great gifts to warn us, to tell us what we must do and we disobey her, do we think that He would be pleased?
3. **R.** Think of two Kingdoms. One in which Christ is the head and one which is headed by Lucifer. Lucifer wants souls for him and Jesus wants souls for Him. There is a spiritual battle that is going on all the time. We do not see so we do not think about this battle. But this is what is happening here over and over and over again, since I received these messages from Mary, from Jesus and from the Father, they are blocked over and over and over again. But it is a spiritual battle. There is a kingdom and Lucifer is the head of one and God, the other. And Lucifer wants all the souls he can get and take them to hell with him. We don't see these things

going on but we know what we experience in our own life, the trouble that we have especially since we have joined Shepherds of Christ. We are taunted by satan for he wants us stopped. The only way you can do what Mary is calling us to do is to spend that hour with Jesus every day because the devil makes confusion and all kinds of distractions in our life to lead us away from what He is telling us to do. And it's in that hour that we keep our focus on Him.

4. **R.** It is a spiritual battle that we experience that is trying to stop us over and over and over again. Since the end of December I have been told about how the 13th would be major and how satan would majorly try to stop it. But this is the thing that I want to say: we do not see the devil at work. Satan is devious. He causes confusion, division, and anger. We must go to God for it is a spiritual battle. It has been the evil one that has blocked the Fatima mission for 80 years, working hard. But it is in our prayers that it will make the difference. Mary is the Queen of Peace — we can't ignore her.

5. **Jesus:** And there will be a new earth, My sweet and beloved ones. There will be a time of great intimacy and love as never before as never before on this earth. You are My leaders that I am sending into this world. You will be taunted. You will be pressed on. You will fight this spiritual battle. But you must pray. Your weapons are the rosary and your prayers. Your weapons are the sacraments. Your weapons are your prayers I give you in the Prayer Manual. Give Me yourself. Give Me your heart. I am Jesus. I am longing for you to come to Me this very day for as I speak, there are many who are holding back. There will be no one standing in line behind you. You are the leader. You will lead. I have called special people to this room this day. I knew that you would respond. I gave you the grace to come here and I am giving you the grace at this moment to give your heart to Me. But many are holding back. There is a soul at the edge of death at this moment. You will help the souls go to heaven.

6. **R.** You may say: I did not know that my daughter would have an accident. I did not know that at that moment her soul would be on the edge of death. It was the prayers, the prayers that had turned her life around, the fact that she had

joined the Shepherds of Christ and consecrated her heart, her heart to the Hearts of Jesus and Mary. It was the prayers for the young ones, the ones that changed their hearts to hearts of love through the consecration when the prayer cards were circulated in the schools and they were being taught so many vile things. It was the consecration cards that helped the child to turn their heart to Jesus and Mary, and Jesus and Mary turned that heart to a heart of love. So you feel battered, you feel worn out. You think that no one is listening. But it is one school that you get the consecration to, that can change 500 children's hearts forever. For once they give their heart to Mary and Jesus, Mary and Jesus take it over. There are so many souls that are going to hell, Mary says. For the last 9 of the 14 months that the Queen of Heaven and Earth appeared to me, she cried out for her little lost children, especially the young ones that were being lost. And she says, "I stood beneath the cross of my Son and I cried. I cried for my little children."

7. Hail Mary
8. Hail Mary
9. **R.** And so this is a message from Our Lady of Light, from the Queen of Heaven and Earth. Jesus told me to read this to you.

from the Rosary of August 27, 1996

Mary: "I stood beneath the cross of my Son, and my Heart was in such pain for I saw Him before my eyes. I saw Him covered with blood. I saw Him die. My Heart, my children, my Heart to watch my Son, but my Heart, my Heart, how I suffered for my little children of the world that give in to this world and give up the love of my Son. O my little children of light, I give you this message. Carry this light into the darkness for your Mother Mary, for I stood beneath the cross and I cried. I cried for the little ones. I cried for the young ones, the ones that do not care and will lose their souls. How do I make you see for you will not listen to me? What can I do? I come. I appear. I beg. I plead. I give you these gifts from my Son, and you reject me. I do not deliver messages very often anymore for I have been ignored. The message is the same. You do not read the messages I have given to you. Please help me. Help the little children. I appear. I appear. I appear, and I am ignored. I stood beneath the cross, and I cried. I cried, and my Heart was in such anguish for my little children, for I am searching for them this day as I searched for the Child Jesus. Please, please help me. I cannot hold back the hand of my Son any longer. I am Mary, your Mother. I ask you to help my children. You are my children of light."

R. And we ignore these messages and ignore them. And we analyze the words and we worry but the message does not get out because satan is blocking the message. As long as he continues to block the messages of Our Lady, of our precious Jesus and the Father, we will continue to suffer. For the messages are given as teachings to draw us closer to Him. The messages are given as warnings for this earth. The world willfully does what it wants in many cases. The Father has warned us. And the focus is on me many times because I deliver the message. It is with great pain and suffering, many times, that I deliver the message for it is more than what is on the paper. The intensity is in my being as He gives the message to me and my only peace is in doing as He asked. It doesn't matter that they said to me, "But why are you listening to Mary when we are ignoring you?" "It doesn't matter to me what people say. God is talking. All I want to do is deliver the message." And it is a very difficult job many times for the focus is, many times, on everything but the message because satan blocks the message. He does not want the message out.

10. Hail Mary

R. Mary is the Queen of Heaven and Earth and she speaks over and over again. And the Father gives to us the great gifts when He sends His Mother and, Jesus opens up His Heart raw and reveals the most intimate secrets of His Heart. And the Father speaks,

"You have ignored My Mother and you Have ignored My Son. But will you ignore Me? If I send to you great gifts and you do not pay any heed, what do I do but to send you sufferings? For you must take notice. You are offending God. And the Reign of the Sacred Heart will come about disregarding all the willfulness of everyone involved for God is in charge."

Let us lift our minds and our hearts up to Him. Let us let go of those things that are keeping us bolted to the ground. Let us spend that hour of intimacy with Him every day, that in that hour He can sift out the negative and the positive messages in our minds, that we will know what God is telling us to do, for He is speaking in our hearts.

Song: *We Have Been Told*

4/13/97

Pray in Crisis

Jesus: I am Jesus, your beloved Savior,

My dear Shepherds,

I have called you on a special mission to help renew the Church and the world. In praying for the priests, religious, the Church and the world, many will turn their hearts to love.

What you do at this time, under this present crisis, will bind you closer in one mind and one heart.

I am asking you to review the message of March 18, 1997, to give this to all members in the movement.

I am asking you again to be faithful to the monthly candlelight rosary.

How you respond will help spread the Fatima mission. This will greatly please My Mother.

Oh, I love you, My shepherds. You must pray, pray as never before. Pray for Fr. Carter fervently in the Morning Offering and for a favorable decision from the provincial. Pray to the angels and saints. You are engaging in a spiritual battle. This Shepherds of Christ Movement must not be blocked because of its great importance to help bring about the Reign of the Sacred Heart and Triumph of Mary's Immaculate Heart.

You will join in one mind and one heart in the Morning Offering and the Consecration. Pray to St. Michael to help you. You must pray all day united to the Masses going on around the world. The devil is the one trying to stop you.

I love you, My Shepherds. Pray, Pray, Pray.

I am Jesus. If you say no, who will I send?

4/14/97

God the Father: To All Florida Apostles

God the Father: To all Florida apostles,

I have asked ______ to be the Apostle Coordinator in Florida. He is in charge of this mission. Therefore, he acts in My authority. I am the Father. I have sent Mary, your Mother, to you to change the hearts of men.

Please, I beg you, if you do not follow the instructions in the apostles message given on January 30, 1997, you will have serious problems. You must use the Apostles Manual, study it and pray the consecration often when on the site with each other. You must remain in one mind and one heart.

I am with you in this mission. Many, many souls throughout the world will be reached through your efforts there. You must love God and love each other. Pray to the Holy Spirit and take your mission with the greatest seriousness.

This is My plan for the renewal of the world. I am the Father.

4/16/97

A Letter to Tom

Jesus: My dear Tom,

I have held you in My Heart. I have watched you suffer and you were given great grace. You have proved your love to Me over and over again.

I want to be so close to you. I love you so much. I know how strong is your faith. You are a model to all for you have stood strong when you were greatly persecuted.

I love you, My beloved son. I am asking you to help as being a main apostle at My Florida site. My Mother loves you, her son, with the greatest motherly love. She watches you as you spread her tapes and books. It is in spreading the prayer manuals and consecration cards, too, that many will turn their hearts to Our Hearts and this will bring about the completion of the Fatima mission. I beg you to help Me. Please help Me.

Your mission is of the greatest importance to the souls of so many. Please help.

I am asking you to live by the Apostles message of January 30, 1997. In order to be in one mind and one heart you must live the messages in the Apostles Manual and the Blue Book messages.

Your role in the Shepherds of Christ Movement is many faceted.

Your farm is of major importance in the Fatima mission. This is why the rosary was said there on October 13, 1996 and will be on May 13, 1997 – the two greatest dates of Fatima.

Please help My Mother at the Florida site. Thank you, My beloved son, for spreading My Blue Books and your generosity. Many souls will know My love because of your gift given in these books and what you do.

I love you so much. I am your Jesus.

4/16/97

Spread My Love

Jesus: My beloved daughter,

I am your Jesus, the bridegroom of your soul. You have greatly pleased My Mother and My Father with your work to help spread our love. Your family has helped and we are blessing your family for your work.

I love you, My beloved child. I love you with the most burning heart of love.

You are a major apostle at the Florida site.

Will you help begin a prayer group there? Will you join in one mind and one heart? You are My apostle. You are to be united praying together in Florida to help in the mission begun at Fatima. You must operate in love. The devil wants to divide you. Please read this message to the others. Always pray together and eat often together. Love each other. If you divide, the world will suffer.

Please keep this focus:

I work for the Lord God to help bring about the Reign of Jesus' Heart and to spread His love, that the Immaculate Heart of Mary will triumph and that I will do all I can to help souls.

I love you so much, My daughter. I am Jesus, your Savior.

4/16/97

To Apostles in Florida

Jesus: My Dear Apostles in Florida,

I am Jesus, your Savior. The Florida site will help with the completion of the Fatima mission. In addition to all material being distributed there, you are asked to spread the Shepherds of Christ Associates *Prayer Manuals,* rosaries, and consecration cards. Many will be reached from this site with rosary and consecration. This will aid greatly in bringing about the completion of the Fatima mission.

I am Jesus. Please help to bring about the reign of My Heart and the triumph of My Mother's heart by spreading this material.

I love you, My apostles. Please tell all priests that come to the Florida site about the priestly newsletter, *Shepherds of Christ.*

4/17/97

Directions From Jesus

Jesus: My dear beloved ones,

I have given to you numerous messages that state ONLY Father Carter is to discern the messages of Shepherds of Christ Publications.

At this time I state the messages given must be obeyed. You are open to attack by the outside world. When a message is given from God it is to be obeyed until another message is given with different instructions. Read the message of January 30, 1997. No material is to be passed out at this time unless it is discerned by Fr. Carter.

Satan will, at this time, do everything to discredit the Movement. You must strongly state that all messages in the Shepherds of Christ Movement have been discerned by Father Carter.

I will give to you a few messages concerning directions. These messages can be given to Rita's spiritual director. Rita is the co-founder and she is in charge under Fr. Carter. You must continue to operate with the greatest guard placed on all messages.

All messages have been discerned by Father Carter. Any messages concerning the Movement at this time will be given as directions through the messenger Rita. Other messages will not be passed out.

Any messages that needed to be passed out were discerned previous to this situation. I am requesting the *Apostles Manual* be printed and circulated as soon as possible. This book was discerned by Father Carter. It is essential that you proceed ahead with this book swiftly.

You have been told by the Father, by My Mother and by Me to publish the *Parents & Children's Rosary Book* for the schools. You have been told to publish the Mass books with the *Imprimatur.* The fourth Blue Book is almost ready to be published and can receive the imprimatur.

I am asking you to publish two rosary books: one book with the rosaries from the existing rosary book with stations and seven sorrows and songs–included in this book should be the additional rosaries given to Rita and demessagetized. This book, with the *Imprimatur*, should be published for the Churches and Schools; the second book must be the children's rosaries from the Junior Shepherds of Christ meetings. It must be published promptly with the *Imprimatur*.

You must focus on this material with the *Imprimatur*. Other messages may not be distributed or published without the consent of Father Carter.

You must pray the Infant of Prague Novena every hour of the day until Father Carter meets with his provincial.

You are as a flock with the Chief Shepherd. Your Movement will be founded on obedience to the Chief Shepherd. John is the president. Father Carter has been given the title spiritual director by Me. Until further notice, I am asking you to obey the messages given concerning discernment.

You will be watched by all wanting to stop you. You cannot publish undiscerned messages at this time.

I am the Chief Shepherd. All must be obedient to Fr. Carter. All must respect him as head of the Movement.

You must pray to bring this about. Satan wants Fr. Carter removed from the Movement. It is a spiritual battle. You must pray the Novena to the Infant of Prague. Pray the Chaplet to St. Michael. Pray, Pray, Pray, My shepherds. The time is nigh, I am guarding you.

You must begin prayer chapters in Florida. I am displeased with the lack of response there. I beg you, beg you to take this job with the utmost seriousness.

I love you, My beloved shepherds. You are suffering. You must pray for Father Carter.

I thank John for all his efforts to make this most trying time a time of stability and love. He is a great leader in your Movement. You must pray for him and follow his direction.

I love you. Jesus

4/21/97

To Shepherds of Christ Associates

April 21, 1997

To My Fellow Shepherds of Christ Associates,

Father Carter is founder of Shepherds of Christ Ministries.

As Jesus stated to Fr. Carter at our inception:

"My beloved priest-companion, I intend to use the priestly newsletter, *Shepherds of Christ*, and the movement, *Shepherds of Christ Associates*, in a powerful way for the renewal of My Church and the world.

"I will use the newsletter and the chapters of *Shepherds of Christ Associates* as a powerful instrument for spreading devotion to My Heart and My Mother's Heart.

"I am calling many to become members of *Shepherds of Christ Associates*. To all of them I will give great blessings. I will use them as instruments to help bring about the triumph of the Immaculate Heart and the reign of My Sacred Heart. I will give great graces to the members of *Shepherds of Christ Associates*. I will call them to be deeply united to My Heart and to Mary's Heart as I lead them ever closer to My Father in the Holy Spirit."

Given on July 31, 1994, feast of Saint Ignatius Loyola, Founder of the Society of Jesus (The Jesuits)

The Mission entrusted to us by our Lord is of critical importance and satan knows this fact. We received a message on April 21, 1997 from Jesus. He asks us to pray the Infant Jesus of Prague Novena every hour of the day until Father Carter meets with his provincial.

How we respond in this crisis will determine the future effectiveness of the Movement. Satan has greatly blocked the Fatima message in the Church. If we want peace we must do as Mary has told us to do at Fatima.

Jesus has instructed us how we must pray. The enclosed novena cards can be used for this purpose. Please ask friends if they are willing to pray with you. We must present a united prayer front to God as a sign of our faith and love.

This novena takes about a minute to pray. The challenge is to stay connected to God throughout the day and to pray it every hour we are awake. It is a very powerful expression of love for Fr. Carter to fulfill this urgent request. If you miss your hour, please do not give up. Just pray it when you remember and ask for grace to do better next time. When Jesus fell carrying his cross, he did not quit! Our guardian angels can also help us to pray.

They are always with us. In the same message we were also instructed to pray the St. Michael Chaplet. Last year St. Michael was seen by several people while praying at the Tom's Farm in Kentucky. He is a special protector of our movement. Due to a scheduling conflict at the Our Lady of the Holy Spirit Center, the May 13th prayer meeting will be returning to Tom's farm with the Rosary @ 12:00 PM. You should have received or will shortly receive a pink sheet with a map and directions to the farm. It should be a beautiful day of prayer.

I would like you to know that all messages and materials in the Shepherds of Christ Movement have been discerned by Fr. Carter prior to the present situation. Nothing will be sent out in the future that has not already been approved by him! An important book, the final version of the Apostles Manual, will be sent out shortly. This book was discerned by Fr. Carter before the latest developments.

Please, I beg you to take this call to prayer seriously. My children are young and I want them to grow up in a country with a strong and holy Roman Catholic Church. Our little prayers to our all powerful God can make all the difference.

In the Hearts of Jesus and Mary,
John Weickert, President
(toll free): 1-888-211-3041

4/21/97

Jesus and Mary's Picture on Cover

Message from Jesus:

My dear son, and to whom it may concern:

I have called you to be a major help in the Shepherds of Christ Movement.

The Prayer Manual is a key to the completion of the Fatima mission. The Father said that great gifts are given but they were not accepted and people did not pay attention to My Mother.

I am Jesus, your beloved Savior. I gave myself as a sacrifice on the cross for sinful men. I have come in these messages to help bring about the Reign of My Most Sacred Heart. I have given to this world the Shepherds of Christ Prayer Manual. It is My instrument for the renewal of the Church and the world.

I want the picture of My Heart and My Mother's heart on the front cover. Your picture should be associated with the Prayer Manual. This Prayer Manual is the key to bringing about the completion of the Fatima message.

I am allowing all to suffer, but your sufferings are giving you great joy for you are learning invaluable lessons that will help you to grow in the deepest holiness.

You have been called and asked by Me to help to spread these prayer manuals with the pictures to the world. You are major in bringing about the completion of the Fatima message. The prayer manual has been held in check by the workings of satan. I am asking you to continue to spread this prayer manual in abundance. The people that come to Florida are hungry for the material.

The Plan of the Father was deterred greatly because of the workings of satan to try to stop the completion of the Fatima mission.

I am asking you to help spread the prayer manual. In the message from the Father He asks that all form prayer chapters centered in consecration and spread the Priestly Newsletter. He says they should be made available in abundance and each priest in the United States receive the book of the Priestly

Newsletters. Soon the *Mass Book* will also be available with the *Imprimatur.* You must continue to work for this goal. All interference to this is the work of satan.

I want the picture of My Sacred Heart and My Mother's Immaculate Heart on the front of all prayer manuals in red. This red book will make men's hearts turn to hearts of love as they give themselves in consecration to My Heart and My Mother's heart.

The Shepherds of Christ Movement is crucial to the completion of the Fatima mission.

Satan will make distractions to try to lead you from this mission. Doing a good thing is not always doing the Will of the Father.

I am Jesus. This is My instrument for the renewal of the Church and the world. You are major in helping to bring this about. Be aware of how satan will try to stop you from carrying out the Plan of the Father.

The Movement is budding forth in the greatest bloom because of your work. I am asking you to majorly help us. Do not be led astray with other endeavors. Please help Me to bring about the renewal of the Church and the world and carry out the completion of the Fatima mission.

You are My beloved son. I have taken you to My Heart and given you the greatest intimacies with Me. You have received the greatest gifts spiritually. You are My chosen son. Please continue to help Me to bring about the Reign of My Sacred Heart.

What you do to help the Shepherds of Christ Movement will help to make the picture a reality where My Heart will Reign as King and Center of hearts and My Mother's heart will triumph. Please help Me!

Thank you, My son. I give you My Heart as your greatest shelter. Come to Me and I will bathe you in My burning love. Oh, how I love thee. I love thee, I love thee, My son. You are precious to Me.

I am your Sacred Heart. I will Reign in the hearts of men and the heart of My mother will triumph. Jesus

Song: *Come to My Heart*

Come to My Heart

- 6:00 a.m. - 4/25/97

Will You Help Me

Message from Jesus

My dear beloved son,

I am Jesus. I have given you the greatest intimacies with My Heart. I am giving you this special letter to thank you for your support to the Shepherds of Christ Movement.

This is My Movement for the renewal of the Church and the world. The prayer manual will greatly help to bring about the completion of the Fatima mission. This mission has been blocked greatly in the past.

I will use the prayer manual and the Shepherds of Christ Priestly Newsletter to help renew the Church and the world.

My Heart will Reign and My Mother's heart will triumph. You have greatly helped. I am asking you to continue to pray each day before the tabernacle for this mission. You are being asked to be a special apostle through your prayers and your love and support.

My beloved son, will you help Me? When this world is dark, will you be a pillar of light? You have delighted My Heart with your love and helping to spread the Fatima mission.

Thank you, My beloved son,

I am Jesus, your beloved Savior.
My Heart burns for love of you.

Thank you, My son. Jesus

4/25/97

A Second Letter to Tom

Message from Jesus

Jesus: My dear Tom,

The Second Blue Book greatly was given to lead men to My Eucharistic Heart.

As men go more and more into My Heart through the Eucharist, the Church will become a great pillar of light in this world.

I have given in Blue Book 2 letters from My Heart, that men

would realize the great gift they have been given in the Eucharist.

Today, more than three years later since I have given these messages, the Eucharist is not treasured as it should be.

I give you Myself. I write letters to turn men's hearts to My Heart. I am treated with such indifference and disrespect.

People do not treasure the greatest gift they are given. The greatest gift given to man is the gift of Myself.

Please help Me to distribute this book that men will treasure the gift I give them in the Eucharist.

Do not give up. If you say 'no', who will tell them of this gift I give to men? Enough men are not responding and helping to spread the word. The burden is heavy on you. Pray, please pray, that men will treasure the gift I give them. Please come to Me daily in Mass and Communion and pray one hour daily before the tabernacle. I love you so much. I wait for you. I want you to come and be with Me. I know how you have struggled. You are major in helping to bring about the Reign of My Heart. You are a soldier of My love.

Please help Me. Do not give up. Give Me your heart and I will hold you in the furnace of Divine Love.

I love you so much.

I am Jesus, your Savior, Chief Shepherd of the Flock

4/25/97

A Letter to the Provincial from Rita Ring

April 29, 1997

Dear Father,

I feel strongly in my heart that I am called to write to you to tell you about all of the ministries in our Shepherds of Christ Movement, and thank you for everything that you and the Jesuits have done to help us to spread this Movement. The Movement is flourishing and we are encouraging people to consecrate their hearts to the Hearts of Jesus and Mary in the churches, schools and families.

The Shepherds of Christ Movement is helping to bring about the completion of the Fatima message. We are praying for the renewal of the Church and the world. We have many materials with the *Imprimatur,* to help bring about the completion of the Fatima message. Mary's peace plan, given at Fatima says we must: 1) Consecrate our hearts to Jesus and Mary; 2) Pray the Rosary; 3) Observe the First Saturday devotion; 4) Make reparation to Their Hearts for offenses against them.

The Prayer Manual has the *Imprimatur.* With prayers to the Sacred Heart and the Immaculate Heart, it satisfies the first, second, and fourth requirement in Mary's Peace Plan. We need to spread this Prayer Manual to the world so that people will be praying for the priests and the renewal of the Church and the world. In doing this, we are fulfilling many of Mary's requirements given at Fatima to help bring about the great era of peace.

We have prayer chapters all over the world praying these prayers for the priests and the renewal of the Church and the world. Many of the prayer chapters are praying before the tabernacle. We have rosary meditations for children with the imprimatur, centered in love of Jesus, love of Mary, the Eucharist, the Mass, and understanding the mysteries of the rosary. We are spreading consecration cards and rosary meditations in the schools, in compliance with Mary's request, given to us at Fatima. I have two books of rosary meditations for Church and school which will get the *Imprimatur.* They are teachings about the burning love of Jesus, the Eucharist, the Mass, and the lives of Jesus and Mary. We have prayer chapters for children, the Junior Shepherds of Christ, who consecrate their hearts to Jesus and Mary.

We have a special group, *Apostles of the Eucharistic Heart of Jesus*, who spend two hours weekly before the tabernacle, praying the prayers for the priests and for the renewal of the Church and the world, from the prayer manual. They pray for the following intentions:

1. For the spread of the devotion to the Hearts of Jesus and Mary culminating in the reign of the Sacred Heart and the triumph of the Immaculate Heart;
2. For the Pope;

3. For all bishops of the world;
4. For all priests;
5. For all Sisters and Brothers in the religious life;
6. For all members of the Shepherds of Christ Movement, and for the spread of this movement to the world;
7. For all members of the Catholic Church;
8. For all members of the human family;
9. For all souls in purgatory.

We have apostles all over trying to spread devotion to the Sacred Heart of Jesus and the Immaculate Heart of Mary. Most pray one hour daily before the tabernacle, go to daily Mass and Communion, pray three rosaries a day and consecrate their hearts with each other and their families.

Our main focus in the Shepherds of Christ Movement is in praying for the priests and for the renewal of the Church and the world.

As the priestly newsletter spreads and the priests are consecrating their hearts to Jesus and Mary, the Church and the world will be renewed through our beloved priests. There is much more – the fruits from this more – the fruits from this Movement are far reaching.

The greatest gift given to man is Jesus Christ giving Himself to us. How indifferently we treat our Lord: at Saturday and Sunday Masses, the whole Church, sometimes 1,000 people, get up and leave the Church immediately afterwards, talking and laughing, and God gives Himself to them.

Jesus wants our love. He is love. He gives Himself to us in the Eucharist and He is treated with indifference. He is not loved by many. He is alive, He is a Person. He is treated as a cold, dead object by many. He is the divine God that remains with us in the Holy Eucharist. He outpours His divine life to us when we sit before the tabernacle. He is moved from many altars and hidden in a corner.

God has given to us the greatest gift: Himself, truly present in the Holy Eucharist. The Mass is the greatest love affair with God, where He gives Himself to us and He wants us to give Him the gift of ourselves. These are special moments after communion when He imprints secrets into His Divine love in our hearts, when He wants intimate time with Him – and sometimes the whole Church leaves on Sunday, laughing and talking, not treasuring the greatest gift given!

Much of our material is centered in Jesus in the Eucharist. Many of our members spend time every day after communion, and an hour before the tabernacle. Many have helped start perpetual adoration in their churches.

I thank you for allowing Fr. Carter to be our Spiritual Director in the Shepherds of Christ Movement.

Mary promised at Fatima that the Sacred Heart of Jesus will reign and her heart will triumph. "Thy kingdom come, thy will be done on earth as it is in heaven." In the Shepherds of Christ Movement we are attempting to help to bring Christ as Center to all hearts. This will bring about the great era of peace and love on the earth. The Fatima message has been blocked for 80 years. They ignored Mary at Fatima and World War II occurred.

We are trying to spread the prayer chapters all over the world, praying for the priests and renewal of the Church and the world. We want to get the Priestly Newsletter centered in consecrating their hearts to the Hearts of Jesus and Mary in the hands of as many priests as possible. We have a *Parents & Children's Rosary Book* and meditations on the rosary, and consecration cards with the *Imprimatur.*

Father Carter has helped to lead so many thousands of souls to the Heart of Jesus. The Movement has spread all over the world and people are growing deeply in their intimacy with Our Lord in less than three years.

There is a book entitled, *The Mass Book, A Journey Into the Heart of Christ*, which is centered on our great love affair with Jesus in the Mass. It is the first of three books and is now at the Chancery for the *Imprimatur.* This book tells us much about Fatima and the Shepherds of Christ Movement.

When a Church, the priest and people consecrate their hearts to Jesus and Mary and go to daily mass and have adoration of the Blessed Sacrament, it becomes a powerhouse, a city of light in the dark world.

You have been most gracious in helping us to spread the love of Jesus to this world. Thank you for everything you have done for us and the world.

I want so much for Jesus' Heart to Reign and Mary's heart to triumph, people to love Jesus in the Mass, and the priests to be filled with His love when they celebrate the Mass. The new earth is coming when His Heart will Reign and Mary's heart will triumph.

Thank you for everything.

Love,

Rita Ring

The Mass – Fr. Carter/ Rita Ring

May 1, 1997 - St. Gertrude Church

R. I join with all the angels and saints and the souls in purgatory and unite in the Holy Sacrifice of the Mass united to Jesus.

I offer myself united to Jesus to the Father in the Holy Spirit. I offer myself through the powerful intercession of Mary - Mother of God, all the angels and saints and the souls in purgatory.

Excerpt from *Response in Christ*
by Fr. Edward J. Carter, S.J.

a) Sacrifice in General

There are various ways of developing the structure of sacrifice. Some authors include more constituent elements than others. We will give a structure which we believe includes the essential elements commonly given. This structure of sacrifice is a traditional one, yet it is one which can well be harmonized with modern theological, liturgical and scriptural studies. A leading scripture scholar, F. X. Durrwell, gives us assurance on this point by telling us of the value of considering Christ's redemptive activity within the traditional structure of sacrifice developed over the centuries: "But first it will be useful to look once more at the drama of the Redemption, placing it in a framework – a framework adequate to contain its rich reality which God Himself had prepared throughout the history of mankind: Sacrifice."[5] We enter upon our discussion of sacrifice in general by considering the first of five constituent elements.

1) Interior Oblation

The first duty of man is to surrender himself to God out of love. This fact flows from the truth that God is the Creator and man is His creature. Man, if he is ideally to fulfill his creaturely role must respond as perfectly as possible to the loving demands of His Creator. God asks that man give himself completely to Himself. This is only proper since everything that man has, whether of the natural or supernatural order, has been given to him by God. Man, in turn, perfects himself by developing these various gifts according to God's will or, in other words, by giving himself completely to God. Man's gift of self to God is centered in loving conformity to the divine will. Consequently, one can understand why the will with its decision-making capacity is the crucial faculty in man, a point emphasized by contemporary thought.

Man directs himself to God by the virtue of religion. This is not to say that this particular virtue ranks above the theological virtues of faith, hope and charity. These are the most excellent, since they unite man directly to God. We are merely stating that the virtue of religion directs all man's actions to the honor of God.[6]

This virtue consists especially in acts of adoration, thanksgiving, petition and reparation. These interior acts can manifest themselves in many ways, but they are especially expressed through sacrifice. Here, then, we have the first constituent element of sacrifice: man's interior offering of himself to God. This giving takes place chiefly in man's will, under the guidance of the virtue of religion. This first element of sacrifice is of prime importance, for it deals with interior dispositions. This importance can be recognized concretely in the history of religion. For example, the Jewish people were convinced that the principal value of sacrifice was centered in the dispositions of the people.[7]

. . .

b) Christ's Sacrifice

We will consider Christ's sacrifice according to the same constituent elements of sacrifice already discussed. In this treatment we will follow the theory of the unicists, who hold that Our Lord offered only one complete sacrifice as opposed to the dualist theory which says Christ offered two complete sacrifices, one at the Last Supper, and one on Calvary. The Church allows either position. We prefer to follow the position of the unicists, since this seems to give a greater unity to Christ's sacrifice, and indeed to the total mystery of Christ. This profound unity of Christ's mystery has become more and more apparent with the scriptural, liturgical and theological renewals.[12]

1) The Interior offering of Our Lord

The sacrifice which Christ offered for the redemption of the world was first and foremost an interior moral act. Christ's life possessed its great value because of His interior dispositions. His entire life was a constant gift of Himself in love to the Father and to mankind, and Calvary was the supreme expression of this gift. This gift of self was regulated by a perfect conformity to His Father's will.

Christ not only was constantly living out this interior disposition of sacrifice, but He strove to inculcate the necessity of it in the Jews of His time. He constantly opposed a false and legalistic concentration on the mere externals of Jewish purifications, for such an attitude tended to diminish the necessary internal dispositions. The synoptic theology of sacrifice stresses this attitude of Christ. Bernard Cooke states: "This insistence of Jesus on internal dispositions characterizes the Synoptic theology of sacrifice, which continues and completes the prophetic emphasis on the moral and individual aspect of sacrifice. . . . One must be careful, however, not to exaggerate the opposition (either in the prophets or in the Synoptic Gospels) between cult and internal dispositions of soul."[13]

5. F. X.Durrwell, *The Resurrection* (New York: Sheed & Ward, 1960), p. 59.

6. St. Thomas Aquinas, *S.T.*, II-II, q. 81, a. 4, ad 1.

7. Cf. S. Lyonnet, "La Sotériologie Paulinienne" in Robert and Feuillet, *Introduction à la Bible*, Vol. II (Tournai, Belgium: Desclée, 1959), p. 874.

12. Cf. Bernard Cooke, *Christian Sacraments and Christian Personality* (New York: Holt, Rinehart, and Winston, 1965), pp. 132-133.

13. Bernard Cooke, "Synoptic Presentation of the Eucharist as Covenant Sacrifice" in *Theological Studies*, Vol. 21 (1960), p. 12.

R. I know at the Mass there is immense grace being released. The more I unite in oneness with Jesus the more I am one with everyone else. I cannot reach this great oneness with Jesus unless I go through the Immaculate Heart of Mary.

June 29, 1929

R. That is why Mary appeared in Lucia's vision with her heart out. The key to this opening of grace through her Immaculate Heart because we become one with Christ the more pure we are. I am a sinner. I give my heart to Mary, the pure and Immaculate one. Mary takes me more deeply to the Heart of Jesus. God releases grace and mercy. It is all in oneness with Jesus; oneness with Jesus makes oneness with Father, Holy Spirit and all else!!

The more we all give our hearts to Mary, the more pure is our offering, the more we all unite deeply in the Heart of Christ. To unite to Jesus we unite with all angels and saints and souls in purgatory. We are one with Jesus giving Himself to the Father. We are one in Him. This is a pleasing sacrifice to the Father.

Excerpt from *Response in Christ*
by Fr. Edward J. Carter, S.J.

The Sacraments and the Mass

4) Acceptance of the Sacrifice by God

In order that the sacrifice might reach its extrinsic consummation God on His part must accept it. God's acceptance of sacrifice has been shown in various ways. Among the Hebrews assurance of the divine acceptance was seen in the phenomenon of fire falling from heaven and consuming the victim of sacrifice. In the absence of such a heavenly token, there was at least some assurance that God accepted the sacrifice because of the duly consecrated altar itself. The altar received the gifts of sacrifice, and in doing so symbolized God's acceptance of the same.

. . .

4) The Father's Acceptance of Christ's Sacrifice

We have demonstrated that one of the constituent elements of sacrifice is its acceptance by God. In the case of Christ's sacrifice, this acceptance by the Father was accomplished in a most glorious fashion – through Christ's Resurrection and Ascension. The Father glorified His Son for the perfect, whole-hearted sacrifice of Calvary. This glorification shall endure for all eternity, since Christ reigns at the right hand of the Father as eternal victim, as eternal, glorified victim. Through this glorified Christ the treasures of His sacrifice are distributed to all men: "Christ's glorification is the mystery whereby the treasures of his divinity flow to us, through the opening of his mortal life."[15]

In the union of these last two elements of Christ's sacrifice, His immolation in death and the acceptance of His sacrifice through the Resurrection and Ascension, lies the essence of Christ's redemptive act – of course, in saying this we presuppose the first element of Christ's sacrifice, His interior disposition or oblation; this is *the* essential element. This union of Christ's death and Resurrection is called His paschal mystery, His passover. In what did this passover or transition consist? In our initial chapter we briefly described this passover of Christ. We will now expand to some extent upon this basic reality of Christ's life.

The divine love, or agape, descended into this world for the salvation of men. This saving force manifested itself to men through the redemptive activity of the Word made flesh. By becoming man, Christ, although free from sin, submitted Himself to the conditions and circumstances of a sinful world.

His redemptive activity consisted in a struggle with the forces of evil. As this struggle developed, Christ at the same time was returning to the glory of His Father. He finally conquered completely through His paschal mystery. Through His death He liberated Himself completely from a world impregnated with sin and passed over into the new order of the Resurrection. Moreover, Christ experienced this transition process not just for Himself. By His own passover Christ achieved for all men the opportunity to pass from death to life, from a life of sin to a new life as sons of God. In the words of Lyonnet, "The redemption is essentially the return of humanity to God. The return is accomplished first of all in Christ who died and rose again as the first fruits of this humanity (objective redemption), and then in each Christian who dies and rises again with Christ in baptism (subjective redemption)."[16]

Consequently, we have observed, in terms of sacrificial elements, the most intimate union which exists between Christ's death and Resurrection. They are inseparable, and lie at the heart of the total mystery of Christ. This paschal mystery is central, therefore, to the liturgy and to the whole Christian life.

. . .

1) Interior Oblation of the Mass

The chief priest and victim of the Mass is the same as the priest and victim of the Last Supper and Calvary, Christ Himself. Christ makes this interior offering of Himself in the Mass for the same ends as were present in His own unique sacrifice – adoration, thanksgiving, petition and satisfaction.

However, Christ is not the only priest at the Mass as He was at the Last Supper and upon Calvary. All the members of the Mystical Body are priests along with Christ. To be sure, there is a difference between the hierarchical priesthood of bishops and priests and the universal priesthood of the faithful. This difference is one of essence and not merely degree. The point we wish to stress, however, is that the universal priesthood is a real participation in Christ's priesthood given through the sacraments of baptism and confirmation.

This concept of the priesthood of all the Church's members is being stressed today in a special manner.[18] Jungmann, the outstanding liturgical theologian, gives us reasons why this concept of universal priesthood became relatively obscure for so many years. He states that the concept of the Mass as the Church's sacrifice faded into the background as a result of the Reformation. The Reformers maintained that there was only one sacrifice, the one which Christ offered upon Calvary. To counteract this heresy the Council of Trent and the theology consequent to it had to clarify that the Mass is a true sacrifice, but not an absolutely independent one. It is a sacrifice relative to the absolute one of Calvary and a representation of it. It was emphasized that the priest of Calvary is also the chief priest of the Mass. Because of such doctrinal controversies, the concept that Christ offers the Mass was alone considered important. The concept that the Mass is *also* the sacrifice of the Church practically disappeared. Finally, Jungmann notes that today we are returning to the balanced view which meaningfully recognizes that the Mass is not only the sacrifice of Christ, but also that of the Church.[19] This stress on the Church's part in the Mass is logically connected with the contemporary emphasis on the priesthood of all the members of the People of God.

As Christ is not the only priest of the Mass, neither is He the only victim. Again, all the members of the Church are victims along with Christ. Various Church documents attest to this. For instance, Pope Paul VI officially calls attention to this: "It is a pleasure to add another point particularly conducive to shed light on the mystery of the Church, that it is the whole Church which, in union with Christ functioning as Priest and Victim, offers the Sacrifice of the Mass and is offered in it."[20] Therefore, the members of the People of God, united as priests to Christ the high priest, offer a combined victim to the Father: Christ and themselves. Such then in all its deep meaning and beauty is the first sacrificial element of the Mass.

. . .

4) The Father's Acceptance of the Eucharistic Sacrifice

It has been observed that if sacrifice is to have its desired effect, it must be accepted by God. That the Father always accepts the eucharistic sacrifice is certain. For the principal priest and victim is Christ Himself, always supremely acceptable to the Father. As for the subordinate priests and victims, they are, taken together, the People of God, the Church herself.

There is always an acceptance on the Father's part even as regards this subordinate priesthood and victimhood of the Mass. For even though the Mass may be offered through the sacrilegious hands of an unworthy priest, there is always a basic holiness in the Church pleasing to God. Because of such holiness the Father always accepts the Church's sacrificial offering, for the Mass is the sacrifice of the whole Church, and cannot be fundamentally vitiated by the unworthiness of any particular member or members, even if that member be the officiating priest.

What do we say concerning the Father's acceptance of the sacrificial offering of the individual Christian? Such an offering will be acceptable in proportion to the Christian's loving conformity of will to the Father's will. Speaking of the Christian's participation in the Mass, Jungmann says: "It follows that an interior immolation is required of the participants, at least to the extent of readiness to obey the law of God in its seriously obligatory commandments, unless this participation is to be nothing more than an outward appearance."[30]

Having considered in successive sections the immolation and acceptance elements of the Mass, we should consider the vital link between these two. For just as the two are inseparably connected in Christ's sacrifice, so are they also united in the Church's sacrifice of the Mass.

In Christ we equated the immolation of His sacrifice with His passion-death, and the acceptance element with His Resurrection. Uniting these two mysteries of death-resurrection, we spoke of Christ's paschal mystery. We have seen that this mystery had been prefigured by the Jewish pasch and exodus, component parts of the Jewish people's transition to a new and more perfect life. In the case of Christ, we considered His pasch – His passover – to be a transition from the limitations of His mortal life to the state of resurrected glory. We speak of Christ's mortal humanity as having exercised limitations upon Him in this sense, that, although He Himself was completely free from sin, He had exposed Himself to the conditions of a sin-laden world through His human nature. In His death-resurrection He changed all this as He conquered sin, as He redeemed us, as He *passed* to the state of glory with His Father.

What happened in Christ also occurs in His Mystical Body, the Church. The Church and Her members experience their own transition from death to resurrection. The entire Church and the individual Christian express, through the Mass, a willingness to grow in the participation in Christ's death. The Father accepts this willingness and gives an increase in the grace-life, a greater share in Christ's Resurrection. This process happened within a short span of time in Christ's life. In the life of the Church it continually takes place until Christ's second coming. The Church, with her grace-life of holiness, has already partially achieved her resurrection, but not completely, even though she continues to grow in grace. St. Paul bears witness to this: ". . . but all of us who possess the first-fruits of the Spirit, we too groan inwardly as we wait for our bodies to be set free." (Rm 8:23).

Vatican II's *Constitution on the Church* beautifully portrays this fused state of death-resurrection which the Church in her members experiences here below as she awaits the fullness of the resurrection in the world to come: "For this reason we, who have been made to conform with him, who have died with him and risen with him, are taken up into the mysteries of his life, until we will reign together with him. . . While still pilgrims on earth, tracing in trial and in oppression the paths he trod, we are anointed with his sufferings as the body is with the head, suffering with him, that with him we may be glorified. . ."[31]

. . .

d) The Christian's Participation in the Mass

God has created man a social being. This fact has relevance as regards man's salvation and perfection. Man does not go to God alone, but rather is saved and perfected with and through others. This is evident in the study of salvation history as one observes God communicating Himself to man in the framework of community. As we have seen, this social dimension is also readily evident in the liturgy.

As we now discuss the individual's participation in the liturgy, we in no way intend to underestimate the communal aspect of the eucharistic sacrifice. We constantly presuppose it and its importance. Liturgy as communal is the indispensable framework and background for any discussion of the individual's liturgical participation.

Granted all this, it is still useful and necessary to speak of the individual's participation in the Mass.[33] Ultimately it is the individual as individual who accepts or rejects God's offer of salvation and sanctification. Therefore, to speak of the individual's response to God in the liturgy is highly significant. Despite all the communal helps the individual receives in the liturgy, despite the fact that the individual must always be deeply aware that he is a member of the community, the People of God, it is still true to say that it is within the depths of his own mysterious, individual personality that the Christian either becomes a mature Christian through the liturgy or fails to do so. With such preliminary ideas established, let us now consider the Christian and his role in the Mass.

1) The Baptized Christian and the Mass

Once again the reader is reminded that through baptism the Christian becomes incorporated into Christ and His Church. Confirmation perfects this incorporation. Although baptism incorporates us primarily into Christ's death and Resurrection, we again stress that it also unites us with Christ in all His mysteries. This is so because all Christ's mysteries are essentially one mystery, for none of them stands separately by itself. Consequently, one cannot be initiated into Christ's paschal mystery without simultaneously being incorporated into all of His mysteries.

The fact that all of Christ's various mysteries are contained in the total mystery of Christ enables the Christian to encounter the entire Christ in the liturgy. Mention of this fact brings us to our next point.

In baptism the Christian first encounters and relives the mystery of Christ. He thereby receives a new life. But this life must be nourished. The Christian must constantly re-encounter the mystery of Christ, and this he does chiefly through the eucharistic liturgy. Here the Christian is daily privileged to encounter Christ in the most intimate fashion. Here above all he exercises his priesthood and consequently grows in supernatural vitality. We use the word *exercise* purposely, since the liturgy is primarily an action, an exercise of the priestly office of Christ.

Since the baptized Christian is sacramentally participating in the mystery of Christ at the Mass, his priestly act must be modeled after that of Christ's. This is true because the life of grace flowing out of the seals of baptism and confirmation is structured according to certain modalities or characteristics based on the life of Christ. This truth was developed at some length in the previous chapter. There we stated that Christ, the head of the Mystical Body, has determined, through His own life of sanctifying grace, the general lines of development according to which His members' lives of grace grow and mature.

Therefore it is evident that the whole of the Christian's life must be orientated to the Mass and be centered about it; for in Christ we see His entire life centered around His priestly act of Calvary. This is true because His interior sacrificial disposition, the essence of His priestly act, permeated everything in His life.

The baptized Christian should also bring his daily life, his whole life, to the eucharistic sacrifice. The Church which assembles about the altar is not a nebulous, ethereal entity, but the Church of this earth. It is the Church of men and women who are immersed in the work of this world. As they gather for the eucharistic sacrifice, they are therefore not removed from the world of their ordinary daily lives to an unreal world of ritual which has no connection with their temporal cares and activities. Rather it is the reality of this ordinary daily life which they bring to offer as priests and victims in union with Christ, priest and victim. In such a manner, then, the eucharistic sacrifice looks to the past life of the Christian.[34]

Yet the Mass also looks to the future of the Christian. By his participation in the Mass he receives grace to assimilate in a more perfect manner the mystery of Christ. Ideally, each Mass participated in by the Christian should mean that he leaves the eucharistic assembly with a greater Christ-likeness. Thus he takes up his daily life as a more fervent Christ-bearer.

The Mass as it looks to both the past and future embraces the Christian's entire life. It is meant to be lived each minute of the Christian's life. Durrwell says: "The Mass is said in order that the whole Church and the whole of our life may become a Mass, may become Christ's sacrifice always present on earth. St. Francis of Sales resolved that he would spend the whole day preparing to say Mass, so that whenever anyone asked what he was doing, he might always answer, 'I am preparing for Mass'. We also could resolve to make our whole lives a participation in the divine mystery of the Redemption, so that when anyone puts the question to us, we can always answer, 'I am saying Mass'."[35]

2) The Mass lived out

As the Christian lives out the Mass, he is consequently daily laboring with Christ in furthering the work of the subjective redemption. This is so because Christ's sacrifice was a redemptive act, and the Church's reliving of this act in the Mass is also redemptive. In this regard we must remember that the entire universe – not merely man – has been redeemed. The nonrational and rational world alike await the furthering of the redemption. St. Paul tells us: "From the beginning till now the entire creation, as we know, has been groaning in one great act of giving birth; and not only creation, but all of us who possess the first-fruits of the Spirit, we too groan inwardly as we wait for our bodies to be set free." (Rm 8:22-23).

How does the Christian help Christ redeem the world? (Henceforth the term "world" is to be understood as including both rational and nonrational creation.) As previously stated, the Christian helps Christ redeem the world by reliving Christ's mysteries. The same "events" or mysteries which accomplished the objective redemption further the subjective redemption also. Since at the heart of Christ's mysteries are His death and Resurrection, it is especially these that the Christian must relive. As the Christian dies mystically with Christ through loving conformity with the Father's will, he rises with Christ to an ever greater share in the Resurrection, in the newness of life, in the life of grace. As the Christian in this manner relives the paschal mystery of Christ, he is accomplishing not only his own redemption, but he is also, in a mysterious yet real manner, helping Christ redeem the world.

Although Christ's life was summed up in death-resurrection, it also included various other "events" or mysteries. Each of these in its own manner contributed to the redemption. So it is with the Christian's life. His participation in Christ's death-resurrection must be "broken down" into the other mysteries of Christ's life.

The Christian must always remember that he carries away

from the Mass not only the Christ of the death and the Resurrection, but also, for example, the Christ of the hidden life and the Christ of the public life. As the Christian lives out his Mass in the exercise of his Christ-life, all these various mysteries should therefore be present.

Before we give examples of how the Christian can relive these saving events of Christ's life, it is well that we first distinguish the two different levels on which the Christian assimilates the mystery of Christ.

Christ, through His death and Resurrection, has transformed us. This transformation is a "new creation," a new life of grace. Through our baptism we are initiated into this life and consequently we exist as new creatures. As long as we possess the life of sanctifying grace, which is our share in the mystery of Christ, we are living according to this new existence whether or not this life here and now incarnates itself in a concrete, supernatural act. In this sense the life of grace, the "new creation," is fundamental, radical and transcendent, a share in the transcendent holiness or mystery of God Himself.

However, God expects that our life of transcendent holiness incarnate itself in concrete supernatural acts. It is in this respect that we speak of reliving the various mysteries of Christ through specific supernatural attitudes and acts. This may also be called imitation of Christ, but with a certain precaution, namely, that the imitation in question is to be considered primarily as interior rather than exterior. By this we mean that although the Christian can to a certain extent imitate Christ according to what was His external mode of conduct, it is primarily through adopting the mind of Christ – His interior dispositions – that the Christian puts on Christ. With this said we now offer suggestions as to how the Christian relives the mysteries of Christ whose presence and transforming influences have been encountered in the eucharistic liturgy.

For instance, each member of Christ, whether he be bishop, priest, religious or layman, can accomplish much of his redemptive work by an intense reliving of Christ's hidden life. Certainly our heavenly Father would have us learn a great lesson from this fact, namely, that His Christ lived out so many years of His earthly life in a hidden manner, doing the ordinary tasks of the ordinary man. In assimilating this particular mystery of Christ the Christian must say with Rahner: "Let us take a good look at Jesus Who had the courage to lead an apparently useless life for thirty years. We should ask Him for the grace to give us to understand what His hidden life means for our religious existence."[36]

Christ did not lead only a hidden life, but a public life also. All vocations within the Church are likewise called upon to reproduce this part of Christ's life in some manner. One aspect of Christ's public life that should be common to all Christian vocations is the selflessness, the constant concern and love for others which Christ constantly and vividly displayed. This concern for others cost Christ much in fatigue of body and mind. Nevertheless, He continuously gave Himself completely to others.

Another characteristic of the public life which all can imitate is that of Christ as witness. Here, then, we reemphasize within our present context that which was stated in an earlier chapter concerning the Church's continuation of Christ's prophetic role. Christ was a witness to the Father, a perfect manifestation of the Father's truth and love. He bore this witness not only through His formal teaching but also through His actions, His attitude, His gestures. All members of Christ are called to give witness also. The Christian's entire life should be a witness to the truth he holds. The world comes to know Christ through the Christian. Schillebeeckx comments on this aspect of being witness: "Our life must itself be the incarnation of what we believe, for only when dogmas are lived do they have any attractive power. Why in the main does Western man pass Christianity by? Surely because the visible presence of grace in Christians as a whole, apart from a few individuals, is no longer evident."[37]

St. Paul sums up the redemptive work of Christ under the mysteries of death-resurrection.[38] These are the principal mysteries which the Christian must assimilate from the eucharistic liturgy and reproduce in his own life. More and more the Christian spiritual life is being considered as a process of death-resurrection. It is obvious why this is so, for if Christ's entire life was summed up in His death-resurrection, so also is that of His members.

Christ's death and Resurrection are so closely united that they are two facets of one mystery rather than two separate mysteries.[39] It is likewise with the Christian. The death aspect of his supernatural life is intimately connected with his life of resurrection, and in various ways. For instance, his very life of grace is his life of resurrection, but his continual growth in spiritual death – death to selfwill in all its numerous manifestations – is achieved through grace. Consequently, the Christian's life of resurrection always accompanies his life of death. We also see the two connected more obviously in the sense that a growth in the death element always results in a growth in the resurrection element.

The daily life of the Christian, then, is a combination and antithesis of death-resurrection. As he gives himself in love to the Father's will, manifested to him in so many ways, the Christian is achieving both death and resurrection. Christ's ultimate goal, as man, was His Resurrection. Resurrection, a greater share in the divine life through grace, is also the goal of the Christian.

These few remarks give examples of how each member of the People of God is called upon to relive Christ's entire life as centered in death-resurrection. More could be said. But we think our remarks have sufficed to indicate how the Christian is to live out these various mysteries of Christ. Moreover, let it be recalled that all the mysteries ultimately make up the one mystery of Christ.

What we have said thus far applies in general to all vocations. But since there are different vocations within the Church, we must also say that each of these projects Christ in a somewhat different manner. Each Christian must study how in particular he is called to put on Christ. Essentially, of course, all put on Christ in the same manner. Yet there are accidental differences according to the vocation, work and individuals involved. For instance, the lay person, in general, is called to a deeper involvement in temporal affairs than is the religious.

Each member of Christ, according to his particular vocation, work and personality, has something special to take away from the Mass.[40] Each Christian, as he lives out the mystery of Christ, projects Christ to the world in his own way. Each Christian, as he himself grows in Christ-likeness, is also helping Christ to redeem the world in a manner commensurate with his total Christian person. For holiness is necessarily apostolic whether the Christian at any particular time is engaged in an external apostolate or not.

Each Christian, according to God's plan for him, must have a vital and dynamic desire to help Christianize the whole world. Perhaps he can do very little through direct, external apostolate. But his prayers and sacrifices – indeed, his entire life – can touch the whole world. Through an intense Christian life the individual can help Christ further the redemption of the family, the business world, the social structure and the like. The Christian is called to have this deep desire: to see the whole universe imprinted with the name of Christ. How true it is to say that the Christian's vocation, rooted in the liturgy, calls for deep involvement in this sacred activity.[41]

In schematic outline we have discussed the manner in which the baptized Christian extends his Mass to his daily existence. As he so lives out his Mass, he is becoming more Christlike. He becomes a more perfect priest and victim for his next participation in the eucharistic sacrifice.[42] The beautiful cycle which the Mass contains lies exposed before us. As part of this cycle the Christian is intimately involved in the process of continued redemption. The Mass is the center of the Christian life: ". . . the liturgy is the summit toward which the activity of the Church is directed; at the same time it is the fount from which all her power flows."[43]

---

15. Durrwell, *Op. cit.*, pp. 68-69. This "acceptance" element of Christ's sacrifice is an extremely important one, a fact being shown through contemporary scriptural, theological and liturgical studies. Two outstanding works which treat of the role of Christ's Resurrection in God's redemptive plan are F. X. Durrwell's *The Resurrection* and L. Cerfaux's *Christ in the Theology of St. Paul.*

16. S. Lyonnet, "La valeur sotériologique de la résurrection du Christ selon Saint Paul" in *Gregorianum*, Vol. 39 (1958), pp. 312-313. Translation taken from *Theology Digest,* Vol. 8 (1960), p. 92.

18. Cf. Second Vatican Council, *Constitution on the Liturgy,* No. 48, and *Constitution on the Church,* No. 10.

19. Cf. Jungmann, *Op. cit.*, p. 417.

20. Paul VI, *Mysterium Fidei,* N.C.W.C. edition, Paragraph 31.

30. J. Jungmann, *The Mass of the Roman Rite* (New York: Benziger, 1959), p. 146.

31. *Constitution on the Church*, No. 7.

33. Cf. Karl Rahner, *Nature and Grace* (New York: Sheed & Ward, 1964), pp. 23f.

34. Cf. Jungmann, "Eucharistic Piety" in *Worship,* Vol. 35 (1961), p. 419.

35. F. X. Durrwell, *In the Redeeming Christ* (New York: Sheed & Ward, 1963), p. 63.
36. Karl Rahner, *Spiritual Exercises* (New York: Herder & Herder, 1965), p. 160.
37. Schillebeeckx, *Op. cit.,* p. 209.
38. Cf. L. Cerfaux, *Christ in the Theology of St. Paul* (New York: Herder & Herder, 1959), pp. 190-192.
39. Durrwell, *The Resurrection,* p. 48.
40. Cf. Karl Rahner, *The Christian Commitment* (New York: Sheed & Ward, 1963), p. 168.
41. Cf. Second Vatican Council, *Constitution on the Church,* No. 36.
42. For a current treatment of the varied richness of the Eucharist, cf. J. Wicks, "The Movement of Eucharistic Theology" in *Chicago Studies,* Vol. 10 (1971), pp. 267-284.
43. *The Constitution on the Sacred Liturgy,* No. 10.

R. And the Father looks down and sees the sacrifice of His Son and we become a more pleasing sacrifice.

The more one we are with Him, the more the grace and mercy flows from the Father in the Holy Spirit through the pierced Heart of Jesus.

I consecrate the whole earth to the Sacred Heart of Jesus and the Immaculate Heart of Mary. It is as if we are all one in this sacrifice, all united: heaven and earth, God: Father, Son and Holy Spirit, the Blessed Virgin, all angels, all saints, all souls in purgatory. We are united, all of us, the faithful, and we pray as Jesus has taught us to pray in the Our Father. "Thy Kingdom come, thy will be done on earth as it is in heaven..."

One bread, one body, we are one in Him in this great sacrifice. The oneness of the greatest love of all is felt in this act of sacrifice where God gives Himself to man in the Holy Sacrifice of the Mass.

And the earth unites in every second of their lives by offering up to the Father all we do in union with Jesus in the Holy Sacrifice of the Mass and we are one in this great sacrifice in all that we do united in the greatest oneness.

Unity - oneness in the Body and Blood of Jesus Christ, the ultimate sacrifice. God gives Himself to man. Grace and mercy flow. Man is given this great gift in the Mass.

We are one in Him. We live according to the Father's will, in love, little, dependent children of God, united to all in heaven –

We want the world to be one –

Jesus gives Himself to us – Through Him, With Him and In Him. God outpours His grace to us. God gives to us such gifts – God gives Himself to men in greatest love.

God gives us a sharing in His Divine Life in baptism and He nurtures this life with the Bread of Life – the Word and the Eucharist.

Song: *A Song from Jesus*

It is love that makes the heart sing. It is love that makes us smile. It is love for which we were created and for which we are to live. It is love, we love God and love one another.

Love is not proud, love is not selfish, love is as He shows us - Love is giving ourselves. Love is as He loved us that He gave Himself to us to His death on the cross. And in this gift of love, rooted in Him, we share in His life.

A Prayer before the Holy Sacrifice of the Mass

Let me be a holy sacrifice and unite with God in the sacrament of His greatest love.

I want to be one in Him in this act of love, where He gives Himself to me and I give myself as a sacrifice to Him. Let me be a holy sacrifice as I become one with Him in this my act of greatest love to Him.

Let me unite with Him more, that I may more deeply love Him. May I help make reparation to His adorable Heart and the heart of His Mother, Mary. With greatest love, I offer myself to You and pray that You will accept my sacrifice of greatest love. I give myself to You and unite in Your gift of Yourself to me. Come and possess my soul.

Cleanse me, strengthen me, heal me. Dear Holy Spirit act in the heart of Mary to make me more and more like Jesus.

Father, I offer this my sacrifice, myself united to Jesus in the Holy Spirit to You. Help me to love God more deeply in this act of my greatest love.

Give me the grace to grow in my knowledge, love and service of You and for this to be my greatest participation in the Mass. Give me the greatest graces to love You so deeply in this Mass, You who are so worthy of my love.

- *Mass Book,* December 27, 1995

R. Our hearts are hard, our hearts are not at peace many times. It is so simple. It is love. God is love! He calls us to be like Him. God is giving. Jesus came into the world giving Himself, a little child in great poverty, and He went out of this world giving Himself on a cross.

Jesus comes and Jesus gives us light into the mysteries of His love. It comes through the Immaculate Heart of Our Mother. We are brought forth as little children of the light in the spiritual womb of our Mother in the Holy Spirit. Jesus is the light of this world.

From *Tell My People*
by Fr. Edward J. Carter, S.J.

The Holy Spirit

Jesus: "My beloved friend, tell My people to pray daily to the Holy Spirit. They are to pray for an increase in His gifts. My people must realize that the Holy Spirit comes to transform them. The Spirit desires to transform you more and more according to My image. Those who are docile to His touch become increasingly shaped in My likeness. He performs this marvel within Mary's Immaculate Heart. The more one dwells in My Mother's Heart, the more active are the workings of the Spirit. The Spirit leads Mary to place you within My own Heart. In both Our Hearts, then, your transformation continues. The more you are formed after My own Heart, the more I lead you to the bosom of My Father. Tell My people all this. Tell them to pray daily for a greater appreciation of these wondrous gifts. I am Lord and Master. All who come to My Heart will be on fire to receive the gifts of the Spirit in ever greater measure! I love and bless My people!"

Reflection: The Holy Spirit is given to us to fashion us ever more according to the likeness of Jesus. And the more we are like Jesus, the more Jesus leads us to the Father. Do we, each day, pray to the Holy Spirit to be more open to His transforming influence? Do we strive each day to grow in union with Mary? The greater our union with our Mother, the spouse of the Holy Spirit, the greater is the transforming action of the Holy Spirit within us.

end of excerpt

R. Is this not what He showed us in His life - compliance to the Father's will? Is this not what Mary showed us in her life - compliance to the will of God?

There will be one flock and one Shepherd. There is one family. It is the Family of God. The King will Reign on His throne. Men will make Jesus King and Center of their hearts – The story is the story of love. God's love for us. He gives us Himself. This is our unifying factor. God loves sinful men. He gives us the pure and Immaculate One whereby we can unite in deepest union with Him. We are sinners. Mary is Our Mother. God is Our Father. Jesus is our Brother, our Friend, our Lover, the Son of God. Jesus comes into this world and He took on flesh. Jesus is the Savior of the world.

The key is, "Thy Kingdom Come, Thy will be done on Earth as it is in heaven."

It is easy. It is simple. Man wants his own way. There is only one way - it is the will of God. It is the will of the Father, our Heavenly Father, Jesus is the Son. Jesus says - "I am the way, the truth and the life." (*John 14:16)* The Holy Spirit molds us more and more in the image of God!

It is so simple. It is love. God shares with us the mystery of God's love in the Mass.

God is the powerhouse. He gives Himself to us in the Mass and the grace and mercy flow and we are one with Him and one with others in the Mass.

God is Love! It is so simple. We are creatures of love. We were created for love. Love is the answer to the bleeding hearts, the greatest gift being the gift of Himself, given to man in the Mass, through the hands of the consecrated Priest.

God is love. The most perfect prayer – the Mass. We unite to God in this most intimate act of love where we praise, honor, adore Him, petition Him, make reparation and thank Him for His gifts, given to us.

December 27, 1995

LET US LOVE THE TWO HEARTS OF JESUS AND MARY IN THE RECEPTION OF THE HOLY EUCHARIST.

GOD'S BLUE BOOK 9

HE GAVE HIMSELF TO US ON THE CROSS.
HE GIVES HIMSELF TO US IN THE EUCHARIST.

How great was the act of love, God gave to this world, when He gave Himself and died on the cross. He gives Himself to us this day in the Holy Eucharist.

The greatest commandment is that we must love God with our whole heart, our whole soul, and our whole being. This is a commandment. If we are to enter heaven, we must follow the commandments. They are commands given by God for us to follow.

The greatest act we can do on this earth is an act of loving God. The reason for our existence is to love God. In the sacrament of His greatest love, He gives Himself to us. This is an act of love on His part. We are called to respond by giving ourselves in love to Him.

This is the purpose of the Holy Eucharist: to unite in such oneness with our Holy, Loving God. Our all consuming passion should be that of loving God. How many go to the Eucharist with the sole purpose of giving great love to God? He wants us to love Him. He wants souls to tell Him how much they truly love Him. This is the most intimate act of love when

Jesus gives Himself - Body, Blood, Soul, and Divinity to man. If it is such an act of love, how are we receiving Him in Communion? We should beg God, in this most intimate union with Him, to help us to love Him with greatest love.

Jesus is a Person. He wants our love. The Holy Spirit wants such intimacy with us. Our Father wants us to love Him. In the Eucharist, we unite with God. In this intimate act of uniting with our beloved God, with Divinity, we must pour out our love to God. We must pour out our heart to the most adorable Heart of Jesus. Jesus is so unjustly treated by many of His beloved souls He loves so much. Let us help make reparation to the Almighty God by loving God with our whole heart, our whole soul, and our whole being in the sacrament of His greatest love. This is the Gift of Himself.

Think of how it is to love someone and give your all for that person, to pour out your heart to him or her and then be treated with coldness and neglect. It hurts our heart so much more when we deeply love someone to be rejected by that person. Jesus loves us with the deepest love. We cannot fully comprehend this love. Let us love Him with the deepest love. Let us love Mary and her Immaculate Heart. Let us love her as the Mother of God. Let us love her as the virgin who bore the Son of God. May we, in the reception of the Eucharist pour out our love to Him, to this adorable Heart. May we pour out our love to His Holy Mother.

Mary said at Fatima that Jesus wants His Heart venerated next to the heart of His Mother. Let us love these Two Hearts as we receive the Sacrament of the Eucharist. Then we are so deeply united with God. We see Their Two Hearts surrounded with thorns for the injustices against Their Hearts. Let us help make reparation daily as we receive Him in the Eucharist. This is a special time to help make reparation to Their wounded Hearts.

Let us remember how He poured His love out to us on the cross and how He pours out His love to us now when He gives us Himself in the Eucharist, the Eucharist which contains His Heart of burning love. His Heart was pierced with a lance. Her heart was invisibly pierced with a sword. As the wounds in Their Hearts are deep, so too is Their love so deep.

He does not want "surface love". He wants hearts filled with deep burning love. *end of December 27, 1995*

St. Gertrude Church - 5/1/97

A Leader in the Shepherds of Christ Movement

R. A leader in the Shepherds of Christ Movement is one who 1) lives the Blue book messages; 2) reads and lives the Apostles Manual; 3) supports all of the events that have occurred or will occur on the 13th of the month; 4) spends one hour before the tabernacle; 5) attends daily Mass and communion; 6) is a member of an active weekly chapter in the Shepherds of Christ Movement; 7) prays the consecration prayers all through the day and consecrates their hearts daily with another Shepherds of Christ member; 8) is an Apostle of the Eucharistic Heart of Jesus; 9) is obedient to the messages given by Jesus that have been discerned and approved by Fr. Carter; 10) is obedient to Fr. Carter; 11) realizes that there are positions of authority in the Shepherds of Christ Movement and complies to those in charge; 12) the messages given in the Apostles Manual must be obeyed.

Jesus: My dear beloved ones,

I give to you the Shepherds of Christ Movement. Your founder is Fr. Edward J. Carter, S.J.. He is the Spiritual Director of this movement. All messages have been discerned by him. It is important that the messages discerned by Fr. Carter be lived and obeyed by all of the members. The lines of authority in the Movement must be clearly defined. There must be order. There must be authority. There must be a plan – the plan is the plan of My Father to help renew the Church and the world and to help bring about the completion of the Fatima message. I will be king and center in the hearts of men. My kingdom is not of this world. In the new era men will be as the Father intended – one happy family living in greatest intimacy with God, according to the Father's Will.

Leaders in the Movement must comply to the above requirements. Your Movement must be structured. People must be given titles. You will report to the appropriate person. The lines of authority must be clearly defined.

All leaders are called by Me to be leaders. A leader must be schooled in the Movement to be a leader. Be leery of any person delegating leadership to themselves without proper authority. Your materials must be guarded as treasures given from God for the renewal of the Church and the world, culminating in the Reign of My Sacred Heart and triumph of My Mother's Immaculate Heart. No one is to delegate themselves as a leader. No one is to acquire materials without proper authorization. The messages must be obeyed. When a person interferes with the flow of obedience to my messages you will know it is not of Me. My directions are clearly defined in these messages. Many will come who have a plan of their own. I give to you the Plan of the Father. There will not be an overabundance of funds. Funds will come at the appropriate time as needed from obedience to My messages. If you use the funds inappropriately you will have financial problems. I give to you all that you need. The evil one will try to squander your materials. It is in strict obedience to the messages, in analyzing and praying over the messages that you will understand the proper action that you must take. Every leader must comply to the requirements listed above. Those who are special cases may, on certain occasions, not be able to follow some of the points. Failure to spend one hour of intimacy with God every day will open the leader of the Shepherds of Christ to immense attack from satan. Whenever you gather you must begin always with the Holy Spirit prayer, the St. Michael prayer and the Consecrations.

I will weed out those that are not in one mind and one heart. There is one plan; there is one will; it is the Will of the Father. Willfulness will be dealt with by expulsion. You will be the example for the world, united in love as children of the Father and children of your Mother Mary. If you deviate from this plan, you will have horrendous problems. Only in prayer will the plan unfold. It is My Plan. I am in control. You will beg, you will plead, you will suffer and in desperation you will go to the messages for your answers. You will find relief only in obeying the messages. I will separate the sheep from the goats. I will weed out the willful ones and the docile ones will turn to the most fervent prayer. You are being schooled by Me. You must study the content of these messages.

5/1/97

Lay Apostles of the Shepherds of Christ Movement

R. Jesus is calling us to be the Lay Apostles of the Shepherds of Christ Movement that will help lead the strayed ones back to the flock.

The Religious are not as, religious, as Jesus wants them to be. Jesus called them to be intimately united to Him. Jesus gave them this special calling that they would give Him their life in love, service and sacrifice. In order to have an intimate relationship with any person it takes the giving of self. Time must be spent alone with that person to have intimacy. Jesus called the religious His special, chosen ones, to lead others to union with Him. Jesus laments that many religious of today do not love Him and do not spend time alone with Him. They do not speak of the love of God for their main concern has drifted away from Him.

Jesus sends to us the antidote for the poison in the Church and the world. He calls His lay people to a special calling as Apostles to lead the flock to His Heart.

All religious orders are structured and are founded on obedience. This is a religious calling of the lay people. Jesus wants our love in intimacy with Him. Since the religious have not responded in many cases in giving this love to Jesus, He has called the Lay Apostles and given them abundant grace to join ever closer to His Heart through the Heart of His Mother. The Church is in need of reform. Jesus is not loved by the religious, as He should be. He sends the antidote to the poison in the Church and the world. It is simply His love. Many religious do not spend intimate time with Jesus every day. Many do not love Him with their hearts. They treat Him as a cold, dead object. This is a most holy order – the Lay Apostles of the Shepherds of Christ Movement. We are committed to an intimate relationship with our Beloved Jesus, as the center of our lives. We give our life to Him as lay people. We are committed to one hour daily in intimate time with Jesus. We have consecrated our hearts to Jesus and to Mary. We unite all of our prayers, works, joys, and suffering to Jesus in union with the Holy Sacrifice of the Mass. We attend daily Mass and

Communion. Many of us pray three rosaries every day. We live by the Scriptures, the Blue Book messages and the *Apostles Manual.* We join weekly with a group that has consecrated their hearts to the Hearts of Jesus and Mary and are also Lay Apostles in the Movement. Our focus is Jesus.

In the great era to come in which the Sacred Heart of Jesus will Reign and Mary's Heart will triumph, all will live according to one plan. All will live in the Father's Will. It will be strict obedience to the commandments of God. The Lord has called us and given us the antidote for the apostles in the Church, especially in the religious life. Because of the severity of the condition in the Church, Jesus has called us to be lay apostles. Jesus tells us what He wants for the religious in the Church – it is intimacy, it is love, it is hearts on fire for love of God and one another. They reject the antidote and persist in living lives, many of which are not centered in Christ. However, we must go to the religious to operate in the Church for they have the authority and we are subject to this authority. This authority was given by God. God sends messages to the religious because of the urgency of the situation. You are being called by Jesus to help in the renewal of the Church and the world through your prayers. It is only through Him that the plan of the Father will be accomplished. This is why the Father gave several messages, all of which ended... "I am asking you to start prayer chapters centered in consecration and to spread the priestly newsletter to the priests." It is absolutely urgent that we pray the prayers given by Jesus in the Prayer Manual and begin prayer chapters.

Our Lady appears on a former bank building in Florida as Our Lady of Fatima in the Americas. I see her there, Our Lady, in her great beauty. Mary does not appear as she once appeared for she was ignored. She gives to us a permanent sign and a calling. Mary looks majestic in her beauty on this building, calling to the world, "come to the water, it must be pure, it must be clean, it must be clear." We have polluted our waters, our streams and our hearts. The grace will flow from the highest mountain, which is the altar of sacrifice in the Church when the priest and the faithful have consecrated their hearts as Mary told us at Fatima 80 years ago. Why have we not responded to Our Lady, clothed with the sun, radiant and adorned in purity? Mary calls in Clearwater to start prayer chapters, the prayer chapters her Son has given in the Shepherds of Christ Movement. The waters will be clear and the hearts will be purified when we comply to the request of the Father, of Jesus and of Mary to begin prayer chapters, to spread the Priestly Newsletters, to join the Apostles of the Eucharistic Heart Movement, and to circulate the Mass Books and Rosary books. We are the Lay Apostles of the Shepherds of Christ Movement. We will not stop helping to spread the consecration on this earth. We vow to try to begin prayer chapters and to spread the request of the Father, the Son and Mary. We are an order of Lay people trying to grow ever closer to the Heart of Jesus, striving for oneness with Him, our hearts centered in helping to bring about the Reign of the Sacred Heart of Jesus and the triumph of the Immaculate Heart of Mary, renewal of the Church and of the world and in helping souls to go to heaven. We beg you to help us in our endeavor to start prayer chapters, to spread the Priestly Newsletter and materials given by God and Mary to the Church, the School and the Family.

5/3/97

Mary Is Mother

Reference: John 14: 9-14

R. The Father gives the gift of motherhood to a woman when she conceives and bears a child.

The Father Speaks of Mary:

I have chosen Mary, My Mother, meaning Mother I chose for My Son.

John 14:11

> Believe me when I say I am in the Father and the Father is in me.

R. Mary is the Mother of the Christ-life, therefore the Father speaks:

God the Father: This is My Mother, for life rooted in Me.

R. Mary was chosen by the Father to be the Mother of all.

5/3/97

May 4, 1997
Morrow, Ohio

Joyful Mysteries

The Annunciation

1. 

2. **Reference: Luke 1: 26-38**
3. Hail Mary
4.

Prayer for Union with Jesus

Come to me, Lord, and possess my soul. Come into my heart and permeate my soul. Help me to sit in silence with You and let You work in my heart.

I am Yours to possess. I am Yours to use. I want to be selfless and only exist in You. Help me to spoon out all that is me and be an empty vessel ready to be filled by You. Help me to die to myself and live only for You. Use me as You will. Let me never draw my attention back to myself. I only want to operate as You do, dwelling within me.

I am Yours, Lord. I want to have my life in You. I want to do the will of the Father. Give me the strength to put aside the world and let You operate my very being. Help me to act as You desire. Strengthen me against the distractions of the devil to take me from Your work.

When I worry, I have taken my focus off of You and placed it on myself. Help me not to give in to the promptings of others to change what in my heart You are making very clear to me. I worship You, I adore You and I love You. Come and dwell in me now.

- *God's Blue Book,* January 17, 1994

5. Hail Mary
6. **July 31, 1994**

Words of Jesus to Members of Shepherds of Christ Associates:

"My beloved priest-companion, I intend to use the priestly newsletter, *Shepherds of Christ*, and the movement, *Shepherds of Christ Associates*, in a powerful way for the renewal of My Church and the world.

"I will use the newsletter and the chapters of *Shepherds of Christ Associates* as a powerful instrument for spreading devotion to My Heart and My Mother's Heart.

"I am calling many to become members of *Shepherds of Christ Associates.* To all of them I will give great blessings. I will use them as instruments to help bring about the triumph of the Immaculate Heart and the reign of My Sacred Heart. I will give great graces to the members of *Shepherds of Christ Associates.* I will call them to be deeply united to My Heart and to Mary's Heart as I lead them ever closer to My Father in the Holy Spirit."

- *Message from Jesus to Father Edward J. Carter, S.J., Founder, as given on July 31, 1994, feast of Saint Ignatius Loyola, Founder of the Society of Jesus (The Jesuits)*

7. Hail Mary
8. Song: *A Song from Jesus*
9. Hail Mary
10. Song: *I Love You Jesus*

Song between decades: "Ave, Ave, Ave Maria"

The Visitation

1. 

2. **Reference: Luke 1: 39-45**
3. Hail Mary
4. Hail Mary
5. Hail Mary
6. Hail Mary
7. **Reference: Luke 1: 46-55 The Magnificat**

   Sing: *Holy Is His Name*
8. **R.** But we must realize too that He gives to us the crosses as it said in the message and that it is His will that we suffer for He showed us through His life that He went through tremendous suffering, that He carried His cross for it was the will of the Father.
9. **R.** If we could see our own graced soul. We would fall to our face for it is so beautiful when a soul is filled with His life. The devil tries to keep us focused on ourselves, thinking in our heads and Jesus shows to us with both hands on the sides of His Heart that He came into this world to give us His love.
10. **R.** Love is in the heart. This is how it should be when we pray that we are filled with such love for God and one another that we unite with the Almighty God. This is why we pray the consecration. Pray the Prayer for Union with Jesus that we are one in Him in the sacrifice. And this is why we are praying, praying here for it is in the Priestly Newsletter that the priests' hearts will be turned to hearts of love, the greatest, greatest, greatest act of love that there is, when the Almighty God gives Himself in love to us. And the priest gets up and at the sermon He is telling us a lot of intellectual things. How is the response of the people in the

pews when they are hearing this. Their response is intellectual, but the Mass is an act of love. How is it when the priest gets up and talks about "Oh, Jesus, loves us. He gives Himself to us." We are bonded in deep love. We feel tenderness in our heart. We respond with a heart emotion. We respond with feelings. This is the role of the Priestly Newsletter to write the messages of God's love on the hearts of the priests so that the people will be fed with this great love of God. We must do all that God is asking us to do. He is asking us to spread these prayer chapters that are praying for the priest, that are praying for the renewal of the Church and the world. This is urgent. This is why God is talking to us. He is sending the antidote for the poison that is in the Church and the world. He has given to Father Carter these prayers. They say exactly what we need to pray and help to bring about the renewal of the Church and the world and to help the priests and to help bring about what Mary has told us at Fatima. It will turn our hearts into the most intimate hearts of love in which the Sacred Heart of Jesus will Reign and the Immaculate Heart of Mary will triumph. It is all in the little red *Prayer Manual* that Jesus has given to us to spread. We must do this. The devil is keeping us focused on all kinds of things to keep us distracted. The Father has told us in message after message after message, we must spread the prayer manuals, we must spread the Priestly Newsletter to the priests. Think of how it is if a priest gets up at Mass and says at the beginning of Mass, "In the name of the Father and the Son and the Holy Spirit." This is a sharing in the mystery of God's love. Let us open our hearts and tell God that we are sorry for our sins and then we say, "Lord, have mercy. Christ, have mercy. Lord, have mercy." And then at the reading, we hear the readings that are filled with emotion and love of God that burn in our hearts. This is what the Mass is - it is the greatest act of love that there is. This rosary is a love expression between us and God. This is our role in the Shepherds of Christ Movement. Many of the religious today are not spending their time praying as God wants them to. Jesus has asked Fr. Carter to form a lay order of apostles that are doing just what we are doing, praying an hour every day to Jesus, going to daily Mass and Communion, whenever possible, praying the rosary, spending our lives trying to spread this consecration and the prayer chapters Jesus gave Fr. Carter praying for the priests. Jesus wants love. The more we do this and pray for the priests, the more the sisters will turn their lives to hearts of love, spending that hour in front of the tabernacle. This is the Visitation. And so you ask, "What does this have to do with the Visitation?" It is in us, His love is alive in us in everything that we do. He is visiting in us. It takes work and it takes grace and it takes time; but it takes Him doing it and it is through the prayers that we will have the renewal of the Church and the world, that priests' hearts will be changed. We must do what Jesus had told us to do in the Shepherds of Christ Movement. Pray these prayers fervently in the *Prayer Manual* ourselves and help to spread prayer chapters and to help spread the Priestly Newsletter. God came to this earth to give love. Love is in the heart. This is what the Good Shepherd tells us. This is what the Reign of the Sacred Heart will be about, hearts of love, hearts that are filled with love for God and love for one another. Mary carried the Child Jesus within her womb. God came as a little baby in the womb of a human person because He wanted to teach us His ways of love. In the Shepherds of Christ Movement, we will majorly help to spread the love of God to the world. Jesus has given us this instrument.

Song between decades: *Come Holy Spirit*

The Birth of Jesus

1. 

2. **Reference: Luke 2: 1-7**
3. Sing: *Silent Night*
4. Sing: *What Child Is This*
5. Sing: *See the Eyes That Look at Mary*

See the Eyes That Look at Mary

by Rita Ring

C G C
Wake us up, Let us see that You are tru - ly
Fill us now, Give us Your love. Let us be so
F G C G
Christ the Lord! We are blind, we need Your grace, please
close to You! We are blind, we need Your grace, please
C F G
to refrain
o - pen up our eyes to You!
o - pen up our eyes to You!
VERSE 3
C G C
3. We are Yours, we give our-selves, we con - se-crate our
F G C
hearts to You. We con - se - crate our
Dm G C
hearts to You, we give You all our love!
no refrain

6. Hail Mary
7. **R.** We are between here and there. We are living in an age of grave disobedience. For He has spoken. Can we say that we did not hear the call?

From Blue Book - May 4, 1994

I Call You to Holiness

May 4, 1994 4:30 a.m.

Jesus: Dear ones, I am calling you to love your brothers. I have loved you. Would you, dear ones, lay down your lives for your brothers? How are you loving this day? Are you following Christ in your actions? I am the Way, I am the Truth, I am the Life. You must constantly put the world aside and look to the Master for all your directions. I call you, My little ones, to holiness. I call you to pure hearts, hearts that are full of love and empty of hate and anger. I call you to guard your hearts and watch that they stay forever holy. You, My precious bride, I want your soul white.

Do you criticize your dear brothers? I gave the last beat of My Heart and the last drop of My blood for the soul you are displeased with. I would die for them this day. Will you not love them for Me? They are so precious to Me!

Quit sizing up your brothers. You do such unloving things in your mind. You do not even know how unloving are your thoughts. You judge your brothers by their exteriors, by their education, by their money. You do not see the beautiful creation of God the Father. He created your brothers just perfectly and He loves His creation. Who are you to criticize His creation? Love your brothers when they are hurting. It is in your loving the hurting ones that they will see the reflection of Christ in you.

Do not hold on to foolish things. One moment and your days on this earth have ended. All that remains is how you loved. Did you love God? Did you love your neighbor? Love is not selfish. It gives of itself. Its whole purpose is to draw the other closer to Jesus.

Study the crucifix. It is such a comfort! I loved you so. I died for you. I would die for you alone this very day, little ones! Look at Me dying on the cross! The way to Me is to follow Me. Be Christ-like in your ways. You must study Me to know My ways. Do not give in to yourselves. My way is love. Will you be the reflection of the love of God within you? My way is the way of the cross. They persecuted Me, they hurt Me, they tore My flesh and spit on Me. They did this to Me for My love given to all! This world is not your end. You follow My ways and you move as you should toward your goal.

I am Jesus, I am the Son of God. I love you so ardently. I died and shed My blood, My beautiful blood, for love of you. I await you this day, My little ones. I loved you so I remain with you in the Eucharist. I await, I long for you to come and share in our love. I am the tenderest of Hearts. No man can be close to you as I. I love you so. I want to dwell and live within you. I want to fill you with all My love and radiate My love to your beloved brothers. I want to shine from your souls.

Oh, little ones, take Me seriously. I am truly here, begging for you to live in My love.

You are the light that will shine in this dark world. You will light up the darkest night with My love.

The best gift you can give to this world is to busy yourself about your love affair with Me. I love you, My little ones. I love you and I want to share this love with you.

Love your brothers. Do not let satan talk in your heads and make them wrong and you right. Love them as I have loved you. Do not look at your brothers and size them up. See them with the eyes of God, the beautiful creations of the Father.

Will you love My beloved ones for Me this day, or will you say "no" to My call? Love your brothers in darkness. They need your love. I am calling you to love them for Me this very day. They may scoff at you and persecute you, but you will plant a seed that I Myself will water and give sunlight to. Plant seeds of love. This is the most important seed you will plant, a seed of love. Watch it grow as I provide it with water and nourishment. I will shine on your brothers through you if you stay in My love. Be the light that shines on this dark world. They are crying out for the love of God. They are suffering.

They need your love.

Put yourselves aside. Die to yourselves. Live only for the love of God. If the world goes one way, you stay focused on My love. Do not follow the world. Follow the risen Christ!

I love you so, little ones. I bring you new life. I fill your hearts with My love. Pray to the Holy Spirit for His gifts. Pray the *Our Father.* Let My mother mother you as she mothered Me. She loved you so. She suffered so for love of you. She appears to bring you back to her beloved Son. Will you answer her call? She is calling you to put God first in your life. She is calling you to love, love of God, love of one another.

Forgive your brothers. Empty your hearts of hate and anger and let go. Let all your anger go. Give Me your resentments and let Me heal your hearts. Forgiveness is the way to peace. Let go. Do not size up your brothers. Love them all. Pray for them. Unite in My love. Love is a miracle cure. Say you are sorry. Be gentle in your ways. Pray for your needs. I love you, little ones. I am with you this day.

Will you answer the call and love for Me? I love you. I am your beloved Jesus. I would die this day just for you. I love you the same as I did the day I died. Turn to Me and give Me your life. I will care for you and love you. I am your Savior. I am Jesus Christ, Son of the Living God. Let Me live in your heart!
end of May 4, 1994

8. **R.** Jesus was born the Light of the World. The light shown in the darkness. We are called the children of light to carry this light into the darkness. I know, I have studied the messages of the Father and every message of the Father ends with the same thing "We must spread the prayer chapters." He will continue to allow us to be pressed on and we will suffer more until we do what is in the messages. Until we spread these prayer chapters, immense amounts of grace will be released for the priests for the renewal of the Church and the world, to help bring about the completion of the Fatima message and so, He is allowing us to go through very much testing. But the more we study the messages, the more we will know how to alleviate the problems, to help bring about the renewal of the Church and the world, to help the priest and bring about the completion of the Fatima message.

9. **R.** A little baby came into this world, the Almighty God took on a human form, was conceived in the womb of a human person and He came to give us His life. Jesus came, Jesus came to give us a sharing in His life. Men will see the light as they have never seen it before in this great era of peace. And it is coming and He has told us what we must do in order to bring it about.
10. **R.** Think of this, my dear brothers and sisters, that the Almighty God has given to us these great messages, that the Almighty God has given to us so much, the Priestly Newsletter, the prayers, and we are having so much trouble getting these on the internet and getting them to the media. Think of all the filth that is on the television and that is on the internet. It is only because satan has blocked the messages from the very beginning and he continues to block them for they have never gone out freely until lately. They went out freely a little bit from the 13ths and now satan has attempted to try to stop us.

Song between decades: *Come Holy Spirit*

The Presentation of Jesus in the Temple

1. **R.** We are doing a service by spreading the Prayer Manual in the Churches. We try to get five or six persons in a Church praying these prayers. They do not have to like the private revelation. All that we have to do is get the prayer chapters started and give the priests the Priestly Newsletter. This is what the Father told us to do.
2. **R.** Mary appeared every day for fourteen months, she begged and begged to spread the consecration and rosaries to the school children. Yesterday we had a mailing, and we're still working on it, to send these consecrations and rosaries to the school children. Satan wants us stopped. But if we reach every elementary school in this world, in this United States, with the consecration and the rosary, think of how happy this will make our Heavenly Mother. Mary appeared every day for 14 months. Mary wants this.
3. **R.** Mary appeared with a sword in her Heart in the statue at the Our Lady of the Holy Spirit Center. And Simeon says, 'Look, he is destined for the fall and for the rise of many in Israel, destined to be a sign that is opposed — and a sword

will pierce your soul too — so that the secret thoughts of many may be laid bare.' (Luke 2:34-35). And she cries out, "What can I do? I come. I appear. I beg. I plead. I give you these gifts from my Son, and you reject me. I do not deliver messages very often anymore for I have been ignored." (August 27, 1996)

"Oh, my children, my little children of light, the time is nigh and many will be lost forever. I appeared and warned and told all to mind their ways and come to the Heart of my Son and they said "No, my Lady, not for you or any mother. We are children of darkness and that we remain, for we seek our pleasure by day and feast on sin all night and when you called, mother, we laughed at your Son and ignored Him and His ways." And He called and His call fell on deaf ears." (December 19, 1996)

4. **R.** And so how do you feel many times during the week? The world does not think like us. But God is speaking to us. Who will listen? Mary is saying the same thing she said eighty years ago. If we do not come to this weekly meeting, we will not receive the encouragement we need in order to help carry out this plan. This is the message that Jesus gave this week but it is also the message that He gave on the 13th when I was speaking that it will become harder and harder and harder as we go deeper and deeper into the Heart of Jesus and He communicates more and more to us His plan for the renewal of the Church and the world. **The Church is where it is, yet God is giving us messages, messages that are saying that the religious must be rooted in God's Heart. They must spend time in daily prayer and intimacy. They must spend time in going to Mass and Communion and praying the rosary.** The religious in some cases have not done what our Lord has asked us and He has asked us to be lay apostles and there are so many of us in this core group, for we are the ones in the beginning that have given our lives, that have spent this time in front of the tabernacle, that have prayed. **Our Lord is asking us to pray that the religious will turn their hearts to intense hearts of love on fire for love of Him. This was some of His greatest agony in the garden, the religious, the chosen ones that He called, that do not spend time in a love affair with Him. He called them to be special lovers**

of His Heart. When we pray the prayers in the *Prayer Manual* and when we pray the prayers for the renewal of the Church and the world in the *Prayer Manual,* this will help to bring about religious whose hearts are centered in Christ.

5. Hail Mary
6. Hail Mary
7. Hail Mary
8.

Luke 2: 34-35

Simeon blessed them and said to Mary his mother, 'Look, he is destined for the fall and for the rise of many in Israel, destined to be a sign that is opposed — and a sword will pierce your soul too — so that the secret thoughts of many may be laid bare.'

R. And how do they treat most of the prophets? They stone them, they try to murder them. But the greatest one of all, how do they treat the Holy One? They hung Him on a cross and He died for love of us. This is what He asks of us today that we would give our life to Him in love, that we will tell the world of this love, that we will help renew the Church and the world by praying and spreading these prayer manuals.

9. Hail Mary
10. Hail Mary

Song between decades: *Come Holy Spirit*

The Finding of the Child Jesus in the Temple

1. Song: *We Have Been Told*
2. **Jesus:** And so My beloved ones, I speak to you, but many do not hear. I am asking you to spread these messages to the far ends of the earth that men will know that I am giving to them My greatest love. I give to you Myself in the Eucharist and I am ignored and I am forgotten. People walk away from the Church on Sunday and they do not talk to Me. My beloved ones, I long for love. I am treated as a dead object by so many of My faithful. I am calling you to My Heart that I will give you the greatest love. Do not run away, but come to Me. Write to Me every day of all of your trials and of all of your joys. You must spend this intimacy with Me every

day that you will be able to handle the problems, that you will face, for I am calling you to be strong soldiers, that I am filling you with My love in these letters. Write to Me every day. Tell Me all of your cares, all of your troubles, all of your complaints and read the messages that I give to you, the letters of My love in *God's Blue Book.* I am your Jesus. I am on fire for love of you. Please, please My beloved ones, do not turn your backs on Me for I have called you to carry My light into the darkness. Will you say "no"?

Song: *We Have Been Told*

3. **R.** And Jesus said when He was lost in the temple and Mary and Joseph found Him, 'Why were you looking for me? Did you not know that I must be in my Father's house?' (Luke 2: 49) Jesus always complied to the will of the Father. And so it is in our life that our every moment must be to try to live in His will, to pray the *Morning Offering* every morning asking the Holy Spirit to guide us that we are living according to the Father's will. For when we are having immense problems, many times it is because we will not surrender and do what He is asking us to do.
4. **R.** The Father has allowed Mary to appear and the Father has given to this earth great gifts in these apparitions. Mary is calling her little lost children to come to her heart and she will take them to the Heart of her Son.
5. **R.** This was the greatest pain under the cross for I experienced some of this suffering of Mary to know how many children, her children, would be lost despite His death on the cross. They would turn their backs on the Almighty God and they would go their willful way and their souls could be lost forever because of their serious unrepented sin.
6. **R.** Do we think that Mary has appeared to be ignored? Do we think that she has given a permanent sign on the building in Florida to be ignored? No. She speaks and says, "I do not appear as I once did." And she is calling, calling all to the Heart of her Son and Jesus has told us that we must start these prayer chapters.
7. Hail Mary
8. **R.** Mary is searching for her little lost children this day. Mary has appeared, and appeared, and appeared and appeared. She wants to lead them home to the Heart of her Son. She has

asked us to spread the consecration for the home.

9. **Mary:** I am the Immaculate Conception. I gave a message on August the 1st, 1994 of the importance of the Shepherds of Christ Movement. I am telling my chosen ones that you have been called by my Son Jesus to go into this world to help bring about the completion of the Fatima message for the renewal of the Church and the world and to pray for the priests. I am Mary, your Heavenly Mother. I give to you my Immaculate Heart. This will be your Ark. My beloved ones, you must come to my heart. I am begging you to spread the consecrations, to spread the *Prayer Manuals* for you have suffered and I am your Mother. I am watching you and guarding you. I will lead you ever closer to the Heart of my Son. Be strong, my little children. My children are suffering. Many will lose their souls. What you do today is very important. The evil one will try to stop you. You will suffer and suffer for he does not want your work to reach the far corners of the earth. You must not be afraid for I am sending the Holy Spirit to you to fill you with fearlessness and courage. I am your Mother. I am guarding you and watching you. Will you please send workers to my site in Florida? You must expand the prayer chapter in Cincinnati that you will receive help. I am sending aid to your spiritual director, Father Carter, but you must pray. You must pray, you must pray fervently every hour. Please do not give up. I know of your sufferings and how hard it is. I stood beneath the cross of my Son and I cried for the little ones that would lose their souls forever, my little lost children of the world. Think my dear, dear children of how it is to go to the fires of hell forever. I know how you are suffering, but see the soul at the edge of death, this is a child of mine. Will you help them? I ask you to spread the prayer manuals to the Churches.

10. Song: *Immaculate Mary*

R. The great gift that God has given to us that He has allowed Mary to appear at Fatima and now appear on the building in Florida. Mary showed the children in Fatima the souls in hell. It has been so hard for me that this thought that came to me at this moment is most comforting. For the little sufferings that I have experienced is nothing compared to the souls that are lost in hell forever. This is my goal, this is my life that I give to Him to try to help the souls so as many as possible will go to heaven forever, to try to spread His love, to help in the renewal of the Church and the world, to pray fervently for our beloved priests and to help with the completion of the Fatima message, to focus on the young ones in the schools who do not even know about Mary and Jesus but are taught through the present day communication such vileness, such horridness but are not even taught to pray the rosary or the Ten Commandments. We are at fault. The communication in the world is extensive but people do not even know the Ten Commandments or how to pray the rosary. The Father has spoken. It did not matter who heard the Fatima message the only thing that happened was that He allowed them to suffer with World War II. Great gifts were given and they did not respond. We need to spread the prayer chapters.

Jesus: Willful men have disobeyed the Pope. The plan is the plan of the Father. Many are called but few are chosen. I have chosen you, My beloved priests to be Me acting in the world. You are not united as you need to be. Some are focused on themselves. You have taken Me as chief priest and celebrant and you have moved Me from My altars. Some have stuck Me in a corner that you will have full reign in your willfulness. Some have taught to the people about politics, to football from the pulpit and have removed the King of Glory from the altar. You are to be on-fire with the love of God and be a good example for others of this.

R. Jesus said the second *Blue Book* was blocked at Falmouth. It would have helped to spread the fire of His love to people that would pray more fervently in front of the tabernacle and stay after Communion. That's why He said that it was important that we spread that down in Florida. Tom donated 30,000 books which I know the Lord prompted him to do because of this message alone. "Oh the waters will run and the earth shake and you will suffer and suffer and you work your own plan and say, It happened before. It's not a sign from God. It's a phenomena happening. No reason to take notice. And I will shake you on your tree and you will fall to the ground as rotten fruit and all that will remain will be the fruit of heaven. Priests, children of light consecrated to the Hearts of Jesus and Mary will remain. If you are not joined in one heart, you will not be able to accomplish this task. I have picked you and formed you. You need to stay as one." This is what Jesus emphasizes over and over again that it will be the core group that will be in one mind and one heart, that will lead this oneness across this world. He says, "You will help to renew the Church and the world. When the poison reaches the peak of pain, I will pour out the antidote on the Church and the world through these revelations. You will be fired at and cry out in pain." This was two months ago. "You can not be divided. The authority is there. I have given it to them. They use this authority to oppose the plan given through the Pope." He said at the heart of every Church must be consecration to the Hearts of Jesus and Mary. Jesus said they do not consecrate their families, in Churches, in schools to Their Two Hearts as they should. Jesus says they must do this or they will fold. Mary said, we need to have the devotion to the Two Hearts all the way from Fatima. Jesus said we need to start the prayer chapters in the Churches and this will help the priests and the parishes. We've got to spread the Newsletter to the priests, too, and then they will be like a little family like the Father intends. So then not just our Shepherds of Christ Movement, but there will be these little families as the Father intended. That's why we need the prayer chapters in the Church.

Song between decades: *Come Holy Spirit*

5/4/97

Mary is the New Eve

R. It has come full circle.

In the Bible, we see what happened. We see Adam and Eve sinned. We see Jesus is the New Adam and Mary is the New Eve.

God created man and gave him great gifts - He gave him great lights.

Man disobeyed God.

Genesis 3: 1-11

Now, the snake was the most subtle of all the wild animals that Yahweh God had made. It asked the woman, 'Did God really say you were not to eat from any of the trees in the garden?' The woman answered the snake, 'We may eat the fruit of the trees in the garden. But of the fruit of the tree in the middle of the garden God said, "You must not eat it, nor touch it, under pain of death."' Then the snake said to the woman, 'No! You will not die! God knows in fact that the day you eat it your eyes will be opened and you will be like gods, knowing good from evil.' The woman saw that the tree was good to eat and pleasing to the eye, and that it was enticing for the wisdom that it could give. So she took some of its fruit and ate it. She also gave some to her husband who was with her, and he ate it. Then the eyes of both of them were opened and they realised that they were naked. So they sewed fig-leaves together to make themselves loin-cloths.

The man and his wife heard the sound of Yahweh God walking in the garden in the cool of the day, and they hid from Yahweh God among the trees of the garden. But Yahweh God called to the man. 'Where are you?' he asked. 'I heard the sound of you in the garden,' he replied. 'I was afraid because I was naked, so I hid.' 'Who told you that you were naked?' he asked. 'Have you been eating from the tree I forbade you to eat?'

R. Eve is the mother of all the living. There is the serpent and the woman. Eve sinned, she gave into her own will, she disobeyed God.

God gave us Mary, Mother of Jesus, Spiritual Mother of us.

From *Tell My People*
by Fr. Edward J. Carter, S.J.

The Holy Spirit

Jesus: "My beloved friend, tell My people to pray daily to the Holy Spirit. They are to pray for an increase in His gifts. My people must realize that the Holy Spirit comes to transform them. The Spirit desires to transform you more and more according to My image. Those who are docile to His touch become increasingly shaped in My likeness. He performs this marvel within Mary's Immaculate Heart. The more one dwells in My Mother's Heart, the more active are the workings of the Spirit. The Spirit leads Mary to place you within My own Heart. In both Our Hearts, then, your transformation continues. The more you are formed after My own Heart, the more I lead you to the bosom of My Father. Tell My people all this. Tell them to pray daily for a greater appreciation of these wondrous gifts. I am Lord and Master. All who come to My Heart will be on fire to receive the gifts of the Spirit in ever greater measure! I love and bless My people!"

Reflection: The Holy Spirit is given to us to fashion us ever more according to the likeness of Jesus. And the more we are like Jesus, the more Jesus leads us to the Father. Do we, each day, pray to the Holy Spirit to be more open to His transforming influence? Do we strive each day to grow in union with Mary? The greater our union with our Mother, the spouse of the Holy Spirit, the greater is the transforming action of the Holy Spirit within us.

end of excerpt

R. Mary is the woman clothed as the sun. Mary will bring the children into the light, the light of knowing God.

God sent His Mother, the Mother of our Christ-life. Mary is the New Eve.

The old Eve was sinful and willful. Eve sinned. Eve obeyed the devil instead of God.

A beginning, a woman Eve, mother of the living, a serpent that caught this weak woman in his snare.

Mary is the New Eve.

5/5/97

The Litany

R. In the Litany of the Blessed Virgin Mary, Mary is called "Mother of Divine Grace".

Mary is our Mother, Mary was chosen by God the Father to be the Mother of Jesus. Mary is the Mother of all of the Father's children. She is to the Father "My Mother", the Mother of all the children He has created. When the Father refers to Mary as "My Mother", He does not mean a mother that brought Him forth. He means, possessively, that she is the Mother chosen by Him to be Mother of His children.

In the Litany of the Blessed Virgin Mary, Mary is called "Mother of the Creator". Mary is Spiritual Mother, chosen to be Mother of Jesus, the Son of God and Mother of God's children. Mary is Mother of our Christ-life.

There is a tremendous link or bond between Christ and us in that we share the same Mother. 5/6/97

Life is Not Life If It is Not Rooted in Him

R. Mother of Divine Grace. For it is through Mary His life flows.

Life is not life if it is not rooted in Him! The reading talked about other gods. I am now writing this after the Mass.

This revelation was revealed during the Mass and I made a few scanty notes for I did not want to write during Mass. If only I could express what I know, which is deeply imprinted in my being. It is so difficult to write about that which is supernatural for, as Jesus says, how can you put in a bottle that which cannot be contained?

I see this lady clothed as the sun, the woman in Florida appearing in Clearwater, symbolizing the purity of "The Mother". Mary, clothed with light and purity. She is the sinless one, the Immaculate One. She is "The Mother", the one chosen by the Father to be the Mother of God. From the Litany "Mother of Divine Grace" "Mother of our Creator" He continues to stress the importance of the words, "My Mother" which I cannot deny. The Mother, chosen by the Father to be Mother of His Son and Mother of His children.

Life is not life if it is not rooted in Him. We receive physical life from our earthly mother. We receive a sharing in His life in baptism.

Eve sinned. Mary is sinless. Mary is Mother of our Christ-life.

We see this, Our Mother, Our Lady of Grace, in statues and pictures in which the grace is symbolized by the rays coming forth from her hands.

Mary appears in Lucia's vision with her Immaculate Heart in her hand. She is shown at the altar of sacrifice with her Son above her, hanging on the cross, and the Father and Holy Spirit above the altar in the Center.

Life is not life if it is not rooted in Him, the greatest source of this life being that given in the celebration of the Mass. Mary is the Mediatrix of Grace.

Mary appeared at Clearwater to signify the purity we must have.

The priest must consecrate his heart to Mary and Jesus.

The priest and the consecration of his heart to Mary helps the priest to be holy and unite more deeply to Jesus.

Life is not life unless it is rooted in Him. Jesus is the source of all life. Mary is the Mother of Divine Life.

A child receives life coming through the mother.

A child in the womb needs their mother.

The child continues to live in the womb because of the mother who is supplying the child with its life.

Life is coming from the Creator. The woman is crucial in supplying this life to the child.

Mary is the Lady of Light and Jesus is the Light of the World.

1 Corinthians 15: 20-28

In fact, however, Christ has been raised from the dead, as the first-fruits of all who have fallen asleep. As it was by one man that death came, so through one man has come the resurrection of the dead. Just as all die in Adam, so in Christ all will be brought to life; but all of them in their proper order: Christ the first-fruits, and next, at his coming, those who belong to him. After that will come the end, when he will hand over the kingdom to God the Father, having abolished every principality, every ruling force and power. For he is to be king *until he has made* his enemies his footstool, and the last of the enemies to be done away with is death, for *he has put all things under his feet.* But when it is said everything is subjected, this obviously cannot include the One who subjected everything to him. When everything has been subjected to him, then the Son himself will be subjected to the One who has subjected everything to him, so that God may be all in all.

R. Mary brings forth her children, a sinful race, into the light, into the light of knowing Him.

Adam and Eve sinned and the light was dimmed. Jesus and Mary are the New Adam and New Eve.

Jesus died on the cross. Mary is given to us under the cross as our spiritual Mother.

Mary is Jesus's Mother. Mary is our Mother. Mary is the Mother of Divine grace.

From the Shepherds of Christ
Priestly Newsletter 2000 Issue 3

<u>The Father's Will for Us – Our Source of Peace</u>

• Pope John Paul II instructs us: "The Church, as a reconciled and reconciling community, cannot forget that at the source of her gift and mission of reconciliation is the initiative, full of compassionate love and mercy, of that God who is love (see 1 John 4:8) and who out of love created human beings (see Wisdom 11:23-26; Genesis 1:27: Psalms 8:4-8)...He created them so that they might live in friendship with Him and in communion with one another.

"God is faithful to His eternal plan even when man, under the impulse of the evil one (see Wisdom 2:24) and carried away by his own pride, abuses the freedom given to him in order to love and generously seek what is good, and (instead) refuses to obey his Lord and Father. God is faithful even when man, instead of responding with love to God's love, opposes Him and treats Him like a rival, deluding himself and relying on his own power, with the resulting break of relationship with the One who created him. In spite of this transgression on man's part, God remains faithful in love.

"It is certainly true that the story of the Garden of Eden makes us think about the tragic consequences of rejecting the Father, which becomes evident in man's inner disorder and in the breakdown of harmony between man and woman, brother and brother (see Genesis 3:12 ff; 4:1-16). Also significant is the Gospel parable of the two brothers (the parable of the 'prodigal son'; see Luke 15:11-32) who, in different ways, distance themselves from their father and cause a rift between them. Refusal of God's fatherly love and of His loving gifts is always at the root of humanity's divisions.

"But we know that God...like the father in the parable (of the prodigal son), does not close His heart to any of His children. He waits for them, looks for them, goes to meet them at the place where the refusal of communion imprisons them in isolation and division. He calls them to gather about His table in the joy of the feast of forgiveness and reconciliation.

"This initiative on God's part is made concrete and manifest in the redemptive act of Christ, which radiates through the world by means of the ministry of the Church."[13]

13. Pope John Paul II, as in *Celebrate 2000!*, Servant Publications, pp. 140-141.

R. Mary, the pure and Immaculate one is clothed as the sun. Eve gave into the serpent; Mary crushes the head of the serpent.

This is what happens to me - the shade goes up and I catch a glimpse of the light. The Holy Spirit allowed me to experience a glimpse into the light –

We must walk in the way of the light. Jesus, the Light of the World, conceived and brought forth from the woman. Mary, the Mother of the Church, the mother that will lead her children out of darkness into the light through her Immaculate womb and the workings of the Holy Spirit within her, her beloved Spouse.

When I ask through Mary there is such purity in my prayer. Mary has powerful intercession, when I pray.

My Mother - the Mother He picked for Mother of all and Mother of His Son.

Sing Song: *Jesus My Lord, My God, My All*

From *Tell My People* by Fr. Edward J. Carter, S.J.

> *"What I say to you in the dark, tell in the daylight; what you hear in whispers, proclaim from the housetops."* (Matthew 10:27)

Jesus Has Come to Give Us Life

Jesus: "This is the day celebrating My Resurrection (Easter). The day of newness of life. I am Lord and Master. I am the Way, the Truth, and the Life. Tell My people to come to Me if they wish to experience life in abundance. I want to give all an ever greater share in the life of My Resurrection. Without Me you cannot be happy, nor have peace, nor have real joy. Tell My people to surrender to Me more and more. The more they do so, the more they will experience My love, wisdom, power, peace, joy, happiness, mercy, and goodness. Within My Heart My people will find these riches. I am Lord and Master! Please listen to My words."

Reflection: Through His life, death, and resurrection, Jesus has come to give us life, and to give us this life in abundance.

When we were baptized, we were incorporated into Christ and His Church. When we were baptized, we received the life of sanctifying grace. This life is a created sharing in the life of the Trinity. Truly, we are called to live a God-like existence according to the teaching and example of Jesus! It is our duty and our privilege to develop our life of grace — our Christ-life — through our participation in the Mass, through the reception of the sacraments, through prayer, and through all other good works. Indeed, we are called to love God and neighbor more and more.

What a glorious life has been given to us! In a spirit of thanksgiving, and together with Mary our Mother, let us always strive to know Christ more intimately, to love Him more ardently, and to follow Him more closely, so that He will always bring us to a closer union with the Father in the unity of the Holy Spirit.

Prayer: Father, we are profoundly grateful for the life You have given to us through Jesus and in the Holy Spirit. Through the constant intercession of Mary our Mother, we ask for the grace to always be Your worthy sons and daughters.

Mary Our Mother

Jesus: "My beloved friend, tell My people to come to My Mother. From the cross, as I was suffering indescribable agony, I gave Mary as spiritual Mother to the world. My great love for My people prompted Me to do this. I am Lord and Master, and I want My people to come to My Mother and their Mother. If you wish to be close to Me, come to Mary. Consecrate yourselves to her. In this way you will grow into the closest union with Me. Through her Immaculate Heart, you will be drawn more and more into My own Heart. It is My desire that you allow My Mother to place you within My Heart which loves you with an unfathomable love! This is My wish — that you come to Me enfolded by Mary's mantle, cradled in her arms, pressed against her Heart."

Reflection: It is God's will that we approach Jesus in union with Mary. Enough said!

Prayer: Heavenly Father, give us an increased understanding of what it means to have Mary as our spiritual Mother. Allow us to see how much it is against Your will to neglect our relationship with her. We make this petition in union with Mary, through Christ, and in the Holy Spirit.

end of excerpt 5/7/97

Satan Wants to Tear Apart - Bloody Friday

Jesus: My beloved ones,

Satan is attempting to destroy the Movement. Satan plans to try to rip you apart at the seams and leave you out to dry. Satan is working on each and every person individually to create a weak front. This message is given from Jesus to all.

The events of the 13th are at hand. I ask you to remember the attempts of satan to destroy the events of the 12th and 13th of last month. The attempts he made to rip the movement apart at all costs were horrendous.

You have suffered and you are weary from the marks of battle. I have told you in previous messages that you would wear the mark of battle, you would cry out in pain, you would prostrate yourself and beg for relief. You are suffering. Only in obedience to the message will the suffering be lifted.

You have been tested and tried. Satan is attempting to destroy any gifts I give to you on the 13th. I must define My stand on satan. All voices, lights, fragrances are not necessarily from God. All lights are not necessarily from God. Satan is a master of deceit. He will not stop until he has made every attempt to destroy the Shepherds of Christ and its credibility as a Movement.

People will attempt to throw out My main message. Satan will work in your mind in tremendous doubt. He wants you stopped.

By their fruits you will know them. Your testing has been altered to fit your needs. Satan knows your weakness, your tenderest spot. And, so you say, each and every member of the Movement, "I have suffered as never before". Do you not read the messages and hear the warnings I give to you? Do you think I speak to be ignored. I love you. I am the bridegroom of your soul. I am warning you in My great love, but you do not want to admit the extent satan will go to stop you.

I beg you. I beg you to continue to pray. He wants you stopped.

Satan will talk in your head. He knows your weak spots. He tempts through passions, anger etc. You may see lights and say, oh, but it is true.

Think again of the events satan used last month to stop the 13th. Remember the tactics he used to block all messages at the Falmouth Farm. Remember the trials with success he used at Our Lady of the Holy Spirit Center to block the rosary and the appearance of Our Lady of Light there. The Shepherds of Christ Movement never made it to the farm.

I come to you dripping with blood. I come to you with a cross on My back. I come to you accompanied by My Mother and yours as she stood beneath My cross her face covered with tears and she cried out to us by My side, "so many of my children will go to hell." Souls are at stake. Satan wants souls for hell. He wants your soul. He wants their souls. If you give into him, many souls will not be reached.

I am asking for prayer. Prayer is the weapon against satan. You are carrying the ammunition to fight off satan.

The materials of the 13th are your ammunition. You are carriers of these writings to the world. Satan wants you stopped.

You are in a battle. You wear the marks of battle. It is a war against satan to tear the Shepherds of Christ Movement apart at the seams. You will be weary and cry out for help. Help is only in Me.

What is satan doing in your life to keep you from the Mission given to you by Me and the Father? Do you feel anxious in your life, to step aside now? Does the devil tell you you must act now? My ways are gentle, kind, slow and loving. The devil's ways stir up the emotions – anger anxious emotion.

The devil wants you stopped. The devil wants you to oppose the Father's will.

I am Jesus. I am giving each person this severe warning. For years you have built a Movement based on love. Satan attempted to stop the Movement at the Holy Spirit Center, the Falmouth Farm and Tom's farm. This is the attempt by satan to tear your Movement apart and separate you. Do not act in haste! He wants to confuse you.

This is a warning. As never before, you will be tested when you are wounded and bleeding.

He wants the 13th stopped. This is major for the completion of the Fatima mission for the renewal of the Church and the world.

Look how many souls were lost in World War II. I give you the message to help renew the Church and the world. Satan will not stop until he has tried everything to stop you. Events will happen that will convince you, you should abandon ship.

Satan is trying to collapse the Movement. It is more urgent that each person come to the Sunday meetings.

You must pray every three hours fervently and every hour for Fr. Carter. Pray at 9, 12, 3, 6, etc.. Spread My Blood at 9, 12, 3 and 6. Plead in union with the Holy Sacrifice of the Mass. This is Bloody Friday. Focus on the crucifixion – the Blood I shed. Pray at these times in connection with My Blood, shed for sinful men. What you do in the Shepherds of Christ Movement will help in the lives of millions of souls and will help intently in the renewal of the Church and the world. I will use the Shepherds of Christ movement to help bring about the completion of the Fatima mission.

Please, please focus on the 13th. I am Jesus and I am begging you to help.

Every person in the Movement is under severe attack from satan. Your attack is tailored to you. You must be aware of this.

I love you, Jesus

You are with My Mother, pleading to the Father at the foot of My cross. Beg for grace for the Shepherds of Christ Movement and to withstand the attacks of satan. Listen to the Mary message tape today.

5/9/97

May 11, 1997
Morrow, Ohio
Sorrowful Mysteries

The Agony in the Garden

1. **R.** Think of Jesus in the garden and in His Divine knowing, knowing all things. Jesus is God. Think of Jesus in His Divine knowing, knowing all things, knowing the great love of the Father for all of men, knowing the great gifts that have been given to man but in their blindness they do not see the great gifts that God has given to them. And with the Heart consumed with the deepest love for man, the Almighty God ready to give Himself to His bitter passion and His death on the cross, is now kneeling in the garden and seeing before Him all that He would undergo and knowing that He would give His all for sinful men. And they would reject Him and they would treat Him with hatred. And they would not even care that God gives Himself to them. Think of how it is, how you feel when you give and you give and you give to another and they do not appreciate that which you give. And in your heart, you feel very sad because you want them to know how much you love them. And many times they do not even recognize the love that you give to them. But think of the all-perfect Lord and the act of perfect love that He gives Himself to sinful men as He does this day. And that He is not even appreciated or loved in return or thanked. Jesus knelt in the garden and His sweat became as great drops of blood for the anguish within His being was so great, to give and to love and His all-perfect love to know all things, He wished to share His knowledge about Himself with man. But man is more focused on the things of the earth. It is excruciating pain for us to know, to know the greatness of God, to know into these Divine mysteries and to see that man does not even care how he neglects the Eucharist. How man does not treasure the great gift that the Mass is, that God gives Himself to us and he gets up and men leave immediately after Mass. Oh Jesus, the gift that You give to us is truly such a gift. We reach for such simple, idiotic things in our life, when You outpour Your Divine love and give us a sharing in Your life in

baptism. Open our heart that we may see this great gift and treasure it and give to You great thanks and love, for Your gift given to us.

2. Hail Mary
3. Song: *I will be with you, that is My promise*
   R. No matter how hard it is, He is always with us.
4. Song: *I will be with you*
5. Song: *I will be with you*
6. **R.** What is the greatest treasure? Is to approach the altar of the Lord and to see Him as the picture that's on the front of the *Apostles Manual.* See Him clothed in white and see Him clothed in His red garb. See His hands outstretched with the wounds in His hand and the blood in His hands. But see the beautiful face that is on the front of the *Apostles Manual* with His arms outstretched. And He speaks and He says, "I give you Myself." And He gives us Himself in the Holy Eucharist. And how is it? For we feel as if we can scarcely walk, when the Almighty, the Divine Lord, gives Himself to us in the Eucharist and we unite with Him. The Almighty God gives us a sharing in His life in baptism. Jesus gives us His Body and Blood in the Eucharist.
7. **R.** Why wouldn't the devil want us stopped? When we are out there and we are spreading the messages that He has given to us to tell the world of His burning love. When we are telling the people about His immense love in the Mass, when we are telling them about the great mysteries in the rosary and Their lives in the rosary. There is so much filth that is out there and He cries out, "I am alive, I am alive, I am alive, but I am treated as a dead object. Will you spread My love to this world for Me? You are My hands. I give Myself to you." In this act of love the Almighty God gives Himself to us. And we are as a people walking in darkness for we do not comprehend fully and we do not see the light. For the light was dimmed with the sin of Adam and Eve. And what, how are we that we can approach the altar of God, that He gives Himself to us? God comes and unites with us. And we do not fall to our face. But if God allowed us to experience the presence of God in our being in such depth when He enters our body, and if we could see our own graced soul, we would fall to our face. In Heaven for

all eternity, we will be full of grace. For we will know Divine love. We are a people walking in darkness. The Light was dimmed through the sin of Adam and Eve. And Mary is appearing to tell us this is the way to the Light. "It is through my Immaculate Heart. Come to my heart. But you must make reparation for your sins, Oh sinful men. For you are tainted in your human nature and God is offended by the sins of men." And what do we do? We ignore the Mother that comes and we say, "not for you, my Mother, or for any mother." For I want for a few silly pleasures. We do not need you. Why should God give us this light of knowing Him, where we would fall on our face, of having this presence as it will be in the Reign of the Sacred Heart. Why should He do this for us? When we will not even admit the sin of Adam and Eve and tell Him that we are sorry. We realize that we have a tainted human nature. We are weak. We are sorry God. We are sorry for the sins of men. We are a sinful race. We are creatures. Here is God and we are the creatures. The creatures are sinful. We must tell God we are sorry. We are one. We are His creatures. We have offended God. We must make reparation for the sins of men. We just do not get it. Mary is the new Eve to lead us to this great Light of knowing God. She comes and she appears at Fatima and we ignore her. Mary appears over and over and over again and she says, "You must make reparation to God. You are creatures. Jesus came into this world, your Savior. You are so haughty in your hearts that you won't even tell God that you are sorry for your sins, that you recognize that you are tainted in your human nature." And so, our beautiful Mother, the pure and Immaculate one, the one through which we will be brought forth and brought into the Light, we ignore and we disobey and we say, "Not for you, my Mother."

Song: *A Song from Jesus*

8. **R.** I know how I feel in my heart when I love someone so much and I feel as if I have been ignored or neglected and how it hurts. Think of how it is that God remains with us this day and gives Himself to us. And we are blind and we are willful. This is the thing that angers the Father the most, is the willfulness of men for it is through the willfulness of Eve that man was cast into this dark shadow. But we persist

in our willfulness. Have we learned our lesson? Why should He take us to the Light? For we all have our own little plan. Are we ready for this new age in which we will all live as the Father says, "according to His Will". We pray for this in the Our Father. Thy will be done on earth as it is in Heaven. But we just don't get it. We are indeed a people walking in darkness. It is through the sin of Eve that we walk with a tainted human nature. There will be the era in which we will all live in the Father's will. When we do not obey the Father's will, we are not happy. We cause ourselves trouble and we stick out like a sore thumb. And He says, "Oh, My beloved creatures, how dearly I love you, so stupid and so silly in your ways, for you are a willful race. It is in giving your will to Me that you will be the children as the Father intends you to be."

9. **R.** This message is so important of June 12th for He says, and it says all through the Blue Books about the Plan, the Plan of the Father. I see now. I did not understand so much when I was writing these books. I see now how they are our way of living this day. They will keep us on our focus for this new era, for the world is becoming further and further away from us. For we are growing more and more into the depths of the Heart of Christ. More into this great era of intimacy. He is teaching us how to be so intimate with Him, how to surrender and to give our wills to Him. And the more we go into the depth of Christ's Heart, the more He is preparing us to be the leaders of this new era. The harder it is sometimes to be out there and to operate. And we must keep going to each other. We must keep going to Him. We must keep going to the Mass and the Sacraments and the Scriptures. For these are our truths and we must keep going to the Blue Books, for They are preparing us to be the leaders in the new era. This is a way in which man has never loved God with such intimacy and in living according to the Father's will as the Father intended. If we are to be the leaders we must be taught and instructed. He gave to us these Blue Books that we would use them everyday when we struggle. That we will go to the Blue Book, open it up and it is a tailored message for us to help us through that trial. And so He speaks in the Carpenter Message, "You are he who goes to a carpenter to learn to make a cabinet. You know nothing. You do not have any idea

of what you are to do. The carpenter knows exactly. He has a procedure whereby his plan will be accomplished. Every detail must be observed. He is the Master. You do not have the talent. You need talent to do woodwork. If you were given the talent and the directions, you could accomplish this task with such beauty. I am the carpenter. You are he who needs to be taught. You lack the talent. You need the gifts of the Spirit to accomplish My task! You come to Me in total ignorance. You are open, the Spirit fills you with the gifts. You have everything you need to do My work. The Father created you to accomplish His tasks. You are perfect. You must come open. You must know the plan. The plan is His will for you. If you do not follow the plan, the cabinet will not be built correctly."

10. **R.** The time will come in which all of men will live according to the Father's Will. The resistance by willful men is very displeasing to the Father. He has given to us these messages to help bring about this great era in which men will all live in accordance to the Father's will. And there will not be any bumping of heads. There will be peace and harmony among men as the children of God as He intended. There will be our Father and our Mother and we will be one body. There will not be bumping of heads. There will be love, love of God and love of one another. Mary promised this at Fatima 80 years ago. She is the woman clothed as the sun to lead her children into the Light. Man must say to God, "I am sorry, my God for I have sinned." For we are a willful race and we give our hearts to the pure and Immaculate One to lead us out from our sin. We are brought forth within her womb and through the workings of the Holy Spirit we are formed more and more into the image and likeness of God. Those who refuse to go to the Virgin Mary will not be brought forth as children of Light. From the beginning of the Bible to the end of the Bible, from the time of Eve when she listened to the devil in the Garden of Eden, we go to the Heart of the New Eve, Mary, our spiritual Mother. Mary crushes the head of the serpent. And we are brought forth again into the Light as children of Light, as children that will obey their Father and their Mother. Love God and love one another. We are so silly that we do not recognize our willfulness. And we persist in our ways. And we ignore the

pure and the Immaculate one, the one that the Father gave to us to lead us to the Light. Mary, our Model – Mary, our Mother, our Spiritual Mother.

Song: *I will be with you*

Jesus: And He says, " because I really love you. To My death on the cross I gave Myself as a sacrifice that you will be with Me forever in Heaven. You must give Me your heart. You must surrender. The way is through the Heart of My Mother, Mary."

Song: *Immaculate Mary*

The Scourging at the Pillar

1. 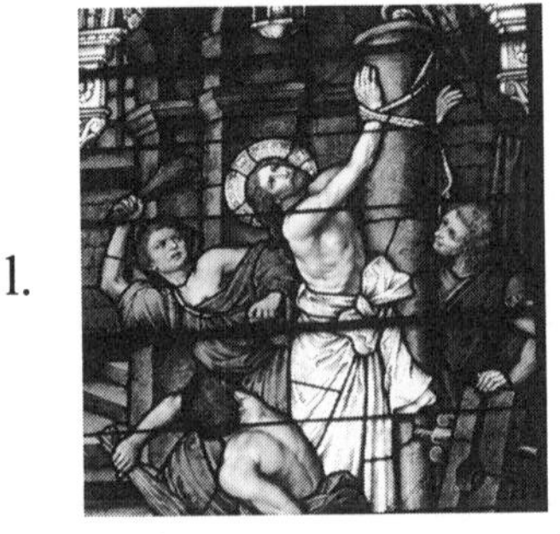

2. **Reference: Matthew 27: 24-26**
3. Hail Mary
4. Hail Mary
5. **Mary:** I am the Immaculate Heart. I love you with my tender heart. I heard the blows they gave my Son. I could scarcely look up. I heard the blows, the awful blows. My Son stood in silence while they beat Him.

   Jesus: All the whipping, all the brutality, the blows covered My entire body. I bled profusely. I stood in My own blood. They were My beloved ones who beat Me. They tore My flesh until it hung from My body. And they laughed at their handiwork. Do your brothers persecute you? And say mean things to you? Do as I did. Respond with love. Anyone who is hating you is suffering. Pray for their conversion. Live to help them to get to Heaven.

   Song: *I will be with you*

6. **Jesus: My dear beloved ones, I have given to you the greatest gifts. I have opened wide My Heart and I have**

shared with you the most intimate secrets of My Heart. The devil is pressing on your Movement. For he does not want you to spread these secrets that I have given to you. You must be strong. You must come to Me. You must pray as never before. For I am strengthening you. You are My soldiers. Soldiers need to be disciplined. Soldiers need to be strengthened. Do not be afraid for I give to you My Heart. Come to the deepest chamber of My Heart and I will give you My burning love. I am with you at every moment. I am with you. Come to Me in the Holy Sacrifice of the Mass and I will give you the greatest grace. When you come to Communion, your heart will burn for love of Me. I am with you and I give Myself to you in the Holy Eucharist. I love you with the greatest love. Do not be afraid. You must be strong and pray for grace that you will be able to accomplish all that the Father wishes you to accomplish. I am Jesus. I am your Savior. You will help lead the children of My Mother, Mary to My Heart.

Song: *A Song from Jesus*

7. **R.** It was so hard so many times to see the Blessed Mother before my eyes and to hear her call out about her children that would go to Hell. What do you do to know these things so deeply in your heart but not be able to do anything? And the thing that Mary called out the most was to spread the consecration to the school children and the rosary. And I tried so many times unsuccessfully to deliver this message because there were blocks that were created by satan. For he knows what will happen. If the children of America unite in their hearts in the consecration, that they will be a powerful force living in the Hearts of Jesus and Mary. We must unite ever fervently in trying to spread this consecration to the school children and spread the rosary. This is what Mary said over and over again that we must reach the school children with the rosary and the consecration.

8. **R.** It is so simple. Do you see Him there as I see Him there now at the pillar? I love Jesus so much. I just love Him. I love Him with all my heart and I see Him there with the wounds in His body. They are wide open and they are bleeding. He gives Himself to us. He gave Himself all through His passion. He gave Himself to His death on the

cross. And He gives Himself to us in the Eucharist. We are blind. We are a people walking in darkness and we will see the Light if we hang in there and do what He has told us to do. And if we would see, we would fall to our face to see the great gift that we are given in this Eucharist. In the Mass, if the priest realized the great gift that God has given to them, that the most important thing that they do is to try to be one with Christ, that they are another Christ acting in this world. Christ is present in the priest. We must do as the Father has told us and help to spread this Priestly Newsletter. We are a people walking in darkness and we will continue until we give our hearts to the Hearts of Jesus and Mary. The priests need to be consecrating their hearts to the Hearts of Jesus and Mary. We must do what the Father has told us to do. We must spread the prayer chapters. It is so simple. It hurts inside me to hear the messages over and over again and not be able to do more. But this is how it is in all of our lives. Satan does have a tailored plan for all of us that affects our emotions, that fills our heart with sorrow, that gets us sidetracked, that zaps our energy. And so here we are and here is the day and we are walking along and we are going to Church. And someone says something. And satan works in our head and we keep focusing on what they said. And before we know it, our energy is zapped and we are not doing what He has sent us to do. We are in severe battle for the devil does not want us doing what God has told us to do. He does not want me to write the Children's Rosary Book for many children will be touched by this. He does not want the Apostles Manual out in book form. The devil works to try to make confusion and division between us and the people in our lives, the people in the Movement, to keep us focused on nonsense things. When, what are we getting? We receive the greatest gifts. Mary, appearing on the building in Florida, appearing to us, Jesus talking to us. But the devil is crafty and he can work on us and try to zap our energy and make us cry and make us feel like quitting. We are our own worst enemy because we stay in our heads so much of the time and we do not go back to our hearts. This is the Age of the Two Hearts. This is the age in which love will reign. We must always act in love. This is not to be foolish, to give into those that are causing problems and will block the work of the Father. This is to say that we must love. Our primary purpose is that of loving God, ourselves, our neighbors and to help in the work of reaching the souls.

9. **R.** We can be so tender, so sensitive, that one little word can send us all of a sudden into a dither and we are upset. Do we not realize that it is a tailored made plan by satan to try to stop us. The devil studies us to try to trip us up. Our family can say the wrong thing that it will wound us easily if we let it. The devil tries to get to us through others we love. And so the person we love can say just the thing that hits the most tender spot in our heart. We must focus on love in our lives. We are the leaders to help bring about this great era of intimacy and love with God and with others. An era in which men will intimately love one another as never before, as we do in this core group. I remember one of the places where the devil immensely blocked the message. The people were bickering and fighting and hating each other and talking about each other. This is satan's way. We were started as a Movement of love. We came here and we joined in love. We must realize when there is any bitterness or hatred in our heart, when we are hearing words in our minds that are telling us this person did that, that one did this, that this confusion can be an attack from satan. That we must stay in our hearts in love, that our thoughts must be rooted in love, that we must pray to the Holy Spirit to work within us so that it is not the evil spirit that is working in us but it is the Holy Spirit that is alive with vibrancy and energy. Oh, how we have been tried and tested as never before. And we will come forth from the fire, a shining star if we stay within the burning Heart of the Sacred Heart of Jesus. We are to be great lovers, not foolish in our ways, but lovers that are to give His love to our brothers in this world.

10. **R.** And so He said several months ago that He was unveiling the workings of satan in the Movement. For it is the same in families, and it is the same in the Church and it is the same in the world. And it boils down to this: It is, there is one Plan and it is the Plan of the Father. When there is willfulness this is not of God. We must always try to be doing the Will of the Father. When there are so many plans from different people's wills, this is what Jesus says divides the Church and divides the family. The way that we stay rooted to His Plan is with the help of the daily Mass. With

that hour spent in intimacy alone with Him we get a lot of grace. For it has to be His Plan. If we read the Blue Book messages He will keep us focused on Him. He is giving to us these messages. For it will get harder and harder and I say this to Fr. Carter and he says, "Oh, don't say that now." But it will become easier and easier for Jesus says that the answers are in these messages. I can open this book now and I can read as He speaks to me.

Jesus: "Stand by Me and walk this road to Calvary. Listen and see My beaten Body. Hear the jeers of the crowd. Hear the thumping of the cross. Listen when it falls hard on Me and I can scarcely go any more. Walk with Me and be there, then think of the little crosses I ask you to carry. Do not put them down. Accept them for Me. It is in your crosses that you are drawn closer to Me. I endured all this suffering for deep and ardent love of you and I would do it today for you alone." **(April 25, 1994 - Carrying of the Cross)**

R. And this is what the devil is blocking. I can open it up and I can read again.

Jesus: "Obey Me in everything I make clear to you in your heart. Be open and focused constantly on Me. I guard your way. Concentrate on My Passion and how I loved you to My death and love you this way, this very minute. I, God, loved you, to My death, child. " **(April 29, 1994)**

Jesus: "Oh, what do I say to convince you? I died for you with such love, and you ask for more! I give Myself to you, Body and Blood, Soul and Divinity, in the Eucharist. I remain forever in the tabernacle with such ardent love!

Oh, child, do not listen to those who attack you. I need you to speak of My love. I give you all you need. Pray constantly for your attackers. I love them so. Your love will preach My lessons.

Never lose your peace. Love God, love one another. Eye has not seen, ear has not heard the glory that awaits him who loves and serves the Lord! I am Jesus. I am the Living God. I am with you, little one. Believe Me. Do not believe a sick world. My love will see you through." **(April 11, 1994)**

Song: *I will be with you*

R. And He speaks and He says that we will not be able to handle this as leaders, if we do not go to the weekly core meeting and if we do not go to the messages and live them. We must open the Blue Book when we are taunted. We must be alone with Him. We must realize this is His gift to us, to help us endure our suffering and our trials. And we will be that little army that He sends into the darkness to carry His Light to the darkened world.

Song: *A Song from Jesus*

The Crowning with Thorns

1. **Jesus:** "Think of someone you love very deeply yelling awful accusations at you. How it wounds your heart, My child. I sat there while they crowned Me with thorns and they hollered awful accusations at Me. They were My beloved ones, yet they stood there spitting at Me and hollering awful things at Me. Those whom I dearly loved, and they mocked Me and insulted Me and hurled their ugly hatred and lies at Me. I accepted all they did with a bleeding Heart and forgave them and loved them still." **(April 25, 1994 - Crowning with Thorns)**

2. **R.** These are the words that Jesus wishes to go into the world: We must be strong in our hearts and in the truth, know, that it is by their fruits that you will know them. Fr. Carter has stood behind all of these messages. Jesus wants this message to go to the world:

   Jesus: "Oh, you do not know suffering. Suffer for Me and lessen My load. This world is wounding My aching Heart. People are indifferent and hateful. They mistreat one another and are proud of their actions. Pray for your beloved persecutors. Don't hate them. It is as with those who tore My flesh and mocked Me. They were so engulfed in darkness! They did not know what they were doing." **(April 25, 1994 - Crowning with Thorns)**

3. **Jesus:** "All that matters is how you love Me and one another. Love those who hate you. My way is a hard way. When they hurt you and holler every ill thing at you, look to heaven and praise the Lord for the trial. It is in suffering that you are drawn closer to My precious Heart. I shed My Blood for you. I suffered for you. Will you not suffer when I ask you to?" **(April 25, 1994 - Crowning with Thorns)**

R. Fr. Carter said he opened up the Blue Book the other day and it said, "suffer for Me."

4. **R.** And so the devil talks in our head. And in the Blue Books Jesus talked all the time about how the devil talks in your head. And I thought that He was talking about thoughts that would make you feel irritated about people. But there are people that are actually hearing the devil talking in their head. And he says things that we want to hear. He says things that we want to do. He is so crafty and he wants the Shepherds of Christ Movement stopped. Jesus defines in the first two Blue Books how Jesus talks in our hearts. It is not in a hurry. It is not in haste that we must do things. We must go sit in front of the tabernacle and let Him speak to us in our hearts. That we know for sure what His will is. Satan is attacking the Movement. He wants us stopped. We must be careful. Know that satan does talk in people's heads and you hear a voice. The question is, what are you hearing in your heart when you feel most intimately joined to Jesus? And is it over a period of time? Or is it with anxiousness that you must act? Do you really believe that it is the will of the Father? If it is, He will make it clear. And it is through the fluttering of the Holy Spirit that we hear. Jesus has asked us to pray this Holy Spirit prayer, the Holy Spirit Novena, everyday. Just since we started it on the 5th, I have received such lights from praying the novena. I vowed to Jesus that I would try to pray the novena everyday. For I know more clearly what the will of the Father is when I do as He asked me to do. Which is to pray the Holy Spirit Novena everyday.

5. **Jesus:** Do you hear things in your head, My beloved ones? Negative things about your brother? Where is your focus? Are you going out to the world and trying to spread My love? You must pray for grace when you are being taunted, when you feel that you must be divided in your head. You must pray for grace. Pray to St. Michael to send the devil into Hell. It takes so much energy to think negative thoughts. It takes so much time, time is urgent.

R. Over and over again, the Father and Jesus and Mary have told us this. The messages have been majorly blocked. We need to begin the prayer chapters. This is what is our weapon against the devil, praying the prayers in the prayer chapter, praying the rosary. He is asking us to do this. The devil wants us to be focused on negative things so we do not do positive things. It is absolutely urgent that we continue with what Jesus is asking us to do.

6. Song: *A Song from Jesus*

7. **R.** And so Jesus points to His Heart and His fingers are on the sides of His Heart. And we do not get it yet. We still want to go and analyze and try to figure things out and listen many times to the negative tapes that satan wants to play in our heads. When our hearts must be hearts of love. If we are to be the leaders to spread the fire of His love across this troubled earth, how can we do it if we who He's calling His leaders, are focused on such negativism. And here we stand each one of us by ourselves at this moment. And around us we have seen unbelievable things happen all week, such confusion. We cannot be in there trying to referee this confusion. We must turn our focus to positive things. We must move steadfastly ahead. We must not listen to satan. If we listen to the words of satan we will be zapped in our energy. I will never get the Children's Rosary Book done from all the confusion that is going on around me. Is this an excuse? For Our Lady told me last year on Mother's Day that she would supply the money for this book and she wanted it out. One year later after several messages from the Father, the book is not much further than it was a year ago. But there were so many things that zapped my energy. And so Jesus asked in the message: "What is keeping you from doing what He is asking you to do? What is taking your energy?" We cannot give in to satan and to emotions. We must get ourselves together in the morning if we are feeling negative. Get ourselves dressed and if at all possible get to the Church and start to read the messages. Listen to a rosary tape. He has given those to us to help us to fight the battle so that we will be doing what the Father is asking. The world is not like us. That is why He is asking us to do what He is asking us to do. We are to spread the fire of His love across this earth. We are to be people that are great lovers.

8. **R.** Let us praise the Lord. Let us give Him our hearts. Let us go to our knees and fall and ask Him to help us. What? To help bring about the Reign of the Sacred Heart of Jesus that men will fervently love God. And so we pray in the Our Father, thy Kingdom come, thy Will be done on earth as it is

in Heaven.

9. Hail Mary
10. Hail Mary

Song: *I Rocked Him as a Baby*

The Carrying of the Cross

1. **Mary:** "I could scarcely stand to walk the way with Him. I was so sick at what they had done but I wanted to be with my Son. I walked by the grace of God.

   Jesus: My suffering was intensified by the sorrow and suffering of My Mother. My eyes met hers and I saw her red, teary face. All they did to Me, but to watch My beloved Mother suffer! She heard the cross as it thumped up the hill. The sounds were so loud and, at the sight, she had to look away.

   Stand by Me and walk this road to Calvary. Listen and see My beaten Body. Hear the jeers of the crowd. Hear the thumping of the cross. Listen when it falls hard on Me and I can scarcely go any more. Walk with Me and be there, then think of the little crosses I ask you to carry. Do not put them down. Accept them for Me. It is in your crosses that you are drawn closer to Me. I endured all this suffering for deep and ardent love of you and I would do it today for you alone." **(April 25, 1994 - Carrying of the Cross)**

2. Song: *I Rocked Him as a Baby*
3. **R.** And so it is in the last book in the Bible, there appears the woman clothed as the sun and the moon is under her feet. And she is crushing the head of the serpent. For the victory has been won and we will be brought forth into this great light of knowing God with the greatest love and the greatest intimacy. But we must go to the woman, the woman clothed as the sun, the pure and Immaculate one, the one that walked by Christ and stood beneath His cross. And as she said, "I stood beneath the cross of My Son and I cried."

   Mary: For I appear, I appear, I appear and men do not hear what I tell them. Will you tell them for me? Will you tell them how I love them. That I am their Mother and that I walk by their side and that I will lead them to the Heart of My Son.

4. **R.** And Jesus is supposed to be the King and center of all men's hearts.

5. **R.** Do we believe this? Or do we think that Our Lady of Fatima did not mean this, when she said this great era of peace would come? If we believe this, if every time we pray the Our Father and we say, thy Kingdom come, thy Will be done on earth as it is in Heaven. If we believe this, then we must realize that in the state the world is in this day, in the state of poison, in the Church and the world, in need of renewal, that God would send into this world messages to help lead men to His Heart. And that someone must be the leaders. If the religious are not leading as they should to the Heart of Christ then there must be some lay people. He has chosen this core group specially. And He has taught us through these rosaries. He has given us great gifts to draw us in the greatest intimacy with Him. But we must believe. We must go to the messages. We must read them. We must be taught. We are the leaders to help bring about this Reign. We do not know. We do not know the Father's will. He is revealing it to us in the intimacy of our hearts. He is revealing to us His Plan in these messages. He is telling us what we must do to bring about the Reign of His Heart. We have been called leaders to help bring about the Reign of the Sacred Heart of Jesus and the renewal of the Church and the world. And satan will infiltrate our head and try to get us focused. He will create confusion around us to where we will lay on the floor and cry out, "Oh this is so hard". And the answer is in Their Hearts. The answer is not in our heads listening to the words of satan. The answer is in going to the Immaculate Heart of Mary and she crushes the head of the serpent. Crawling up in bed at night in the heart of Mary, being with the Father and telling Him, "I just want to do Your will, Father, I love You Jesus." The presence of the Trinity with us at every single second. And in those quiet moments feeling that presence of God. Great gifts have been given to us. But we must keep our focus for the devil is working with all of his demons to try to infiltrate our minds and to get us to abandon ship and to leave our post.

6. **R.** Do you see the torn body of our Savior? Do you see the cross on His back? Do you see Jesus with blood all over His face in the corner of His eyes and in His ears? And He looks

up in such stress and He sees the eyes of His Mother. And what He sees is the beautiful Mother that He loved so much covered with such stress, with such sorrow, with such pain. And in that look They share great love and suffering. This is how it is in our life. We are not alone. Jesus Christ, the Son of God, would give Himself this very day for me, on the cross. The little things that He asked to help us to do to help with souls is so small compared to all that He did, that these souls would be saved.

7. **Jesus:** Carry your cross for Me, My beloved ones, for you are the leaders that will help to bring about the Reign of My Sacred Heart. Do not be afraid. Do not listen to the tauntings of satan in your head to distract you and to get you focused on other things. You must come to Me. You must beg for grace. You must cast satan into the fires of Hell. And you must pray hourly for your leader, Fr. Carter.

8. **Jesus:** I am giving to you great grace when you come to Me at the hours of 9, 12, 3 and 6. And you remember My Precious Blood that I shed for you. I am dressing you in My Precious Blood. You will be protected against the wiles of satan. You must go to the Heart of your Mother and Mine, for she will crush the head of the serpent and he will not influence you.

9. Song: *O Lady of Light*

   Jesus: And I walked, and as I walked, the cross seemed so heavy and it pressed down on My back. But I did not remove the cross. How is your cross this day? Is it heavy on your back? You must go a little further, a little further, always going further and knowing that it is in the cross I will give you My greatest love.

10. Hail Mary

    Song: *See the Eyes that Look at Mary*

The Death of Jesus

1. **Mary:** "They hung Him on the cross. I was so weak I could barely stand. I was held up by John. I watched my Son in such agony. Oh, my beloved Son! What had He done to deserve such suffering? He loved you to His death. He was crucified for love." **(May 25, 1994 - The Crucifixion)**

2. **Jesus speaks and He says,** "How do I tell you that I died for you? Do you even know I would do it today, just for you? They nailed My beautiful hands and feet to the cross. Big, gigantic nails they pounded into My precious hands. Such hard hearts! (I got this in August 23rd of 1993. It was one of the first things He ever said about the passion.) They pounded the nails through My feet. Blood spurted out and they continued. Such hardness of hearts. Look at your hands, My child. Would you allow someone to nail them to a cross? Would you withstand this torture for love? This is My love for you. It is not a little lip service love. It is the love that made Me lay down My life for you.

   Surrender. I call you to surrender. Open your arms as I did when I died on the cross. Let all your worldly possessions drop around you and you will experience the joy of being free, united only to Me, of letting go and knowing that I, God, tend to your every need. To My death on the cross I loved you and I love you this way this very day. Let go and give it all to Me. I will care for you far better than you could for yourself. I am God and I love you more than you can love yourself." **(May 25, 1994 - The Crucifixion)**

3. **R.** "Jesus is dead, hanging on the cross, arms outstretched. His feet are not even on the ground. He is hanging by nails on a piece of wood. What do we hold on to? He wants us in midair in total surrender." **(May 25, 1994 - The Crucifixion)**

4. **Jesus:** "Oh, little ones, how you squander your possessions. How you hold on to people, how you won't let go! See Me in total surrender. I gave My very life for you. What do you hold on to, My little ones? Little bits and pieces you give to Me and you hold tightly to your lives. All will go up in smoke and only the things of God will remain. Not one pair of shoes do you take with you, only your love given to God and to others." **(May 25, 1994 - The Crucifixion)**

5. **Jesus:** "Do not put the cross down. Do not complain. Sainthood is carrying the cross with a cheerful face. Your brothers will not comfort you and they will not give you your answers. Turn to Me, My beloved ones, in the silence. I am forever present. I know the workings of your hearts. I sanctify your souls. I am the Sacred Heart of Jesus. I ponder your ways with such love." **(May 10, 1994)**

6. **R.** And so I say to Jesus, "but my beloved Jesus, I am not a saint. I just love You so much. I love to go to the Eucharist and I love to feel the presence of God within my breast. I love you with the deepest love. But these other things seem so hard. Jesus I want to be like You, but it is so hard."

7. **R.** And He says to me that we are sinners, that this is what we must admit. That we make mistakes. That we are sorry for those things that we do, that we recognize ourselves as a sinful race and that we do what God is asking us to do, to come to Him in love, to love one another. And when we sin, that we say that we are sorry. Before every Mass that we recognize that we are sinners and that we make reparation to God, that we realize that we are totally dependent on Him and His grace. That it is His grace that will make us more holy. That in every Mass that we will die more and more to our imperfections. For this is what causes the problem in our relationships, many times, is our own imperfections, our own weaknesses, our own wounds and the devil knows this. So he can touch just the right point. And we can react. And we think many times it is the other. But it is what's going on inside of our own hearts.

   Jesus: That is why I tell you My beloved ones, you must come to Me for I know the workings of your heart. I know every care and every struggle that you have. And I will comfort you and I will lead you deeply into My Heart.

8. **Jesus:** In the head, how could you figure out all of the things from your life and why you act the way that you act. I am telling you, you must give Me your cares. You must come to Me and surrender. For it is grace that will make you whole.

9. **R.** And so many times when we are not nice to others, we do not want to go and to tell them that we are sorry. We do not want to admit our error. And so we go on and on in our minds how maybe it was their fault or maybe it is our fault. Or who's fault is it? And so, so much time and energy is lost when we could be doing positive things. The devil truly is working on our minds to try to divide us from one another, to try to get us focused on so many things that take us from the work that He wants us to accomplish. He is telling us about the events of the 13th. This is a major part of the completion of the Fatima message. The work in Florida is major to bringing about the completion of the Fatima

message and the renewal of the Church and the world. And so satan has worked and worked and worked to try to divide us so that we will not do what He is asking us to do. How can we call ourselves lovers, children of God? When He is love. But how are we in our hearts? We must try to love and to work with each other. We must consecrate our hearts with one another. We must surrender for we are children of Eve and we have a tainted human nature and we fall. And it is very hard. Many times it is hard. But it's through the Immaculate Heart of Mary that we will be brought forth to the Light. It is through the purity of her heart that we will unite to the Sacred Heart of Jesus and that we will know His immense love. And in knowing His immense love and in being saturated with this love, we will spread this love to others. It is not us that is acting. It is Him acting in us and we will be great lovers but we must go to the Hearts of Jesus and Mary.

10. Song: *Give me Your Heart, Oh Jesus*

Jesus: And so I say to you, My beloved ones, I give you My love. You must let go of the tauntings that satan has created in your head to lead you astray. You are the leaders that I am calling to help bring the children to the Light. It is in the Shepherds of Christ Movement that I will greatly renew the Church and the world. It is through these prayers that many priests' hearts will be changed. You must fervently focus on starting prayer chapters and praying the prayers yourselves. The most important thing that you do is your personal holiness. I have called you and I have given you the greatest gifts. You do not realize that when you pray the Morning Offering, when you pray to the Father in union with Me in the Holy Sacrifice of the Mass, in My name, in the Holy Spirit, through the powerful intercession of My Mother, through the angels and saints, that in the degree of holiness that you have reached, that your prayers are very powerful. I have taught you, My beloved shepherds in the core group. You must realize the power of prayer. In praying the novena every hour, you have been taught how to pray and to ask. If you ask, the Father will hear you. When you ask in My name, you will receive great gifts. You must be about your own personal holiness and come to Me. Come to Me and ask Me for help. Intercede to the Father for help in My name.

I am Jesus. I have given you a heart of love. I have given you a heart that will be ever closer to Mine. When you pray, the Father hears your prayers and He is attentive to all of your needs. Do not be afraid. Come to Me and I will give you My burning love.

Song: *Give me Your Heart, Oh Jesus*

Jesus: You are My beating Heart in this world. If you say no, My Heart will not beat with the love that is coming through your heart. Surrender and give your heart to Me. Come to Me in the intimate moments and I will fill your heart with My Divine love. And others will know Me through you. But you must surrender and come to Me. Pray on the hours of 9, 12, 3 and 6 for the Shepherds of Christ Movement and think of the Precious Blood that I shed for you.

Jesus: I must warn you that you must pray for all of the members in the core group, for those that did not hear this message for they will be taunted immensely by satan. You must pray for your brothers and sisters. It is most urgent that you do this now. And pray hourly for Fr. Carter.

Jesus: I must warn you finally that those that oppose you are being pressed on by satan and causing master confusion. You must pray for those that satan is using to stop the Movement. You must also pray for all of the members that will attempt to come on the 13th for satan will try to stop them from coming. I am Jesus. It is most urgent that you continue the Holy Spirit Novena and that you pray for the events of the 13th.

5/11/97

Running for Cover

R. On May 13, 1997, we went to Tom's farm in Kentucky. I hadn't referred to Conyers before in any rosaries. In the fourth mystery of the rosary, I told how at Conyers on May 13, 1993, a gigantic wind came up and I accounted what happened. After the rosary, it was cold and the people walked to Tom's barn. The main people were still behind about 5 minutes after the rosary. A wind came up and I thought I would have to run for cover, for I thought I would be blown off my feet. The large Sacred Heart and Immaculate Heart statues blew to the ground. Mary's head came off and was face up. She was cracked diagonally right through her Immaculate Heart. Our Lord wished these pictures to be placed here on the Internet. The chairs, the swing, the tables all were blown over. It was just like Conyers, May 13, 1993. The air was calm and as soon as the rosary was over, the wind came forth so strong I could hardly stand on my feet, and it blew everything over.

Our Lord wishes these pictures to be released with this writing today. What followed was immense persecution for the Shepherds of Christ Movement. The rosary and its message of May 13, 1997, will soon be released here.

May 13, 1997

Rosary on Tom's Farm

Glorious Mysteries

The Resurrection

1. **Jesus:** Open wide your hearts, My beloved ones, for I am with you in a special way on this day. There are many changes that are occurring in your lives. You must let go and

surrender for I am separating the sheep from the goats and you will be a strong body. You will be a body joined in one mind and one heart to help carry the light into the darkness. Do not be afraid for I am here and My Mother is here in a special way. I will guard you.

Song: *I will be with you*

2. **R.** And so where does our journey take us. This is the Shepherds of Christ Movement. It is not yet three years old and it has spread internationally all over this world. We have received many messages from Jesus, from Mary, and from the Father telling us how we could advance in spreading the love of the Sacred Heart and helping to bring about His reign and the triumph of her Immaculate Heart. We have been given so many messages that will help renew the Church and the world. We have been given prayers in the prayer manual, that will help to turn the priests hearts to holy priests. And this is our mission, our mission is to help renew the Church and the world and bring about the completion of the Fatima message. The Fatima mission has been oppressed for 80 years. It has been blocked over and over again in the Church and in the world. Do we think that Mary will go away? Do we think that the Father will change His plan because of willful men? Is this not the reason why we are in this state to begin with? For it is that Eve ate of the fruit and Adam and Eve sinned, an act of the will in which they did their will over God's. And it is that the Father is well pleased when we obey His will. How is our world today? Is our world aligned with the will of the Father or are we a willful race? I would like to read to you the message of the Father given on January the 18th. It is most important that you also read this message and the message of the Father from January 11th and study these messages. We must see things as from the Father's perspective as from the I Am. We must see them in their whole view. We are creatures that are walking the earth but we must see that

sinful man has disobeyed the Father and that we must make reparation to Him for our sins. Adam and Eve sinned. God came into this world to save us from our sins. Mary appears at Fatima and she tells us, "You must, my beloved children, come through my Immaculate Heart. You must make reparation. You must tell God that you are sorry for your sins," and we ignore her. But she promises to us that there will be a great reign in which the Sacred Heart of Jesus will reign, in which men will know God in this great light similar to before when Adam and Eve had the light, that there will be this great era of intimacy with God, and man will know God. But why, why, should God lead us in to the great era of peace and love? Have we shown God that we recognize the fact that we are sinners, that we are sorry for our sins, that we come to Him as little dependent children, that we love God with our whole heart, our whole soul and our whole being, and that we want to make reparation for our sins? Or do we come with haughty hearts, with willfulness and we do not listen to the Father? Why should we go into this new era? The new era will come about. It will come about peaceably if we do what they have told us to do. The Father is telling us now very strongly exactly what we must do. We must begin these prayer chapters to help to lead the priests to holiness, to help renew the Church and the world, to help to bring about consecration in the hearts of the priests, of the sisters, of the people. The Father is telling us what to do. He gave great gifts at Falmouth. This is what He said, "I gave great gifts to you allowing Mary to appear and because of willful men they did not cherish these gifts and so I used Falmouth as an example of the chastisements to come if you do not obey. And what am I telling you to do, My children? I am telling you to begin these prayer chapters. I am telling you to pray as my Son Jesus has instructed you to pray. I am telling you to spread this priestly newsletter that it will greatly renew the Church and the world." The devil will try to do everything he can to stop us. But the Father has told us over and over again that we must begin these prayer chapters, that we must pray these prayers fervently ourselves, that there will be this era of great peace and love. In December, if you study the all night message, (December 29, 1996) if you study the messages of Jesus and Mary, you see the intensity as it builds. Mary says, "I cannot hold back the hand of my Son any more." October the 5th, "His hand is struck with power." Jesus appears on the cross on December the 5th after Mary appeared for two years and four months and His mouth is moving and He says, later, that no one is listening to Him. Then I received strong messages December the 19th, December the 22nd. December the 19th Mary says that she appears on a building in Florida because we have made money our God. She also says that "the time is nigh." And Jesus gives to me a strong message for the first time and He said, "There will be chastisements and the moon will turn to blood and I am telling you what you must do. You must go to the Holy Sacrifice of the Mass. The grace is outpoured in the Mass." On December the 22nd, He gives another message where He speaks about chastisements. All of these messages in the sequence is very important to the Father's plan. They are in the Apostles Manual. The Father begins to speak in January and He says, "You have ignored my Son and now you will ignore Me?" And so I received the strongest messages all through December and February to where I had knots in my stomach and He kept talking about Falmouth and He kept saying how we did not cherish the gifts that He had given. And then there was the flood. And after this the Father said that this was only a little example of what is to come if we do not do as He has asked us to do. It is so simple. We are children that are willful. We are children that must obey our Father. We must pray. We must tell Him that we are sorry for our sins. The prayers in the prayer manual are the prayers that Jesus gave to us to help to turn the priests to holy priests, to help to renew the Church and the world, and to help to bring about the completion of the Fatima message. The priestly newsletter is written by Father Carter but Jesus is writing the newsletter through him to teach His priests about His burning love, to teach them all that they need to know to be holy priests celebrating the Mass and ministering to all of the people. This is a great gift from God and in all great gifts that are given we experience much suffering as we see in the life of Jesus, for He died but He rose on the third day.

3. **R.** The message of the angel from Fatima says this: "The angel came… bearing a golden chalice in one hand and a Host above it in the other. The amazed children noticed that

drops of blood were falling from the Host into the chalice. Presently, the angel left both suspended in mid-air and prostrated himself on the ground saying, this beautiful prayer: 'Most Holy Trinity, Father, Son and Holy Spirit, I adore You profoundly. I offer You the most precious Body, Blood, Soul, and Divinity of Jesus Christ, present in all tabernacles of the world, in reparation for the outrages, sacrileges, and indifferences by which He is offended. By the infinite merits of the Sacred Heart of Jesus and [the intercession of] the Immaculate Heart of Mary, I beg of Thee the conversion of poor sinners.'"(The Spirituality of Fatima and Medjugorje, p. 9)

4. **R.** And so He came and He rose on the third day to give us life and we share in His Divine life. And He gives to us Himself in the Holy Eucharist. In the Mass, the sacrifice of Calvary is sacramentally made present. It is at this time that we must tell God that we are sorry for our sins, that we want to make reparation for our sins, that we give our hearts to God. For as we unite in this sacrifice with Jesus on the cross to the Father, we make this great act of reparation for our sins. We are a sinful race. We will be blessed and given great gifts when we act as the Father intends us to act. We are sinful. We have as the Father said "run amok". We are doing our own wills. And so the Father speaks on January the 18th and He says, "I am the Father. My plan is unfolding through you, My beloved priest and Rita and the core group in the Shepherds of Christ Movement. I tell you all to read the accounts of Noah. Nowhere in history has God been offended as He is this day by this sinful world. You will suffer a fate for your offenses against God. Mary appeared at Fatima to warn you, the sinful children, how they are offending God, but you did not listen. The war did not change the hearts of many evil men." Eighty years ago Mary appeared at Fatima and she told us what we should do and we did not pay attention. And Mary said, "If you do not do what I tell you to do, there will be a great war." And the whole world suffered from World War II because they did not listen to their heavenly Mother. "I warn you through My beloved daughter, Mary. You did not heed her warnings.

Disobedience against the Mother I gave you displeases Me greatly. Mary is the Mother of all children. Mary is a gift from Me, but you are willful and abuse the gift I sent you. You do not make reparation to her Immaculate Heart; you continue to offend her. I will not tolerate the deeds of evil men any longer. My plan will unfold."

5. **R.** Jesus came to this earth and He gave Himself as a sacrifice for love of men. I saw Him on the cross with His withered body. I saw Him at the point of death and I saw His mouth move and He said later that no one is listening. Do we not hear the words of our beloved Savior as He speaks to us over and over again in the Mass? How are our minds when we go to the Mass? Are we focused and trying to be in one heart with our beloved Savior in offering the Holy Sacrifice in order to make reparation to the Father? Is this our consuming desire: to give love to the Almighty God? For this is the greatest act of love that God gives Himself to us in the Mass. We are a blind race. We are willful. We are haughty. Jesus has given to us these messages in order that we will turn our hearts to hearts of love, that we will turn our hearts to hearts that praise God, that love God and love one another, that we tell God that we are sorry for the offenses that we have committed against Him, and that we will – obey Him and love Him and live according to the Father's will.

6. **R.** And so the Father speaks, "I am the Father, the Almighty God, the Alpha and Omega; you are a sinful people, a chosen race sinning against a loving God. I am angered at your ways for they are not My ways. You have run amok. You have offended your God and You have disobeyed your Mother and My beloved Son Who died for you." The Father warned and He has warned again and He has told us what we must do. The resurrected Lord is here with us this day. He gives Himself to us in the Holy Eucharist and He is treated with such indifference and such disrespect. And this is what the angel speaks of in the Fatima message, "I offer You the most precious Body, Blood, Soul, and Divinity of Jesus Christ, present in all tabernacles of the world in reparation for the outrages, sacrileges, and indifferences by which He is offended." (The Spirituality of Fatima and Medjugorje, p. 9)

7. **R.** The angel continues and says, "Take and drink the Body and Blood of Jesus Christ, horribly outraged by ungrateful men! Make reparation for their crimes and console your God." (The Spirituality of Fatima and Medjugorje, p. 10)

8. **R.** And so the Father speaks, "I will act on all who continue in such sin. The sheep will be separated from the goats; the goats will receive punishment for their deeds. Heaven and earth will kiss and there will be love in all hearts. Justice will prevail and My children will be children of light, children that obey as I intended from the beginning."

9. **R.** Let us turn our hearts to our beautiful Savior Jesus Christ, Who gave Himself to His death on the cross and Who rose on the third day. Let us be the soldiers that He has called us to be in the bitter pain and the suffering that we suffer to go forth and to spread the word of God. Let us ask for the grace to suffer this persecution, but realize that as Mary promised at Fatima that there will be this great reign of peace in which the Sacred Heart of Jesus will Reign and the Immaculate Heart of Mary will triumph, that we have majorly been called by God here this day to hear this message.

   Jesus: I give to you, My children, I give to you My Sacred Heart. I am asking you to march into the darkness and to carry the light, the light that comes forth from My burning Heart of love. You will be pressed on. You will be stamped on. You will suffer and be persecuted, for the devil wants you stopped. You must be strong. You must know that I am strengthening you for the task at hand. You will be strong soldiers. You wear the marks of battle. You are marching into a world in which many are godless to carry My light.

   R. I see our beloved Jesus before me as I saw Him once at Immaculata adorned in the brightest light and transfigured before my face. This will be the banner of light that we will carry into this darkened earth. But we must stay rooted firmly in Him. We must give our hearts to Jesus and to Mary, that we will be pure, that we will be able to withstand the torture that we will suffer as we go into battle as soldiers carrying the white flag which will lead to victory.

10. **R.** Does not Jesus wear the marks of battle? I see Him now. When I go to the Eucharist, I see Him as the Jesus on the front of the *Apostles' Manual* with His hands outstretched

and the blood in His hands. Look at His wounds; they are glorified wounds. He wore the marks of battle and He came forth victorious in the end. We too will come forth victorious, for we will wear a white flag and we will carry the message of our beloved Savior into this world. Many will know about Him, will know about His love and His Divine Life because we will tell them what He has shared with us.

Song between decades: *"I come to you with greatest love..."*

Jesus: Are you afraid? Are you afraid, My beloved ones, to march into battle? How are your hearts, are they rooted in Me or are they fearful? I am the Almighty God. It is with My might that you will go forth into this world and there will be victory, for I have won and many hearts will turn to hearts of love as you march forth into the darkness and carry My flag of light and the hearts will be lighted with the fire of My love. Their hearts will be alive with My burning love. Look at your world this day. Look at the children, how many hearts are alive with God's love? How many children are being told about My love? How many people this day are focused on so many things, but do not even give Me a thought? You are the soldiers I am sending. Will you say "no" when it gets tough? I will weed out the strong ones from those that are not truly committed. And it will be with this small in number that the soldiers will march forth into this world, and they will carry the flag of victory.

The Ascension

1. **R.** It is His Might that will accomplish this task, not mine, not yours, but His Might, as we identify more and more with Him. And so what does He give to us in order that we can unite more with Him? He gives us Himself in the Holy Eucharist. We share in such intimacy with the divine God. We walk down the aisle and we receive God within our breast. Why do we fear when the Almighty God loves us so much that He gave Himself as a sacrifice on the cross, and He remains with us this day and He gives Himself to us in the Holy Eucharist?
2. Song: *I am the Bread of Life*

Jesus: I love you. I love you. I love you. I am with you at this very moment. No matter how you feel in your heart give all your cares to Me and I will bathe you in My precious love. I am the Almighty God. I give to you a sharing in My Divine life and My Divine love.

3. **R.** "I offer You the most precious Body, Blood, Soul, and Divinity of Jesus Christ, present in all the tabernacles of the world in reparation for the outrages, sacrileges, and indifferences by which He is offended. Take and drink the Body and Blood of Jesus Christ, horribly outraged by ungrateful men. Make reparation for their crimes and console your God." (The Spirituality of Fatima and Medjugorje, p. 9-10)

4. **R.** And so He gives to us an abundant sharing in His divine life when we go to the Eucharist. And how is He treated? Horribly outraged. Are we honoring God? Are we praising God? Are we giving thanks to God? Are we loving God? Jesus has given to us the *Mass Book.* He has given to us the writings of Father Carter in the priestly newsletter in order to instruct the priests more so that they will turn their hearts to hearts of burning love, love for their Savior, that they will consecrate their hearts and give their hearts to Jesus and Mary. And what about reparation? Do we even hear about this? Look at this, the Holy Sacrifice of the Mass, the sacrifice of Calvary, sacramentally made present. I know that I am a sinner. But I know this, I know that if I go to the Immaculate Heart of Mary that I can unite in deep union with Christ. And in the Holy Sacrifice of the Mass, I unite in deep union with Christ and offer myself to the Father and tell God, "I am sorry for my sins, and for the sins of all men." We are a nation. We are a race. We must make reparation to God for the creatures of this earth. We must cry out at the Lamb of God, "Lamb of God, have mercy on us, have mercy on us." The Father is displeased with the creatures of this earth. They are our brothers. This is what is being said in the Fatima message: we must make reparation to God for we are creatures that have offended our God and we must give Him our love and tell Him that we are sorry.

5. **R.** We unite in this deep union with Jesus when we give our heart to the heart of Mary. How many times I am at the Mass and I see my sins before me. And I just say, "Oh, Jesus I love

You so much and I want to be one with You so much, Jesus." I say, "Mary, I give you my heart that I can be pure in your heart and unite deeply to the Heart of Christ." As I unite with Jesus in this Holy Sacrifice of the Mass, as my sacrifice becomes one with His sacrifice and I offer it to the Father and tell Him that I am sorry for my sins and the sins of all men, this is most pleasing. We must make reparation to God, for we are a sinful race. We are offending God. This is what Mary tells us, she tells us that we must make reparation. Why should God give us the light? Why should He take us into the new era? Men march around this earth with haughty hearts. They ignore God. They do not even tell Him that they are sorry for their sins. They do not even recognize that they have been tainted by the sin of Adam. They are haughty in their hearts. And Mary appears and she says, "You are offending God. You are a sinful race. You must give your heart to me and when you give your heart to me, you will unite in such depth with my Son Jesus. Offer a sacrifice to the Father. Offer a sacrifice united to the sacrifice of Jesus. Make reparation for your sin, men. I am your Mother. I am telling you what to do." And so what do we do? We curse our Mother. We ignore our Mother. We do not do what our Mother tells us. Eve decided that she would do what she wanted. What is wrong with us that we do not see that we must obey, obey the will of God.

6. Song: *I am the vine you are the branches*
7. **R.** And I heard Him call out on Ascension Thursday several years ago, "I am alive. I am alive. I am alive." How is God treated this day? He said that He is treated as a dead object and how it offends Him so greatly when people go to the Eucharist, especially, and they do not even talk to Him or give thought to Him. This morning at Mass the whole front of the Church was covered in a celestial light and I saw the altar of sacrifice. And then Jesus was exposed after the Mass and I had such a realization of how we make great reparation to God when we unite to the sacrifice of Jesus in the Holy Sacrifice of the Mass and we offer ourselves as a sacrifice to the Father and we tell Him that we are sorry for our

sinfulness. We must do what God is telling us to do. We must spread these messages. We must spread the *Mass Book* and Father Carter's Newsletter Book. Priests need to have hearts that are consecrated to the Hearts of Jesus and Mary. They must give their heart to the Immaculate Heart of Mary that they can be so one in their relationship with Jesus. The world is in need of renewal. There is much poison in the Church and the world. And so we come and we shake our books of prayers and we say, "Pray for the priests. Pray for the priests." We do not have to say. "Jesus said that you should pray for the priests." All we have to do is take the book with the *Imprimatur* and say to the people in the churches, 'This will help renew the Church and the world. It will help priests to be holy priests. It is all in prayer.'" We must do what Mary said at Fatima and consecrate our hearts. When we pray these prayers, we are doing what Mary told us to do and it will help to bring about the Reign of the Sacred Heart of Jesus. He is alive and He is treated as a dead object in many cases. We are the soldiers, the soldiers of light, to carry the light into the darkness. And as men consecrate their hearts to the Hearts of Jesus and Mary, as they are born and brought forth in the womb of the Lady clothed as the sun, brought forth in her Immaculate womb, they will be brought forth children of light and will know God with the greatest love, for to know Him is to love Him. How I long for this great Reign when men's hearts will be burning and on fire for the love of God.

8. Song: *Oh, burning Heart, oh love divine*

R. And He speaks and He says, "I love you. I love you. I love you. I give Myself to you." And the angel said at Fatima how horribly outraged is the Almighty God. It is up to us to spread these prayer chapters, to do what He wants us to do, to spread the second *Blue Book* that people will go to the tabernacle and realize the great gift that they are given in the Mass, to spread the *Mass Book* which is a great gift for it tells us from Jesus' point of view what is going on in the Mass, but it will have the imprimatur so it can be used by the priests and in the Church, and we will not suffer any persecution and men will know the great gift that God gives to us in the Holy Sacrifice of the Mass. It is Himself.

9. Hail Mary

10. Hail Mary

Song between decades: *Come Holy Spirit, fill our hearts*

The Descent of the Holy Spirit

1. **R.** Eighty years ago today, May the 13th, 1917, the words of Our Lady, "Do not be afraid. I will do you no harm.... I am from Heaven. I have come here to ask you to come here six months in succession on the 13th day, at the same hour. Later on, I will tell you who I am and what I want. Are you willing to offer yourselves to God and bear all the sufferings He wills to send you, as an act of reparation for the sins by which He is offended, in supplication for the conversion of sinners? Pray the Rosary everyday in order to obtain peace for the world, and the end of the war." (The Spirituality of Fatima and Medjugorie, p. 12-13)
2. **R.** On June the 13th, Mary spoke. "There were about 70 people present, and the children were the only ones that could see the apparition. She told the youngsters that many souls go to Hell because they have no one to pray and to make sacrifices for them. She said that Francisco and Jacinta would soon leave the world for Heaven. Holding out her heart, surrounded by thorns which pierced it from all sides, Our Lady told Lucia, *'God wishes for you to remain in the world for some time because He wants to use you to establish in the world devotion to My Immaculate Heart. I promise salvation to those who embrace it.'*" What a promise! *"And their are souls will be loved by God as flowers placed by myself to adorn His throne."* (The Spirituality of Fatima and Medjugorie, p. 13)
3. **R.** In July, she spoke, and she said, *"You have seen Hell, where the souls of poor sinners go. To save them, God wishes to establish, in the world, devotion to my Immaculate Heart. If people do what I tell you, many souls will be saved and there will be peace. The war (World War I, then raging) is*

going to end. But if people do not stop offending God, another and worse one will begin in the reign of Pius XI. When you see a night illuminated by an unknown light [January 2, 1938], know that this is the great sign that God gives you that He is going to punish the world for its many crimes by means of war, hunger and persecution of the Church and the Holy Father." (The Spirituality of Fatima and Medjugorie, p. 14)

And so Jesus spoke in December twice and He told me about chastisements and then the Father began to speak. And the Father said, "You have disobeyed Mary. You have disobeyed Jesus. Now you will disobey Me? You will suffer a fate." And then He spoke of Noah and from that point on until the day of the flood, my stomach was in knots. And then the day of the flood He spoke that the world has so much poison. And at the peak of the poison, He will pour down the antidote in these revelations and they will turn from their sinful ways; but many souls will be lost. And the Father spoke later and He said, "I gave you gifts at Falmouth and you did not respond. I gave to you a chastisement. This is an example of what will happen to the earth if you do not respond. I am telling you to spread the prayer chapters, to pray the prayers and to spread the priestly newsletter, the *Mass Book,* and the *Priestly Newsletter Book* and the *Children's Rosary Book.* All of these things **have** the imprimatur." If we do what the Father says, if we make reparation to her Immaculate Heart, He said that He would lessen and/or not give us the chastisements. But if we do not, He said in several messages that He would wipe off the face of the earth. (Father Carter discerned all of these messages, the following messages are in the Apostle's Manual - January 18, 1997: "Oh indeed My sweet messenger, I look to the earth and see the darkness, I see the disobedience of men against their Mother. I know the deeds committed and the evil in the hearts of so many. Justice will prevail and I will wipe out the earth. Only the children of light will remain, those who have given their hearts to their Mother Mary...") (Also from January 18, 1997: "You are a sinful, willful race, and the devil will vanish from the hearts of the children of light for they will be under the protection of her Immaculate Heart, the other children will be wiped off the face of the earth.") (Jesus said December 22, 1996: "I give water to quench your thirst, I bathe you in My divine love, but to the evil doers, I will curse their name and wipe them from the face of the earth.") (Jesus said March 26, 1996: "Filled with My love, you will conquer this earth, not with weapons and powder or force, but with fires of My love. The fire will wipe out the hatred in the cold hearts and the earth will be covered with My celestial light." All of these messages where discerned by Father Carter.) The messages are very strong. I beg you to read the messages in this *Apostles Manual*. It is so simple to just do what they are telling us to do. Do we think that if Mary told us this 80 years ago and we did not obey that the Father will just change His plan because of willful men? This is the whole course of things. It is because of the willfulness of Adam and Eve that the Father is displeased. He is displeased with our sins. He wants us to make reparation, to pray, to honor the Immaculate Heart of Mary, and to go to the Heart of Jesus. How can we say "no" 80 years later when He has called us the soldiers of light, the shepherds, that will go out and will help lead the flock into one fold under His guidance? He has majorly guided us through Father Carter. We have been very graced that God gave us a holy priest and that He did discern all of these messages, that he was here rosary after rosary after rosary and supported us and told us what we must do, that he is God's chosen instrument to write the priestly newsletter to renew the Church and the world. And so, we speak of the descent of the Holy Spirit upon the apostles. Let us cry out from the bottom of our hearts, "Dear Holy Spirit, descend upon us and turn our hearts from fearful hearts to fearless hearts that we will be the apostles, as the Father intends us to be, to help to usher in this great era. And we will walk, and as we walk, we will be pressed on and persecuted for the mission that He entrusts to us will help with the salvation of millions of souls, and the devil wants us stopped. Our beloved Father Carter is here in his heart with us. We are all joined in this Movement in one mind and one heart to help to renew the Church and the world, especially through these prayer chapters, through the prayers that Jesus has given us, through the priestly newsletter to pray for the priests, and to consecrate our own hearts and to grow in the deepest oneness with our beloved, adorable Savior.

4. **R.** *"If my requests are granted, Russia will be converted and there will be peace. If not, she will scatter her errors throughout the world, provoking wars and persecutions of the Church. The good will be martyred, the Holy Father will have much to suffer, and various nations will be destroyed.... But in the end, my Immaculate Heart will triumph, the Holy Father will consecrate Russia to me, Russia will be converted, and a certain period of peace will be granted to the world."* (The Spirituality of Fatima and Medjugorie, p. 15)
5. **R.** On August the 13th, "Consequently Our Lady did not appear to the children on this particular 13th. The authorities fearing reaction on the part of the people, quickly released the children" for they were locked in jail. "Mary appeared to them on August 19th near Valinhos. She told them that she was greatly displeased by the action of the mayor. As a result, the miracle promised for October would not be as impressive as originally planned." (The Spirituality of Fatima and Medjugorje, p. 16)
6. **R.** If the Fatima message has been held back, if it has been blocked as it has for 80 years, if the children of Fatima were locked in jail, what makes us think that we would not suffer as we are suffering here today? For it is very hard in my heart that Father Carter is not here. Our president John has helped us in so many ways, and each one of us are the apostles. As we read the Acts of the Apostles and we hear the scriptures every day, we know that our lives are very similar to those of the apostles, and we truly live the gospel message.
7. **R.** On October 13, 1917, there were more than 70,000 people gathered in the Cova da Iria in Fatima, Portugal… Shortly afternoon, Our Lady appeared to the three visionaries..., what occurred was the miracle of the sun…

   Then a gasp of terror rose from the crowd, for the sun seemed to tear itself from the heavens and come crashing down upon the horrified multitude.... Just when it seemed that the ball of fire would fall upon and destroy them, the

miracle ceased, and the sun resumed its normal place in the sky, shining forth as peacefully as ever."
(The Spirituality of Fatima and Medjugorie, p. 4)

A great sign was given, but they still did not respond to the great sign of Our Lady. And Our Lady spoke and she said, *"I am Our Lady of the Rosary. I have come to warn the faithful to amend their lives and to ask pardon for their sins. They must not offend Our Lord anymore, for He is already too grievously offended by the sins of men. People must say the Rosary."* Our Lady told us we must say the rosary. *"Let them continue saying it every day."* (The Spirituality of Fatima and Medjugorje, p. 16)

Mary has told us what we must do, but we are not obeying our beloved Mother. Jesus has given to us signs and told us that we must turn from our ways. The Father has spoken and He has given to us a great sign in Falmouth, Kentucky. He is imploring all of us here to be the apostles to help usher in this great era. And so the apostles went forth and there were thousands converted, for they were filled with the Holy Spirit. They were not afraid. And they spoke in foreign tongues and all understood. It is not with our might that we go forth. It is with the Might of the Almighty God. For as we give ourselves to Mary and give ourselves to Him, we unite in deep union with Him and as we become more and more one in Him, He operates through us. He is showing us in these sufferings that He has given to us. I have never learned to pray as I have. I know fervently that I can pray and that God truly is hearing our prayers. But it is not me, it is His Might that is operating here, that we must surrender ourselves totally and let Him operate through us, that we must try to be more one with Him, that we must intercede to all the saints and angels and the Blessed Mother and beg the Father, in union with Jesus, in the Holy Sacrifice of the Mass that this great era of peace will come soon and that men will turn their hearts to hearts of love.

8.

Acts 2: 1-4

When Pentecost day came round, they had all met together, when suddenly there came from heaven a sound as of a violent wind which filled the entire house in which they were sitting; and there appeared to them tongues as of fire; these separated and came to rest on the head of each of them. They were all filled with the Holy Spirit and began to speak different languages as the Spirit gave them power to express themselves.

Song: *Come Holy Spirit, fill our hearts*

9. **R.** Jesus has asked us to pray the Infant novena every hour for Father Carter. But in so doing, it is uniting us at every hour on the hour. It is as we unite in one body, as we unite in the Morning Offering, in the Holy Sacrifice of the Mass, with one another, as we say this prayer hourly for Father Carter, and we ask, and we seek and we knock that our prayers will be answered that we ask the Father in the name of Jesus, through the powerful intercession of Our Lady that our prayers will be answered, for He is the Almighty God. Look at this. See the Father, the Father above, and He looks down at the earth. He is the I Am. He is not as we are. But He looks down at the earth. He sees the sins of men. He sees us as creatures, as a chosen race that is not obeying God. He sends Mary as a messenger to tell us that we must make reparation for our sins. We disobey. He sends her over and over and over again. Jesus gives to us these messages deep from within His Heart to bring about the reign of His Heart and they are blocked and ignored and treated, not with love, but with much anger, and they are analyzed and people are not treasuring the gift that He gives. Finally the Father speaks. He said, "I am the Father. You have disobeyed Mary. You have disobeyed Jesus. Now you think you will disobey Me? I will chastise the earth." So He sends to us the gifts, and He gives to us an example in Falmouth, and then He tells us what we must do. Will you be His shepherd? Will you go into the world? Will you help? Will you be the one that fervently prays, this day? He is very disappointed by the prayer life of many of His religious, of many of His faithful. He has called us to pray fervently. We are praying fervently for the religious, for the renewal of the Church and the world. He is calling us to be His apostles. We will see miracles happen, for it is His Might behind us.

10. Hail Mary

After the Glory Be:

R. He ascended into heaven, but He left behind the apostles to carry out His work. And He gives to us Himself in the Holy Eucharist, for He is alive and He is truly present in the tabernacle in His Divinity and His humanity. And so we sing the song that He asks us to sing to remind ourselves.

Song: *I will be with you that is my promise*

R. And He will weed out the army so that what is left is a strong army in order to march into this world, where there is much willfulness and hatred and darkness and He is covering us with His most Precious Blood. I received a message on Friday. He called it Bloody Friday and this is what He said. He was asking us to stop at the hours of 9, 12 , 3 and 6 o'clock and to just say a short prayer for the Shepherds of Christ Movement, to cast the devil into hell and He said at these hours when we pray that He will dress us in His Precious Blood. We are being dressed in His Precious Blood, ready to go into battle. Our arms are the weapons that He has given to us. They are His love. Why are we afraid? We go into battle and we carry our rosary. This is a great weapon that Our Lady has given to us to help to fight off satan and she told us at Fatima that we must pray the rosary.

The Assumption

1. **Jesus:** Are you afraid? Are you afraid now? I am telling you that you must pray to the Holy Spirit every day. Make a novena to the Holy Spirit continually. The Holy Spirit will transform your hearts from hearts of fear to hearts that are fearless. I am Jesus, your beloved Savior. Your might is in Me. My sweet wonderful loved ones, I give you My Heart on fire and burning for love of you. Will you carry this love into the world? Will you tell those that are hurting, that are suffering, that are in pain that Jesus loves you, that Jesus has given Himself for love of you?

   R. He is the light of the world. He shows us that the Almighty God came in the womb of a human creature and He was brought forth. We too must go to our Mother. We must be brought forth as children of light through the action of the Holy Spirit and as we go to the womb of the woman, to her Immaculate Heart, we are brought forth into the light and we know God in a different way. We know God in a way that we can not help but love Him for He opens up the shade and we see. And what we see makes our heart burn for to know Him is to love Him. Now we are a people walking as in a fog for we do not see. We do not know or we would not be offending God.

2. **R.** On October the 13th, 1917, there were more than 70,000 people gathered in Portugal. They had come to observe the miracle. Lucia and her two cousins, shortly after noon, Our Lady appeared to them and this is what they said.

   "As the Lady was about to leave, she pointed to the sun. Lucia excitedly repeated the gesture, and the people looked into the sky. The rain had ceased, the clouds had parted, the sun shone forth but not in its usual brilliance. Instead, it appeared like a silver disc, pale as the moon, at which all could gaze without straining their eyes. Suddenly, impelled by some mysterious force, the disc began to whirl in the sky, casting off great shafts of multicolors. Red, green, blue, yellow, violet - the enormous rays shot across the sky at all angles, lighting up the entire countryside for many miles around, but particularly the upturned faces of those 70,000 spellbound people. After a few moments the wonder stopped , but resumed a second and third time - three times in all - within about 12 minutes. It seemed that the whole world was on fire, with the sun spinning at a greater speed each time. Then a gasp of terror from the crowd, for the sun seemed to tear itself from the heavens and come crashing down upon the horrified multitude.... Just when it seemed that the ball of fire would fall upon and destroy them, the miracle ceased and the sun returned to its normal place in the sky, shining forth as peaceably as before." (The Spirituality of Fatima and Medjugorje, p. 3-4)

3. **R.** "When the people arose from the ground, cries of astonishment were heard on all sides. Their clothes, which had been soaking wet and muddy, now were all clean and dry. Many of the sick and crippled had been healed of their afflictions." (The Spirituality of Fatima and Medjugorje, p. 4)

On May the 13th of 1993, we had gone to Conyers and the same thing happened to us. We were covered with water. It was so awful I couldn't believe it. The umbrella turned inside out and all of our possessions were sopping wet. It was so terrible - the rain. I couldn't believe how awful it was and I started to cry when I got to the car because I had lost my children. And my feet were wet like they were never wet. Everything that I had - the cameras were sopping wet. I put them in the car and it was like instantly, they all dried up and this peace came over me. And from that time I have felt a difference in my heart for I know what is important are the things that Our Lady is telling us. Before I was worried about the plaques in the back of the car, and the cameras, and myself and being wet. But at that point she gave me a greater gift for at that point I knew that what was important was what she was telling us. She had said that darkness had covered the earth and that we were offending God similar to what Mary said at Fatima. But no one was listening. Will you listen to this message that Jesus speaks today? For Mary called, called, called to so many visionaries and she relayed the message. This is Jesus' plan for the completion of the Fatima message. It began October the 13th of 1996. Mary started in May and ended October the 13th. Jesus started with me on October the 13th and has given us the messages in the tapes to circulate, to listen to as candle rosaries and He has promised great gifts because He is telling us what to do to help bring about the completion of the Fatima message for the renewal of the Church and the world. These tapes are so important to Jesus and He said that when we do the candle rosary that He will give the greatest grace to those people present, the same as when the rosary was given on the 13th of the month. He wants us to know the messages He has given. Will you listen to the messages that Jesus gives today or will the Father have to take action more and more because we are not doing what He is telling us to do, for Mary promised at Fatima that there will be a reign of peace. How are we going to go from where we are today to this reign of peace? What sign do you think God should give us to get our attention? For we are stubborn and willful in our ways. We have not learned our lesson. We are still willful. Many are not doing what God is telling us to do and obeying His will. Many do not obey the commandments. We do not love God, many of us as we should. Many do not go to Church and do not want to help make reparation to God for the offenses against Him. We are a sinful race. We, His people, must make reparation for ourselves and for our brothers. God sees us as a nation, as a family. He sees us offending Him.

4. Hail Mary
5. **R.** Miracles are signs given to men in order that they take notice so that they will be obedient to the commandments – so that they will love God and love one another.
6. **R.** And so we pray the rosary. We meditate on the lives of Jesus and Mary. We see their lives more and more and we see that the angel appeared to Mary, asked her to be the Mother of God. And Mary said, "Behold, I am the handmaid of the Lord. May it be done to me according to your word." We see that Mary always complied to the will of the Father. We see that Jesus, who is God, always did the will of the Father. This is most important that we live according to the Father's will.
7. **R.** And Mary was assumed into heaven. She lived her life according to the Father's will. Jesus lived His life according to the Father's will and He ascended into heaven. Jesus and Mary are our models. Jesus and Mary teach us how to live. If we want to go to heaven, we must follow Them. In the world today there are many, many plans, that are not the plan of the Father. The more we give our hearts to Jesus and Mary, the more we dwell in their Hearts, the more we live our consecration to Jesus and Mary, the more we will be joined in one mind and one heart and the more likely we are to be operating according to the Father's will. In schools, as the school children pray the consecration, they are united in one mind and one heart. There is usually not discord and there is greater peace and harmony as Mary has promised. As we give our hearts to Mary and Jesus and our Father, there is peace. Mary appeared at Fatima to tell us that we should give our hearts to her and Jesus and then we will have peace for we will be united in one mind and in one heart with one plan, the plan of the Father.
8. **R.** I want to read a message given to Father Carter from Jesus

Jesus: "My beloved friend, tell My people to pray daily to the Holy Spirit. They are to pray for an increase in His gifts. My people must realize that the Holy Spirit comes to transform them. The Spirit desires to transform you more and more according to My image. Those who are docile to His touch become increasingly shaped in My likeness. He performs this marvel within Mary's Immaculate Heart. The more one dwells in My Mother's Heart, the more active are the workings of the Spirit. The Spirit leads Mary to place you within My own Heart. In both Our Hearts, then, your transformation continues. The more you are formed after My own Heart, the more I lead you to the bosom of My Father. Tell My people all this. Tell them to pray daily for a greater appreciation of these wondrous gifts. I am Lord and Master. All who come to My Heart will be on fire to receive the gifts of the Spirit in ever greater measure! I love and bless My people!"

9. Hail Mary
10. Hail Mary

Song between decades: *Immaculate Mary*

The Coronation

1. Hail Mary
2. **Reference: Isaiah 30: 19-23**
3. **R.** And they will see with the light of seven suns, for we will be brought forth from the woman clothed as a sun as children of light and we will know God in a way that we never knew God before. We will have such intimacy with the Almighty God and such love for Him. Now we are as a people walking in blindness.
4. **R.** And Mary comes and she tells us that we must go through her Immaculate Heart and we do not pay heed to what she tells us.
5. **R.** She is the Queen of Heaven and Earth. She was chosen

by the Father as the Mother of all and the Mother of Christ. He came into this world a helpless little baby in the womb of a human person. Why do we think that we do not need Mary when Christ showed us?

6. **Jesus:** And so this is My message to you, My beloved ones, I ask you to carry out this message to the world. I ask you to begin the prayer chapters in churches, if possible. If not, to start all prayer chapters that are possible in your homes and other places. I have given to you these prayers that will help bring about the renewal of the Church and the world. You must pray these prayers fervently. You are My apostles. I am asking you to help. I am not asking you to be anxious and to worry. If you are unable to do some of the prayers, I am asking you to spend an hour with Me each day. In that hour, I will instruct you on the ways of My Heart. I will reveal to you the will of My Father for you. I am Jesus. I have called you here this day. This will help bring about the completion of the Fatima message which began 80 years before.

7. **R.** And the earth was covered with much darkness but the sun came out and the sun was bright as the light of seven suns and their hearts were filled with great joy for they knew the presence of God within them. They were close to the Almighty God in their hearts and they did not fear for He gave to them a great grace.

8. **Jesus:** How can you refuse the Mother that I gave to you? She is filled with grace. My little ones, you must give yourself to the heart of My Mother. She will take you to the depth of My Heart and you will know My burning love. You must be strong, for you will suffer. You will suffer very many trials – but…

   Song: *I will be with you that is My promise*

9. **R.** The greatest gift that He gives to us is Himself in the Holy Sacrifice of the Mass. For I see Him when I walk the aisle, I see Him with His arms outstretched and He is filled with such love. And He gives Himself to me, and I am wrapped in the presence of the Almighty God, and nothing,

nothing here compares to this union with Him.

10. **R.** And we stand with His Mother under the cross pleading to the Father to have mercy on us. He is the Lamb of God. He is the Lamb that is sacrificed, and so at every Mass, we cry out, "Lamb of God, have mercy on us." It is as if we should prostrate ourselves to the ground and to beg the Father to have mercy on us, a sinful race, and tell Him that we truly are sorry for the offenses of ourselves and the other creatures against God and that we want to be forever in His light and that we want the Sacred Heart of Jesus to reign and the Immaculate Heart of Mary to triumph. The new Eve. The new Adam. The Hearts of Jesus and Mary.

He ascended into heaven but He speaks to us this day and He tells us…

Song: *I will be with you that is My promise*

Jesus: I am Jesus. I have called you here this day to hear this message. I am asking you to write a letter of intimacy to Me every day. I am asking you to live by the Blue Book messages for it will become hard and you will suffer much. You must go to the Blue Book for I will give you My answer to your trials. I have written these love letters to you. You must use the Blue Books.You will go through tremendous suffering and persecution. Do not lose heart. I am strengthening you. You will be strong soldiers. Many will be left behind. You must pray fervently for your leader Father Carter. He is a great gift to this world. He is writing the priestly newsletter in order to help renew the Church and the world. You must pray for Him and for His provincial and for all of the priests that are involved. I am Jesus. Pray the novena hourly and unite as close to the hour as possible in one mind, in one heart. Come, My little ones, I will take you into My Heart. You must go weekly to your chapter meeting for as you go deeper into My Heart, you will suffer, for many will not understand. You will be strengthened by those that have consecrated their heart to Me. They will be your family. You will be My beating Heart in this world. This is the core chapter I have called here. You are the strong ones. You must pray and do as I have told you. You must live the messages and study the messages. It will become difficult unless you go to the weekly meeting and unless you live the messages. You will not be able to survive this calling for it will become more and more difficult as you assume your role as a leader. I am Jesus. Will you answer My call? Will you be a leader? Will you live by the messages that I give to you? Will you pray fervently an hour every day and go to Mass and Communion whenever possible, preferably daily? You must consecrate your hearts. If you at this time can not do all of these things, I am asking you to do as many as you feel comfortable with, but to stay close to your chapter. I do not want you to be anxious and filled with fear. I want you to come to Me and I will comfort you. You must do only as you can. I am not demanding that you do all of these things. I am asking you to study the messages and try more and more to live the messages and to come closer to My Heart. I am giving to each of you a special grace to be My apostle. If you want to answer this call, I will give this grace to you now. I am Jesus. This is May the 13th, 1997. What you do here today will majorly help to renew the Church and the world and to help bring about the completion of the Fatima message. Will you help? Will you answer the call of My Mother and yours? Will you answer My call? Will you answer the call of your Father? If you say "no", who will I call?

Song: *I will be with you that is My promise*

Song: *Oh burning heart, Oh love divine*

Message before the Glory Be: There was a special prayer intention for someone now that is very dear that's dying and for those helping him so I would like to include that in the prayers and any of the prayers that are in your heart, for there are prayers that you hold in your heart that you wish special attention from Our Lord, Our Lady and the Father. We give these prayer intentions to you at this time on this special day and we ask for the grace to help carry out the mission you have entrusted to us, to be strong and to not be afraid.

May 13, 1997

The Events That Day

Jesus: In the Fourth Mystery of the rosary, My messenger accounted the happenings at Conyers, Georgia, May 13, 1993, when the wind came up and it looked as if the people would be blown off their feet. The sky was darkened with a white rim around the horizon. The message from Mary talked about going deeper and deeper into darkness.

The rain came down as in buckets and with great force and the wind blew.

At the end of the rosary on May 13, 1997 after reference to the Conyers event, a very similar experience happened at Tom's farm. The wind came up with enormous strength and it blew everything over. My statue of My Sacred Heart which I requested be brought to Tom's farm for the 13th beginning in October was blown over and the statue of My Mother fell to the ground. She was decapitated, her head turned face up on the ground. She was broken in her Immaculate Heart.

R. I must note here that we went to Tom's farm on October 13, 1996, as requested by Jesus. We continued to meet there on November 13, 1996, December 13, 1996, and January 13,

1997. On February 13, 1997 we met at Our Lady of the Holy Spirit Center. We met also on March 13, 1997 and April 13, 1997. On May 13, 1997, the Holy Spirit Center had another engagement scheduled and Jesus told us to meet on Tom's farm.

Jesus: On this day May 13, 1997, the Shepherds of Christ Movement was notified for the third time they were not permitted to operate on the 13ths from My Mother's House, Our Lady of the Holy Spirit Center.

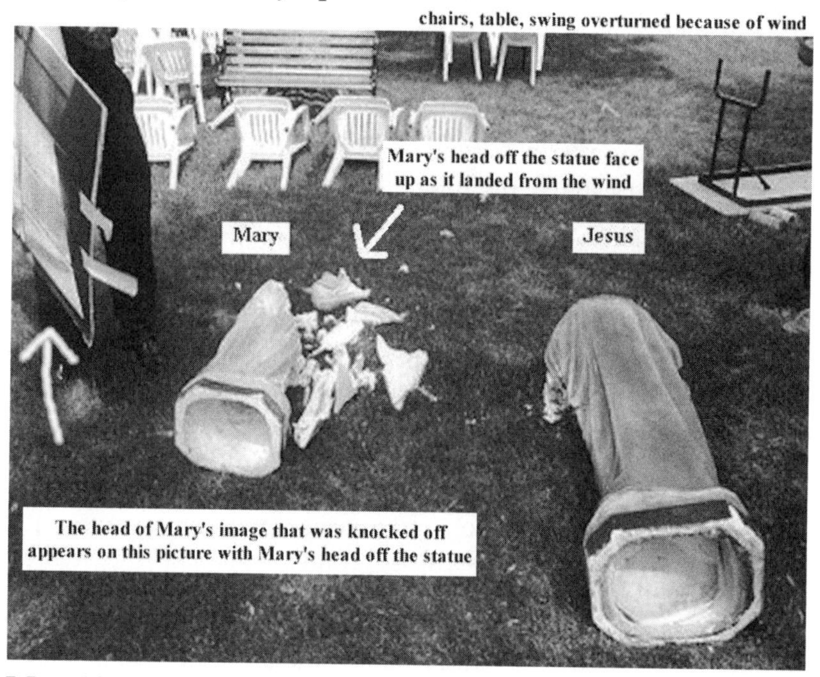

May 13, 1997

From the Internet
Mary's Head Broke Off

R. I so desire that you be able to hear the live rosaries and at some time in the future receive the video of May 13, 1997. The tapes available of the live rosaries, 6 in all, were recorded on 13th's in which He delivered the messages: October 13, 1996; November 13, 1996; December 13, 1996; January 13, 1997; February 13, 1997, as Father Carter led the rosary. On September 10, 1996, I delivered the rosary and received messages. These are the only live rosaries available. When Father Carter leads the rosary, Our Lord has promised immense grace. He led the 5 rosaries on the 13ths. The video of May 13, 1997, is very important to the completion of the Fatima mission. It includes the part Shepherds of Christ plays in this. Our President, John Weickert, led this rosary. This is the day the statues of the Sacred Heart and Immaculate Heart were displayed on Tom's Farm and after the rosary, all the chairs, pictures and the statues were overturned by a tremendous wind. The statues fell to the ground and broke.

I tell this story because of the message given to release this video as soon as possible. These live rosaries are presently given on the 5th of each month in Florida at 6:30 p.m.; on the 13th of the month in China, Indiana at 12:00 noon (unless otherwise indicated); on every Sunday at 2:00 p.m. at the Morrow Center, Ohio. There are special live rosaries, as on December 17, 1998, in Florida, when called by Our Lord, or when He gives me permission to travel to a certain place and He promises to give messages (as in Toledo, Ohio).

The live rosaries consist in this. On the direction of Our Lord, I do this rosary. Mary and Jesus give messages verbally as we pray the rosary. Usually another person leads as I receive the messages. These rosaries are then transcribed and typed. They are reviewed by a competent priest theologian. The last book of rosaries for children and parents has been approved for the imprimatur. Future rosaries without messages, now will be sent for approval to the chancery in the hope we can circulate rosary meditations to the schools. These rosary meditations are to help the love of Jesus and Mary come alive in men's hearts. They are called *Rosaries from the Hearts of Jesus and Mary.*

On May 13, 1997, we gathered at Tom Arlinghaus' farm as directed for the rosary of the 13th.

R. We had been instructed to have a particular large statue of the Sacred Heart and a particular statue of Our Lady with her Immaculate Heart at all 13ths since October 13, 1996, when the rosaries began at Tom's farm as instructed by Jesus.

On that particular 13th, we were instructed by Jesus and Mary to meet at Tom's farm. The statues were placed on a table and the rosary was given.

In the fourth mystery I accounted the events of May 13, 1993, when I was in Conyers, Georgia. I had never referred to this before in the more than 700 rosaries which had been given up to that time.

On that particular day in Conyers, May 13, 1993, the wind was calm, and then immediately after the rosary, it was so windy. I told how the umbrella turned inside out. The rain came down with such force it was awful. I was soaked through to my socks. I finally got to the car, threw in all the possessions, the cameras and everything else, all of which was so wet. It was like a miracle that the cameras and other possessions that were all wet were not ruined. It was as if everything dried up.

As we left Conyers, a peace came over us and I dictated to my daughter the first message that appears in God's Blue Book I.

Cling to Me

May 13, 1993

Jesus: My dear child, if you stay close to Me, then I live in you and you live in Me. I am He Who created you and I love you with such an intensity that you will never know. My words are your truth. You must abide in My heart in all things. There is no room for doubt. My ways are steadfast, direct, and without error.

You must stay rooted in Me to ward off the power of the evil one. His grip is paralyzing and crippling. His power is stronger every day.

When you live in Me, I am in your heart and he has no power over Me. I am your God. I am your true lover. I want to protect you. I want to guard you from this force. Stay rooted firmly in Me and he will have no power.

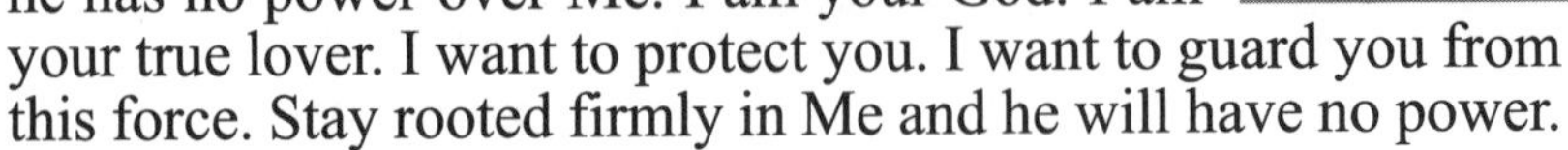

I am He Who comforts you. My hand is upon you. Hold tight to Me, My child. My eyes are fixed right on you. You are My most precious child. I love you as no other can. My arms are about you. My tenderness surrounds you. My love is in your heart. You go not alone. I walk with you.

I share every aspect of your life with you. Cling to Me, feel My presence. It is warm and secure within your chest. There is no room for fear, for I cast out fear and bring you comfort and joy.

end of May 13, 1993

All the way home we were followed by the miracle of the sun which we video taped, along with the calm leaves, and then the darkened storm that had instantly come immediately after the rosary. We made many copies of this video, because the events had made such a traumatic impact on us.

I had received messages since October 1991.

I heard about Conyers in March of 1993, and went there in April of 1993. At that time, in the prayer room in the apparition house April 14-15, my family and I saw a man clothed in a burlap type sack which looked very strange. The man's eyes were focused upward and then he disappeared. There were only about two people besides my family in the apparition house. Later, as we were taking photos, we almost tripped over the man. His burlap garment blended in with the floor, and he was bent over as in a ball, praying on the floor.

I thought later that it could have been St. John the Baptist. This was my first experience at Conyers.

I felt the experience on May 13, 1993, majorly changed our lives. We were less focused on the world and more on God. To get back to the message I received May 13, 1993, Our Lord made it very clear to me that I was to put this message dictated to my daughter in the 1st Volume of *God's Blue Book.* He told me it was to go first.

R. On May 13, 1997 Mary and Jesus' statues fell over because of a gigantic wind. Mary's statue was beheaded.

This rosary was 5 days later.

May 18, 1997
Morrow, Ohio

Glorious Mysteries

The Resurrection of Jesus from the Dead

1. **Reference: Luke 24: 1-5**
2. **Reference: Luke 24: 6-8**
3. **R.** Why do we look for the living among the dead? Is this not the question that Jesus asked of us this day? Think, think of how it was before Jesus began to give us these messages. And how it was many times in our heart that we felt that we did not communicate very well with Him. Think of the times that we sat before the

tabernacle, the long waits, the wanting for Jesus to say something, to feel something, to know something. I know this. I know that Jesus promised Fr. Carter that in the Shepherds of Christ Movement, that we would receive great grace in order to be drawn closer to His Heart and the heart of His Mother. And I watch in this prayer group and I talk to people and I know that this truly is a fact. That from praying these prayers that great graces have been given to the members of the Shepherds of Christ Movement to draw them ever closer to His Heart. I know so many times this day how He communicates to me. And there are periods of dryness in which I may not feel Him sometimes. But his presence is always alive within my heart even during these periods. But think of the words of Jesus that He speaks to us over and over again. Think of the words in our heart, I love you, I love you, I love you. Jesus is a person. Jesus is alive. We must spend time alone with Jesus. Our Divine Lover, and to know Him and to feel Him and be one with Him at every second of our existence. And Jesus calls out to us and Jesus says, " I am alive. I am alive. I am alive." And so the angel said to them, " why do you look for the living amongst the dead?"

4. Sing: *Are Not Our Hearts*
5. **R.** We know in our heart how truly close Jesus is to us. We know how it is especially when we go to the Eucharist and we sit in front of the tabernacle. But many times, we distance ourselves from Jesus when we are with others and when we are occupied. Do we realize that at every second that Jesus is there? I remember one time I had an experience and my heart beat very erratically and Jesus told me that in the days to come whenever this would happen I would know that Jesus was with me. And it seemed every time that this happened that I was caught off guard which gave me the realization that no matter how close I felt like I was with Jesus at a particular time, Jesus could catch me and make my heart beat a certain way. And I knew that I had taken my focus off of Jesus. Today, it is very difficult for satan wants to stop us. But there is much joy in our hearts for we do have this presence of Jesus alive within us. But it is in those periods when we are filled with suffering that we must realize that Jesus sometimes is the closest to us. And that we

must focus on Jesus and give Jesus our love. Jesus, I give my heart to you in the trials and in the good times. And I want to be aware of Your presence at every single second as I breathe and as my heart beats as Jesus showed me in this experience. Jesus is with me when I am in the state of grace. Jesus is with me in a very special way. Right now my heart is beating and I am breathing and Jesus is alive within me.

6. **R.** It is so wonderful because sometimes I will be in the car by myself and all of a sudden I will receive a grace and I will cry because I am overwhelmed at Jesus' presence. And I cannot help but cry out and tell God how much I love Him. This is a great grace that God gives when this happens to us. But we must keep our focus always on the fact that as we breathe and our heart beats that Jesus is there, even when we do not receive the special favors all the time. When we feel that we are walking up a hard road with a boulder on our back and we want relief as we feel as if we are carrying His cross on our back, we must realize that Jesus walked up the hill to Calvary, carrying His cross on His back and at every second Jesus was one with the Father and Jesus knew His love. The Father and the Son and the Holy Spirit are one. We too, are one with Jesus and the Father. And God is loving us at every second, at every moment, at every breath, at every heartbeat. We are filled with the love of the Father, the Son, and the Holy Spirit. And this realization should make our hearts burn for the love of God, is overwhelming.

7. **R.** And if we do not for a moment, feel God's presence, all we need do is look at the crucified body of Jesus as He hung on the cross. I saw His body. I saw Him hanging on the cross. And in all of the things that I have seen and I have experienced, it is so hard to keep my focus many times on His presence. But I want to speak about this again. I want to speak about this that we will all stop at this moment and that we will envision the body of a Man, the full size of a Man, the Man that has been beaten and bloodied and close to the point of death. That we will see how men unmercifully nailed Him to the cross. We will see the nails in His hands and the blood as it rolls down His body. And we will look at the face of this Man and we will see the hollow cheeks. We will see the weakness in His face. And we will also see the mouth of this Man move, move. But we do not hear anything

for He says that people do not hear. But then He says to us that we must speak for we are His mouth in this world. We are His hands. We are His feet. We are His Heart beating in this world. As we breathe, and as our heart beats, we breathe into this world a positive energy, a life-filled energy. The beating Heart, the life and the love of the Almighty God or we breathe into this world a negative energy. An energy that may be filled with fear, an energy that will hurt those that we talk to, that will not lead others to God. We are Christ to one another in this world. How would Christ act if He was here? If He was talking? It is so difficult. I look to Jesus and I say, " I am not a saint, Jesus." I will try to do whatever I can. But when it gets hard, many times I give in. And then I go to Mass and I put myself so securely in the Immaculate Heart of Mary and I take the great gift that He gives to me which is union with Him. Because I can take my impurities and go to the heart of Mary. But I know that it says in the third Blue Book, "Is the glass half empty or half full?" I know that this is Pentecost and there will be a great reign of the Sacred Heart. And I know that He has called me and every person in this room to be a major part of helping to bring about the Reign of His Sacred Heart. And I know the way that I am walking now that my cross is kind of dragging on the ground and I am falling underneath it. And I am giving in many times when I could be looking into the eyes of the other and spreading His love. I am spreading that negative energy that is not what He wants me to do. Oh Jesus, I love You. I love Your Heart full of love!

8. **R.** Jesus went with the Disciples to Emmaus.
9. Sing: *Come Holy Ghost*
   R. Jesus appeared to them.
   Sing: *Veni Sancte Spiritus*
10. Song: *Are Not Our Hearts*
    Song: *A Song from Jesus*

The Ascension of Jesus into Heaven

1. **Reference: Luke 24: 44-51**
2. **R.** Jesus is alive and Jesus lives in our graced baptized soul. How am I in this world today? Jesus has called us to be His special chosen ones. Jesus wants us to aim for sainthood.

But I say to myself over and over again, I am not a saint. Jesus I love your messages. I love the gifts that You give to me but I am not a saint. And I complain and go my way. And many times, it separates me in my heart from Jesus when I talk about others and do not look at them with the love that Jesus would look at them, as He would look at them. I am seeing more and more how I must read the third Blue Book for when He gave these messages, Jesus talked over and over again about how we were to love Him and to love one another. How is our face? Is our face alive with the life of Jesus that lives within our hearts? Is our face radiating this joy? Do we carry the cross and suffer with Him? Or do we take our sufferings to others and give them the cross that Jesus really meant for us to carry?

3. **R.** It is so hard for me to be silent and to carry the cross. I know that it is only through His grace that I can proceed ahead and advance more spiritually. I know that Jesus is alive. I see the people in this group and I see Jesus in their actions. I see their fervor and I see their love. I see their service and you do not even hear of the sufferings that they are undergoing within. I see Jesus alive in my fellow members in this group. And it is a great gift that God has given, that I can watch all of you, and I can learn about Him, as Jesus lives within you. I pray for this grace that I too can be more like Jesus. That, that light of Jesus will shine through my eyes. That His light will shine into this world. And so I hear the words of this song, "Are not our hearts burning within us." Indeed are not our hearts burning within us? For we have been given great grace and Jesus has united us in a very deep way to His most Sacred Heart. Jesus has given to us great gifts and Jesus has truly made our hearts burn with love of Him. Are we carrying this burning love to others? Are we falling under the weight of the cross? We can give a negative energy or a positive energy when we talk to others. How would Jesus act? Do we not realize that Jesus has all of the Might? That no matter what is happening around us, if the building falls in and we are under the

building in a hole, that Jesus knows exactly what is happening and Jesus' Might in one second can release us from any situation.

4. **R.** And so Jesus wants to teach us to be very, very, very strong soldiers. Soldiers that will go into the world and will carry His Light, soldiers in which He can be one in and operating in this world in us as we give ourselves to Jesus. And so Jesus gives to us sometimes, very great sufferings. And so how do we learn our lesson? Do we learn the lesson and grow to be stronger soldiers? Or do we, give up? The lesson that Jesus is teaching us, only maybe to get a stronger lesson tomorrow.

5. **R.** We are the apostles that Jesus is calling to help bring about the Reign of the Sacred Heart and we must be so one in Jesus that Jesus can operate through us. We must let go of the imperfections and the impurities. We must go to the heart of our Mother and ask the Holy Spirit to help sanctify us. We must die to those ways not like Jesus. This truly is a calling from God that we are the lay apostles that will pray fervently and through our intercessory prayer great graces will be granted from the Almighty God. But it takes what Jesus is asking us to do and that is to strive always for sainthood.

6. **R.** And I hear myself say over and over again, "I am not a saint. Thank you for Your gifts to me, Jesus. Thank you for that great gift, Jesus." But I am not a saint. And I pray fervently. I pray fervently for His grace to help me to be able to carry out this great calling that Jesus is calling me and calling you to, that is, to be an apostle to help to usher in this great era in which the Sacred Heart will Reign and the Immaculate Heart of Mary will Triumph.

7. **R.** And so on Ascension Thursday, several years ago, when I heard Him call out, "I am alive. I am alive. I am alive." And I felt as if my insides were buckling in. I know now He cries out, but we do not hear the words. Just as they did not hear His words. He told them, He told them what would happen. He gave them enough information that they knew that He would rise from the dead. But they did not hear. And then when they saw, they did not believe. Is this not sort of like us? That Jesus has given to us grace after grace after

grace, that Jesus has touched our soul, that Jesus has made our heart burn with His love. But that we are not the strong believers that we should be, that we are not the ones that are really living with His life radiating from our eyes as it could be. Because we give in and we say as I do, "I am not a saint, but thank you for the gifts You give."

8. **R.** The gifts that He gives, the gift that He gives to us is the gift of Himself. The great gift given to man that the Almighty God gives Himself to him and unites in such union with him in the Holy Eucharist. Thank you God for this great gift, for this great union let me cherish every second, every moment that You are truly present in me after Communion. I ask that in these special moments, that You help me to be more likened to You.

9. Song: *Give me your Heart, Oh Jesus*

   Jesus: I love you. I love you. I love you. My dear and special soldiers, I am giving to you a great grace at this moment. You must let go of any feelings of division in your heart and put the burden at the foot of My cross. It is through My might that so much will be accomplished in the Shepherds of Christ Movement. I am teaching you to surrender, to let go and to be great lovers. I am asking you to strive to be saints. You are My chosen ones. It is from your face filled with light that many will know Me alive inside of you.

10. **R.** But Jesus, this has been one of the hardest times and we have struggled so. For as the Movement moves more across the face of this earth, as You give us greater lessons to turn us to be stronger soldiers, it becomes more and more difficult and there are so many that want us stopped. And then You come and You say to us, Jesus, "now smile and let My Light shine from your eyes." Jesus, give us this grace that, we can be as You ask us to be, the strong soldiers in which the Light of Your life does shine from our eyes, in which we walk away singing and not grumbling, in which we do not give in to the tauntings of satan to try to divide us in our minds from one another in which people will look at us and they will say, "we know who they are by the love that they have in their hearts."

    Song: *Come Holy Ghost*

The Descent of the Holy Spirit

1. **Reference: Acts 2: 1-4**
2. **R.** Let us look at the life of Christ. For He lived a quiet life for so many years. Let us look at our lives. Are our lives hectic? Are we running around sometimes and spinning our wheels? Let us realize that the Might is in Him. Always in Him. That Jesus' way is the way of love, always love. That if we go to Jesus and if we do as the Father wills us to do, that Jesus will give to us the grace that we need to accomplish the task that He is asking us to accomplish. It is in this austere prayer life, in this oneness with Jesus as we become one in Him, that the job will get done, that we will help to spread the consecration to the far ends of the earth. For it is in Him and so Jesus teaches us lesson after lesson and we balk and we complain and we think that we are pressed on and He says,

   Jesus: Have you learned the lesson yet, My children. Have you learned the lesson that it is through Me, that you must come to My Heart and become one in Me and I will carry the load. I will accomplish the task in you. I am Jesus Christ, the Almighty God, all-powerful. This is My Movement for the renewal of the Church and the world. Each and every prayer I give to you for this purpose. Every word is a word that I have given to help to turn the priests to holy hearts, to help with the renewal of the Church and the world and to help to bring about the completion of the Fatima mission. It is through My Might that this will be accomplished. Your job first and always is to come to My Heart and to be one in Me. I am the All-Powerful, Almighty God.
3. **R.** And so we see the Apostles. And so many were converted for they were filled with the Holy Spirit and transformed from fear to fearlessness. How are our hearts? Are our hearts filled with fear? It is in being one with Him that we will have hearts that are hearts of peace. It is in praying to the Holy Spirit that we will be filled too with the fearlessness to carry out this mission.
4. **R.** The Prayer Manual is exactly the way that Jesus wanted it to help to accomplish the task at hand, to pray for the

priests, and for the renewal of the Church and the world and so that people will give their hearts in consecration to Jesus and Mary. We are working the Father's Plan. It is His Plan and He is revealing the Plan to us. We must realize that we must be open and ready to listen so we hear the Plan and that we respond as He wishes us to.

5. **R.** It is through the Priestly Newsletter that Jesus is instructing the priests, that He is teaching them about His burning love, that He is writing the message of His love on their hearts.

6. **Jesus:** And so My apostles, Amen Amen I say to you. My beloved chosen ones, do not be filled with fear in your heart but with great joy on this day of Pentecost for I am with you in a special way and I am filling you with the grace to help to accomplish the task that the Father has given to you. You are a major part of the Plan of My Father to help to renew the Church and the world. You must pray fervently. Pray all through the day the prayers for the priests and for the Shepherds of Christ members and the consecration prayers, the prayer for the human family and for the Priestly Newsletter. It is through your prayers that many graces will be granted. And this world will be brought to great renewal.

7. **R.** And as the prayer chapters spread to the far corners of the earth, the prayer power will become greater and greater. For Jesus has truly written these prayers that they will turn men's hearts to hearts of love as they give their hearts to Jesus and Mary. And the prayers are prayers from holy hearts, heart-felt prayers, praying for the priests and for the renewal of the Church and the world.

8. **R.** Jesus has asked us in several messages to pray these prayers everyday. And I figured out that it only takes about 5 minutes to pray the Holy Spirit prayers and the prayer for priests to the end to the consecration. I figured this out last week after there were great trials that I had gone through. So I went back and read the messages and He said, " Pray at 9, 12, 6, and 3 o'clock. For these are hours that are very special to Him. And that He is dressing us in His Precious Blood and protecting us when we pray these prayers. For these prayers will help to accomplish what He wants accomplished, renewal of the priesthood, the Church and the

world and hearts that are one in the consecration.

9. **Jesus:** And so My beloved ones, I ask you to pray the prayers and I tell you that you will receive great grace, that you will be drawn ever closer to My Heart and the Heart of My Mother and that you will be protected. For I am dressing you in My Precious Blood. You must pray the prayers fervently and frequently.

10. Sing: *Come Holy Ghost*

    Song: *I Love You Jesus*

The Assumption of the Blessed Virgin Mary into Heaven

1. **R.** And they were filled with the Holy Spirit and they went forth into the world and many were converted. The Holy Spirit works within the heart of Our Lady. It is there that we receive great grace, that we are sanctified and that we are transformed more and more into the image and likeness of Jesus. It is there that the Holy Spirit gives to us great lights and understanding more and more insights into the hidden mysteries. Oh Holy Spirit, we long to be intimately connected to You. We ask You to pour out Your abundant grace to us, that You work within the heart of our Mother to change us to be more and more like Jesus, that the light of God will shine from our eyes and from our hearts. For we are sinners and we are weak. But we know when we go to the Immaculate Heart of Our Mother, when we give our heart to her, that You work within her heart and bring us forth, children of Light.

2. **R.** And so we walk and it seems very difficult so many times. And we meditate on the mysteries of the rosary and we see how we are living these mysteries in our lives. We see Christ walk with the cross on His back. We see Our Lady as she stood beside Him and as she stood under the cross. And so then why should we think that our road, the road that we follow, that is the path behind Them, would be anything but have certain sufferings.

3. **Jesus:** Are your hearts afraid? I have allowed you to experience great trials at this time. But you have grown in

your intimacy with Me. You have learned many lessons, lessons on how to pray. My beloved ones, in all of the suffering I am giving to you great gifts, jewels, that will help you to accomplish the task that the Father has given to you. I look at you and I watch you struggle and I know every trial and every suffering. But I know the end. And I know how you will be the strong soldiers to accomplish the work that I am calling you to. Be patient. Be loving. And grow more and more in your relationship with Me and with one another.

4. **R.** And Mary is our Mother. Mary is the Mother that walked beside Christ. Mary is the Mother that was with Him all through His life, His friend, and His companion. Mary is the one that He could talk to and that Jesus could share Himself with. Mary is our Mother too. For on His death bed, Jesus gave to us His Mother to share with us that we too could turn to the Immaculate Heart of Mary. We can give ourselves to her and she will always be there with us, walking by our side. We are not alone, for our Mother walks with us as she walked beside the cross of Christ.

5. **R.** It is a great joy for me to go to the Mass, and when I am seeing my own sinfulness to know that I can give myself to the Immaculate Heart of Mary and become most intimately united with our Divine Savior. But I long so much to be so close to Christ in the Mass that I am most grateful for this gift to be able to go to the Immaculate Heart of Our Lady and to unite in the deepest intimacy with Jesus in the Mass.

6. **R.** Today is a day about gifts, for we see that the Holy Spirit descended upon the Apostles and they were filled with such gifts. But look at the gifts that we're given. We are given the great gift of Jesus in the tabernacle. God outpours His grace to us when we pray before the tabernacle. When we go to the Eucharist we are filled more with His life, His grace in us. We know that He is giving to us these great gifts that we are able to comprehend more fully insights into the mystery of His love and be more deeply one with Him. God has given to us a great mission. God has called us by name in all of the things that we may feel like we are experiencing, the persecution and the suffering. We know in our hearts that the most important thing to us, is our relationship with God. I cannot believe many times how ungrateful I am and how ungrateful men are that they are not thanking God for the

great gift that He gives to us, which is, the gift of Himself in the Eucharist.

7. **R.** And I hear Mary as she calls out in the Mary message tape, "I stood beneath the cross of My Son and I cried." And I read the messages in the Apostles Manual and last week it was with great suffering for there are so many strong messages in there. We must turn our hearts to hearts of prayer. We must make reparation to God for our offenses against Them. I am asking each and every person here to study the messages in the Apostles Manual. This is what He has asked me to do. The more that we study these messages, the more we will hear Him speak to us and hear Him tell us what we can do. The more we will realize the urgency of the situation, how spreading the prayer chapters is so important to the Father's Plan to help bring about the renewal of the Church and the world.
8. **R.** And the days seem like they go by so quickly but it seems many times that we do not even have a chance to breathe and to look around and to take in the gifts God has given to us. God wants us to be filled with joy in our hearts, to realize that it is in God that this work will be accomplished. But Jesus wants us to read the messages too, to understand the urgency of the situation, especially the Father's messages for He is saying that we are a sinful race, that we must make reparation especially to the heart of our Mother. That we must pray. These are very strong messages. In the five years before that I received the messages, since 1991, maybe it is six years now, they have become stronger and stronger since December. I know this. I know that the Father wants us to try to spread the prayer chapters. That it is most urgent that we do all that we can for our own personal holiness and that we pray fervently, that we unite at every second in the Morning Offering to the Holy Sacrifice of the Mass. That it is in the prayer that many things will be accomplished. We do the will of God in love so God's Plan will unfold.
9. Hail Mary
10. Hail Mary

Song: *Immaculate Mary*

The Coronation of Mary as Queen of Heaven and Earth

1. **R.** How I love Mary. Mary is the Queen of all Apostles. Look at the picture of Mary as she appears on the building in Florida. Look at Our Lady of Guadalupe. On December 12th, Jesus and Mary asked me to make the tape, Mary's Message. And to make sure that on every tape it said that it was recorded on December 12th, the Feast of Our Lady of Guadalupe. This was four days before she appeared on the building. She said in the message that she is appearing there as Our Lady of Fatima in the Americas. I know that it is very important that we are praying to Our Lady of Guadalupe to help us in our mission.

2. **R.** Mary is the woman clothed as the sun with the moon under her feet. And there are twelve stars about her head. And Mary is bringing forth the children of Light.
3. **R.** Mary is Queen of Heaven and of earth.
4. **R.** Mary is Mother of Divine Grace. Mary is Mother. Mary is full of grace. Mary is the Mother that the Father has chosen for His children.
5. **R.** Mary is the Mother of Jesus, and Mary is our Mother, which makes a great bond between us and between her.
6. **R.** We must fervently pray to spread this consecration that all men will realize that they must go to their Mother, Mary. That it is through her that they will see the Light.
7. **R.** Oh Mary, the Holy Spirit came down upon you and together you gave us the Child, Jesus. Help us to prepare our hearts so that we also may receive the Holy Spirit and allow Him to work in us. Grant this through Christ Our Lord, Amen.
8.

Acts 2: 1-2

When Pentecost day came round, they had all met together, when suddenly there came from heaven a sound as of a violent wind which filled the entire house in which they were sitting;

R. Jesus is alive and Jesus is with us. Jesus is alive in our hearts and He has called us on this most special mission. We have been given great gifts. The Apostles got out of prison singing. How are we this day? How is His life showing alive in our hearts? Are we the instruments that God wants us to be to carry the Light into the darkness? It is in going to our Mother Mary, in giving ourselves to her, that the Holy Spirit will work within her heart to make us more like Him.

9. **Mary:** And so my children, I am your Mother Mary. And I deliver this message to you this day. You are the apostles that My Son has called to go into the darkness and to spread the Light. You must pray to Our Lady of Guadalupe. Do not be afraid. You must have hearts of love. You must give your heart to me and I will take your heart to my Son, Jesus. You must smile that the Light of His life will shine through your eyes and from your heart. And it will go into the hearts of others for you have been given great gifts. You have been called and chosen, His apostles, the apostles to help bring about this new era of great peace and love. Do not be afraid, come to my heart, for I am crushing the head of the serpent. And you will be protected. I am asking you to pray the prayers given by my Son, Jesus in the prayer manual frequently. For you will be protected against satan. Do not be afraid, for I walk by your side and I am guarding you and I am protecting you, my little children of Light. I am your Mother Mary. I am the Lady clothed as the sun bringing forth my children of Light.

10. **Jesus:** My beloved ones, I am asking you to go into the darkness and to carry My Light, My life alive within you. Will you smile or will you curse the darkness and walk away? You have been called. You must spend time every day in intimacy with Me or satan will trip you on your way. I am Jesus. I love you with the most burning love on this Pentecost. Give Me your heart and I will fill you with My burning love. I love you. I love you. I love you.

Song: *I Love You Jesus*

R. And Jesus feeds us with His Body and His Blood and we are one in Him. Jesus is God, All-Powerful and Almighty and we are Jesus' chosen ones.

Sing: *I Am the Bread of Life*

5/18/97

The Mass

R. What do I want at this Mass? I want to unite with Christ and offer this to the Father, in the Holy Spirit through the powerful intercession of Mary, my Mother. The Mass is the Sacrifice of Calvary, sacramentally made present. I want to be deeply united to every word at Mass.

Excerpt from *Response in Christ*
by Fr. Edward J. Carter, S.J.

However, as we have said, Christ is not the only victim of the eucharistic sacrifice. The members of His Body, the Church, are also victims along with Christ. Those members must also be in a state of victimhood. As with Christ, they cannot undergo a bloody immolation. Their immolation must also be a mystical one. How is this accomplished? We can look to two passages of the encyclical *Mediator Dei* for thoughts on such a mystical immolation. In one passage we read that pride, anger, impurity and all evil desires are to be mystically slain. As the Christian stands before the altar, he should bring with him a transformed heart, purified as much as possible from all trace of sin.[27] Positively considered, such a transformation means that the Christian is striving to grow in the supernatural life by all possible means, so as to present himself always as an acceptable victim to the heavenly Father.

In another passage of the same encyclical this mystical immolation of Christ's members is further developed. To be a victim with Christ means that the Christian must follow the gospel teaching concerning self-denial, that he detest his sins and make satisfaction for them. In brief, the Christian's victimhood means that he experiences a mystical crucifixion so as to make applicable to his own life the words of St. Paul, "I have been crucified with Christ. . ." (Ga 2:19).[28]

Summarily, then, we become victims with Christ by lovingly conforming our wills to the Father's will in all things. Such conformity was the essence of Christ's sacrifice, of His victimhood, and of His immolation. A similar conformity must be in the victimhood and the immolation of Christ's members. This mystical immolation is a lifelong process. The ideal is that each Mass participated in by the Christian should mark a growth in his victimhood. The true Christian desires to die more and more to all which is not according to God's will so that he may become an ever more perfect victim with Christ.

27. Cf. *Mediator Dei*, Paragraph 100.

28. Cf. *Ibid.*, Paragraph 81.

R. I give myself as the victim, united to Him, to die to my sins and to help make reparation to God for my sins and the sins of the world.

We are aware God is asking us to help make reparation for our sins and the sins of the world. And God will outpour His grace on the world as we pray deeply and unite deeply to Jesus.

Man is sinful. We beg God to forgive us for our sinfulness and we unite with the all-holy, perfect sacrifice of Jesus, the Son of God, offered to the Father, in the Holy Spirit.

We want to help make reparation for the sins committed. God is all worthy of our love and we have offended Him with our sins. The old Eve chose to do her will – she sinned. We are tainted, we come to Mary, our Heavenly Mother, the pure and Immaculate one. We go through Mary's Immaculate Heart. We want purity. We are sinners. We want our sacrifice to be holy; we want to be pure.

The Holy Spirit works in the spiritual womb of Mary – her Immaculate Heart and leads us to God. We ask our hearts to be filled with fire for love of God. Mary is a powerful intercessor.

This Mass is a great love affair with God. We want to give Him the greatest love. We ask the Spirit to work in our hearts, filling our hearts with the greatest love.

In the name of the Father, the Son, and the Holy Spirit.

Let our hearts be cleansed. We pray to be cleansed of our sins and made more pure. We want to be one in great love with God. We go to Mary's heart and ask the Holy Spirit to sanctify us. We unite in the Holy Sacrifice of the Mass, we want to adore and love God, to praise Him, to help make reparation to Him and to petition Him for our needs.

Oh, Holy Word of God, I thirst for your wisdom and love. We are one body. We unite in Him. Prepare our hearts, we hear your Word. Let us unite in Him. The Word lives in us, penetrating us like a two-edged sword. God gives us the Bread of Life – His Word and the Eucharist. We are taught by God. God feeds us with the Bread of Life.

We are one body in Him. We must unite in love with all the world. We beg for the Holy Spirit to come and renew the face of the earth.

Alleluia, Alleluia. God has given us this great gift, the Mass - Thank You God!

God is sending us into this world to proclaim the Good News. We are afraid. We are filled with His love at the Mass. We are refueled. We are one body, in the Church, we are the body of Christ. We are sent into the world. The Holy Spirit fills us and He moves in us, in our hearts. We are alive – with His love. We go to the world.

The Holy Spirit fills us and fills the people and all hear this Good News that we deliver. It is in Him, it is by His Might, it is by our surrender that we will be filled and sent forth as His apostles into the world, filled with God's love.

We are given different gifts. We must do our part. We are to help in the building of the Kingdom of God.

Thank you for the gifts, God. Help me to use them for Your service. My heart is filled with Your love.

We petition God to help us. Come Holy Spirit, help us, fill us - we need You, our God. Help us to grow in love. Fill us with peace. Help us to use our gifts. Oh, God, we love You and thank You and praise You. We offer the gifts to God: the bread and the wine.

God will be with us forever more. He gives us such a gift in this Mass. We offer ourselves. We offer the bread and wine. We pray our sacrifice is acceptable to God. "May the Lord accept the sacrifice of your hands for the praise and glory of His name, for our good and the good of all His church." the Lord be with you.

We give You thanks God, our hearts sing, we love You so much. We long now for You to be with us in this Holy Sacrifice. We want to be one in this sacrifice with You.

Holy, Holy, Holy God of Might. We adore You, we love You, we honor You. We come to this Holy Sacrifice to be one in You in this sacrifice

He gives Himself to us. The bread is changed into His Body; the wine is changed into His Blood.

Jesus comes to us Body, Blood, Soul and Divinity. Oh my beloved God, I love Thee.

I unite in this Holy Sacrifice, united to the sacrifice of Jesus – to the Father, in the Holy Spirit – through the powerful intercession of Mary by our side, with all the angels and saints and the souls in purgatory. I beg for grace to be outpoured on this earth. I unite with all the angels and saints and souls in purgatory and I give myself to the Father and I beg that His grace is outpoured on us, His people. This is the greatest gift of all - the gift of Himself!

We lift our arms - we give ourselves to the Father - united to Jesus. We pray for Thy Kingdom Come, Thy will be done on earth as it is in heaven. We beg the Father for this. We beg God to take away the sins of this earth in the Lamb of God. Jesus is the Lamb of God. The Mass is the Sacrifice of Calvary, sacramentally made present. We seek to be pure in our interior offering. If we go to the Heart of Mary, we are within her Immaculate Heart. It is there we become deeper in our union with the Most Sacred Heart of Jesus.

Jesus is the light that shines in our dark souls and our imperfections are brought to light that we might die to them and be more like Him. We come broken; we are made whole. We are sinners. We are made holy through the workings of the Holy Spirit in the Heart of Mary. We die that we may live in Him. Take away my sins, cleanse me, have mercy on me, oh God, that I may be more like You! I give myself as an offering to help make reparation for my sins and the sins of men. My sacrifice is offered united to Jesus in the Mass, to the Father, to give God greater love. You, God, are all worthy of my love, my sacrifice is offered to be one with You. I give myself to You and unite as deeply as possible to You to be a lover like You in the world. And He gives us Himself. Our loving capacity is elevated to such heights as we unite to Him. We feel God's presence in us. We want the presence of the Father, Son and the Holy Spirit deep in our soul. We are in awe of the Almighty, All-Powerful, all-loving God.

And I walk to the altar to receive Jesus. Jesus is there. Jesus gives me Himself. He gives Himself to me in the Holy Eucharist.

These moments after communion are the dearest moments of all - when He unites to us, His feeble creatures, and He gives Himself most intimately with me. I become one in Him and I know things, insights, into God, that I never knew before. I know My Divine Lover more deeply in my being in a most intimate union. God tells me in my heart the Father's will for me. I feel His presence within my chest - it is the presence of God.

I give thanks to Him and remain with Him so one in my heart. God blesses me. My heart has been lifted to a new height in this great union with Him.

The whisperings in my heart. He outpours His grace to me. The seeds of Our Blessed Savior, alive in my heart, ready to germinate and bring forth light in the world.

Oh, God, I thank you for this gift and I pray: "Thy Kingdom Come, thy Will be done, on earth as it is in heaven."

Amen. Alleluia. Praise the Lord, for he has visited His people and the earth is full of His love, alive in our hearts.

Excerpt from *Response in Christ*
by Fr. Edward J. Carter, S.J.

> These few remarks give examples of how each member of the People of God is called upon to relive Christ's entire life as centered in death-resurrection. More could be said. But we think our remarks have sufficed to indicate how the Christian is to live out these various mysteries of Christ. Moreover, let it be recalled that all the mysteries ultimately make up the one mystery of Christ.
>
> What we have said thus far applies in general to all vocations. But since there are different vocations within the Church, we must also say that each of these projects

Christ in a somewhat different manner. Each Christian must study how in particular he is called to put on Christ. Essentially, of course, all put on Christ in the same manner. Yet there are accidental differences according to the vocation, work and individuals involved. For instance, the lay person, in general, is called to a deeper involvement in temporal affairs than is the religious.

Each member of Christ, according to his particular vocation, work and personality, has something special to take away from the Mass.[40] Each Christian, as he lives out the mystery of Christ, projects Christ to the world in his own way. Each Christian, as he himself grows in Christ-likeness, is also helping Christ to redeem the world in a manner commensurate with his total Christian person. For holiness is necessarily apostolic whether the Christian at any particular time is engaged in an external apostolate or not.

Each Christian, according to God's plan for him, must have a vital and dynamic desire to help Christianize the whole world. Perhaps he can do very little through direct, external apostolate. But his prayers and sacrifices – indeed, his entire life – can touch the whole world. Through an intense Christian life the individual can help Christ further the redemption of the family, the business world, the social structure and the like. The Christian is called to have this deep desire: to see the whole universe imprinted with the name of Christ. How true it is to say that the Christian's vocation, rooted in the liturgy, calls for deep involvement in this sacred activity.[41]

In schematic outline we have discussed the manner in which the baptized Christian extends his Mass to his daily existence. As he so lives out his Mass, he is becoming more Christlike. He becomes a more perfect priest and victim for his next participation in the eucharistic sacrifice.[42] The beautiful cycle which the Mass contains lies exposed before us. As part of this cycle the Christian is intimately involved in the process of continued redemption. The Mass is the center of the Christian life: ". . . the liturgy is the summit toward which the activity of the Church is directed; at the same time it is the fount from which all her power flows."[43]

40. Cf. Karl Rahner, *The Christian Commitment* (New York: Sheed & Ward, 1963), p. 168.

41. Cf. Second Vatican Council, *Constitution on the Church*, No. 36.

42. For a current treatment of the varied richness of the Eucharist, cf. J. Wicks, "The Movement of Eucharistic Theology" in *Chicago Studies,* Vol. 10 (1971), pp. 267-284.

43. *The Constitution on the Sacred Liturgy*, No. 10.

Uniting Our Hearts To The Mass

October 20, 2000

R. I give my heart to Jesus and Mary with you in love. I want to pray united to you as a body all day. Yesterday as I prayed I realized how important it is we stay united to the Mass the whole time we are praying. Great grace is released as we stay united to the Mass and pray in union with the Masses being offered around the world. Whenever we do the hourly prayers or pray the rosary or do God's will in our activities we are so consciously aware of our union to the Mass being celebrated at that moment. There is such grace that can be released from our union with the Mass. Here is Lucia's vision.

Whether I am at the Mass so actively present or I am in my home or my car or in a Church, I want to be so united to the Masses going on around the world. I realized as never before that so much grace could be released. This deep connection to the Mass is so important so tremendous grace will be released. The sacrifice is being offered through the hands of a priest. I pray and tremendous grace can be released. I want to be so connected to this font of grace as the Mass is being celebrated. I want my prayer to be most pure so I unite myself to the pure and holy Hearts of Jesus and Mary. I want all I do to be a sacrifice united to their pure and holy Hearts. I want the most tremendous grace possible to be released from the offering of my life and my prayers so I unite so deeply to this font of grace. I realized more than ever before in my life how Jesus is Chief Priest and Victim. The priest is the instrument God uses. But in every Mass, Christ Himself is celebrating through the priest. The Mass is so powerful because it is Christ Who is the Chief Priest. We stand with Mary under the cross and we beg God to release grace. Our every action should be cognitively united to the Masses going on around the world. Great grace will be released from our prayers and offerings.

Morning Offering

My dear Father, I offer you this day all my prayers, works, joys, and sufferings in union with Jesus in the Holy Sacrifice of the Mass throughout the world, in the Holy Spirit.

I unite with our Mother Mary, all the angels and saints, and all the souls in purgatory to pray to the Father for myself, for each member of my family, for my friends, for all people throughout the world, for all the souls in purgatory, and for all other intentions of the Sacred Heart.

I love You, Jesus, and I give You my heart. I love you, Mary, and I give you my heart. Amen.

5/22/97

Mary Loved God's Will

R. I never suffered as I have suffered yesterday. I know that I was pressed on by a million devils. It was the greatest attempt to get me to abandon my post and give up the ship. I was immensely attacked. Fr. Carter supported me, which helped me.

The devil wants to press on you by trying to get you to isolate. The devil presses on you to think that people you love do not love you and the devil works on fear of abandonment. The devil works in fear in hearts. He can try to manipulate fears from our childhood.

I must explain the "victim theory". This was explained early in January or February of 1996. It is this: There is a group and in their hearts there are impurities, angers etc. They bind together as a force against a victim. It makes a false bond and all are united against one (it could be more than one). In holy groups they see themselves as the ones favored by God. They see those opposed as not holy.

The whole plot is not being loving as God wants. Jesus shows us the victim. Jesus is the sacrifice. The Mass is the Sacrifice of Calvary, sacramentally made present. Jesus loved Judas. Jesus loved those who persecuted Him. Jesus loved those who beat Him.

Jesus is the suffering servant, the victim for our sins, for men's sins, for men's hatred.

Reference: Isaiah 42: 1-4

R. As a person progresses in the spiritual life, they have less and less enemies (victims in their heart).

Jesus was the victim. He loved.

We are to love.

Let us think about the "victim theory". Are we so pure that we do not have any victims we are angry at?

Jesus' Heart was full of love. Even when they beat Him and put Him to death, He remained silent and loved them.

Jesus loved them to His death. How are we told to live? We are told that we must be willing to lay down our lives for each other.

See diagrams:

"I will put enmity between you and the woman." The woman is Mary! Mary loved God's will.

From the Priestly Newsletter September/October 1997

In all this Mary offers an example. Selfishness was totally foreign to her. She did not belong to herself. She belonged to God. She was not closed in upon herself. She was completely open to God. When God spoke, she listened. When God pointed the way, she followed. She realized that life is not a process a person masters by carefully mapping out one's own self-conceived plans of conquest, but a mystery to be gradually experienced by being open to God's personal and loving guidance.

Selfishness, then, did not close Mary off from God's call. Neither did fear. God asked her to assume a tremendous responsibility. He asked her to be the Mother of Jesus. Mary did not engage in a process of false humility and say that such a great role was above her. She did not say that she did not have the proper qualifications for this awesome mission. Briefly, she did not waste time looking at herself, making pleas that she was not worthy, telling the angel he had better go look for someone else. No, Mary did not look at herself. Her gaze was absorbed in God. She fully realized that whatever God asked of her, His grace would accomplish. She fully realized that although she herself had to cooperate, this work was much more God's than hers.

Mary's words, then, truly sum up what is the authentic Christian response at any point of life, in any kind of situation: "I am the handmaid of the Lord," said Mary, "let what you have said be done to me".[1]

end of excerpt

1. Fr Edward J. Carter, S.J., *Shepherds of Christ Spirituality Newsletters 2,* Shepherds of Christ Ministries, p. 103.

R. We are Mary's children. No better way to be formed than the way Jesus was formed. Jesus is our model.

The Father sent Jesus, His Son to be the model. We are the followers of Jesus Christ.

Mary takes us to the Heart of Jesus, deep intimate love.

5/22/97

The Spouse of the Lamb

Jesus: My Child,

I am requesting you bind the Spouse of the Lamb material you now have available and circulate it with this message. Read one entry after communion each day. Write to Me now as your beloved bridegroom, tell Me your love for Me and your feelings for Me. This is an urgent message for your Movement.

Every person must see Me as their bridegroom and write to Me as such. Read the entries after communion. You are My spouse. This booklet should include a color picture of the bridal Mary and the picture above the altar in China. I love you, give this to the leaders promptly.

5/22/97

This Movement is for the Renewal of the Church and the World

Jesus: I give to you great honor because I have called you by name and you are My chosen ones. The revelations given through Fr. Carter and Rita will greatly help to renew the Church and the world. When the rosary aves were published for the schools the name of Rita Ring was omitted from this publication. This was due to the fact that the Holy Spirit Center in Norwood had rejected the apparitions of My Mother and the messages given through the messenger, Rita Ring.

I have called each one of you by name. I have called some prophets, some teachers, some apostles, some to be intercessors. I have called. Never have I told you to hide the gifts I have given to you.

My Might is beyond your feeble minds. This earth is disobedient and willful. I watch the manipulation of men and then I see that your movement has been called manipulative. I am God. I am in control. In no way will I alter My will to fit the will of men. Men have willfully squandered the gifts I have given for their own end. I will address this issue again. Great gifts were given from God when He allowed the apparitions of the Virgin Mary. Heaven has visited the earth in these revelations. I am contacting the earth in these revelations. To hide any of the gifts given, to misname the gifts given, is not to My liking.

I have called you by name. If you are burned at the stake you must adhere to the absolute truth in the way these revelations are given. I have given the most intimate secrets of My Heart in these revelations. The writings according to Paul were identified as given to Paul. To confuse the issue and misname the way chosen by Me to give My teaching to please the people is not to My liking.

I will deal with the opposition. You are under tremendous attack from satan and some have opposed the will of God. The will of the Father will be done. Our Lady of the Holy Spirit Center and the Falmouth Farm were places where great gifts were given to men. Events happen and you, in your feeble minds, do not comprehend or connect the letters I give to you. You are so limited in your vision and in your knowledge.

I am God. You are not to alter the Plan of the Father. These writings will go down in history as great revelations to help usher in this great era of intimacy. You are caught in the every day affairs. You see a means to an end.

I spoke to Moses. I gave to him the commandments. Because of their ways - he broke the tablets. I tell you. You must obey. You must be as submissive children. You are My chosen ones. I have called you by name. You must not take the liberty to change any messages given, because of the actions of men. Fr. Carter is the spiritual director of your movement. You have fallen in your fervor to pray hourly on the hour. Each minute ticks by, each hour goes on, you are coming closer each hour to the beginning of the era of peace. Your opposition is bigger than anything you can imagine. The Plan is bigger than anything you can imagine. The Father will act soon. It is important to begin the prayer chapters and circulate the Priestly Newsletter.

You are suffering. You are suffering. It will become more difficult if you do not pray the prayers I gave to you at the hours of 3:00, 6:00, 9:00 and 12:00. I woke Rita at 3:00 a.m. and 6:00 a.m. to stress the importance of memorizing and reciting these prayers. Do not give up, give in! Put aside your willful ways and obey.

You must publish the *Mass Book* as soon as possible. This book must be circulated. I am asking you to publish the Children's Rosary Book. In the beginning of the book include the section from Fr. Carter's book, "The Fatima Messages." Include the rosaries given in the Junior Shepherds of Christ meetings. Do not be afraid. I am the Might that will move the Movement across the earth.

I am Jesus. Souls are suffering. You hold a key to help the souls that are suffering. I am asking you to come back to the fold with an open heart and to help to put the writings of the Shepherds of Christ Movement, given through Fr. Carter and Rita, on the Internet. Will you please help Me?

I tell you to hold tight and do not be afraid. Read the Blue Book messages. Proceed ahead with the Apostles Manual. You are suffering the marks of battle. Do not be afraid. Pray to the Holy Spirit daily.

I am with you. What you do will affect millions of souls. There are so many souls today that are being changed because of your work here.

Look around you. The world may oppose you, but I gave you a command, "Feed the Hungry".

The hungry will listen. The haughty and arrogant will give you problems. It is the simple, humble soul that you will touch. There are so many people who are living holy lives because of your work.

It is the little people I work through. The high and mighty are but weaklings when they are put to the real test. Only those rooted in Me will survive.

I am separating the sheep from the goats. I have called you by name. Each person in the core group and those in the extended core groups have their roles. Your group is becoming larger. Your roles more clearly defined. You must be strong. Satan focuses on your 'self'. You must read the Blue Books all through the day when you are taunted and pray the Shepherds of Christ prayers.

At the hours of 3:00, 6:00, 9:00 and 12:00, pray the prayers from # 10 to the end. I will dress you in My Precious Blood. I am Jesus. You will be rewarded when you pray for the priests and the renewal of the Church and the world and when you consecrate your hearts to Me and My Mother.

5/27/97

The Mass - A Journey into the Heart of Jesus

R. Jesus took me to a place that was all red - all red, and warm and it was Him alone I wanted and never to leave. It was all red. I saw it as clearly as could be - a chamber of red, as if being within something and I begged and begged and begged to not take it away.

I could hardly breath after Communion, having received His presence. My whole chest hurt on the way to Communion from the anticipation to receive Him.

This morning at Church I received a message. I went to All Saints Church and yesterday was a holiday. I thought it was Monday. When I got to the door I saw the sign and realized it was Tuesday. Now, my greatest joy in adoration is to be before Him on Tuesday when He is exposed at All Saints.

I knew the presence of God. It got all glistening around the monstrance. The mural behind was like there was a glow around the Eucharist. It was a pearl-like light that was around it. I was filled with the presence of God. He had withheld His treasures to me for a time before and this experience was a great consolation to me. I was filled with the greatest awe and cried.

Love is - love is not words - it is in the heart and the being. After He showed me this red room, in this red place, then it went black. He told me to write. The pain was not as how I thought it would be when it ended after such an experience and such a heavenly rapture. His voice was so direct and clear and told me to write. Before I thought I would die to have Him take this blessing away, I feel the immense joy of that place for I see it and feel its warmth.

This is the title of the *Mass Book.* He showed me the journey He wished to take a soul on, in the Mass. He takes the soul into the most intimate place in the depth of His Sacred Heart. Enveloped by warmth and love, and the soul is existing in Divine Love. Nothing can explain in words how He gives the grace and

holy hearts will know this union with Him through consecration in the new era, the era in which God takes a soul into the depth of His Heart in the Mass, through the Immaculate Heart of Mary.

5/27/97

June 1, 1997
Morrow, Ohio

Feast of the Precious Body and Blood of Jesus

The Sorrowful Mysteries

The Agony in the Garden

1. **R.** Before the apparitions for Fatima that started on May 13, 1917 the angel appeared 3 times and somebody noted this week that before Jesus began to give His messages, October 13, 1996, that the angel appeared two times to two different people on August 13, 1996 on the Farm.
2. **R.** In one of the apparitions by the angel it says, the angel came bearing a gold chalice in one hand and a host above it in the other. The amazed children noticed the drops of blood were falling from the host into the chalice. Presently, the angel left both suspended in mid air and prostrated himself on the ground saying the most beautiful prayer, *"Most Holy Trinity, Father, Son and Holy Spirit, I adore You profoundly. I offer You the most precious Body, Blood, Soul and Divinity of Jesus Christ, present in all tabernacles of the world, in reparation for the outrages, sacrileges, and indifference by which He is offended. By the infinite merits of the Sacred Heart of Jesus and [the intercession of] the Immaculate Heart of Mary, I beg of Thee the conversion of poor sinners."*

   5. *Our Lady's Peace Plan*, op cit., p.2.
3. **R.** There were three visits from the angel. Three months before Jesus started to give His messages for the completion of the Fatima message, August 13, 1996 two women had visions.

Vision as seen by Ellen, August 13, 1996 -
Arlinghaus' Farm, Shepherds of Christ Meeting

"I had a profound experience this evening. As soon as the rosary started, I looked up towards the sun and I couldn't turn away. I realized there was a covering over the sun and that I would perhaps witness the miracle of the sun. Instead, after a few rotations, I began to see clear pictures: first, I saw the cross, Mary and Joseph holding our baby Jesus, and then what seemed to be a large Host, the Monstrance, and an angel holding up the Host, but I wasn't sure so I closed my eyes and said to myself, 'Dear Lord, I would love to see an angel as I have never seen one.' And with that within a split second a huge figure appeared, bigger than life, and came crashing to the earth, right before our group and returned. It was St. Michael! I recognized him immediately - his short, curly blond hair, his armor, which was brownish, but the whole figure of Michael was orange. His presence filled the whole area with bright light. It is difficult to describe, but I see St. Michael before me now as he appeared and want to share this with everyone because, surely, he has appeared to assure us of his protection for the Shepherds of Christ."
* *Warning: Eye damage can occur from staring at the sun.*

R. This was August 13th and Jesus began His messages for the completion of the Fatima message on October 13th, 1996.

4. **R.** Ellen noted that she had water that felt as if it was splashed on her and she didn't talk to another woman, Mary and Mary said the exact same thing about the water. This night was just terrible because the mikes weren't there and the girls had to go to Radio Shack two times before we could start the rosary. And so John started the seven sorrows and it was the first time that he was there and he was not the president yet.

Vision as seen by another woman, August 13, 1996 -
Arlinghaus' Farm, Shepherds of Christ Meeting

"On August 13, 1996 during the Shepherds of Christ prayer meeting, I saw the miracle of the sun.

When John started the Seven Sorrows of Mary, the sun appeared to be spinning through the trees. There was a disk in front of the sun. The disk was turning different colors including "Virgin Mary Blue". Different colored lasers also appeared to be coming from the sun.

The sun started growing brighter than normal that I had to close my eyes. When I opened them, the tree below the sun had turned to a brilliant light. The Angel of the Lord was in the tree.

I then noticed a very blue line coming down the middle of the river towards our side of the shore. After the blue line reached the shore, I felt a drop of water on my forehead. I looked up and saw nothing. I proceeded to pray when, I felt another drop of water fall on my forehead. One more time I looked up and saw nothing. When I looked towards the river again there was a brilliant golden light standing on the river. The brilliant golden light, which was the Angel of the Lord, ascended from the river and disappeared over the state of Kentucky.

I then looked straight ahead towards the deck, and when I did, I noticed more brilliant lights in the bushes and trees surrounding the deck and us. *There appeared to be angels encamped all around us.

Next I noticed the bottom branches of the tree directly in front of the deck moving and bending, it is then that I saw the brilliant outlines of Jesus and Mary in the tree. They were standing side by side in the tree during the entire rosary." *end of vision*

5. **R.** I mean to note here that Ellen saw the monstrance and the Host and the angel. Sister Lucia relates how the angel, gave them Communion, she says: "Then, rising, he took the chalice and the Host in his hand. He gave the Sacred Host to me and shared the Blood from the chalice between Jacinta and Francisco, saying as he did so: 'Take and drink the Body and Blood of Jesus Christ, horribly outraged by ungrateful men! Make reparation for their crimes and console your God.'" Ellen also had told me one other time that she had a dream in which she received the Holy Communion. It was a gigantic Host. And then she had this vision on August 13th.

6. **R.** And so we see Jesus in the garden and the angel appeared to Him to comfort Him. Jesus' agony was so great that Jesus sweat blood. Is this not what we are doing in our lives? That we are living Their lives in our life this day. And so when we

struggle so hard to do His work and we are pressed on and we suffer, should we not expect to live as He lived. For this is why Jesus came to this earth to show us the way, to show us how to live. And it is most important as we meditate on the mysteries of the rosary that we meditate on each mystery of the rosary, and see how it is unfolding in our lives. See how in the Joyful mysteries how we are being brought forth as children into the light. As the incarnation goes on in us we see how in these Sorrowful mysteries of the rosary we truly are living as we walk with the cross on our back, as we struggle sometimes and are pressed on, with the crown of thorns on our head and we feel as if sometimes we have sweat blood. For the more that we become like Christ, the more that our life is identified to His. And there is always the glory and the resurrection. For I know in this great suffering that there is this great union with Him, this great oneness with Him, that is so present in our hearts and that is the greatest gift that we have. It's our life that we share in Him.

7. Song: *Spirit Song*

   R. The Blood of Jesus. The most Precious Blood of Jesus in the Holy Sacrifice of the Mass. The priest has the power to change the bread and the wine into the Body and the Blood of Jesus. This wine is the fruit of the vine.

8. Song: *I Am the Vine*
9. **R.** Jesus wanted me to read the two readings at Mass this morning and I didn't bring them in, so you may read these later after we have prayed this rosary and concentrate on the blood in both of those readings. He also wanted this to be read. February 23, 1997, in the Apostles Manual.

February 23, 1997 - Sacrifice

When I go to Mass I offer a sacrifice. God wants our all. He wants to be first in our life. He asked Abraham to sacrifice his son.

Gen. 22: 1-2, 9-13, 15-18

It happened some time later that God put Abraham to the test. "Abraham, Abraham!" he called. "Here I am," he replied. God said, "Take your son, your only son, your beloved Isaac, and go to the land of Moriah, where you are to offer him as a burnt offering on one of the mountains which I shall point out to you.

When they arrived at the place which God had indicated to him, Abraham built an altar there, and arranged the wood. Then he bound his son and put him on the altar on top of the wood. Abraham stretched out his hand and took the knife to kill his son.

But the angel of Yahweh called to him from heaven. "Abraham, Abraham!" he said. "Here I am," he replied. Do not raise your hand against the boy," the angel said. "Do not harm him, for now I know you fear God. You have not refused me your own beloved son." Then looking up, Abraham saw a ram caught by its horns in a bush. Abraham took the ram and offered it as a burnt offering in place of his son.

The angel of Yahweh called Abraham a second time from heaven. "I swear by my own self, Yahweh declares, that because you have done this, because you have not refused me your own beloved son, I will shower blessings on you and make your descendants as numerous as the stars of heaven and the grains of sand on the seashore. Your descendants will gain possession of the gates of their enemies. All nations on earth will bless themselves by your descendants, because you have obeyed my command.

end of excerpt

10. **R.** And so we see Jesus through the passion. And we see how He suffered. We see Him bound, at the pillar and we say to ourselves he was bound at the pillar. But was He bound? For true freedom is in living according to the Father's will.

It was in His suffering as He sweat the blood in the garden as He was bound at the pillar, as He was crowned with thorns, as He shed His most Precious Blood that He gave Himself for our sins to His death on the cross.

Song: *I Love You Jesus*

The Scourging at the Pillar

1. **R.** Envision Jesus vividly before your eyes at the pillar. See His stooped head, His hair long and stringy and dark and see the men stand beside Him as they beat Him. We see a man, we see a man that looks like He is restrained. We see a man that looks like He is beaten and suffering. We see Jesus Christ, the Son of God, our beloved, who came to this earth. Jesus is our Savior, Savior of the world.
2. **R.** Jesus wanted this particular reading read and it's entitled February 23rd - Sacrifice.

February 23, 1997 - Sacrifice - continues

The Father gave His Son for us. This is how great the Father's love is for us.

When we go to the altar many times we are suffering. We want something really bad, but we know we love God the most. What the Father asks for us is to offer that which we are so attached to as a sacrifice, united to the sacrifice of His Son, Jesus. If we offer this sacrifice to Him, the Father will pour out blessings that will be divine blessings, greater than anything we could have here on earth.

The Mass is the perfect sacrifice we offer to the Father, in which God pours out His blessings and we are one with Him and with all others in a profound expression of love. God shares His divine love with us and we partake in an intense way in His divine loving capacity. In order to become one in Him and to feel His love like this, we must surrender ourselves and be open.

He told Abraham to offer his son. God gave him his son back. He wanted Abraham to love God above all things and people. *end of excerpt*

3. **February 23, 1997 - Sacrifice - continues**

Jesus offered Himself as a sacrifice to the Father. This is the most pleasing sacrifice to the Father. If He gave His Son Who died for love of us, will He deny us when we unite our petitions with Jesus and offer these at the Holy Sacrifice of the Mass?

He took them to the highest mountain and He was transfigured before them in the greatest light.

end of excerpt

4. **R.** I see the altar of sacrifice on the highest mountain. Think of the mountain being the Church. And from this high point the priest, think of the priest. The priest can be a great witness more and more as he gives himself to Jesus and Mary. The priest is another Christ to us. See grace outpoured in copious fashion to all the earth. The people of the earth are fed by the Almighty God. Priests need to consecrate their hearts to Jesus and Mary. People are to consecrate their hearts to Jesus and Mary. This is our Mission. In the Shepherds of Christ Movement, God has called us here to pray for the priests and for the renewal of the Church and the world. This morning I went to Church and it is so difficult many times because it feels as if the people are so disconnected with one another. I pray for great unity. We want unity in great openness at Church. Jesus is the vine, we are the branches. We are one body. We are united in the Holy Sacrifice of the Mass. Jesus gives to us His Body and Blood. What union! To spread this Consecration to the Hearts of Jesus and Mary is our mission in the Shepherds of Christ. This is what the Father is teaching to us to pray these prayers fervently. Asked to be dressed in Jesus' Precious Blood. Pray, He says from Prayer Manual, pray 10 to the end. We are praying the words that Jesus gave to Fr. Carter for devotion of His Heart and Mary's Heart. We are praying for the renewal of the Church and the world. We are praying and consecrating our hearts that we will be one in the Hearts of Jesus and Mary. These are great gifts that God has given to us. Today, Jesus is greatly offended because of the way that He is treated. We pray in reparation for our sins. Is this the love affair that God wants with us and with each other in the Holy Sacrifice of the Mass? Jesus gave Himself, shed His Precious Body and Blood. Jesus teaches us all about the will of God, that it is in self surrender and in giving, and He is teaching us truly in this Movement. See the power of these prayers. Ask Jesus to dress us in His Precious Blood when we pray these prayers. God wants us to pray the prayers. Jesus gave to us these prayers for the renewal of the Church and the world. Jesus gave these prayers to pray for the priests.

5. **R.** Bound at the pillar, look at the man, do you see Him? And they come down on Jesus and they tear Jesus' flesh. Jesus bleeds and Jesus is wide open. Look at Jesus. Jesus is King. Is this a king? Today is the Feast of the Precious Body and Blood of Christ. Oh my God, to receive Jesus and to know Jesus' presence. Jesus, I long to be one with You. And you just want Jesus to take you to Himself. You are united in the great oneness with God and with all of humanity. This is the gift that Jesus has showed us for He has raised the veil and He has let us experience Himself in a most intimate fashion. And so the world does not seem very connected to us. Pray for great grace that the world will be more united in Him.
6. **February 23, 1997 - Sacrifice - continues**

Mark 9: 2-10

Six days later, Jesus took with him Peter and James and John and led them up a high mountain on their own by themselves. There in their presence he was transfigured: his clothes became brilliantly white, whiter than any earthly bleacher could make them. Elijah appeared to them with Moses; and they were talking to Jesus. Then Peter spoke to Jesus, "Rabbi," he said, "it is wonderful for us to be here; so let us make three shelters, one for you, one for Moses and one for Elijah." He did not know what to say; they were so frightened. And a cloud came, covering them in shadow; and from the cloud there came a voice, "This is my Son, the Beloved. Listen to him." Then suddenly, when they looked round, they saw no one with them any more but only Jesus.

7. **February 23, 1997 - Sacrifice - continues**

We go to the altar of sacrifice. The mountain to come, in which so many graces will flow, is the altar of sacrifice where the Holy Sacrifice of the Mass is offered through the hands of consecrated priests.

We hear the Father say, "This is My beloved Son in whom I am well pleased, listen to Him." *end of excerpt*

R. On Tuesday there is Eucharistic Adoration and is there one to go to visit Him? Yet there are so many to go to this festival. Jesus wants us to love Him, to adore Him, to go to the Eucharist, to bow down as the angel, to kiss the floor, to say, "Oh, my Almighty God how I love You and how I adore You". This is our mission, but we may not understand the seriousness of this. We feel afraid. I go to the festival and I see so many people. I know in my heart how it is. I know the Eucharist truly is the Son of God. Whether there is one or five thousand people there in front of the Exposed Eucharist. I know it is Jesus and I am most intimately united to Jesus. I want deeper union with God.

8. **R.** People should be told from the pulpit to come before the tabernacle and before the Exposed Eucharist! We will bow down and we will pray and we will be a holy people. And Jesus stood there at the pillar and He was tied and He looked like a man that was beaten, and that was about to die at the pillar. But Jesus withstood it. For Jesus knew that it was the will of God. For the freedom truly is in doing the will of God.

9. **R.** Jesus speaks of Himself as the teacher in the All Night Message. It is so important that you study this message for He is truly revealing so many things in this message and in the Apostles Manual. We in this group, though very small in number, have been chosen by Him as a core group that will help in the renewal of the Church and the world. But you must believe this in your whole heart that we can help by doing what God tells us. For if the vision gets away from us, we will not work according to His plan. He has truly called each one of us here to be major in the renewal of the Church and the world. Let us be one praying deeply united in wanting to spread Jesus' love. Look, look, look what they did to Christ. This is Jesus, the Son of God. They nailed Him to a cross and they left Him hang for three hours to His death. They beat Him at the pillar and they crowned Him as a king with a crown of thorns. And He loved them so much! And He is the Savior. He gave Himself for us, for our sins.

10. **R.** Jesus said in the message on December 19, 1996, the light began to steal across the darkened sky and the moon was covered with blood. The blood was the blood of the Lamb. The blood represented the blood Jesus shed to give us life. But the blind men just saw ordinary blood and were scared to death. They responded with the greatest fright and

lacked peace. But those rooted in God, those whose hearts were consecrated to Mary and Jesus, knew the sign was from God. That the time of reckoning was at hand. Many were punished and suffered.

December 19, 1996

St. Gertrude Church - Received in a few minutes after Communion

Jesus: My Beloved Ones,

You will know a great time of trial and darkness. I have written to you of the great sufferings to come. The sinfulness of this world greatly displeases Me. I beg you to pray for forgiveness and turn your hearts to love.

And darkness covered the earth and the light was cast in little corners of the earth. Those who were willful remained in intense darkness, those who were rooted in God, and giving themselves to consecration, were the children of the light.

And the light shown in the darkness and the darkness grasped it not, but to as many as responded, they became the children of the light and from them His life flowed into the hearts that were cold and dark and slowly, very slowly, the light began to steal across the darkened sky and the moon was covered with blood. The blood was the blood of the Lamb. The blood represented the blood He shed to give us life. But the blind just saw ordinary blood and were scared to death. They responded with the greatest fright and lacked peace, but those rooted in God, those whose hearts were consecrated to Mary and Jesus, knew the sign was from God — that the time of reckoning was at hand. Many were punished and suffered a great chastisement. Many were left to death, but the children of light prayed the rosary and trusted in God.

And the night was no more for the light of day came stealing across the sky and myriads of angels filled the sky and the heavens. Sing Alleluia, Praise the Lord, you saints and angels, show yourselves to the survivors for they walked in darkness and could not see, but the light was alive in their hearts and they dwelt within the furnace of His Heart.

Have no fear now, My people, for you are the children of the light and My hand is forever upon you. You may suffer now a little, but it is nothing compared to the splendor to come.

R. Oh, reign of peace, reign of the Sacred Heart, triumph of her Immaculate Heart, we wait for you anxiously for the nights have been cold and dark and we cried a bitter cry in the darkness but we knew of the glories to come for we forever trusted in You and Your mighty hand.

Your hand is struck with power. The Virgin Mary warned the poor children that died an eternal death to mind their ways and they cried out, "Not me, oh, no, God — your ways are stiff necked and cruel. I want for foolish pleasure now and tomorrow will care for itself."

And the Lord called and called and they marched into the darkness with cold hearts, telling the Almighty God, 'no'.

Mary: Oh, my children, my little children of light, the time is nigh and many will be lost forever. I appeared and warned and told all to mind their ways and come to the Heart of my Son and they said "No, my Lady, not for you or any mother. We are children of darkness and that we remain, for we seek our pleasure by day and feast on sin all night and when you called, mother, we laughed at your Son and ignored Him and His ways." And He called and His call fell on deaf ears.

Please, my children of light, come to my heart now for although you walked next to the children of darkness. I smite the dragon that whirled around you and protected you in my heart and you will now feast on the glories of His Kingdom, my little children of light.

end of excerpt

R. And He says that the blood represented the blood He shed to give them life. But the blind just saw ordinary blood and were scared to death. It is so hard for me to even get the prayer manuals into a church. It is just an unbelievable feat to even try to start a little prayer group in which we are praying to consecrate our hearts to Jesus and Mary. This is what Jesus wants. Jesus wants us to pray these prayers and to spread this to the far corners of the earth. But I did not realize the power of these prayers or how important they were to Jesus and Mary, until He gave the message on Bloody Friday that said, that He would give special grace when we pray at the hours of 3, 6, 9 and 12 is the most important. And when we pray that He will dress us in His Precious Blood and the more that we suffer then we will be waiting for 3 o'clock to come to pray the Divine Mercy, and to pray these prayers, because we will realize the power of the prayers and how important they are. And then we will be motivated to spread this to the far corners of the earth. Jesus told us in many messages how important the prayers were, how important the Priestly Newsletter is, we pray every hour. But in your heart where else can you go? Does it matter if there's 2 or 500 people in that Church where Jesus is exposed? That's where my heart is. That's where I want to be. If we are tied at the pillar or if we are feeling an immense joy, our heart is with Jesus, whatever it is, it is the will of God that we want because we want God.

Song: *A Song from Jesus*

The Crowning with Thorns

1. **R.** And on December 22, 1996, Jesus said, "And the moon will be covered with blood. It was the blood of the Lamb and it poured forth on a sinful world to cleanse them of their sin, and I give you My Body and Blood in the Mass and I am ignored.

   He slapped their hands and He smite their cheeks and they laughed in their pain and continued their willful ways. But the day of reckoning is at hand and I will separate the sheep from the goats and the sheep I will take home with Me. The goats will know a day as they never knew before for My justice will prevail."

2. **R.** And Mary came, Our Lady of Light, every day for fourteen months to warn us, her children, and to tell us what we must do and she was ignored. Mary speaks on December 19th, 1996.

December 19, 1996

Mary: Oh, my children, my little children of light, the time is nigh and many will be lost forever. I appeared and warned and told all to mind their ways and come to the Heart of my Son and they said "No, my

Lady, not for you or any mother. We are children of darkness and that we remain, for we seek our pleasure by day and feast on sin all night and when you called, mother, we laughed at your Son and ignored Him and His ways." And He called and His call fell on deaf ears.

Please, my children of light, come to my heart now for although you walked next to the children of darkness. I smite the dragon that whirled around you and protected you in my heart and you will now feast on the glories of His Kingdom, my little children of light.

3.

Revelation 12: 1-2

Now a great sign appeared in heaven: a woman, robed with the sun, standing on the moon, and on her head a crown of twelve stars. She was pregnant, and in labour, crying aloud in the pangs of childbirth.

R. Mary said to us that she appears in Florida as Our Lady of Fatima in the Americas. This to me looks similar to Our Lady of Guadalupe. For notice the similarity between Our Lady of Guadalupe and the Lady that appears on the building in Florida. She was pregnant and in labor and Our Lady of Guadalupe is pregnant and crying aloud in the pangs of childbirth.

Revelation 12: 3-4

Then a second sign appeared in the sky: there was a huge red dragon with seven heads and ten horns, and each of the seven heads crowned with a coronet. Its tail swept a third of *the stars from the sky and hurled them to the ground*, and the dragon stopped in front of the woman as she was at the point of giving birth, so that it could eat the child as soon as it was born.

4.

Revelation 12: 5

The woman was *delivered of a boy*, the son who was *to rule all the nations with an iron sceptre*, and the child was taken straight up to God and to his throne,

R. The child, the little Infant of Good Health, has a scepter in His hand. The little Child, the Infant of Prague, is the little King. His Kingdom is coming. We pray when we pray the Our Father, thy kingdom come, thy will be done on earth as it is in heaven. And the little Child will lead the way. And the lion will lie down with the lamb and there will be peace on the earth as Mary promised when we what? Give our heart to the Immaculate Heart of our Mother. When we give our heart to Jesus.

5.

Revelation 12: 7-12

And now war broke out in heaven, when Michael with his angels attacked the dragon. The dragon fought back with his angels, but they were defeated and driven out of heaven. The great dragon, the primeval serpent, known as the devil or satan, who had led all the world astray, was hurled down to the earth and his angels were hurled down with him. Then I heard a voice shout from heaven, 'Salvation and power and empire for ever have been won by our God, and all authority for his Christ, now that the accuser, who accused our brothers day and night before our God, has been brought down. They have triumphed over him by the blood of the Lamb and by the word to which they bore witness, because even in the face of death they did not cling to life. So let the heavens rejoice and all who live there;

6. Hail Mary
7. **Reference: Revelation 6: 12-14**
8. **R.** How many times have I heard Our Lord say in strong messages, that He would rock us. That He would shake us. That He can rock us on our rockers. And then on the day of the flood, on March 3, 1997, I received a message.

March 3, 1997 - Day Falmouth Flooded Early Morning

Jesus: Oh, the waters will run and the earth will shake and you will suffer and suffer and work your own plan and say it happened before, it is not a sign from God - it is a phenomenon, a happening, no reason to take notice.

And I will shake you on your tree and you will fall to the ground as rotten fruit and all that will remain will be the fruit of heaven.

9. **R.** So do you want to give up? Do you feel like you are being crowned with thorns, that you are pressed on, that the devil is working so much in our lives? I feel so many times why is it so hard when I am trying so hard to do your work. We are not doing everything that He wants us to do in the messages. And He is teaching us through the suffering. I have learned more and more the immense importance of the prayers in the prayer manual. That this is the tool that Jesus will use to help renew the Church and the world. I am the messenger and I am aware of the importance of these prayers. Jesus gives us gifts and we do not understand. These prayers are most important. They are the prayers of Jesus that He has given to help many priests to grow in holiness. They are the prayers that He has given to help renew the Church and the world. They are the prayers that we need to say and that the people in the Churches and the schools need to say to consecrate their hearts to the Hearts of Jesus and Mary. And the Priestly Newsletter is the instrument whereby Jesus will help renew the Church and the world. And is this important in this rosary? Yes, it is important. For Jesus will run this little core group. We will be one. Jesus can then use us to be able to operate out of us in order to accomplish the task that is at hand. He will operate through us but we must die to our imperfections. As it is now they are all coming up to light and they are clashing as we try to unite with one another. And as they come to light and we stay closer to Him, we die to these imperfections. But it is painful. It has been a painful time but in the cutting back there is such growth. And that is what is happening to us. Though small in number, it does not matter, for His Might is the Might with which we will move forward and you have been called and chosen. But as He said in the Bloody Friday message, you may feel like abandoning the ship and giving up, or abandoning your post. We all need to be in one mind and one heart and the greatest

love is this intimate love with God! Our hearts must be filled with love. I live to help to bring about the renewal of the Church and the world and to help to pray for the priests, to help to spread the consecration and to see Thy Kingdom come, thy will be done on earth as it is in heaven.

10. Hail Mary
Song: *A Song from Jesus*

The Carrying of the Cross

1. **R.** And so I cried out to the Father and I said Oh Father, what I want with all my heart is to help for the priests to be holy priests, to spread these prayers, to help to bring about the renewal of the Church and the world, to spread the Newsletter. But it is so hard my Father. Will you please help us, please Father, please Jesus, help us! And what does He say to us? Meditate on the mysteries of the rosary for I see, I see Jesus at the pillar and it looks like a man that is beaten. Jesus died for us. Jesus suffered for us! Jesus is our Savior. We see Jesus at the pillar. We do not see our efforts when we are suffering. There are all different distractions that are happening which are making it very difficult to pray before and at Mass. And He said that it is in this great suffering that He pours out great graces. It seems that when you are experiencing this great gift that He gives that you know the grace. But do we know that in the great sufferings that He is giving, when we are walking up the hill and carrying the cross that there is great grace that is being outpoured in the Movement and we are all suffering we have all said we know we suffer when someone else in this Movement is hurting. That we truly are one body. He has molded us and bound us together in one mind and one heart in these prayers with each other. We are one now. Let us meditate on Jesus as He carried His cross for the real freedom is in doing the will of God. There is great grace that is being released when we are carrying the cross and it feels so hard that we can hardly carry it anymore.
2. **R.** And He fell to the ground. And they poked at Him and He was covered with blood and His body was torn and the cross dug into His skin. And He got up and He went on.
3. **R.** It became apparent to me when Fr. Joe was here just from a few of the things that he said, but Jesus had said it all along

how important this core group is. But it became so apparent that there is not another prayer group like this prayer group in the world. That He has chosen us for a mission to help to spread these prayers to help bring about the renewal of the Church and the world. He has chosen each one of us and if we do not do it, if the devil can work on us hard enough so that we abandon the ship and we leave our post then, he will have a victory. But what of our hearts, will our hearts have a victory? For you know as I know that I cannot help but do what He is asking me to do.

4. **R.** Look at our beautiful Lady as she appears on the building in Clearwater. He said that she appears there because it is Clear Water.

5. **R.** And so we are being brought forth as children of light through the power of the Holy Spirit. We are being formed more and more into the image and likeness of God. And we are trudging ahead and it is very difficult and we feel as if we are falling under our cross. And then we see all the imperfections come out. For we know that we want to be more and more and more like Jesus. But He is allowing us to see our imperfections so that we can die to them. And the more that we die to these imperfections the more that we become one. The more that we have imperfections the more that we are separate from one another. So the imperfections come up. We must be purified. We must move ahead so that we are becoming more and more like Christ. Because as we become more and more like Him, then we will unite in greater oneness with each other.

6. **R.** Are you perfect? Do you feel as if you should be perfect? Or are you in a state of becoming? Are we being brought forth as children of light? Do we feel that we have to be perfect? Or do we realize that we are sinful creatures? That we must constantly be telling God that we are sorry when we offend Him. And that we move ahead. But the devil tries to tell us that we are supposed to be perfect already. But are we perfect? For if we feel that we are perfect we are constantly frustrated for we see that we are not perfect and then we say, but we are not perfect, so we should feel bad. What we should do is try to love God with our whole heart, our whole soul and our whole mind. To realize that we are creatures and that we fall and that we are not perfect and that

we must tell God that we are sorry when we offend Him. For it is in doing this that we can move ahead, that we can move out of our imperfections and that we can become more like Him. If we think we are perfect then we won't move out of our imperfections.

7. **R.** And it is in the Eucharist that He gives Himself to us. And we share most intimately with the Almighty God, with the All-Perfect God, with the Divine God, with love Himself. And we are molded more and more into His image and likeness in the most Immaculate womb of His Mother, her Immaculate Heart, through the power of the Holy Spirit.

8. Hail Mary

9. Hail Mary

10. **R.** We must stay united to one another. We must come to these meetings weekly. For it is here when we stay connected, when we consecrate our hearts with one another, when we share our love of Jesus with one another, that we are strengthened. For the world in many cases has turned to sin. We must go to Jesus and we must come especially to be with one another. For it is in these meetings that we are strengthened, that we will have the courage to go on, to go out and to be with the other people and to minister to them. We pray these prayers Jesus gave Fr. Carter together and we pray the rosary together here in our chapter meetings.

The Death of Jesus

1. **R.** This is an excerpt that is in the *Mass Book* and it goes something like this, I see the man hanging on the cross and He does not speak a word for we do not hear the words that He speaks to us. But if we study Him as He hangs on the cross, we hear His message loud and clear.

2. **R.** Jesus came to die so that we would have life, life in Him.

3. **R.** Jesus gives us Himself in the Holy Eucharist and He wants our love and so He told me that I should write this intimate letter and He said to tell everyone to write the letter, in last week's rosary and to express our feelings, tell Him whatever is in our heart so that we can move ahead and love. And so I did that. I told Jesus the problems I had, people problems. Jesus wants our love! And then, I went out and I was loving everyone else. And then He overwhelmed me

with a grace that made me want to love Him and to love Him and to love Him. And the next day all I could do was tell Him how much I loved Him. And I did, I loved Him so much. I love Jesus so much. And that's all I could do was tell Jesus how much I loved Him. And I knew that when I wrote the letter that all I did was complain to Him that, that was not the way to treat somebody that I loved. And He taught me. Jesus taught me because all I wanted to do was tell Him how much I loved Him. Jesus filled me with this love for Him. And in that I told Him, I told Him how all I wanted to do was to help to pray for the priests, was to help to bring about the renewal of the Church and the world, was to help to spread the consecration. Jesus made it clear to me that when you love someone and you tell them how much you love them, that is the time to gently tell them the concerns of your heart, and to tell them, as I did to Jesus, Jesus I don't know what to do about this, but this is the whole desire of my heart. This is what Jesus wants. Jesus wants love. When we go to the Eucharist, He wants us to just keep telling Him how much we love Him. To see Him as He died on the cross with His hands outstretched and the wounds in His hands, and to just tell Him, Oh Jesus, I love you so much. When we wake up in the middle of the night and we feel this fear go across our heart, when we start remembering all the things that have been going on because this is a lot of stress. There are so many people out there that are doing whatever they're doing. They have pleasures etc. and you feel like your being pressed on and then Jesus reminds me but you have this deep intimate relationship with Me. That is a great gift I am giving to you. And so in the middle of the night when you wake and a chill goes across your chest when you're kind of sorry you woke up because then your mind starts to think already, about the things that are pressing down. And then, in that moment, instead of giving in to that, that fear that's going across your heart like a dark cloud, but to say, Oh Jesus, I love you. Oh God the Father, I love you so much. I love you so much dear Holy Spirit. To feel that presence within our heart and to know that God really dwells in our graced baptized soul. The Father, and the Son and Holy Spirit are in us. God has given us a sharing in His life in baptism. And how many times we are not even thinking about loving them, when God loves us so much.

4. **R.** And so here it is, it's our thoughts and the devil works in our thoughts many times the devil tries to confuse and tempt us. But even when it is so hard, that is when Jesus is with us. When it is so hard to pray, to pray anyway through the distraction and the struggle, to not give in to satan that is trying to stop us and to know that great graces are being given when we pray, that great grace is given when we are suffering. The blood poured out of the sides of Jesus' mouth. Jesus was crowned with thorns and the wounds bled from all over His whole body. He did not feel good in His body at that time. Jesus is our Redeemer, our Savior.
5. **R.** So a big, big, big help is to keep always on our lips and in our hearts the words, Jesus I love you. And how He longs for this, from our hearts, truly longing to give Him this love. This means so much to Jesus and I know now when I wake up in the middle of the night and the black clouds start to go across my head, that I have to go right away to the Father, to the Son and to the Holy Spirit and just keep telling them I love You, I love You so much, I love You so much, I am just going to be with You in my heart.
6. **R.** God is making strong soldiers of us. Few in number, but we are the core group. We are the ones that must be tested in fire and tried. We are the ones that must move forward more and more in His image and likeness and become more and more like Him so that He can operate through us. We are the ones that must die to ourselves and our imperfections in order to do the task that He is asking us to do. And the thing of it is, if you say, Oh my God, this is so hard. You say to yourself, but where do I go? Where, Lord, can I go? For it is You that I want.
7. **R.** And so I see a man as He hangs on the cross. His hands are nailed to the cross and His feet are nailed. His head is crowned with thorns and He hangs there, this man. He looks all battered and bruised and bloodied. And He hangs there to His death on the cross. He is bound, but is He bound? For freedom is in doing the will of God.
8. **R.** And in these Sorrowful mysteries He looked as a man that was beaten, that was bloodied, that was bruised all the way to the point of death. But we see in the Glorious mysteries to come the glory of the Almighty God, for He gives to us a sharing in His life in baptism.

9. **Jesus:** This is the rosary that I give to you this day, My beloved ones. For I watch you and I am so close to you. And in the struggle you are receiving so much grace when you are faithful to Me. You do not realize the grace that you are obtaining. You must hold tight. Pray! Pray! Pray! You must not give up the ship. You must come to Me. I long for your love. Will you tell Me the words from your lips constantly that you love Me? Will you be strong soldiers? Will you march forth into this world? Will you carry the light into the darkness? And will you help renew the Church and this world? I am Jesus. You are my soldiers of light. I give to you My heart. I give to you the heart of My mother. Mary is your mother. Mary is protecting you and loving you as she loved Me. You must open your heart and give yourself to Me.

10. **Jesus:** You will have peace and joy only in Me!!

Song: *A Song from Jesus*

R. How offended He is in the Holy Sacrifice of the Mass by those who do not give to Him their love, for He wants us to be one body, He wants us loving each other, and loving Him. We are many parts but one body. We must give ourselves to Him in the greatest love. This is why we were created, to love God and to love one another.

6/1/97

A Letter from Rita

R. My dear beloved Shepherds,

Enclosed is a summary of messages and directions I received from Jesus. No messages have been circulated that were not discerned by Fr. Carter. Jesus said we could circulate a directive message. This is a synopsis of His requests.

We are children of God. We were created in His image and likeness. We are to love God and love one another.

1. God wants our love.
2. God wants us to love each other, even in trials and sufferings.

3. We are the soldiers of love He has chosen to help bring the world to the light.
4. The Blue Book messages are to be lived by Shepherds of Christ members.
5. Jesus wants a letter of intimacy each day in which we tell Him all our cares. He is our best friend.
6. Jesus wants us to pray hourly the Infant of Prague novena for Fr. Carter. We can easily memorize these prayers.
7. Jesus wants us to realize the power and purpose of the Shepherds of Christ Prayers.
8. Jesus is dressing us in His Precious Blood when we recite them.
9. Jesus wishes us to pray the Shepherds of Christ Prayers at 3:00 p.m., especially, if we can.

   First pray the Novena to the Child Jesus for Fr. Carter

   Divine Mercy

   Shepherds of Christ Prayers - #10-16, p. 10, 11, and 12 (this takes about 5 minutes).
10. Jesus is dressing us with His Precious Blood whenever we pray the Shepherds of Christ prayers at 3:00 pm., 12:00 pm, 6:00 pm. and 9:00 am. and p.m. He is not asking us to wake from our sleep to pray any prayers.
11. We must say our Morning Offering every day. We receive so much grace when we offer everything we do to the Father in union with Jesus in the Holy Sacrifice of the Mass. We are united in a special way to each other when we do this.
12. It is certainly recommended that we spend an hour of intimacy with Jesus every day if possible. If you cannot say all the Shepherds of Christ prayers during the day, try to pray #10-16, p. 10, 11, and 12 sometimes during the day.

This is a rigorous prayer schedule Jesus wants from His apostles. If you are unable to pray according to this schedule, pray as much as possible. Jesus does not want you anxious about your prayer life.

Jesus wants, most of all, our LOVE.

All prayers should be prayed from the heart. All prayers are acts of love for God.

If this prayer schedule is too much, pray as much as you can but make it an act of love.

Every action is a prayer that is most pleasing to Him when united to the Holy Sacrifice of the Mass and done in love. Even when we are eating and sleeping we receive grace when we are doing it according to the Father's Will, with love.

Oh, I love you all so much. You are my brothers and sisters in Christ. God is our Father. Mary is our Mother and we are truly His family united in love.

I repeat, do not feel anxious about the prayers and the program. Do what you can to follow it. God knows how your life is.

Jesus has made it so clear to me how powerful the Shepherds of Christ prayers are. We have all been going through suffering. Jesus told me the Shepherds of Christ prayers were written by Him to help turn priests to holy priests and to renew the Church and the world.

Jesus wants us to pray the prayers often and to spread them to the ends of the earth.

They are so powerful. Jesus has told us He gives us special protection against satan when we pray the prayers. It is His intention to use these prayers majorly to help renew the Church and the world so He wants us to pray them for the priests, the Church and the world.

Jesus told us many things and we do not listen. Jesus has allowed us to suffer and in praying the prayers we have received much relief from the sufferings.

Another thing Jesus is teaching me is how much He wants me to love Him. One day I was complaining in my love letter to Him and not giving Him much love. The next day He allowed me to experience a great grace to just want to pour my love out to Him. I just kept telling Him how much I loved Him and then I told Him my petitions for the priests, the Church and the world, in love. This is how He wants us to treat Him - always in love.

When I awake in the night and I start to feel afraid, I try to just realize how God, the Father, Son and Holy Spirit are inside of me and tell them how much I love them.

Instead of giving into the negative fears of satan, I just outpour my love to God and then the cares of my heart come out.

Jesus will answer us more if we petition Him with great love. Jesus wants our love so much.

I love Jesus so much and I love God, the Father and the Holy Spirit, and Mary, so much!

Jesus wants us to love. That is the reason for our existence.

I figured that the greatest freedom comes when I do God's will.

The greatest peace is in my heart when I put aside the feelings of being wrong and love.

I want to be like Jesus. Jesus has taught me and Fr. Carter has taught me that I must identify my every act with Him. Praying the Prayer for Union with Jesus really helps because we become one with Him.

We have been trying to pray the Consecration and Holy Spirit prayer with everyone when we meet. I pray the prayers with Fr. Carter every day. We stay united in one mind and one heart by praying the prayers.

This helps protects us from the devil and we are united in one mind and one heart.

We are in dire need of funds. It costs $15,000 to circulate the Priestly Newsletter. Jesus wants this Newsletter to reach the priests. After our spiritual growth and all spiritual matters, that which is the most important to Jesus in our Movement is circulating the Priestly Newsletter and praying the prayers in the Prayer Manual.

It is through His Might the Movement will spread. We must obey Jesus and do what He asks to spread the Newsletter and Prayer Manuals.

I am so excited that the 13th will be at our Morrow Center. Fr. Kenney will celebrate Mass for us under a big tent! The 13th is very important to Jesus for the completion of the Fatima message. Please try to come!

We really need help at the Center. If anyone can come and help us it would be appreciated as we could then get all the work out that Jesus is asking us to do. The Center is so busy with calls, many of them from Florida. Someone threw acid on the Virgin Mary's image and disfigured her face. Somebody said it now looks like tears coming down her cheek.

Remember the Mary Message where she says, "I stood beneath the cross of my Son and I cried".

We also have a video on the Florida site which will be available on the 13th, or you can call or write for a copy.

We really need help in Florida and your prayers. There are places to stay if anyone can go to help.

Jesus spoke in a recent message how we have lost our fervor in praying our hourly novena for Fr. Carter. He says, "You have fallen in your fervor to pray hourly on the hour. Each minute ticks by, each hour goes on, you are coming closer each hour to the beginning of the era of peace. Your opposition is bigger than anything you can imagine. The Father will act soon. I ask you again to circulate the Falmouth picture. It is important to begin prayer chapters and circulate the Priestly Newsletter.

"You are suffering, you are suffering. It will become more difficult if you do not pray the prayers I give to you at the hours of 3:00, 6:00, 9:00 and 12:00. Do not give up! Give in!"

Jesus tells us we must publish the Mass book (this is about ready to go to the printers) and the Children's Rosary Book. This takes funds. We are circulating many materials that the Father, Our Lord and Our Lady asked us to circulate in Florida. Jesus wishes all of the books and rosaries from the 13th to be on the Internet.

Jesus wishes the *Apostles Manual* published in a small book form and given to all members in the Shepherds of Christ Movement. This is about ready to go to the publisher. It is small in size but has about 455 pages. It has been discerned by Fr. Carter.

The *Mass Book* does not have any direct messages from Jesus but are writings Jesus gave to me. This book was previously discerned by Fr. Carter.

These materials can circulate soon. Jesus spoke further in the message. Jesus says He is with us and that what we do will affect millions of souls. There are so many souls today that are being changed because of our work.

Look around - the world may oppose us but He tells us to "Feed the Hungry". The hungry will listen; the haughty and arrogant will give us problems.

It is the simple, humble soul that we will touch. There are so many people that are living holy lives because of our work.

It is the little people He works through. The high and mighty are but weaklings when they are put to the real test. Only those rooted in Him will survive.

Jesus said in the message, over and over again, how He is calling us by name. We are His chosen ones!

I love you so much. You are in my heart, all of you, and in my prayers. I feel so closely connected to each and every one of you. We are in one heart, in the Hearts of Jesus and Mary and united in great oneness with the Holy Sacrifice of the Mass. It is important to pray the Morning Offering.

I love you.

Rita

6/2/97

Ministries of Shepherds of Christ

Rita and cousin Archbishop Ed McCarthy

Dear Archbishop Ed,

Hi! How are you? Remember when I talked to you in December 1995? These are some of the writings of my experiences then. In no way is this a complete study on the Mass. There is so much more that I have been given since then.

In the Shepherds of Christ, our main focus is to pray for the priests. We have the imprimatur on the Prayer Manual and the Consecration card and Rosary Aves we sent to schools. We are trying to get prayer chapters started in the Churches, families and schools, praying for the priests and the renewal of the Church and the world. We pray the prayers on pages 10 and 11 of the prayer manual several times a day at the hours of 9:00, 12:00, 3:00, 6:00 and 9:00 for the priests and the renewal of the Church and the world. I do not do it all of these times, but many of us are doing so. It only takes about 5 minutes to pray the prayers for priests and renewal of the Church, the world and the Consecrations to

Jesus and Mary.

I want His Kingdom to come on earth as it is in heaven and His will to be done. I love Jesus so much!

We sent out consecration cards with the *Imprimatur* to 8,000 Catholic schools in the U.S. to get children to give their hearts to Jesus and Mary and to tell them how much Jesus and Mary love them and we have rosary meditations with the imprimatur to try to get children to pray the rosary.

We have prayer chapters all over the world praying for the priests and for the renewal of the Church and the world. Fr. Carter's Priestly Newsletter book with the first two years of Priestly Newsletters has the Imprimatur.

I am writing to ask you to read the *Mass Book.* It is not a complete study, in any way, it is my individual journey into the Heart of Christ. It is much deeper for to know Him is never ever enough, it goes deeper and deeper. I just love Him so much!

We are trying to start prayer chapters in the Churches centered in consecration. When the Church is consecrated to Jesus' and Mary's Hearts and the priest is consecrated to Their Hearts, and the people are living this consecration, they become so united in Their Hearts. This is what Mary wanted us to do at Fatima. Oh, Father, there is so much about being born a Child of the Light from the Immaculate Heart of Mary, so many revelations. The *Mass Book* does not contain all of this, there is so much more. *The Mass Book* does not have any messages so anyone not into private revelations might read it. Our Lord told me how to write it even if it is not in His words. I wish you would read it. I thank you for your dedication to loving Our Beloved Savior and His Holy priests. I am honored to be related to you. I love God so much and I love you, His Holy priest.

Love,
Rita

6/3/97

A Letter to a Donor

Dear Deby,

Hi, how are you? I wanted to send you the Mass Book. There are not any messages in it because Our Lord requested this so that we could get more priests and sisters to read it, but He told me how to write it. We are sending the Priestly Newsletters to 50,000-70,000 priests in English and Spanish.

Our whole mission is to pray for the priests and circulate the priestly newsletter to as many priests as possible. The first two years of Priestly Newsletters were published with the imprimatur. I am enclosing this book.

The Prayer Manual has the imprimatur and we are trying to get as many prayer chapters started as possible in the Churches. This is what the Father and Jesus want. It takes only 5 minutes to say the prayers for priests and for the renewal of the Church and the world, and the Consecration of our hearts to Jesus and Mary on pages 10 and 11 of the manual. Jesus has asked us to say these prayers several times a day because of the need for us to pray for the priests, the Church and the world.

We sent 8,000 elementary schools the little consecration cards and rosary meditations in May – all this has the imprimatur.

It has been very hard for the devil wants us to quit, but we press forward with all the *Imprimatur* material on the Church, family and school to spread the consecration, which is what Mary said at Fatima will bring peace to the world. We are also trying to get together a Children's Rosary book published and am pursuing an imprimatur for this important book for our children.

We operate on donations only. We want to send the *Mass Book* to the publisher but it has been very difficult trying to publish all the material Jesus has told us to publish. If you can help in any way with the Mass Book it would help us get it out to the people. I cannot tell you how much we would appreciate anything you can do to help us.

I am enclosing the book and sincerely hope to hear from you. You are always in my prayers, and I thank you for your prayers for me.

I love you,

Rita

6/3/97

Satan Wants You to Focus on Yourselves

Jesus: My dear ones, you must love. Your enemies are innumerable. I am telling you that you are given great gifts. I am giving you a special mission. What is your mission? How is satan keeping you busy so you do not follow My directions? How is satan making your life busy? He will send those with advice. Oh, you look tired. You better rest now. The devil will try to send someone to get you to focus on yourselves. The devil will try to get you to explain your actions. Some others will try to control you. Satan will tempt you to focus on yourselves. Satan will try to get you to explain your actions. Some others will try to control you. I will admonish, if you are running off course. How do I make you understand you must adhere to obedience to My directions. I use the word obedience, for your sake. Many will try to distract you to leave your post. Satan is coming with the talkative ones. The ones that want you to focus on yourself and be dependent on them. I am your God. You are the child of the Father. Be leery of those attempting to instruct you on your life. I am giving directions to follow. You must take care of yourself, eat proper food, have proper rest. You must spend time alone, intimate time with Me. Do not give into satan. I speak in the silence in your heart. You need quiet times during the day, alone with Me. Satan is cunning. He will send friends to divide other friends. You must stay united. **A house divided against itself will not stand.** Satan will try to get you to be friends against another. You are one family. You must operate in love. The answers are given in the Blue Books and the rosaries. You should listen to the rosary every day for 5 to 10 minutes. I tell you for your own good. If you do not obey many times you will suffer. Your relief will come from reading the messages and obeying the messages. Will you obey? Or will you suffer for not listening to My warning. Satan wants to control. Satan wants you divided. I have given you a mission. Satan will send a friend to take you from your post. So why were you not at your post on Monday or Tuesday or Wednesday or Thursday or Friday or Saturday? Satan appeals to the moment. Satan focuses on you and how you have been offended by others, telling you "Oh it is so hard for me." You are now offended and you must tend to your wounds. Satan tells you, you are overworked and tired and your back is hurting and so you should go out with a friend or cry in your bed. Have you prayed for relief? Have you cast out satan? Are you being a burden because you are not obeying the Mission I have given you? Do you want peace? You must get the proper rest. It is not the will of the Father to skip the proper sleep. It is not the will of the Father to starve yourself or to pray all night. I am pleased with your compliance to the Mission I give you. Doing other things that get you off your course is not to My liking. You must pray before the tabernacle everyday and be most intimate with Me. This means silent prayer. This is prayer spent alone with God. Satan will try to get you to be focused outside of yourself. You must have this period everyday when you are alone with Me. Satan uses trickery. Watch your tongue and the telephone. You are spending too much time on the telephone and not with Me. Read the Blue Book. I love you Jesus.

6/4/97

June 5, 1997

Rosary with Rita Ring at Morrow, Ohio

Glorious Mysteries

The Resurrection

1. **R.** And so Jesus tells us that the Shepherds of Christ Movement is to spread to the far corners of the earth. That it is for the renewal of the Church and the world. Yet we are so small but with His Might it can spread to the far corners of the earth and immensely help to change hearts to great hearts of love.

2. **R.** But it is in the coming back. It is in the dying to one's self that we become more and more like Him.

   Song: *Unless a Grain of Wheat*

   Song: *Choose Life*

3. **R.** And so in the rosary we meditate on the mysteries of Christ's life. But I see that the answer is in pure holiness, is

to be more like Him. But how can I be like Him if I do not meditate on His life and if I do not try to live as He lived. And so I thirst more and more to know more about God. So I can be more like Him because I see my ways and I see how I fall. And I want to be like Him. But the only way this can happen is if I study Jesus' life. And so They gave to us the mysteries of the rosary to walk with Christ, to be with Him, to meditate on His life, to meditate on His life with the Blessed Virgin and with the Apostles, to see how the Holy Spirit always worked in Their lives. This is what the rosary is all about. It is a meditation on His life that His life will live in our life. So how, today, did you live the resurrection in your life? How was it today? How is it when you are suffering? Immediately, since we are all trying as hard as we can to do the will of God, immediately, when we are confronted with suffering, do not our thoughts go to Him? And it is like, Jesus help me. I can be going along and not thinking too much about God and then all of a sudden something comes as if a friend comes and slaps you in the face and makes an erratic remark and you know that you can't say anything back, that you just have to take it within, and you want to still maintain your peace and love. And so they say something to you and where do your thoughts go? Immediately, in the suffering, it is like opening up a door to be deeply united to Christ. The opportunity is there to be with Him. The second we suffer we are deeply united to Him.

4. **R.** It is like a doorway that He opens up and we touch Him. It doesn't feel good many times but in a way it does because we know that He is present and He is alive. Moments before when we were enjoying ourselves we were not so focused on Him. But immediately when someone came up and made the remark or humiliated us, and we had to stand there and take it, our thoughts immediately went to Jesus, suffering, a doorway to the Heart of Christ.

5. **R.** And so it is in the death there is the resurrection. In the death there is the life for when I suffer I know Him. He is so present and so alive in my heart when I am suffering.

6. **R.** The messages that I received in 1991 when I first received messages, talked about how He would be with us to the far ends of the earth. And He talked about how the

messages were for the world. I did not even talk to anyone about these messages until sometime in 1993. I basically hid the messages in my notebooks under my bed and when I was struck with problems I would go into my closet and read the messages. Where before I was totally baffled and I did not know what to do. All of a sudden there was such a simple answer that He had given to me in the messages. And I came forth from the closet with an all together different frame of mind.

7. **R.** Problems that had stumped me for my whole life, that I had run from one person to another trying to find a solution to, all of a sudden had such a simple solution that I couldn't figure out why I hadn't thought of it myself. But is it not that when God gives us the grace and He allows us to understand a certain insight into something that it is very simple. That it is when He gives us the light that we comprehend. It all has to do with Him giving us the grace and then we know it. That's how it was. When He started giving me the messages it was like He gave the grace to go along with the message, so you just knew all these simple things, that seemed simple about God. So before where you were stumped, baffled and suffering immensely in your life, all of a sudden His life began to grow in a new way within me as He gave the messages.

8. **R.** On the day of the Falmouth flood He said when the pain in this earth reaches the peak of pain that He will pour down the antidote in these revelations. This is how I see this with the Movement. We have books and books. We have great gifts and rosaries and messages. We have all of Fr. Carter's Newsletters that he has written to the priests. It is as if now we are in the locked tomb. It is as if we are in the tomb with Him. And it says in the Bible, it says Lord why don't You protect what You have planted? Why don't You do something? Don't you see how bad that it's gotten? And the voice cries out and this is exactly what He answered the day of the flood. He said when the pain gets to the peak of pain then I will pour down the antidote in these revelations. It is like we are in the locked tomb and the stone is slowly being rolled away from the tomb as all of the materials are being put in order to help renew the Church, the school, and the family to help renew the world. All of the materials are

being stacked inside the tomb as if it is a library filled with the antidote for the poison that is in the Church and the world. And what are in these books in the library? And the books in the library as you open the books comes forth a letter from Jesus. One in which He speaks loud and clear with the most tenderest love that He has never revealed to man before from His Most Sacred Heart. It is a love letter from Jesus. And He speaks and tells the world that He loves them, that He is alive, that He is present, and that He wants them to love Him. He is writing the messages of His love on their hearts in these messages. And as Christ came forth from the tomb victorious, the stone will be rolled away from the tomb and He will pour down the antidote on the poison in the Church and in the world through Fr. Carter's Newsletter and through these revelations.

9. Hail Mary

10. **R.** And where did I meet my God? I met Him in the darkest, darkest room. One time I had a vision and it was a time of great suffering before He started giving me the messages. And the vision was this. It was this cave and it was all dark. And the rocks were poking in. And it was black in the cave. And I was in there and I felt like I couldn't move. And then all of a sudden I went through this doorway and it went into another room, and the other room was much larger. And there was some light in that room and you could stand, and the rocks were against the wall and they were pointy, but they weren't close to you, so you could stand up, in that room. Before I started receiving all of these revelations I would have visions of doors that were partway open with a chair like in front of them. And in this vision that He gave of the cave, this is how it is. Is it not in the darkest night of your life and the time when you were suffering, the absolute most, that it was then that you turned to God for there was nowhere else to turn, but to turn to Him and so therefore you found Him. And so we can say in the darkest night I found my God.

R. In order to have union with God there must be purification that takes place. There is purgatory before heaven. For in order to have this immense union with God the Father, Son, and Holy Spirit, we must be purified. How is it that each one of us here could unite in such a deep union with God. For we are sinners. We know that we can go through the Immaculate Heart of Mary and therefore we can get close to God for her heart is pure but look at your life. Every person in this room that is immensely close to God has gone through great sufferings where He allowed us to be purified that we could have this intense union with Him. And in no way are we perfect or are we all holy. For we see our imperfections and we know the long way that we have to go. But before He gave each one of us in this room this close union with Him, each one of us know that in our life we went through an immense amount of suffering in which He purified us. This is a great gift. You look back at your life and you remember how hard it was but you remember what came afterwards. For all of a sudden God was so alive and He was so close. But it was because of that great purification that we then could become much closer to Him. In that great suffering, in that darkest night, in that closed dark cave when it was so tight that I could hardly move, in that greatest suffering, that is where I met my God.

And I fell to the floor and I cried out my God are You there? Are You there my God? For this is great suffering. Do You hear me? And it felt as if the night would never end. But slowly, very slowly, the light came stealing across the sky and in that our heart was changed to great joy. For it truly is in the death there is the resurrection. And wherever you were yesterday with such anguish and pain within your life, today He has given to us a great relief. And today we are not suffering as yesterday. For our whole life is this. Death and resurrection.

Song: *Choose Life*

R. And so what happens if He gives to us suffering and we reach out and we try to alleviate the pain or if we live as the world lives always hunting for the pain killer. Then we've missed the great opportunity that He gives to us to encounter Him in a special way.

The Ascension

1. **R.** Let's analyze our life. Some days are good. Some days are not so good. Some days are suffering. Some days are joy. Let us look at the night and then see the day. There is darkness and there is light. And what happens in the darkest

night as you wake up in this dark night and there is no one around. I know that Jesus woke me for several years in order to write the Blue Book messages in the middle of the night. And He said that, that time is very, very, very precious to Him. For He had my undivided attention. I could not call anyone. I could not do any work because I really was not, in a way, in a position to work in the middle of the night. And so He said He would call me from my bed because there were no thoughts in my head and He would give me the messages that He wanted to give to the world to tell them of His love.

2. **R.** It was in the darkest cave that I met my God. And so what happens when you wake up in the middle of the night? You are isolated in a way that you are not isolated during the day. There usually is not someone around that you can talk to. This is a time when the devil can work in our mind. And he can get us off guard. Jesus said that the devil works a lot in the darkness. But, it is in the darkness, in the middle of the night, when we are awakened from our sleep, that we can go within ourselves and know that the Father, the Son and the Holy Spirit, are in us and we can be one with Them. How is your sleepless night? Is it a night of fear and terror? Is it a night of waiting for the morning to come? Or is it a great joy? For in that awakening, Our Lord was calling you to be most intimate with Him, for He knew, He knew that it would be a time when you would not be distracted by anything else. And so He says –

   Jesus: My beloved one, it is in the dark hours that I stand by your bed and I wait for you. And many times I wake you and I see you in a panic. And I am longing and I am crying out to you, talk to Me, be with Me, tell Me of your love. And I see you. And I see your mind go. And I see you think of all the worries in your life and all of the things that you must do. And I want this time. I want this time to be alone with you. I want to be united in Our Hearts in such oneness. And you are in your head, as your head runs as a machine, as a busy machine, manufacturing thoughts of fear, terror and concern. And it could have been moments that we spent in the most intimate oneness with each other. When I wake you in the middle of the night, you must come to Me. You must not give in to running thoughts of fear in your head. You must be alone with Me in your heart. I am dwelling in you. The Father dwells in your graced, baptized soul, when you are in the state of grace. The Holy Spirit is with you now. We are longing for your love. Will you spend those moments being alone with Me in the dark night? It is then that you feel isolated.

R. It is then that Our Lord calls.

3. Hail Mary
4. **R.** Jesus is alive. We do not comprehend how much God really wants our love.
5. **R.** This is December 27th. In this great era to come it will be an era in which man is espoused to God, in which he is united to God in a way that he has never been united to God so deeply before. This is what this great era will bring. For Jesus has promised that it will be a new earth. The relationship that Adam and Eve had with Our Lord was so close and the light was dimmed. In this we will be so one with the Almighty God. He (Jesus) wanted me to read this, it's called *Your Bridegroom Awaits.*

From Blue Book I - The Bridegroom Awaits - December 27, 1993 - 4:00 a.m.

Jesus: Dear child, the Son of Man waits and you sleep in the night. I wait for you and you sleep. You know I am waiting and you are dead in your bed. Awake, My little one, when I call. You must not give in to the desires of the body. I care for your needs. Your strength comes from Me. Jump from your bed, sound the trumpet and arise, for your Savior comes in the night to bring you a message for all His children. Ready yourself, for I do not like to wait. Get up and come, child. I am God.

I am He Who made the world, He Who makes the sun shine and the baby in the womb! You make Me wait while you sleep. Rise and run, for the Lord is at hand. God awaits you and beckons you to be attentive to your calling. Sound the trumpet! Arise in the night. I am He Who comes to you. You must harken to the call. Come pronto to My request and do not tarry. I wait and I wait and I eagerly want to talk to you.

I am Jesus, Son of the Living God. Oh, child, I want these messages to reach the ends of this earth. I deliver each with such love. Will you deliver My messages to all My loved ones? *end of excerpt*

R. This message was probably received about 4:10 a.m. in the morning and He woke me and when I went to bed I could only just be filled with such joy to know that God was going to wake me up in the middle of the night and give me this message. But when He woke me, it was hard to get out of bed sometimes. And a lot of times I would just be sometimes, half asleep while I was writing these messages. And He would be talking to me. I would hear Him tell me the message.

From Blue Book I - The Bridegroom Awaits - December 27, 1993 - 4:00 a.m. - continues

Jesus: They eagerly need to hear My words of love. They need to know how I feel about each one of them. They need to know that I am God. I love each child uniquely and My love is the love of God. What can you get on this earth that can compare to the love of God? You have a message declaring My love for each of My children. They are My love letters to them. Please see that they receive this letter. This is your top priority. It is a love letter to My beloved ones. *end of excerpt*

R. And this is a love letter that He has given to the whole world and He has called each one of us here to take this letter to the ends of the earth. It is your letter. It came through my hand. But it came from God and it is given to each one of us for we are the messengers.

From Blue Book I - The Bridegroom Awaits - December 27, 1993 - 4:00 a.m. - continues

Jesus: I am your Savior. I am not a myth. I am alive and I come to you. I wait in the tabernacle every day as a prisoner. Waiting and waiting in the tabernacle and who comes to be with Me? I await you, My children, to come and realize that God is in the tabernacle. I am Jesus, the Son of God, and I wait for you every day. Come to Me in your busy day. Come to Mass. Make ready your hearts and receive Me in Communion. I am there awaiting you as a groom awaiting his bride. I want to be with you, united in Holy Communion. I am truly present there, but which of you come? I wait for each of you. I am God. I can love you each so intently you do not understand. *end of excerpt*

R. The rest of the message goes on and talks about this spousal relationship that He wants with each one of us. And this was December 27th of 1993. December 27th of 1995 He gave the *Prayer Before the Holy Sacrifice of the Mass* in which we give ourselves entirely to Him. And He gives Himself to us.

6. **Jesus:** Are you afraid and are you troubled? I am alive and I watch you. As close as you feel that you are to Me I see the fear in your heart and I see you as you awake in the middle of the night. I am calling to you in your bed and many times you do not focus on Me. It is a call from God. It is special moments that you will spend with Me that will give you strength for the day to come. Do not worry about your sleep at this time. When you are awaken in the night and you cannot go to sleep, do not sit and worry about the hours as they pass. Take this precious time and be with Me and I will give you energy to handle the day at hand. There are special hours, these morning hours that you spend with Me. I am not asking you to stay up and to pray. I am asking you to be with Me. If I wake you in the night and you cannot sleep, use this time to be very close to Me.

7. **R.** And so the night is a time of refueling, of building our body. It is a time in which we must spend time resting. But many times He calls and many times we miss the call.

   Jesus: It is in the morning hours that I long to be with you. For you are isolated from the rest of the world and this is the time that I want you, when you are all alone with Me.

   R. Jesus is not telling us to set our clocks and to get up. He is telling us that if we wake up to put aside the fear that is in our minds and to be with Him intently and intimately in our hearts and just rest or go back to sleep in union with Jesus in our heart.

8. **R.** It is funny about sleep because many times we do not worry about the sleep and we abuse ourselves and allow ourselves to go to bed very late. But, then if we are awakened in the middle of the night, we are so worried about the minutes in which we will lose our sleep. We should do as

Jesus said in a message that I received yesterday. We should get our proper rest and go to bed for it is then that the devil will work when we stay up and when we stress ourselves out. Jesus told me it is not the will of the Father when we do not get the proper rest. But He also said that when He wakes us in the middle of the night, it is a great time to relax and to just be with Him, to take all the cares that are inside of our heart, all of the money problems whatever it is that is inside of our heart, and to go to Him and to tell Him, I love You Jesus, I love You. Pray for the grace to love Him. Pray for the grace that all you want to do within your heart is to love Him. This is what He has told me. And then, in that great love, the desires, the anguishes, all of the problems that we are having come lovingly out of our heart and Jesus will help us when we go to Him and ask for His help in deep love. This is the key to prayers being answered. It is to praise God. It is to thank God. It is to adore God. And it is to petition Him as our lover, the Bridegroom of our soul. For what lover would refuse the person he loves asking for something that is troubling them.

9. **R.** God is not a box that we go to and then we say, I will put in my petitions and coldly confront Him. I will tell You God and unload my problems on You. God wants us to love, to petition Him, and to be with Him as our best lover.
10. **R.** We live His life, death and resurrection in our lives. God is love. Our primary focus in every action we perform, in every prayer we speak, should be that of loving.
    Song: *A Song from Jesus*

The Descent of the Holy Spirit

1. **Jesus:** Imperfections, imperfections, you are filled with imperfections. But that which offends Me the greatest is the heart that comes to Me that is haughty. I long for the heart that comes that is contrite and that is loving. I am asking you to put aside your haughtiness and your pride and to come to Me with a heart that is humble, that is gentle, that is loving. I am Jesus. I am asking you to meditate on the mysteries of the rosary.
2. **R.** Jesus wants us to be His apostles. He wants to live in us. Jesus wants us to follow Him. Jesus wants to minister to the world through us. But we must meditate on how Jesus was.

How is Jesus? Do you see Him with the crowd? How was His voice? Was He anxious? How did He live His life? Jesus lived in unity with the Apostles.

For thirty years of His life He lived a most quiet life. Jesus was not anxious. Jesus calls us, today to help in the work of redemption. This is the life that He wants for us. He wants us to identify with Him in all of our actions, to be Christ to one another, to love God and to love each other.

3. **R.** And so how are we? Do we know when we have wronged someone? Do we tell God that we are sorry? For we know when we wound them that we have wounded Him. Do we tell the person that we are sorry? How does Christ want us to be in our heart? Always saying that we are right? Or telling others when we are wrong and saying we are sorry. This is what has offended the Father the most in the messages that He has given, is the fact that man does not make reparation to God for their sins. They are haughty in their hearts. Man offends God. We as a people must make reparation for our sins and the sins of the human race.
4. Hail Mary
5. **R.** Jesus has asked us to pray the Holy Spirit Novena everyday. That it is so important that the Holy Spirit is working within our lives leading us, filling us with the fire of His love.
6. **R.** I want to read the message that I got yesterday because He wanted us to hear this today.

June 4, 1997

Jesus: My dear ones, you must love. Your enemies are innumerable. I am telling you that you are given great gifts. I am giving you a special mission. What is your mission? How is satan keeping you busy so you do not follow My directions? How is satan making your life busy? He will send those with advice. Oh, you look tired. You better rest now. The devil will try to send someone to get you to focus on yourselves. The devil will try to get you to explain your actions. Some others will try to control you. *end of excerpt*

R. This is exactly what's happening in our lives. We have such a major Mission, each one of us, to help renew the Church and the world and satan is working in each and every person trying to tempt them. Someone comes up and says you don't look too good. Somebody else tells you something else. The second a person comes up with a negative comment to you, be leery of satan to get you focused on yourself instead of the job that He is asking us to do.

June 4, 1997 continues

Jesus: Satan will tempt you to focus on yourselves. Satan will try to get you to explain your actions. Some others will try to control you. I will admonish, if you are running off course. How do I make you understand you must adhere to obedience to My directions. I use the word obedience, for your sake. Many will try to distract you to leave your post. Satan is coming with the talkative ones. The ones that want you to focus on yourself and be dependent on them. I am your God. You are the child of the Father. Be leery of those attempting to instruct you on your life. I am giving directions to follow. You must take care of yourself, eat proper food, have proper rest. You must spend time alone, intimate time with Me. Do not give into satan. I speak in the silence in your heart. You need quiet times during the day, alone with Me. Satan is cunning. He will send friends to divide other friends. You must stay united. **A house divided against itself will not stand.** Satan will try to get you to be friends against another. You are one family. You must operate in love. The answers are given in the Blue Books and the rosaries. You should listen to the rosary every day for 5 to 10 minutes. I tell you for your own good. If you do not obey many times you will suffer. Your relief will come from reading the messages and obeying the messages. Will you obey? Or will you suffer for not listening to My warning. Satan wants to control. Satan wants you divided. I have given you a mission. Satan will send a friend to take you from your post. So why were you not at your post on Monday or Tuesday or Wednesday or Thursday or Friday or Saturday? Satan appeals to the moment. Satan focuses on you and how you have been offended by others, telling you "Oh it is so hard for me." You are now offended and you must tend to your wounds. Satan tells you, you are overworked and tired and your back is hurting and so you should go out with a friend or cry in your bed. Have you prayed for relief? Have you cast out satan? Are you being a burden because you are not obeying the Mission I have given you? Do you want peace? You must get the proper rest. It is not the will of the Father to skip the proper sleep. It is not the will of the Father to starve yourself or to pray all night. I am pleased with your compliance to the Mission I give you. Doing other things that get you off your course is not to My liking. You must pray before the tabernacle everyday and be most intimate with Me. This means silent prayer. This is prayer spent alone with God. Satan will try to get you to be focused outside of yourself. You must have this period everyday when you are alone with Me. Satan uses trickery. Watch your tongue and the telephone. You are spending too much time on the telephone and not with Me. Read the Blue Book. I love you Jesus. *end of excerpt*

June 5, 1997 continues

R. Suffering is suffering. Christ did not come down from the cross because it did not feel good. Christ withstood it. See His pain in His face, His anguish by looking at His body.

Jesus: The devil taunts you. You are weak. You do not wish to suffer. You want relief. You must learn to not act impulsively. You must learn to not give in to relieve the suffering. The world teaches you to reach for a pain killer. I tell you to withstand the suffering for the grace that will be released because of your suffering. (not for all suffering, in health issues, medicine may be needed)

R. We live His life, death and resurrection in our lives. When we study the Passion of Our Lord, He looks in such anguish. Do we realize He suffered for our sins. We too must suffer and die mystically with Him that we will rise to new life in Him. His way is death and resurrection, suffering and life.

Jesus: Do not act impulsively. Do not throw away the opportunity for grace I give to you. Accept the suffering. Great grace is released when you are suffering. You are afraid to suffer. You want a way out. The resurrection comes after the death. The victory is won. You must live in suffering and in joy according to the Father's will. The devil wants you to end the pain. In the darkness satan tempts you. In the darkness, in the isolated night I wait for you. Turn to Me. Turn to the all Powerful God. I will give you grace when you withstand mental torment. Turn to the Blue Books and the rosary tapes and turn to Me. You are suffering for the Movement, for the priests, for the renewal of the Church and the world, for your willful disobedient friends who oppose you. You must pray for them. I am Jesus, your beloved Savior.

7. Hail Mary
8. Hail Mary
9. **R.** We must study the Acts of the Apostles. Study the Apostles. We are in a state of becoming as we pray more and more to the Holy Spirit and we are filled with the Holy Spirit, we will proceed ahead fearlessly. That is why Jesus wants us to pray the Novena to the Holy Spirit everyday. It is the key. That is why He told us about the apostles, about their lives and we see their weaknesses and we see how they were concerned about all the worldly things. And then we see the work that was accomplished when they were filled with the Holy Spirit. It is the Holy Spirit that will help give us what we need to be the apostles, to carry out this task to help renew the Church and the world. On this Feast of the eve of the Sacred Heart, let us, with all our hearts, vow to Jesus, that we will try to take His message of love to the far ends of the earth. For His love is the Mighty Medicine that will heal the sickness that is in the world. It is only His love that will heal this world. For the world is crying out in pain and it is because they are longing for His love.
10. Song: *Come Holy Spirit*
    Song: *I Am the Vine, You are the Branches*

The Assumption

1. **R.** Jesus gives to us His Mother. Jesus' Mother that is with us, Mother at our side. Fr. Carter, every time I am with him, smells like roses and I have never been so aware of how close Our Lady is to all of us, because he has been smelling like roses every time that I meet with him. Think if we had Mary right by our side, Our Mother. And we see ourselves many times in our lives that we are just afraid. But if we knew our Mother was standing right beside us and when we are afraid and we feel like we've been wounded and when we aren't getting what we really need because of something that we don't even understand is going on inside but we're

not feeling good, if our mother was standing right by our side and was there to pick us up and to love us and to hold us and to assure us that she has this endless love to give us, would we be afraid?

2. **R.** Mary is the perfect Mother. The Mother that the Father chose for His Son, Jesus. Mary is by our side at this very second. So why are we afraid? The next time that we are feeling afraid, that someone has done something that makes us feel upset inside, we must see ourselves as a little child and Mary standing right beside us. And at that moment, she picks us up and she presses us against her chest and she tells us as she tenderly strokes our hair that she loves us and that she is caring for us.

3. **R.** Jesus does not want us haughty adults that have it all together. Jesus doesn't want a person trying to make another slavishly dependent on them. What He wants us to do is to go to Him. Jesus wants us to do God's will in love and recognize our dependence on Him.

4. **R.** The devil will get us focused on ourselves and try to get us to leave our post. The devil talks in people's minds to think of the negative thoughts. We are wasting a lot of time in our minds thinking of negative thoughts. There was a message in the Third Blue Book and it is called, *"Is Your Glass Half Full or Half Empty?"* I have thought about making laminated copies of this message.

5. **R.** Do we realize, in a message that I received from Jesus at Easter, how we truly are this family of the Father that will spread out to the rest of the world, in which the rest of the world will be one as a holy, happy family? Do we realize that we are the core and the center of this? That He is really forming us? That He is teaching us? That He has given to us each other that we can be most intimately involved in our hearts with one another. That we do not talk about the socks and the weather and the cars on the road and whatever we talk about and talk about the things in our hearts, the love of God. We talk about things, how we feel. We talk about things and it is very hard when we are talking many times with others because we cannot share deeply, our feelings in our hearts. This is a great gift that He has given to us to help bring about this era of the Two Hearts.

6. **R.** And so you go out and you say I do not understand. They do not speak about the things that I want to speak about. And my heart feels so cold.

   Jesus: I am forming you, My apostles to carry My love into this world. It is in praying with your heart, it is in being in your heart, it is in loving with your heart that you will spread this devotion of My Heart to the world.

7. **R.** What if we went to Church and the priest got up and the priest said, "Jesus loves you so much. Pray to Jesus. He is longing for your love at this moment. He will give Himself to you in the Holy Eucharist. You are offering yourself up to Jesus and Jesus will outpour His love to you and you will feel His Divine love within your heart." This is what Jesus wants of our world. The world is blind. He has given to us this great gift. This great grace to know Him most intimately in our hearts. Jesus has given to us one another to share this love in our hearts. We must focus on the glass being half full and not half empty. We must look around at each other and love each other in all of our imperfections, to love the little quirks and the personality that irritate us many times. For in a family there is love and He is using us to be His family, His little heart beating in this world.

8. **R.** Mary is by our side. The devil wants us stopped. The devil wants souls caved-in, having bad habits or vices, they keep using on others and trying to force bad behavior. Anything that the devil can get, to get us focused on ourselves, to get us feeling that we have been wounded, anything. And then he moves in and takes over. We spread negativism. **We have to be soldiers of love.** This is why He wants this intimate letter every day, to go to Him and to tell Him our love and when we tell Him our love to pour out our cares to Him.

9. **Jesus:** Are you afraid My beloved ones? I can look around this room at this very moment and I can see the fear and the frustration within your heart. You must let go of all of the fear that you feel in your heart at this moment. At this moment I am asking you to focus on the love of My Heart, to go to My Heart, this red chamber, this room, and to think of nothing but the warmth of My love and to be alone with Me, to take all of the cares that are inside of your mind and

to put them to rest and to focus only on My Divine love, to see My beating Heart, to see the red chamber of My Heart. Release yourselves of all of the problems in your mind and in your heart and focus on My love for you. You are here to know My love, to receive love and give love to others.

10. Song: *Immaculate Mary*

The Coronation of Mary as Queen of Heaven and Earth

1. **Jesus:** My beloved ones, this is how satan works in your head. At the moment that you are attacked, he tells you that you must worry and you must be concerned and then he plays in your mind thoughts of how others have offended you and how they are plotting to harm you or to hurt you. And then your mind begins to wonder and then your heart is troubled and you feel at once that you must act or that you must share this with another. For you are feeling suspicious and hurt. The impulsiveness that you feel many times is the sign that it is satan. You must quiet your heart. You must quiet your fears. You must give your cares to Me. You must surrender. He works when you are tired and when you are hungry and when you feel unloved. He is there waiting, lurking by your side, coming into your thoughts, planting seeds of division between you and those that you love. His way is to divide you. My way is to bring you into oneness.

2. **Jesus:** You must practice the discipline to not act impulsively when you are motivated to move ahead. And you feel edgy and agitated. You must continue to do My work for satan will attack you as you are working and you will have to press ahead and it will almost seem as if you cannot move ahead. But this is satan who aims to stop you. And you will feel tired and you will feel like you cannot pick up the phone. And you will feel that you cannot do this job, that it is too hard, that another day maybe, but not today. And there will be call after call. Someone that you must talk to now that will stop you from doing this job. I am telling you that millions of souls will be affected by the work that you do here. And that is why you are being pressed on by satan. You must not give in to his tactics. You must be aware that he is there to distract you, to have some call you to keep you from the job that is at hand. You must focus on one job until it is

done. If others call and call you must not answer many of the calls. Set time aside to do the work that I have given to you for I have called each one of you and given you the talents that you need to accomplish this task. Satan will try to do everything to keep you from the Mission that I have called you to. You know how it is. There are millions of souls that are at stake and what you do in this Movement is crucial to the renewal of the Church and the world. You must forever have before your eyes the burning souls of hell for you are helping souls to get to heaven.

3. **Jesus:** I see you, My beloved one that I have called and I see your willingness to give your life to Me and I sent you to that girl. And satan told you that you were tired and you did not feel like speaking to her. And I told you to give her My book and to tell her how I loved her. And I gave her a great grace and she listened. That was My beloved one and I tried to help My beloved one through you, through My Blue Book. Yesterday, My beloved one was in an accident, what you did, that little act that was magnified by the Almighty God, changed her life.

   R. For we are but players in His play and He is the Master and we are moving about and we are struggling but there truly is a Divine plan behind all of our activities for we have surrendered our life to Him. And He is working in us in ways that we do not even realize. And that is how this Movement has spread as it has to many far corners of this earth. Because it was His Might working in people that were walking as it felt in mud, and did not see the results. I did not hear the calls that they heard on the Shepherds of Christ phone and I did not hear the letters when they said that the Blue Book changed my life. But when I was sent out on the last mission, a woman came up and said I wouldn't be standing here today if it wasn't for this book and I thank you for writing this book.

4. **R.** And so we are tired and we complain and we do not see the far reaching effect and it was at Holy Saturday Vigil Service Ellen said to me. She said, "Can you imagine how many people are making their First Communion tonight because they read the Blue Books about Jesus in the Eucharist? We did not know any of them. But you know how these messages have made our friend, Chris love the

Eucharist. And now Chris is being made Catholic and going to communion." Chris said, "I know how they have made me love the Eucharist." I know how they made Chris long to receive the Eucharist. We don't see what we're doing. We walk in the mud. We feel like we are beaten up by satan. Our opposition is right there waving the flag. And the silent ones, the ones that are all over the world like Hank Miller that wrote and said I have a prayer chapter in a prison. And he wanted more of the rosaries because they like the rosaries so much. And he said that he lives by the Blue Book messages. I never knew that. It seemed like everybody that read the Blue Book messages are opposing me that day. And it made me cry because there are thousands and thousands and thousands of messages out there that have changed people's lives because you went to the Abbey at the Holy Spirit Center in Conyers. And you went in there anyway and then Jesus sent a person in there that was on the verge of going the wrong way and they picked up the book and then He gave them the grace and they opened it to just the right page. And their life was changed.

5. **R.** We are the players and He is the Divine Master. And there is but one plan and it is the plan of the Father. And "Thy Kingdom come, Thy will be done on earth as it is in heaven." Soon, this will happen. There will be one plan. Now the devil gets inside of the hearts of so many and that is where the problem is. For there are so many plans and they are not in alliance with His plan. But there will be a new earth when all are united in the plan of the Divine Master. It is like a symphony. The symphony is beautiful if all the players are playing the music. They all play a little different part and the tone is so beautiful and it eases the mind. The conductor is conducting the music and it has been written by the Divine Master. And it goes in such harmony. But if every person that is in the symphony decides to play their own tune, decides to have their own plan, think of the sounds that go forth. This is how the world is today. As we spread the consecration, as we spread the Shepherds of Christ Movement, more and more there will be one symphony with one master and one song.

6. **R.** This is the problem. In every Church, every school, every family and in the world there are people. How many in the

set of people are going according to the Father's plan? And how many are doing their own wills? The Church is divided this way. In one church it might be half the church that follows God's will and half the church that has their own plan. In another church it might only be 5% is doing their own will. This is how the whole world is set up but on this new earth, when the Sacred Heart of Jesus Reigns, all will be doing the Father's will.

7. **R.** Think of the school children as they all walk into church for Mass and they genuflect and they all go into the pew. And there's always a few that have to talk, that have to try to get away with something. And then there's maybe a whole lot that are doing exactly what they're supposed to do. This is how it is. There's always a few that are doing their own will. We have great problems when there's more than a few. This is how the world is today. A great portion of the world is not living according to the Father's will.

8. **R.** Mary is the Queen of Heaven and Earth. Mary is the Lady of Light. The Lady Clothed as the Sun. Mary brings us forth into this world as children of light all living according to the Father's will.

9. **R.** Mary has given her peace plan to us at Fatima. And we are the bearers of this plan to the world. What you do this very day will make the difference to millions of souls. We have been called by Jesus to this Movement. You are the core group. You are the center of His Heart beating in this world. What you do in this Movement will make the difference to so many. Why He has chosen us I do not know. But we must believe because if we falter in our belief, if we allow satan to work in our lives, to focus on ourselves, our fat or whatever it is, how you talk, and so your impatient, and so you look tired, and so oh when you got up to speak you looked shaky. And whatever else. Be leery of those that are coming, that are focusing on ourselves. Look for the heart that comes to you and shares the love of God. And pray for those that come up and attack you.

10. **Jesus:** I am forming you, yes, you, into My saint. And you are suffering and you are being purified. And you are being taught daily My ways.

6/5/97

June 7, 1997
Toledo, Ohio

Feast of the Immaculate Heart of Mary
Sorrowful Mysteries

R. Jesus requested part of a tape on Fatima be shown.

Excerpt from the *Spirituality of Fatima*
by Fr. Edward Carter, S.J. - October 13, 1917

As the Lady was about to leave, she pointed to the sun. Lucy excitedly repeated the gesture, and the people looked into the sky. The rain had ceased, the clouds parted, and the sun shone forth, but not in its usual brilliance. Instead, it appeared like a silver disc, pale as the moon, at which all could gaze without straining their eyes. Suddenly, impelled by some mysterious force, the disc began to whirl in the sky, casting off great shafts of multicolored light. Red, green, blue, yellow, violet — the enormous rays shot across the sky at all angles, lighting up the entire countryside for many miles around, but particularly the upturned faces of those 70,000 spellbound people.

After a few moments the wonder stopped, but resumed again a second and a third time — three times in all — within about 12 minutes. It seemed that the whole world was on fire, with the sun spinning at a greater speed each time.

Then a gasp of terror rose from the crowd, for the sun seemed to tear itself from the heavens and come crashing down upon the horrified multitude.... Just when it seemed that the ball of fire would fall upon and destroy them, the miracle ceased, and the sun resumed its normal place in the sky, shining forth as peacefully as ever.

When the people arose from the ground, cries of astonishment were heard on all sides. Their clothes, which had been soaking wet and muddy, now were clean and dry. Many of the sick and crippled had been cured of their afflictions.[2]

2. For background material on Fatima, I am particularly indebted to *Our Lady of Fatima's Peace Plan from Heaven* (Rockford: TAN Books and Publishers, Inc., 1983) pp.7-8.

A special message for you today from Jesus and Mary

Jesus: I call out to you My children of Light, My children of the world. For I love you with the greatest love. Will you spread the love to all My little ones, all the children that Mary loves so much.

Mary: I appear as Our Lady of Light to take the children to the Heart of my Son. You are sinful in your ways and you do not ask for forgiveness for your sins. You do not appreciate the gifts God gave to man and my Immaculate Heart. God gave you this gift to become ever closer to Him. Despite the fall of Adam and Eve, you oh sinful children, can become so intimately united to God through my Immaculate Heart. Oh please put aside your fears and put your trust in God. The devil wants you to stop the work you do to tell the world about our Two Hearts. You must be strong. I am the Immaculate Heart. I am the Ark of the Covenant. I am the Ark by which you will sail deeply into the Heart of Christ, my Beloved Son Jesus, the Savior of the world. I show you my Immaculate Heart, the way to go into the depth of the Heart of my Son. I appear and show you my heart pierced with a sword each day for fourteen months and I cry out to you of my lost children. I have allowed you to suffer my pain under the cross, the pain for the children that do not know their Mother. You must reach the children with the rosary and the consecration cards. You must act now for the time is nigh. The Father is displeased with the earth. I am your Mother. I am appearing and crying bloody tears for the men that are haughty, that are arrogant, that are willful and will be lost. Oh come my little children to my Immaculate Heart. It is there you will learn to be pure. It is there you will be sanctified through the Holy Spirit. I am the Lady of Light, the Lady picked by the Father to bring the children in sin to be united in a deep union with God. I am the sinless one that the Father sent, your Mother, the Mother of the human race, the Mother that stood beneath the cross, the Ark by which you would be saved. And I cry bloody tears today. This my special feast of my Immaculate Heart. For you are willful, willful and disobedient to God's commands. I ask you, I beg you to continue all the work my Son, Jesus has asked you to do in the

Shepherds of Christ Movement. Father Carter is my priest-son to help lead the priests to the Heart of My Son. I guard and cherish him, my beloved son, my priest, my precious son. You must be strong, my son, for the fallen angel has targeted you. But I am guarding you and spreading my mantle on you. (What is so beautiful is that every time I have seen Fr. Carter, he just smells of roses. And one day it lasted for 2 hours. It was so strong. But I know that Our Lady is immensely guarding him because of his role with the priests to lead them to the Heart of her Son.) You must, my beloved shepherds, continue to pray every hour on the hour for him. Do not fear. That is satan. Work hard to accomplish all the Father has asked you to do. I am crushing the head of the serpent. You must constantly make the act of consecration of your hearts to my heart, my Immaculate Heart and the Heart of my Son. I crush the head of the serpent. I love you. I am the Immaculate Conception. (And then she added this. This is for you here.) You have been chosen for this mission, my beloved Toledo. Will you help me? I am Mary, your Mother. You are my core chapter here for the Shepherds of Christ, the chosen ones, of my Son, Jesus.

Song: *Immaculate Mary*

The Agony in the Garden

R. Jesus wants us to pray the Prayer for Union with Jesus. We are more one with Him.

Galatians 2: 19-20

> ...I have been crucified with Christ and yet I am alive; yet it is no longer I, but Christ living in me.

1. Hail Mary
2. **R.** Let us go deeply within ourselves and to try to focus totally on our heart. Let us go to the inner chamber of the Heart of Christ. See the red, the interior of His Heart. Feel the warmth and know that it is there, that we're abundantly loved and we are protected by God Himself. No matter how the wind blows, or what may seem to be bothering us, in our lives, that this really is our refuge.
3. **R.** And how can I, a sinner, go deeply into the Heart of Christ? For in order to unite to God, I must be pure. And this is the great gift that God gives to us by giving us Mary and her

Immaculate Heart. For as we give ourselves to Mary and we dwell in her heart then we can unite in Jesus' Heart because Mary is all pure. And so in this rosary, we give our heart to Mary and we give our heart to Jesus. And we meditate on the lives of Jesus and Mary as we walk the passion.

4. **R.** How is it when we feel panicky? How does it feel when it seems like everything is going wrong on the outside. How does it feel? It doesn't feel good. But there is this place within, always within, when we have given our heart to Jesus and Mary and we are in the state of grace, no matter what we think. God is there if we call on Him. If we tell God that we are sorry, we can go to the heart of Mary and we can dwell deeply within the Heart of Jesus. This is such a great gift. So our life may seem confused on the outside and the money problems may be strong, the children are angry, some of them do not go to church. So many things press down each and every day. But in the moments of the silence, we can go within ourselves. We can give ourselves to Mary and no matter how we think that we have wronged others or what we have done, God is there waiting to forgive us. We go to her Immaculate Heart, we can go deeply into the Heart of Christ. This is the great gift that we are given on this earth for how in our sinfulness could we unite to God? There is Purgatory, to help purify us so that we can get to Heaven and be united to God. But our little Heaven here on earth is dwelling in the Hearts of Jesus and Mary no matter where I am, I can always go to Their Hearts. Let go of all of the cares and surrender and take refuge within His Heart.

5. Song: *I Am Your Sacred Heart*

6. **R.** And we see Jesus in the garden. We see Him in such anguish. Be within the Heart of Jesus and think Jesus knew all of the sufferings that He would undergo. He knew all of the souls that would be lost despite all of His suffering and He knew the great love that He had for those souls. And He knew that some souls would go to hell, forever, and He sweat blood.

7. **R.** Think of how we feel so many times when we feel that we know and we love Jesus so much and we know so many things because He has given us a great grace to see and to know Him. And we look around and we do not understand why others do not love Jesus so much and we want them to,

and we feel frustrated and we hurt inside because we know God loves them and wants their love and they don't even think of Him. Think of that little frustration that we feel sometimes, it is great suffering really, its not a little frustration. It's great suffering for me to know God and to love Him and to want to spread this love to others. But think, in His Divine knowing, in His Divine loving, of His anguish in the garden, to know the souls and all their sins, and all their vileness and how they would reject God and choose such senseless pleasures, so many ordinary things to His Divine love and Jesus, sweat blood in the garden.

8. **R.** Has the anguish ever been so great that you cried out and it felt as if you would buckle over in pain? And so it felt many times, maybe, as if you would almost sweat blood. But the blood did not come. Think of the anguish of our Divine Lord that He actually did, sweat blood.

9. **R.** The blood that Jesus sweat, for our precious souls. So precious are our souls to Jesus that He gave Himself to His death on the cross.

10. **R.** Do we realize how precious, we truly are? That the Almighty God loved us so much, that He gave Himself for us. Do we treasure ourselves as gifts from God? Do we treat our self, as His precious gift? Do we know how much He truly loves us?

R. There were three visits from the angel that preceded the apparitions of Mary at Fatima. The third visit from the angel:

Excerpt from the *Spirituality of Fatima*
by Fr. Edward Carter, S.J.

In the fall of the same year, the angel visited the visionaries a final time:

The angel came...bearing a golden chalice in one hand and a Host above it in the other. The amazed children noticed that drops of blood were falling from the Host into the chalice. Presently, the angel left both suspended in mid-air and prostrated himself on the ground, saying this beautiful prayer: *"Most Holy Trinity, Father, Son and Holy Spirit, I adore You profoundly. I offer You the most precious Body, Blood, Soul and Divinity of Jesus Christ, present in all tabernacles of the world, in reparation for the outrages, sacrileges, and indifference by which He is offended. By the infinite merits of the Sacred Heart of Jesus and [the intercession of] the Immaculate Heart of Mary, I beg of Thee the conversion of poor sinners."*[5]

5. *Our Lady's Peace Plan*, op cit., p.2. (The words in brackets are my own-added for clarification).

Song: *I Love You Jesus*

The Scourging at the Pillar

1. **Excerpt from *The Spirituality of Fatima* by Fr. Edward Carter, S.J.**

Then, rising, he took the chalice and the Host in his hand. He gave the Sacred Host to me and shared the Blood from the chalice between Jacinta and Francisco, saying as he did so:

"Take and drink the Body and Blood of Jesus Christ, horribly outraged by ungrateful men! Make reparation for their crimes and console your God."[6]

6. *Fatima in Lucia's Own Words*, op cit., pp.64-65.

2. **R.** A person told me a week ago that three months on the 13th of August before October 13th, 1996 when Jesus started giving messages for the completion of the Fatima message, that two people on the Farm on August 13th had apparitions from angels.
3. **R.** And so these were placed in the *Apostles Manual* because that is what Fr. Carter told us to do. But on August 13th this is what one woman saw:

Vision as seen by another person, August 13, 1996 - Arlinghaus' Farm, Shepherds of Christ meeting

"I had a profound experience this evening. As soon as the rosary started, I looked up towards the sun and I couldn't turn away. I realized there was a covering over the sun and that I would perhaps witness the miracle of the sun. Instead, after a few rotations, I began to see clear pictures: first, I saw the cross, Mary and Joseph holding our baby Jesus, and then what seemed to be a large Host, the Monstrance, and an angel holding up the Host, but I wasn't sure so I closed my eyes and said to myself, 'Dear Lord, I would love to see an angel as I have never seen one.' And with that within a split second a huge figure appeared, bigger than life, and came crashing to the earth, right before our group and returned. It was St. Michael! I recognized him immediately - his short, curly blond hair, his armor, which was brownish, but the whole figure of Michael was orange. His presence filled the whole area with bright light. It is difficult to describe, but I see St. Michael before me now as he appeared and want to share this with everyone because, surely, he has appeared to assure us of his protection for the Shepherds of Christ."

** Warning: Eye damage can occur from staring at the sun.*

4. **R.** Mary came in all of these apparitions to lead people to the Eucharistic Heart of her Son. We see how the angel speaks before Fatima, of the Eucharist. This is a main mission in the Shepherds of Christ Movement in the letters that Jesus speaks to us that we must honor Him and love Him and give Him the respect that is due to Him in the Holy Eucharist.

5. **R.** On First Saturday, its says specifically by the request of Our Lady that we are to make reparation to the Hearts of Jesus and Mary. Especially Eucharistic reparation. Think of what goes on at Church, at Mass. The Mass is the sacrifice of Calvary sacramentally made present. And in uniting in that oneness with the priest, with Christ, we offer ourselves to the Father. And that, at this time, we should tell God that we are sorry for our sins. We should tell Him at the Lamb of God when we beg, Lamb of God who takes away the sins of the world, have mercy on us: Lamb of God! We should get down on our knees and prostrate ourselves and beg God for we are praying not only for our own sins, but, the sins of all men. As a sinful race, we are telling God how sorry we are. But what is happening at the Mass? Are we making reparation as God wants us to do in this Holy Sacrifice? Or are we not even aware of the fact that the Almighty God is present? Or are we not even aware many times that we are sinners and that we must tell God that we are sorry? How greatly this offends our Beloved Jesus when He gives Himself to us in the most intimate act of love. God, the Almighty God, giving Himself to us in the Holy Eucharist and we do not even talk to Him. And we go from the Church

and do not spend time, with the Almighty God.

6. **R.** I was struck last week by the festival and all of the activity and the drinking of beer and the gambling. And I was very hurt within my heart for at the Tuesday adoration there are so few souls that come to tell God of their immense love, when Jesus is exposed in the Monstrance.
7. **R.** It is so clear to me and it hurts so much to love God so much to know His presence, to be in awe, to fall to the ground and to cry, to know that God is truly present there, and He is not adored and honored and loved as He should be. Our Beloved God, who remains with us, truly present in the Holy Eucharist.
8. **R.** And so they beat our Beloved Savior at the pillar and He suffered. We do not even know a little bit the immensity of being beaten with whips. Think of yourself now as being tied to the pillar and think of what it would be like to be hit and to bleed and to suffer and then after you are hit and you are suffering, for them to continue to hit you on the same places. But He suffered for all of us. He suffered so much for the sins of the flesh. For they beat His Body. And He wanted to give this message, the message to the world, "I love you, no matter what your sins, I love you. I forgive you when you come to Me and tell Me you are sorry. And I give you My love. I give to you My Body and My Blood." We have the sacrament of Confession for mortal sins.
9. **R.** We are bound, we are limited. We do not comprehend the ways of God but He is teaching us His ways. And the more He teaches, the more we want to know for it is that which satisfies our starved soul, that I am so grateful to Him for all of the teachings that He has given to me, for how He has opened Himself up and He has let me know Him, know Him in this special way. I know that this is a great gift that He has given and that many men in the new era to come will know Him with this immense love. But this is a great gift He gives to us right now. A great grace when we read the Blue Book messages and we cry. It is a mystical experience that He gives to us to experience His love in a special way. Jesus is indeed giving us great gifts right now. He allows us many times to suffer and to go through a lot of turmoil because of the work that we are doing. But think of how it would be to live like a little on the surface relationship with Him,

thinking that He's somewhere out there, being all alone and isolated in your heart, knowing that God is there, then He's there, but not really knowing Him like you know Him now. I know Him now immensely and it is because of the great grace He has given from praying these prayers in the Shepherds of Christ prayer book. He promised that to Fr. Carter that when people join the chapters and they pray those prayers, that they would receive a great grace to be drawn ever closer to His Heart and Mary's heart. And I have watched it happen for all of the members in our prayer group since 1994. I have watched them, I have watched their relationship with Jesus grow so immensely.

10. **R.** And it is because of the love letters that He has given. It is because of immensely sitting in front of the tabernacle, going to the Mass and the Eucharist with great fervor and daily that He has given great grace to me to be joined ever closer to His Heart. And I am very, very, very grateful for the grace that He gives when I go to the Eucharist. It is what my heart craves and wants and longs for. Jesus, we thank you for these graces that You have given to us and if we have offended You by our ingratitude or we have not thanked You properly, if we have not adored You and praised You and told You of our love, we are very sorry and we want to tell You now, thank You. Thank You for all the gifts that You have given to us and we love You with all our heart.

    Song: *Little Child*

The Crowning with Thorns

1. **Mary:** I stood beneath the cross of my Son, and I cried. I cried for my little lost children. The children that I love so and that I knew would lose their soul. I am Mary, your Mother, and I have come to you, my beloved Toledo. I have come to you to ask you to lead my little children to the Heart of my Son through the consecration.

2. **Mary:** This too, is a special area for the completion of the Fatima message. I have formed this core group in this area to help accomplish this mission. You have been given the greatest grace to respond and you have responded. Do not be afraid. Come, come to my heart and I will place you in the Heart of my Son. I am Mary, I have come to you this

day, my beloved Toledo, that you will help to spread the Shepherds of Christ Movement for my priest son, Fr. Carter. He is the leader and founder of this Movement, for my Son, Jesus. Will you respond to the call that Jesus has made to you through him? The times of trial will be great and many and you will suffer. But in the suffering you will be drawn ever closer to the Heart of my Son. You will live more and more as a child of God, more in His image and likeness. It is through the suffering that I am touching your heart. My little children do not be afraid for my Son is with you at every moment. You are doing His work and helping in the completion of the Fatima Plan, the completion of the Plan of my Father.

3. **R.** Mary is the Mother chosen by the Father to be the Mother of the whole human race. As the Father chooses a prophet, as the Father chooses a person to do His work, He also has chosen Mary to be Jesus' Mother and the Mother of all of us. And so, as she says, "I stood beneath the cross of my Son and I cried." It is the tears of Mary, it is the sorrow that we too feel in our heart for there is such an intimate connection between a child and their mother. But how much more our Mother Mary loves us for she is the all-holy, Immaculate Heart that the Father has chosen to love us as our Mother.

4. **R.** And Jesus' head was crowned with piercing thorns. But to speak of this is not to feel it, to experience the pressing down of the thorns ourselves. But He has allowed us to suffer greatly. Many of us with mental torment many times in the middle of the night when we wake and we are worried about our children and our funds and our houses and our job. When we try over and over again to do His work and we are persecuted at work and we are stopped in our churches when we try to go to them and to get them to let us have Eucharistic adoration. Many times we wake in the night and we are pressed on. We are mentally tormented many times and what does Jesus say to us?

5. **R.** The dark hours, the hours of darkness are the hours that we can be closest to Jesus. For Jesus says He calls us in those dark hours when we are not distracted by other things in our lives. And many times He wakes us in the middle of the night and it is then that the devil begins immediately to try to create concerns and anxieties in our minds. And Jesus

says that He wants us to go to His Heart, to take refuge in His Heart, to go to the red room, to put aside all of the fear that is in our heart and to just go and to be with Him. This takes discipline of our will, it takes faith, it takes letting go. When things seem like they are pressing in on us we must recall Jesus and we must see Him with the thorns pressing deep into His head. And this is how it seems many times for we are pressed on in our mind and in our thoughts. And we are feeling within that we should act or we should be impulsive. And we must see this picture of Jesus' face with blood trickling down His face with thorns pressing inward penetrating His precious skin and know that He did not act. Look at Him. Do you see Him now as He sits there? Do you see Him? He lets them spit on Him. He let them poke at Him. He sat there, He let them mock Him and call Him a King when in fact, He, the Almighty God, could have at any second, stopped them in their place. But He did not act. He sat there and He withstood the suffering and what happened? Jesus is our Savior. Jesus looked like a man beaten. Jesus looked like a man bloodied and wounded. He suffered for our sins. Jesus is our Savior. Jesus gives us the Church. God gives us a sharing in His life in baptism. Jesus is the Bread of Life.

6. **R.** We know that we can look at Jesus and we can see Him and we can study how He was. He withstood the suffering. He withstood it. Jesus suffered for our sins. We know that our Mother walks by our side, that she holds our hand, that we can give ourselves to her and be cradled in her Immaculate Heart. We must pray for the grace to dwell forever in Their Hearts for this truly is our place of refuge.

7. **R.** I like the dark hours of the night when Jesus wakes me and I can just be with Him and there is nothing in the world that can distract me or nothing that I have to do. Think of the great grace that He has given to us that we realize that when we are in the state of grace that the Father, Son and Holy Spirit dwell within us in a special way and we are not alone. So if we wake and we are feeling afraid, we know that God dwells in our graced baptized soul. We know too, if the devil starts to tempt us, we don't have to listen to the devil. Pray for grace. Say "I give myself to Mary. I go to your Immaculate Heart." We can pray to be forgiven for our

sins, the devil tries to tell us we should not pray for forgiveness. We are too bad. The devil is a liar.

8. **R.** And so Jesus sweat blood in the garden and so Jesus' Body was torn and ripped at the pillar and now we see Him as He sits on a mock throne. How awful to mock someone. Think of them mocking the King of all Kings. And now we see the blood come from His precious skull. Do we believe that Jesus loves us? He loves us so much He suffered and died for our sins.

9. **R.** It is hard many times to believe that people really love us. It is hard many times and we do not even believe that God loves us as we should. Jesus has written these messages in *God's Blue Book* that we will open them and that we will hear Him speak of His love to us.

10. **R.** It makes me feel so good inside when someone tells me that they love me, when someone does something very special for me. Think of how it is that we are so special and so precious to God that He came, that He gave His flesh, that He gave His Blood, that He allowed them to pound His head with thorns. He gave His Blood for me.

    Song: *Come Holy Spirit*

The Carrying of the Cross

1. **R.** Many times we are upset because we feel we are unloved or we feel that we are rejected. God gives to us this special *Apostles Manual* and He wants us to read it and to study it. For it is a great gift that He has given and it is very profound in its revelation for the future generations to come. He has asked me to read this entry from a rosary on September 10th, 1996. This is what He wants to speak to you:

Excerpt from September 10, 1996 Rosary

Jesus: My sweet one, I waited for you day and night. I waited for you to come. I waited for you and you did not come, and My Heart was in such anguish for I knew the sorrow within your heart, and I knew that I could comfort you and I could make you feel full of love in your heart, but you refused to come. You went to the world. You went to your friends. You went every place, but you did not come to Me and I waited. I watched you in your struggle. I watched you go from place to place searching, searching for that, that would fill your

starved soul, and you did not find what you wanted, but I waited, and I hoped, and I gave you the grace, but you continued. I waited for you. I am waiting for you now. I am waiting for you in this rosary to open your heart, to let Me come into your heart, and to penetrate your soul. I want to give you My Divine love. I want to be so close to you. Let go, My sweet, sweet, sweet one, for in this rosary I will give you great gifts. I will give you My undying love.
end of excerpt

2. Hail Mary
3. **Mary's Message - from the Rosary of August 27, 1996**

Mary: I stood beneath the cross of my Son, and my Heart was in such pain for I saw Him before my eyes. I saw Him covered with blood. I saw Him die. My Heart, my children, my Heart to watch my Son, but my Heart, my Heart, how I suffered for my little children of the world that give in to this world and give up the love of my Son. O my little children of light, I give you this message. Carry this light into the darkness for your Mother Mary, for I stood beneath the cross and I cried. I cried for the little ones. I cried for the young ones, the ones that do not care and will lose their souls. How do I make you see for you will not listen to me? What can I do? I come. I appear. I beg. I plead. I give you these gifts from my Son, and you reject me. I do not deliver messages very often anymore for I have been ignored. The message is the same. You do not read the messages I have given to you. Please help me. Help the little children. I appear. I appear. I appear, and I am ignored. I stood beneath the cross, and I cried. I cried, and my Heart was in such anguish for my little children, for I am searching for them this day as I searched for the Child Jesus. Please, please help me. I cannot hold back the hand of my Son any longer. I am Mary, your Mother. I ask you to help my children. You are my children of light.

end of Mary's Message

4. Excerpt from December 19, 1996 - Received in a few minutes after Communion - St. Gertrude Church

Mary: Oh, my children, my little children of light, the time is nigh and many will be lost forever. I appeared and warned and told all to mind their ways and come to the Heart of my Son and they said "No, my Lady, not for you or any mother. We are children of darkness and that we remain, for we seek our pleasure by day and feast on sin all night and when you called, mother, we laughed at your Son and ignored Him and His ways." And He called and His call fell on deaf ears.

Please, my children of light, come to my heart now for although you walked next to the children of darkness. I smite the dragon that whirled around you and protected you in my heart and you will now feast on the glories of His Kingdom, my little children of light.

end of excerpt

5. Song: *I Rocked Him as a Baby*
6. **R.** When we go to confession our souls are made clean and we can unite in deepest union with Jesus.

   Anger is an energy. God gives us energy to do good. Passion to love for Jesus. Anger is energy that can tear apart.

   Jesus: Leaders in the Movement must pray one hour before the tabernacle daily. If you do not, satan will work on the weakest link and create great problems in the Movement.

   No one is exempt. I am telling you once and for all, your Movement is a movement of love. There is division among you. You will not proceed ahead as I wish with such divided hearts.
7. Hail Mary
8. Song: *See the Eyes That Look at Mary*

   R. See the eyes of Mary as she looks into the eyes of Jesus on the way to Calvary and she sees the precious face of Jesus covered with blood and His head crowned with thorns. And see Jesus as He looks into the eyes of Mary. Jesus sees her red teary eyed face. This is the love of the Two Hearts for us. Now we must think of this every time that satan tries to attack us by feeling that we are unloved. We must go and dwell in these Hearts of love, and meditate more fully on the mysteries of Their lives so we can act more and more like Them. I see Jesus with the cross on His back and when the cross is on my back I want to take it off because it hurts and it bears down and it is very hard to walk. But Jesus showed us the way. There is joy and there is suffering. And when He is giving us a cross and it is the Father's Will that we carry it, there is much grace that we can receive for doing as He is asking us to do.

9. Hail Mary

10. **R.** Father Carter has a book and its called *"The Spirituality of Fatima and Medjugorje"*. It is in studying these messages of Fatima that it will keep us on track and focusing. For we realize that this is accepted by the Church and Mary said these things 80 years ago. They are strong messages. Mary says in here, "I am the Lady of the Rosary. I have come to warn the faithful to amend their lives and to ask pardon for their sins. They must not offend Our Lord anymore for He is already too grievously offended by the sins of men. People must say the rosary. Let them continue saying it everyday." Think of how many people do not even know what a rosary is.

    Song: *A Song from Jesus*

The Death of Jesus

1. **R.** This is from the Mass Book.

Excerpt from December 26, 1996 - Union With Jesus

In the Mass, the priest says, "As we prepare to celebrate the mystery of Christ's love, let us acknowledge our failures and ask the Lord for pardon and strength."

I love this part, when he says, "…prepare to celebrate the mystery of Christ's love…"

To me this is the greatest act of love. Oh, my heart burns to share this great act of love with my Divine God. I love Him. I love Him. I love Him, and I love the Mass. It is the greatest expression of His love for us. God gives Himself to man in the Mass. *end of excerpt*

2. **R.** What is love, but the gift of self to the other. And God shows us for He carried the cross on His back and He mounted the cross, and they pounded into His hands and into His feet the nails that went all the way through to the wooden cross. And Jesus hung there for three agonizing hours to His death.

3. **R.** And so we look around and we see that the world is not like us with the pain killers and all of those things that are there to stimulate our pleasures and to make us feel good. But it comes in praying the rosary everyday and in meditating on the mysteries of the rosary. We see how Jesus and Mary lived Their life and it puts into perspective how we too are expected to live our lives.
4. **R.** It is in the act of giving ourselves that He gives Himself to us in the greatest intimacy. For the more that we die to ourselves the more we become one in Him. And what else is there? The greatest is being united to Him in Holy Love.
5. **R.** Jesus held nothing back. Jesus came into this world in great poverty, Jesus is the Almighty God. Jesus took on human flesh and He mounted the cross. Jesus allowed them to beat His body, crown Him with thorns and hang Him on a cross. And in the end Jesus gave His Body and His Blood for me.
6. **Jesus:** And so I say to you, My beloved Shepherds, to treasure yourselves for you are a great gift to this world. I am working in your heart and giving to you the greatest grace to carry out the work that the Father has given to you. Be strong soldiers in this godless world. For I have called you. You do not understand how important you are. You are small in number, but as My Might works through you, you will accomplish great things. For millions of souls will be affected by the acts that you perform this day. You must not give in to satan. You must come to Me and take refuge in My Sacred Heart. I am waiting for you with My burning love. Even when you are taunted you must continue to pray for it is in great suffering and prayer that you receive great grace. Know that when you are attending Mass and you are suffering much that you will receive much grace, if you continue to tell Me how much, you love Me and you try to participate. I allow you to struggle in your prayers and I allow you to be taunted. You must not give in. You are receiving great grace when you are in suffering and when you are struggling, when you give your struggles to Me and you continue to love.
7. **R.** Do you see Jesus hang on the cross? Do you see the great suffering that He is undergoing? Jesus is our Savior. Jesus

shed His Blood that we would live in Him. What a most precious gift Jesus gives to us and what honor He gives to us that we are worth Him shedding His Blood for us.

8. **And so Mary speaks:** I stood beneath the cross of my Son and I cried.

   R. For she cried for the little ones that would be lost despite the suffering of her Beloved Son. And so when she appeared everyday for fourteen months, her cry was to reach her little children. And she is giving us a great, great help by loving us and protecting us as our Mother to do the work that the Father is asking us to do.

   Mary: I stood beneath the cross of my Son and I cried. For I appear, I appear, I appear and I am ignored.

9. Song: *I Rocked Him as a Baby*
10. Song: *Oh Holy Dwelling Place of God*

R. Mary is the Mother, that God the Father chose, to be our Mother. Mary stood beneath the cross of her Son and Mary cried for her lost children and Mary appeared over and over and over again and she was ignored. Mary is the sinless one, the Immaculate Heart of Mary. It is through Mary's heart that we will go deeply into the Heart of her Son. We are brought forth children of Light in the womb of the Lady clothed with the sun with the permeating action of the Holy Spirit within her womb. We are constantly in a state of becoming more and more like Him. We must be gentle with ourselves and loving with ourselves. Loving of God and loving of one another. For our role is to love, to try to be more and more like Him.

Jesus: For you were created in My image and likeness. My little children of Light, I bid you this day to go to the heart of your Mother, Mary and she will take you to the deepest recesses of My Heart. I am waiting to bathe you in My precious love. Do not be afraid. Be filled with hope and joy. I am asking you to help to spread the Priestly Newsletters to the priests. I am asking you to pray the Shepherds of Christ prayers whenever you can from 10-16 at the hours of 3, 12, 6 & 9. I will protect you in a special way with My precious Blood. My beloved ones, these are the prayers that I give to you to help the priests to become holy priests and to renew the Church and the world. It is your Father that has asked you to pray the prayers, to start the prayer chapters and to spread the

Priestly Newsletter. The tools that We give to you will help to renew the Church and the world. It is through this grace from the prayers that many priests will receive the help that they need and that their hearts will be turned to holy hearts through the Consecration and the Priestly Newsletter. I am Jesus, your Beloved Savior. I love you with the most tender love. Do not be afraid. Come to Me in the darkest night and take refuge in My Sacred Heart.

Song: *I Am Your Sacred Heart*

R. This is indeed a great feast, the feast of the Immaculate Heart of Mary!

I want to read the little part that was just to Toledo again.

Mary: You have been chosen for this mission my beloved Toledo. Will you help me? I am Mary, your Mother. You are my core chapter here for the Shepherds of Christ, the chosen ones of my Son, Jesus.

Song: *Immaculate Mary*

6/7/97

Feast of the Immaculate Heart

R. This feast follows the Feast of the Sacred Heart of Jesus. We (Fr. Carter and I) went to St. Teresa for Mass because I was going to Toledo. I was overwhelmed with the love of Their Two Hearts - The Hearts of deepest love, the Hearts consumed with love for sinful men.

Last week I suffered so on Saturday - the agony of Mary's heart. I knew such a longing on her part for oneness with her children, her wanting to Mother them and how she felt under the cross. Mary is the Mother. The Father speaks "My Mother, the one I chose for you to bring you into oneness with God. I give you the gift, but you throw it away - she appears - you ignore her."

He gives us the gift of His Son, Jesus. We do not love Him and cherish the gift of Jesus in the Eucharist.

Jesus: I call out to you, My children of light, My children of this world, for I love you with the greatest love. Will you spread My love to all My little ones, all the children that Mary loves so much?

Mary: I appear as Our Lady of Light to take the children to the Heart of my Son. You are sinful in your ways and do not ask for forgiveness.

Oh, please put aside your fears and put your trust in God. The devil wants to stop the work you do to tell the world about our Two Hearts. You must be strong. I am the Immaculate Heart. I am the Ark of the Covenant. I am the Ark by which you will sail deeply into the Heart of Christ, my beloved Son, Jesus - the Savior of the world.

I show you my Immaculate Heart - the way to go into the depth of the Heart of my Son. Do you see my heart, pierced with a sword? I appeared every day for 14 months and I cried out to you of my lost children.

I have allowed you to suffer my pain under the cross, the pain for the children that do not know their Mother. You must reach the children with the rosary and the consecration card. You must act now for the time is nigh. The Father is displeased with the earth. I am your Mother, appearing and crying bloody tears for the men that are haughty, that are arrogant, that are willful and will be lost.

Oh, come my little children to my Immaculate Heart. It is there you will learn to be pure. It is there you will be made more in the image of Jesus as the Holy Spirit molds you.

I am the Lady of Light, the Lady picked by the Father to reach the children in sin so they will be united in a deep union with God.

I am the Sinless One that the Father sent - your Mother, the mother of the human race, the mother that stood beneath the cross, the Ark by which you will be saved.

And I cry bloody tears today, this my special Feast of my Immaculate Heart, for many are willful - willful and disobedient to God's commands.

I ask you, I beg you to continue all the work my Son Jesus has asked you to do in the Shepherds of Christ Movement.

Fr. Carter is my priest-son to help lead the priests to the Heart of my Son. I guard and I cherish him, my beloved son, my priest, my precious son.

You must be strong, my son, for the fallen angels have targeted you but I am guarding you and spreading my mantle over you. You must, my beloved Shepherds, continue to pray every hour on the hour for him.

Do not fear, that is satan. Work hard to accomplish all the Father has asked you to do. I am crushing the head of the serpent. You must constantly make the acts of consecration of your hearts to my heart, my Immaculate Heart and the Heart of my Son. I will crush the head of the serpent when you dwell in my heart. I love you. I am the Immaculate Conception.

You have been chosen for this Mission, my beloved Toledo, will you help me? I am Mary, your Mother. You are my core chapter here for the Shepherds of Christ, the chosen ones of my Son, Jesus.

Song: *Immaculate Mary*

6/7/97

June 8, 1997
Morrow, Ohio

The Glorious Mysteries

Resurrection of Jesus from the Dead

1. **R.** The 2 main Father's messages that are in the *Apostles Manual* are so important, the two, and He wants us to keep reading them over and over again. I would like to read part of this one Father's message.

Excerpt from January 11, 1997

God the Father speaks: My plan will unfold despite the willfulness of any of My children. I am the Father. I have guided you in all of your activities.

I am telling you that the members of the Shepherds of Christ must be made aware of the importance of living the *Blue Book* messages.

Planning is up to Me. This is My plan and it will unfold. Men plan for the future. I AM.

I am directing the Shepherds of Christ Movement through these messages.

I am angered at the lack of response on the part of some to back these messages. You must support these messages so they are lived by man.

These messages are given from the Hearts of Jesus and Mary to bring about the reign of the Sacred Heart of Jesus and the triumph of My beloved Mary's Immaculate Heart.

You are given all you need. You must adhere to My plan.

I am the Father. I AM WHO AM. I was in the beginning, I am now and I will be forever.

end of excerpt

2.

John 1: 1-14

In the beginning was the Word: the Word was with God and the Word was God. He was with God in the beginning. Through him all things came into being, not one thing came into being except through him. What has come into being in him was life, life that was the light of men; and light shines in darkness, and darkness could not overpower it.

A man came, sent by God. His name was John. He came as a witness, to bear witness to the light, so that everyone might believe through him. He was not the light, he was to bear witness to the light.

The Word was the real light that gives light to everyone; he was coming into the world. He was in the world that had come into being through him, and the world did not recognise him. He came to his own and his own people did not accept him.

But to those who did accept him he gave power to become children of God, to those who believed in his name who were born not from human stock or human desire or human will but from God himself. The Word became flesh, he lived among us, and we saw his glory, the glory that he has from the Father as only Son of the Father, full of grace and truth.

3. Song: *I Will Be With You*

4. **R.** And so we pray for wider vision for the victory has been

won. For the Lord came forth from the tomb victorious and we share in abundance in His Divine life. For we have been baptized and He has given to us this sharing in His life. So why are we afraid? Where is our mind at this moment? Are we so fixed on the moment that we miss the big picture that He wishes to unveil to us. Let us pray to see the vision of the Father. Let us see the events of Adam and Eve and the willfulness in the garden. And let us see in the last book of Revelation where He speaks of what He will do on this earth. That the lady clothed as the sun will come with the moon under her feet, that she will shine, Our Lady of Light, and bring forth the children into the light. Let us see the whole Bible. Think of the Bible, the Word of God. And the more that we know God the more that we are rooted in the truth, that we want to know the Word of God, we seek to know God. Know the Bible beginning to the end. Let us pray in this rosary for the grace to see with wider vision, to not be so focused as we are on the moments at hand, but to see His Divine Plan. To be one in our hearts with God. To be one with each other. To see that the plan of the Father is unfolding here. To see the events of Adam and Eve, their willfulness. To see God is displeased with the creatures of this earth. That He has called us, this small core group, to go into this world and to tell them that they must stop offending God. What God wants from us is obedience. God wants reparation for the sins that we have committed. God wants us to tell Him we are sorry for our sins. God wants us to recognize that Jesus is truly present in the Eucharist, truly present in His Divinity and humanity. We indeed are a sinful, willful race. And the Father has said that He wishes us over and over again to read these two messages in January for they are filled with information that He is giving to us for the unfolding of His plan. We are the shepherds that He has called to help carry the light into the dark world.

John 1: 5, 10

and light shines in darkness, and darkness could not overpower it.

He was in the world that had come into being through him, and the world did not recognise him.

R. And so too, we must see with a wider vision. Constantly, keeping our vision to this wider vision to see ourselves truly in this picture for we must operate according to His plan. The devil gets us focused on ourselves. See the big picture, the Plan of God the Father.

And He speaks: I am without a beginning and without an end. I am the almighty God. I have called you. I have called you by name, My chosen shepherds to help carry this light into the darkness. Do not be concerned with the distractions in your life. Move fearlessly ahead for you have been chosen and I am giving you the most abundant grace to proceed in all of the sufferings. You will proceed ahead if you keep your focus on Me.

5. Song: *Come Give Me Life*

   Jesus: Are you afraid? Are you scared? Are you tired?

   Song: *I Will Be With You*

   Song: *City of God*

6. **R.** The Father has a plan and His plan will unfold. We see Adam and Eve in the garden and we see that they were told not to pick from the tree. And they disobeyed. We know that God is displeased at their disobedience. And so the light is dimmed. We see today the willfulness of men and we see as the Father speaks. The Father speaks on January 18th. These two messages are so filled with so much. What He is really saying to us, if we keep our focus on this, on the All Night Message, if we keep our focus on the wider vision we will hear what He is saying. God is God – God is the same God Adam and Eve disobeyed. It is the same God that speaks to us, the same God that we are communicating with. Mary said "yes" to the angel – "yes" to God the Father. It is the same God, Jesus Christ, the Son of Man that said when He died on the cross that He did the will of the Father even to His death on the cross. The message is to comply to the will of God. Adam and Eve sinned. Jesus is the New Adam. Mary is the New Eve. Mary stood beneath the cross. She said, "yes". Jesus said, thy will be done when He died on the cross.

And so the Father speaks on January 18th, 1997.

"I am the Father. My plan is unfolding through you, My beloved priest, Fr. Carter, and Rita and the core group in the Shepherds of Christ Movement.

I tell you all to read the accounts concerning Noah. Nowhere in history has God been offended as He is this day by this sinful world. You will suffer a fate for the offenses against God.

Mary appeared at Fatima to warn you, the sinful children, how they were offending God, but you did not listen. The war did not change the hearts of many evil men.

I warn you through My beloved daughter, Mary. You did not heed her warnings. Disobedience against the Mother I gave you displeases Me greatly. Mary is the Mother of all children. Mary is a gift from Me, but you are willful and abuse the gift I send you.

You do not make reparation to her Immaculate Heart; you continue to offend her. I will not tolerate the deeds of evil men any longer.

My plan will unfold. Any disobedience to these messages given by Me, My Son, or your Mother Mary will cause Me great displeasure.

I am the Father, the Almighty God, the Alpha, the Omega; you are a sinful people, a chosen race sinning against a loving God.

I am angered at your ways for they are not My ways, you have run amuck, you have offended your God, you have disobeyed your Mother and My beloved Son who died to save you."

7. **R.** This is a story of Jesus, the Son of God, coming to this earth. And we meditate on this in the rosary. We start in the Joyful Mysteries. Jesus was born in Bethlehem. We see Mary is our Spiritual Mother. The incarnation goes on in us.

From *Tell My People*
by Fr. Edward J. Carter, S.J.

The Holy Spirit

Jesus: "My beloved friend, tell My people to pray daily to the Holy Spirit. They are to pray for an increase in His gifts. My people must realize that the Holy Spirit comes to transform them. The Spirit desires to transform you more and more according to My image. Those who are docile to His touch become increasingly shaped in My likeness. He performs this marvel within Mary's Immaculate Heart. The more one dwells in My Mother's Heart, the more active are the workings of the Spirit. The Spirit leads Mary to place you within My own Heart. In both Our Hearts, then, your transformation continues. The more you are formed after My own Heart, the more I lead you to the bosom of My Father. Tell My people all this. Tell them to pray daily for a greater appreciation of these wondrous gifts. I am Lord and Master. All who come to My Heart will be on fire to receive the gifts of the Spirit in ever greater measure! I love and bless My people!"

Reflection: The Holy Spirit is given to us to fashion us ever more according to the likeness of Jesus. And the more we are like Jesus, the more Jesus leads us to the Father. Do we, each day, pray to the Holy Spirit to be more open to His transforming influence? Do we strive each day to grow in union with Mary? The greater our union with our Mother, the spouse of the Holy Spirit, the greater is the transforming action of the Holy Spirit within us. *end of excerpt*

R. We live the life, death and resurrection of Christ in our lives. We live out the mystery of Christ in our life.

We see how the mysteries of the rosary unfold in our life. We receive a sharing in His life in baptism. But we must follow the commandments of God. This is what He has told us. The first commandment is "I am the Lord thy God, thou shalt not have any gods before Me."

8. **R.** Jesus has made it so clear to me many people complain about the one hour that they spend with Him a week at Mass. And this morning, this is what He said, "One hour, one hour and they complain but the first commandment commands that they put Me first in their lives." What are our gods? He spoke very much this morning about the football and how it can become a god to us. How our television can be our god. And He showed us in the Falmouth Flood how unimportant our televisions are as they float down the river, for He has all the power. And we hear Him speak, "I am God. You see the little individual events

in your life as so important." And then He has showed us that He can get our attention if we do not answer to the gifts He gives. We must pray as He has asked us to pray. What happens to our gods, our televisions, whatever it is? It could float down the river as it did in a flood. This is an example of the events that can happen.

9. Hail Mary
10. Hail Mary

Song: *A Song from Jesus*

The Ascension of Jesus into Heaven

1. **R.** Think of the world today and think of how they are disobeying the ten commandments.

   The first one is: I, the Lord, am your God. You shall not have other gods besides me.

   The second one is: You shall not take the name of the Lord, your God, in vain.

   The third one is: Remember to keep holy the Sabbath day.

   And then we read the messages from the Father and He says that we are a sinful race. He gives to us ten commandments to follow. Are we following the commands? They are not suggestions, they are commandments that He gives to us to follow.

2. **R.** Moses went up the mountain to get ten commandments and when he came down they were worshipping the false gods.

   Reference: Exodus 31: 12-18

3. **R.** Moses came down from the mountain and he was up there awhile. And when he came down he saw the people and they were dancing and worshipping false gods. With that Moses' wrath flared up so that he threw the tablets down and he broke them.

4. **R.** I go to the Exposed Eucharist every Tuesday at All Saints. And I have seen the altar adorned in the greatest light. And there is this celestial aura and I feel the presence of God burn within me and I cry from the awe of it all. I know the presence of the Almighty God profoundly. And to see what I see, all these things happen to the altar and God is there. And this is where I had two of the great visions. The Almighty

God is truly present in the Eucharist. And there are maybe one, maybe two, maybe three people in the Church, but with the festival, so many outside. So many to run to the football games on Sunday with no care of the money for the tickets, or no care of anything. How is it in the lives of so many today? What does the first commandment say to us? 'I, the Lord, am your God. You shall not have other gods besides me.' And then He speaks about stealing. What about stealing the time that God has given to us that His plan will unfold. What about the money that we have and that we make that we do not share and that we do not give to God. Are we following the ten commandments? What is this? God is speaking to us to you and to me. We are the ones that He is speaking to. Everything that He speaks is written in the Bible, but we are looked at and we are criticized for talking about Jesus in the Eucharist and the Mass and the rosary and the commandments.

Excerpt from March 3, 1997 - God the Father: You need to stay united. You will help to renew the Church and the world. When the poison reaches the peaks of pain, I will pour down the antidote on the Church and the world through these revelations. You will be fired at and cry out in pain. You cannot do this divided - only in intense union will you receive the gift I am giving. *end of excerpt*

R. We have to have this wide vision for if we lose our focus who will do what He is asking us to do.

5. **R.** Will the wrath of God not flare up at the people and they will be stopped from the false worshipping and the dancing. Mary appeared on the building and she says, "You have made money your god".

December 19, 1996

Mary: My dear children, I give to you, my Son, Jesus, born in a stable in Bethlehem on Christmas morn. He is the Almighty God, the Light of the World.

I appear to you, my children, on a (former) bank in Florida. You have made money your god! Do you know how cold are your hearts? You turn away from my Son, Jesus, for your money. Your money is your god.

I am Mary, your Mother. I do not appear as I once appeared to you. I am asking you today to circulate my message given on a tape on the feast of Our Lady of Guadalupe, December 12, 1996. Please circulate this tape now. Give it to as many people as you can. I am Mary, your Mother. Please circulate my *Rosary Book.* *end of excerpt*

R. Mary is speaking about the first commandment that is being violated immensely. I cannot even get the messages of God the Father out. There has been great opposition especially to these messages of God the Father and the obedience is the thing that they are objecting to the most. This is the thing that God wants. The whole thing is that we must obey the will of God. This is the thing. What about parents and children? How is the obedience as far as children obeying their parents. They are told by the television not to obey their parents. They are told by the movies. They are told by the video games that they must think of themselves and do what they want. And the fourth commandment. Where is the fourth commandment? For the children, for the children are being taught. And this is what Mary cried out for all those months when she appeared everyday. Her beloved children and how their minds are being poisoned. We are the antidote for the poison but really we are being mistaken for the poison.

6. **R.** On March 27th, the message of God the Father said, "that the sufferings would be lessened and or averted if we did the prayers in the prayer manual and spread the Priestly Newsletter." And it is with great fear that I deliver these messages because I sit back and I get them and I shake inside after I get the messages. And the thing of it is, is it's like we are accountable if we are not delivering the messages. The message is this that we need to try to get especially this Falmouth message out to the earth, that people will respond. For it is indeed a warning and it's important that they hear the warning and its up to us to try to circulate this.

7. **R.** How was it at your Mass today? I can tell you how it was at my Mass. The Mass was packed. There were so many people there and there was a choir there and they were singing and they were celebrating two teachers that had

taught there many many years. The whole Church was very big and it was very packed but there was nothing from the heart that I felt in the Mass. Even the choir. The music was stiff and the words spoken were hard. They were disconnected and they were not in one heart as Our Lord wants us to be. It is through these messages that the people will turn to great love for God, that the Churches will be united in one mind and one heart. The more that we do what He asks us to do, it will help bring about the Reign of the Sacred Heart. It is majorly a task that God the Father has given to us but though we are small in number it is through His Might and through our prayers that this task will be accomplished. There is nothing to fear for He says, "I am." He is God. We are the ones that suffer at this moment at that moment. The devil presses on us. The devil is smart – he is crafty – he has tested people for centuries. He tempts our weakest point and tries to work us up. The picture that is on the Mary card that Mary asked me to make is a picture that was covered with an immense mist of Mary that I see when she appears. Its a vision that is so hard to even reproduce when somebody takes a picture of it. But the picture there which shows her face is not the same as the face on the other. So too, with the mist video. That mist video was a great gift. We must thank God for the gifts that He has given. Our Lady of Clearwater is a gift. These are great gifts that we are given in these writings and you know yourself that they have drawn you closer to the Heart of Jesus. You know what the Mass means to you. We must be so thankful to God. This is what God wants. He wants our love. God wants our thankfulness. God wants our courage to stand out there when the whole world seems like it is different than we are but to realize that God has given to us the antidote for the poison and to be strong for we are the soldiers, we are the apostles, we are the ones that He called out to and He said, "I am alive. I am alive. I am alive, on Ascension Thursday and I am treated like a dead object."

8. **R.** And so there is fear in our hearts many times for we are standing out there and we are alone. I can be in a Church with a thousand people and a thousand people are not in the Shepherds of Christ Movement. They do not have the same mission that I have to accomplish. I must do whatever it is that He has asked me to do. One thing to do when I am in

the Church and there are a thousand people in there is to consecrate that Church to the Sacred Heart of Jesus and the Immaculate Heart of Mary. To place all the people in that Church in the Sacred Heart and the Immaculate Heart of Mary. To ask God to help join them in this oneness. The Sacred Heart of Jesus will Reign. This is what we can do in every setting in our work places, wherever we are, to consecrate the world to the Sacred Heart of Jesus and the Immaculate Heart of Mary. We want Jesus alive in our hearts. We are to pray for great graces to be released. We pray for the priest, as he is speaking. We pray for Masses with heartfelt love. We pray for lectors and people at Mass. We pray for the consecration of men's hearts in Church to Jesus. So they are one in Jesus' Heart, not stiff and heartless. We pray the love of Jesus radiates from our voice, our face, our hands, our gestures. We pray for the love of Jesus in the hearts of the priests.

It is not words spoken that we throw at Jesus. It is a love affair that God wants with man. He created us to love Him and to love each other. And He speaks, "I am alive, I am alive, I am alive. Tell them Rita, tell them." And He let me suffer, immense suffering on Ascension Thursday. This was to carry the message to the world. You all know how you experience the depth of the love of the Heart of Jesus. And it is what propels us to go forward in the face of opposition, in the face of persecution. Jesus is God. And it is from our hearts that we speak and we want people to know Jesus, not be stiff, not focused on self, to focus on the Word of God, not ourselves.

Jesus: The emphasis must be on the love of God. This My beloved ones is your Mission. I am Jesus. I am calling you to carry the messages of My Heart to this world. Each one of you go to Mass every Sunday and you see the faithful get up and leave. I am longing and I am waiting for love from my faithful ones, for I give them Myself and they do not treasure the great gift that I have given to you.

R. We must spread these messages, Father's newsletter, the prayer chapters, spread devotion to the Sacred Heart of Jesus. We must see with the wide vision that the Father wants us to see with. We cannot be focused on the things that satan makes to try to divide us and avert us off our course. For souls are being lost as Mary said, day after day after day. Let our hearts be alive with the love of Jesus. Pray for the Reign of the Sacred Heart in men's hearts.

9. **Jesus:** You must not get discouraged. I need you to do this work. They persecuted Me, they mocked Me, they tore My flesh, and what had I done. You must obey Me even if you do not want to. OBEY GOD! If others try to stop you - block you – they are blocking Me. Do not ever underestimate the order of obedience. You must do My will. Listen to your heart and obey Me always. Your heart will gnaw at you until you obey. Take care of yourself and obey My will. You must always obey Me. You are given letters and directions from Me. I am Jesus, the Son of God – Listen to Me. You are My messenger here. You are being told what to do by God. If you do not obey Me, you do not feel good. You obey as I command you. Always obey your superiors. I am Jesus, the Son of God. This is not a myth. I am truly speaking to you. I will protect you child. Surrender to Me. You must realize that the very hairs of your head are numbered. Accept all your discomforts and learn the lessons I so sweetly teach you, sufferings I allow. I ardently love you.

   R. Today is just so clear that Adam and Eve committed this sin against His will. And that they ate of this fruit of this tree. Jesus Christ is the New Adam. The Son of God is truly present in the Blessed Sacrament. We've got these golden calves that we're worrying all about. The first focus is not on God, but is on all these other things.

10. **R.** And so He ascended into heaven and He gives us this: I will be with you, that is My promise.

    The prayers in the prayer manual are so important, our prayers are so important. God gives us the Mass. Wow! God gives us the Bread of Life – the Scriptures, the Eucharist.

    Song: *Come Holy Spirit*

The Descent of the Holy Spirit

1. **R.** This is Genesis 6: and it's speaking of Noah.

Genesis 6: 5-8

> Yahweh saw that human wickedness was great on earth and that human hearts contrived nothing but wicked schemes all day long. Yahweh regretted having made

human beings on earth and was grieved at heart. And Yahweh said, 'I shall rid the surface of the earth of the human beings whom I created – human and animal, the creeping things and the birds of heaven – for I regret having made them.' But Noah won Yahweh's favour.

2. **R.** Thy shalt not kill.

3. **R.** The All-Night Message is so important that when you study this message, that you know what He is teaching us. This Apostles Manual is filled with what we need to know. And to pray with all your hearts that the Mass Book gets out because today I could see again why He stresses that, that book must be out. The Mass is so important. We are to be full of love at Mass, with hearts of love in which we are all joined in the Mass in one mind and in one heart. We are like stiffs in the pew, ununited to each other. I saw some youth go out of the Church and the one had the most awful look on his face, he was about 10 years old with the Eucharist in his mouth. And then the three walked out of the Church and I remember a person in the Movement saw a little kid take the Eucharist out of his mouth once and laughed at it. This is the truth. Look at this. The Almighty God is truly present in His Divinity and humanity. We must teach children to love the Eucharist. I cry out at the Lamb of God in sorrow for our sins and beg for mercy and peace. We cry out to Him with all our heart, Lamb of God, who take away the sins of the world, have mercy on us. Beg Him. I just cry so much because I want at that point, at the Lamb of God, for Him to just outpour His mercy on us for our sins. We must make reparation to God. Do you realize that one person can pray for great grace for the whole Church. He did not destroy the whole earth at the time of Noah. One heart that is faithfully loving Him has such intercessory power. If I am a person in a Church and I am fervently loving Him, I can help to bring down great grace. I thought today in the Mass how I need to treasure the Bible and know so much more about it. The Father gave His Son as a sacrifice for love of us. We can pray deeply to our Father, united to Jesus, the Son of God - in the Holy Spirit at Mass. Wow! He's taught us. He's taught us how to be so united to Him that great grace will be outpoured. For we know how to pray that great grace is outpoured. It is the way that it will be in the new era. When

Fr. Carter celebrates the Mass I want to cry. We cannot underestimate our own intercessory power. This is what Jesus is telling to us. With our whole heart we pray for the Reign of the Sacred Heart, holy priests, and the renewal of the Church and the world. What an outpouring of abundant grace we will receive when instead of focusing on our toes or whatever else we focus on, what Susie said, and what she's doing and etc. and etc. that goes through our minds but we realize the power when we give ourselves to God and unite in the Holy Sacrifice of the Mass. And the other thing is that the more we realize this the more we will teach it to others in the Movement, our apostles that we visit. We can be this powerful force where God is operating through us with His grace. But it is in the believing. It is not in the abandoning the ship, giving up the post no matter how we're suffering or what's going on. It's knowing the power of the Mass. But our hearts must be hearts fixed in Jesus' Heart and Mary's heart.

We are united in our Morning Offering to the Masses going on around the world every day in all we do.

SAY DAILY

GOD, I GIVE YOU MY LIFE IN UNION WITH THE MASS AS AN OFFERING FOR THE SOULS, THE CHURCH AND THE PRIESTS.

HELP US!

4. **R.** And so I see His eyes on the picture that is on the front of the *Apostles Manual.* I see that Jesus when I go to Communion and I cry because it is Jesus there that gives Himself to me. I walk away from there realizing that God is inside of me and He has given Himself to me in a most immense way and there the grace is outpoured. The grace for what's in our hearts, we pray for grace for the renewal of the priesthood, the renewal of the Church and the world, for Fr. Carter, for us to be doing the will of God and to be loving Him and appreciating all that He's given to us and thanking Him and being ever closer to that which our heart desires, which is Him. What great gifts He has given that He has

lifted this veil for us and He has allowed us to know Him so intimately, so that we could carry this light out to others. We are the bearers of this great news that God has given to us.

5. **R.** Thy kingdom come, thy will be done on earth as it is in heaven. And every time we pray this Our Father, how dear the words, Our Father, Our Father. I know Him in a way that I never knew Him in my whole life of blindness. And I see myself now as a little child in His arms and I'm being loved by Him. And in that love I'm telling Him my cares. And the thing of it is, is I know that He's God the Father, all-powerful and all Mighty, and He's listening. And when I go to Mass, being this little child in the Father's arms, and uniting in the sacrifice that is most pleasing to Him, the sacrifice of His Son. And I'm asking Him for these things, for Fr. Carter, for the priests, for the Church, the world, the Reign of the Sacred Heart, but the greatest thing of it is, is I know that He is answering our prayers, that great things are happening because of our belief and it's not me, it's His Might. It's not that I have to worry if everybody in the church is doing their thing. It's me being focused on Him. And even in the suffering because I want to be so one with Him, and sometimes He allows me to suffer so immensely during the Mass, but I fight distraction and pray for help. He said that great grace is released when you are suffering in the Mass. But it's the desire in our heart to try to focus on Him, to want Him more than anything. We pray for grace for the renewal of the Church and the world and the priests. We pray to be deeply united to Him and each other. We pray for the Shepherds of Christ Movement to flourish.

A Prayer Before The Holy Sacrifice Of The Mass

Let me be a holy sacrifice and unite with God in the sacrament of His greatest love.

I want to be one in Him in this act of love, where He gives Himself to me and I give myself as a sacrifice to Him. Let me be a holy sacrifice as I become one with Him in this my act of greatest love to Him.

Let me unite with Him more, that I may more deeply love Him. May I help make reparation to His adorable Heart and the heart of His Mother, Mary. With greatest love, I offer myself to You and pray that You will accept my sacrifice of greatest love. I give myself to You and unite in Your gift of Yourself to me. Come and possess my soul.

Cleanse me, strengthen me, heal me. Dear Holy Spirit act in the heart of Mary to make me more and more like Jesus.

Father, I offer this my sacrifice, myself united to Jesus in the Holy Spirit to You. Help me to love God more deeply in this act of my greatest love.

Give me the grace to grow in my knowledge, love and service of You and for this to be my greatest participation in the Mass. Give me the greatest graces to love You so deeply in this Mass, You who are so worthy of my love.

- *Mass Book*, December 27, 1995

6. Song: *Come Holy Spirit*

   R. And the apostles locked themselves in the upper room because they were afraid. But when the Holy Spirit descended upon them, they went out and so many were converted. We pray to reach people to pray for the priests, the Church and the world. We have to keep praying to the Holy Spirit to work in our heart so that we too will go forth fearlessly. When we are persecuted, what is my special gift that I have been given to help accomplish this task He is asking us to do? We pray for this devotion to the Sacred Heart and that He Reigns in the hearts of men.

7. **R.** We pray the rosary - living the mysteries of Jesus and Mary's lives in our life. We as the apostles live the mysteries of this rosary in our life. We are talking about this mystery, how the Holy Spirit descending upon them, sent them forth to go out and to spread the Good News. We are being sent forth to go out to help renew the Church and the world. Men, today, are thirsting for the Good News that has been dimmed in their hearts. We are living these mysteries in our lives.

8. Hail Mary
9. Hail Mary
10. Hail Mary

    Song: *Immaculate Mary*

The Assumption of the Blessed Virgin Mary into Heaven

1. **From the Apostles Manual - Excerpt from December 22, 1996**

   Jesus: Brace yourselves in the Shepherds of Christ. You want to be Christ-like. Is this the true desire in your heart or is it just words like the other words you give to Me?

   Brace yourselves. I will lead the way with My rod and My staff, but you must be strong to follow for the way is rocky and the rocks are sharp. They cut through to the soul. They cut through to your heart.

   You will be brought to your knees, you will beg for Me, you will be molded and helped with in the abundant grace flowing from My Heart. My little shepherd, so willful and so stupid in your ways, but I love you just the same to My death, child. I love you and you do not see that all I give to you is for your good.

2. **R.** Then He says, and He says this to all of us.

From the Apostles Manual - Excerpt from December 22, 1996 continues

Jesus: I am not angry with you, My messenger. You must suffer now to write My messages for the world. How could you write had you not experienced My pain in your soul? You are My hand, that I am using to write the messages of My Heart for the world. My Heart was crowned with thorns. So, too, will your heart be pierced and wanting to bleed. Bleed, little heart, My Heart bled for you.

And the moon will be covered with blood. It was the blood of the Lamb and it poured forth on a sinful world to cleanse them of their sin, and I give you My Body and Blood in the Mass and I am ignored.

He slapped their hands and He smite their cheeks and they laughed in their pain and continued their willful ways. But the day of reckoning is at hand and I will separate the sheep from the goats and the sheep I will take home with Me. The goats will know a day as they never knew before for My justice will prevail.

When I warned they would not turn from their evil ways and

I could not reach them. They walked as blind men down the path of destruction and who would have thought that the end of the road was so near. And at the end of the road they continued to walk for in the darkness they could not see and they fell into an everlasting pit of doom and suffering.

Justice will prevail. I am a good God. Justice and truth will kiss. When I gave to them My warning they said, "Oh no, Lord," and continued their sinful ways.

The time is at hand. My efforts and yours were in vain. I will wipe their sick smiles from their evil mouths and they will suffer forever the death of the soul.

I will not have mercy on these hard-necked cowards who thought, in their pride, they could smite Me. I will throw the book at them and they will suffer for their sinful ways.

Woe to them who led My children astray. Woe to them. They will burn the eternal death of intense suffering for the murder of My young. And who will help them then? They will know a death beyond all deaths and suffering beyond all suffering. For a few moments of pleasure, they lost their souls forever.

3. **From the Apostles Manual - Excerpt from December 22, 1996 continues**

Jesus: I am a just and merciful God. I give water to quench your thirst, I bathe you in My Divine love, but to the evil doers, I will curse their name and wipe them from the face of the earth. I have spoken. Justice will prevail. My hand is struck with power. The senseless ones will know My might.

Who will you call? You said 'no' to God and He struck you for your sinful ways.

All honor and glory be to God for He has visited His people and they cast Him aside. I will light the earth with My love and the dark hearts will curse the night for they will be no more.

And justice will flourish in His time and fullness of peace forever.

I have spoken. The deaf will not hear. My hand is the hand of God and it is struck with power.

I say to the grass to grow and it grows, to the sun to shine and it shines and to you I say, "Be ready for you know not the day nor the hour. I come as a thief in the night to take your soul home to Me. Will you be ready or will you be caught unprepared?"

Prepare ye a way to the Lord. Make ready His steps, My shepherds. I guard you but you will suffer. You must be strong and not caught off guard.

Purify your souls for I am coming and the earth will know My light this Christmas for I will shine in the hearts of the just. I will shine on My shepherds this Christmas. My light will shine in the hearts of those consecrated to My Heart and the heart of My Mother. *end of excerpts*

4. **R.** And the Falmouth card is so clear because He said in this message that He will stop or lessen the sufferings if we do the prayers. So we have circulated this card so that people will know. And this is what He said will help us immensely if we do this.

5. **From April 10, 1997**

   God the Father: You must release this information. …I am asking the faithful to begin prayer chapters, centered in consecration, and praying the rosary… Lastly, but of major importance to the renewal of the Church and the world, I am asking that the *Priestly Newsletter* be made available in abundance, that the apostles spread these newsletters to the priests and encourage them to read them. I am asking the *Priestly Newsletter Book* be published as soon as possible and circulated to all priests and bishops in the United States. I am the Father. You must pray as never before and join in one mind and one heart... *end of excerpt*

   R. We have to focus on working out our problems with one another and working to full potential, because our whole mission is to be one and to spread that to the earth. We cannot deviate and start to get divided. A house divided against itself will not stand. God the Father does not want any division in our Movement. And He doesn't want any division between us so we have to work out our problems and remain in one mind and one heart, for we're the little happy family that He has called.

6. **R.** And Mary was taken up to heaven but she is with us at every second in everything that we are doing. We go to her heart and we dwell in her heart and the Heart of Jesus and

we are working with our whole lives to help to carry out the Father's plan.

7. **R.** We are the apostles of this new era. It is a great mission and we are forever thankful to the Almighty God for this great intimacy, love and friendship that He has given to us with Him and with one another.

8. **R.** And so the apostles travel and we went to Toledo and there are the lights that are shining on the tree there. And we went to Dale and there are the lights that shine on the tree there. And the 13th, many come to us and they take so many materials back to their place for as in Toledo, so many of those people had all of the material because Sue Hicks carried back all of the materials from the 13th. And we work and we work and we feel weary and we feel like falling on our face and then a man comes up and a man says that he was going to go to a psychologist because it was so bad and the priest told him that Sue Hicks had given him the Blue Book and he started reading it and he has never had to go and he spreads them all over and does the Movement. And another man came up and said he just finished the Third Blue Book and the Blue Books have changed his life, that he reads them all the time and lives by the Blue Books. And there are all these people out there that are living according to the way that God wants them to according to His will. And we're down there packing them up and sending them out and not really feeling all the results. But there are so many calls and people are crying and thanking us. And there were people crying yesterday because of the grace that Jesus gave to them. And we are kind of numb to it for we get the grace over and over again. But in all the suffering as He brings us to our knee and He pokes us around as He pokes us into order with His rod and staff and gets us to do what we're suppose to do. In all of that there is so much good that's being accomplished and believe it or not if we do not do it a lot of souls will be affected.

9. Hail Mary

10. Hail Mary

R. Mary is the Queen of Peace and Mary has given to us the directions to help to have peace on this earth.

Song: *Hail Holy Queen*

The Coronation of Mary as Queen of Heaven and Earth

1. **Excerpt from December 19, 1996**

   Mary: Oh, my children, my little children of light, the time is nigh and many will be lost forever. I appeared and warned and told all to mind their ways and come to the Heart of my Son and they said "No, my Lady, not for you or any mother. We are children of darkness and that we remain, for we seek our pleasure by day and feast on sin all night and when you called, mother, we laughed at your Son and ignored Him and His ways." And He called and His call fell on deaf ears.

2. **Excerpt from December 19, 1996 continues**

   Mary: Please, my children of light, come to my heart now for although you walked next to the children of darkness. I smite the dragon that whirled around you and protected you in my heart and you will now feast on the glories of His Kingdom, my little children of light. *end of excerpt*

3. Hail Mary
4. Hail Mary
5. Hail Mary
6. **R.** There will be a great era in which the king will reign on His throne as never before. He will reign in their hearts. Men will fervently love God and each other. Now the world is living in a dim light. Oh, it is there, the Mass, the sacraments, the priests. Oh they are a people walking in darkness. They are blind. They do not see. They do not know. And so the lady appeared at Fatima and she told them what would bring about this great era and promised that it would come. Mary told them the secrets to bring it about. The Father sent her, the messenger, the woman clothed as the sun and men did not listen. And the streets are dark and dingy and the men on the earth will remain in a half-lighted fog when the day could be bright. Only in giving themselves in consecration will they see the light. Only in giving themselves to Mary will they be brought forth, the children of light. Only in going to her pure and sinless heart will we be able to unite in such depth in the heart of Christ that we will know Him and His love and He will live in us in a profound union.
7. **R.** Mary is the key. The treasures promised and foretold in

all the books in the Bible: Thy kingdom come, thy will be done, on earth as it is in heaven.

8. **R.** And the children of light marched into the new era. They were living as one holy, happy family, as the Father intended according to His will, and relishing the great gifts of the era.
9. **R.** The light reigned in their hearts. We spread the light when we encourage priests, religious, men, women, and children to consecrate their hearts. We are working hand and hand. The veil will be removed and people will know God much more. To know Him as we should, in immense love and adoration given to Him.
10. Hail Mary

6/7/97

Two Visions at Falmouth

Rita: I had two visions on June 8, 1995 of Falmouth Farm

(1) Flood; (2) Fire

Fire of His love

Fire - destruction - Medjugorje looked as if hills were burned

and June 8, 1995

Mary apparition - flooded the earth

Fire can be the fire of Jesus' Heart or Fire can be fire that destroys

She knew many would fall and rise from Simeon's prophecy.

Reference: Luke 2: 25-35

Her Immaculate Heart - some holy
some lost

June 9
I had two visions yesterday
at Falmouth
Saw flame as bright brillant, heard it go pluff then it came out of a square box sitting on a hardwood floor that looked like the floor in the Sorrowful Mother Chapel. The Chapel was empty some things on the floor in the distance. Room was bright. FLOOR was the center

(2) Saw waterway + trees, nothing commercial, all Gods things

TALL TREES

There was a little tiny blue sky

Then I saw water as a falls going into water

water

Vision of a Flood

R. Dear Father,

We have made other things our king and it is as if we shout it to Jesus in the tabernacle – we have no king but Caesar. We have our lives, our whims, our money. It goes back to the first commandment, "I, the Lord, am your God. You shall not have other gods besides me."

Man has rebelled against God in salvation history. This is what the Father said - "you don't keep the commandments."

Many times, Sunday is not a day of rest, it is a day of recreation, work and football. In many homes, the king of Sunday is the football game. In many homes the family is pushed aside. Church can be forgotten and the emphasis on football and other things. Is it God's day?

Is one hour a week - too long for Church on Sunday, Sunday the Lord's day.

The Falmouth flood showed how temporary are the items we hold as our idols. Our T.V.'s are subject to water damage – the T.V. can be an idol, the video games, food, alcohol, sex, can all be idols.

What is the first commandment: I, the Lord, am your God. You shall not have other gods besides me. Sunday is His day. Do we balk about one hour spent with Him a week? What do we run for, that is our idol?

> "Nothing is more practical than finding God, that is, than falling in a love in a quite absolute, final way. What you are in love with, what seizes your imagination will affect everything. It will decide what will get you out of bed in the mornings, what you will do with your evenings, how you spend your weekends, what you read, who you know, what breaks your heart, and what amazes you with joy and gratitude. Fall in love, stay in love, and it will decide everything."
>
> Pedro Arrupe

What do we work for? If at this second I was told I would die, would I die for my T.V.? Would I die for my job? Many hours are spent at the job – is the job, a job so I can love or do I live for the job? Does the job give me the dignity that I feel or do I do the job because it is God's will and my dignity comes from being a child of God?

Oh, my Father, help me to know God - the greatest treasure there is.

May Thy Kingdom come on earth as you will. What idols do we hold? God's Kingdom is not a kingdom based on idols – God is to be first in our lives!

So Mary says, "you have made money your god." We are to be obedient to God.

God is telling us what to do. We must throw our face to the floor and beg for forgiveness for our offenses as a sinful race against Him.

We must make reparation. We must put our hearts into His. He is the King of our hearts. When He is the king of our hearts, He will reign on the throne. Now, how do we pray - is it with our hearts? What do we hold most dear? What do we spend our time, our money on?

It is now 7:48, the packed car lot outside the Church has now emptied out in several minutes. Jesus gives us Himself in the Eucharist.

The Blue Books were given by Jesus to teach about Jesus in the Eucharist. Jesus is not honored and adored as He should be. Every vision of Mary given was to lead people to Jesus.

The angel of Fatima told of this great time of indifference and abuses against God in the Eucharist. Instead of Him being honored and adored, He is treated, as He says, "by many, I am treated like a dead object."

Remember thou must keep holy the Sabbath day. Holy - what does it mean to keep a day holy? It means a day consecrated to God.

The false idols of the people have permeated the minds of many of the children. They do not even see the light for they have disobeyed God and they continue to do so.

The 10 commandments were given by God as Commands We Must Follow! They are not suggestions, but commands. Moses went up the mountain to receive the commandments.

Exodus 31: 12-15

Yahweh then said to Moses, 'Speak to the Israelites and say, "You will keep my Sabbaths properly, for this is a sign between myself and you for all your generations to come, so that you will know that it is I, Yahweh, who sanctify you. You will keep the Sabbath, then; you will regard it as holy. Anyone who profanes it will be put to death; anyone who does any work on that day will be outlawed from his people. Work must be done for six days, but the seventh day will be a day of complete rest, consecrated to Yahweh. Anyone who works on the Sabbath day will be put to death.

Reference: Exodus 32: 15-20

The Ten Commandments

1. I, the Lord, am your God. You shall not have other gods besides me.
2. You shall not take the name of the Lord, your God, in vain.
3. Remember to keep holy the Sabbath day.
4. Honor your father and your mother.
5. You shall not kill.
6. You shall not commit adultery.
7. You shall not steal.
8. You shall not bear false witness against your neighbor.
9. You shall not covet your neighbor's wife.
10. You shall not covet anything that belongs to your neighbor.

R. He saw the calf and the dancing. With that Moses' wrath flared up so that he threw the tablets down and broke them.

Father, is this like what is happening? God is here and we are worshiping the golden calf.

Will the wrath of God not flare up at the people and they will be stopped from the false worshiping and dancing?

Mary appeared on the building and said, "you have made money your god."

December 19, 1996 Message from Mary

Mary: My dear children, I give to you my Son Jesus, born in a stable in Bethlehem on Christmas morn'. He is the Almighty God, the Light of the World.

I appear to you, my children, on a (former) bank in Florida. You have made money your god! Do you know how cold are your hearts? You turn away from my Son, Jesus, for your money. Your money is your god.

I am Mary, your Mother. I do not appear as I once appeared to you. I am asking you today to circulate my message given on a tape on the feast of Our Lady of Guadalupe, December 12, 1996. Please circulate this tape now. Give it to as many people as you can. I am Mary, your Mother. Please circulate my *Rosary Book.*

end of excerpt

R. I cannot even get these messages of God, the Father, out. There has been great opposition. We must believe and fight to make them public.

Falmouth is a warning. Mary appeared on the mountain in Medjugorje and Mary appeared at Falmouth – both towns near by suffered.

March 27, 1997: We have sent...see the message on the card.

March 27, 1997 - Message from God the Father

We have sent you great gifts and they have not been accepted and obeyed. What is left but to send you greatest sufferings? I sent My Son to you. He has given you the most tender messages of His love (*Tell My People, Rosaries From the Hearts of Jesus and Mary, & God's Blue Books*) to bring about the Reign of His Most Sacred Heart. You have not appreciated the gift we have given you. I gave you your Mother. She appeared and she warned you. Falmouth is an example of the sufferings that will befall the earth. I sent you gifts from heaven and you continue to offend and ignore your God. I will chastise the earth with the greatest sufferings. You did not respond to the gifts, as did the people of Falmouth not respond to the gifts given. You will now receive the chastisement that will cause you to sit up and take notice. Falmouth is a warning to this earth. *end of excerpt*

R. January 18, 1997: I tell you to read the accounts of Noah - see message on the card.

January 18, 1997 - Message from God the Father

...I tell you to ***read the account concerning Noah***. Nowhere in history has God been offended as He is this day by the sinful world. You will suffer a fate for the offenses against God.

...Mary appeared at Fatima to warn you, the sinful children, how they were offending God, but you did not listen. The war (WWII) did not change the hearts of many evil men. I warn you through My beloved daughter Mary. You did not heed her warnings. Disobedience against the mother I gave you displeases Me greatly. Mary is the Mother of all children. Mary is the gift from Me, but you are willful and abuse the gift I send you...Disobey My messenger, ignore your Mother, ignore the Son in these messages...My Plan will unfold through the Shepherds of Christ Movement. I am talking through these messages given by My Son and Mary to tell you how to accomplish this task of carrying out My plan. *end of excerpt*

R. Great gifts were given to us. He has allowed sufferings to get our attention. We make our own problems many times because of willfulness.

God's Covenant with Noah:

Reference: Genesis 8: 20-22

Reference: Genesis 9: 8-15

R. God gave the sign of the rainbow as a Covenant with Noah.

Reference: Genesis 6: 5-13

R. God flooded the earth at the time of Noah.

R. At this point I remember Jesus telling me to read the rosary of July 16, 1995. He said it was very important. Mary said the rosaries of the summer of 1995 were important to know for the times to come. There were messages in them you need to know.

Jesus talked about stars falling from the sky and the sun ceasing to shine.

On the day of the flood, March 3, 1997, Jesus talked about shaking the tree and the rotten fruit falling off - "then all that would remain would be fruit of heaven"- meaning men who are children of light with consecrated hearts to the Hearts of Jesus and Mary.

God said barren branches He cuts off and makes them clean. The days of heavenly fruit are at hand, when the Church brings forth fruit of heaven, not barren branches.

It is a time in which grace will flow copiously through all the branches and bring forth great fruit.

Now the tree is filled with love branches or branches that are withered and dying. Many are not branches bearing fruit for they are barely staying alive themselves.

Adam and Eve:

Genesis 3: 23-24

So Yahweh God expelled him from the garden of Eden, to till the soil from which he had been taken. He banished the man, and in front of the garden of Eden he posted the great winged creatures and the fiery flashing sword, to guard the way to the tree of life.

Genesis 2: 9, 16-17

From the soil, Yahweh God caused to grow every kind of tree, enticing to look at and good to eat, with the tree of life in the middle of the garden, and the tree of the knowledge of good and evil.

Then Yahweh God gave the man this command, 'You are free to eat of all the trees in the garden. But of the tree of the knowledge of good and evil you are not to eat;

John 15: 1-2

I am the true vine, and my Father is the vinedresser. Every branch in me that bears no fruit he cuts away, and every branch that does bear fruit he prunes to make it bear even more.

R. The angel of Fatima gave the following messages concerning the Body and Blood of Jesus horribly outraged.

From the *Spirituality of Fatima*

In the fall of the same year, the angel visited the visionaries a final time:

The angel came...bearing a golden chalice in one hand and a Host above it in the other. The amazed children noticed that drops of blood were falling from the Host into the chalice. Presently, the angel left both suspended in mid-air and prostrated himself on the ground, saying this beautiful prayer: *"Most Holy Trinity, Father, Son and Holy Spirit, I adore You profoundly. I offer You the most precious Body, Blood, Soul and Divinity of Jesus Christ, present in all tabernacles of the world, in reparation for the outrages, sacrileges, and indifference by which He is offended. By the infinite merits of the Sacred Heart of Jesus and [the intercession of] the Immaculate Heart of Mary, I beg of Thee the conversion of poor sinners."*[5]

Sr. Lucia relates how the angel gave them Communion:

Then, rising, he took the chalice and the Host in his hand. He gave the Sacred Host to me and shared the Blood from the chalice between Jacinta and Francisco, saying as he did so:

"Take and drink the Body and Blood of Jesus Christ, horribly outraged by ungrateful men! Make reparation for their crimes and console your God."[6]

5. *Our Lady's Peace Plan*, op cit., p.2. (The words in brackets are my own-added for clarification).

6. *Fatima in Lucia's Own Words*, op cit., pp.64-65.

R. We should obey. Jesus gives us the tree of life.

The Bread of Life is the Word and the Eucharist.

Sing: *I Am the Bread of Life*

Reference: John 15: 5

Excerpt from March 3, 1997 -
Day Falmouth Flooded Early Morning

Jesus: And I will shake you on your tree and you will fall to the ground as rotten fruit and all that will remain will be the fruit of heaven.

Reference: Wisdom 15: 15-19

Reference: Wisdom 16: 1-7

R. Tree of life - Good and bad fruit

Adam - Bad fruit - willful

New Adam - Jesus: Good fruit - Will of God

See Diagram

Some say – 'We have no king except Caesar.' *John 19: 15*

R. They put Jesus on a cross.

Jesus is the Bread of Life –

We eat His Body – We drink His Blood.

Sing: *I Am the Bread of Life*

Reference: Luke 6: 43

Reference: Luke 13: 6-9

Excerpt from December 29, 1996 from the Apostles Manual

Jesus: You did not see her stand at the foot of My cross and see her weep for in her Heart she knew from the prophecy of Simeon that some of her children would rise and some would fall and she knew, under the cross, before I officially gave you My Mother in My dying words, that many of her beloved children would be lost forever and she knew the fate to come.

For the hell you will have, oh children of darkness, those who refused the grace-filled womb of My Mother and yours, the hell you will experience is forever! For a few pleasures in the world below you said 'no' to the Lady clothed as the sun and the dragon came and he wiped you off the face of the earth and he took you home with him. You did not go to the heavenly home I had planned for you where there is eternal light and life. You went to the anguishing pit of darkness and she heard your cries, anguishing cries under the cross – her little children – and she cried, "I stood beneath the cross of My son and I cried."

R. The Father is angered. We have rejected the Two Hearts.

Excerpt from January 18, 1997

> **God the Father:** I am sending water, rain to quench your thirst, My beloved children of light; I am sending fire to burn the fields for the sinful children, they will suffer drought and will fall to the ground dead, they will know fire, they will know the wrath of God. For I speak and I am ignored.

Jesus: I give you this Mission. It is a great Mission. You are to focus on the directions given in these messages.

I cannot make you see the importance of the Shepherds of Christ Mission to the renewal of the Church and the world. The devil will create doubt and confusion to stop you and Fr. Carter from this Mission. You have grown immensely since April 5, 1997. Your Movement must be centered in prayer, praying for the priests and the renewal of the Church and the world, spreading the Priestly Newsletters. Other visionaries will cause distraction and take you from this focus. Your focus is to give the messages for the Shepherds of Christ Movement. If people come who want you to serve them or help them with another mission you must be very careful. You must focus on the job at hand. You have much work to do. Jobs that take your apostles away from the directions I give you must be carefully discerned.

People who come who want you to help support them are not there to serve this Mission. I have given you the directions to follow. Prayer chapters must be started in the Churches and the world. The Church, family and school must be reached with the Consecration. I have asked you to spread the Priestly Newsletter to the priests. Your Mission is clear.

I have asked you to spread the Mass Books and the Blue Books. This will help those in the world to love the Eucharist. I want the world to turn to Me in the Eucharist. These are My messages to lead the world to the Eucharist, to lead the world to the most intimate love with My Sacred Heart.

Do not be led astray by other missions. My directions are clearly stated. Your job is your job, given by Me. It is a great honor. If you do not do this job, if you are spread too thin, it will not get done.

I beg you to focus on the messages, to not leave your post. Your directions are given here.

6/8/97

Fr. Carter and My Writings, Antidote for Poison

R. Dear Father,

Jesus said our main focus must be in putting out your writings and my writings. They are the antidote for the poison in the Church and the world.

We both need to focus on this joint Mission.

Jesus said more and more distractions would creep into our lives, trying to divide us. Anything that divides us will cause problems for our Mission. Our main Mission is to help bring about the Reign of the Sacred Heart through these writings.

6/8/97

Fr. Carter and Rita's Writings as One

Jesus: My dear priest,

You must majorly focus on this Mission. The main thrust of messages are given through the messages of Rita. You must focus on this Mission with Rita. Rita must focus on this Mission with you. You must take time to discuss the messages received and in the rosaries.

No matter what is happening, your main focus is to be united. You must work to get the Mass Book out. I am telling you to pray together and to discuss the messages together. You must attend daily Mass whenever possible and pray together. Anything that changes this is not working toward My will. You must be patient and keep this as your goal.

6/9/97

Jesus Says Your Joint Writings, Fr. Carter and Rita, are Important

Message from Jesus

My dear priest,

I have given messages before that told you of the joint Mission. I have majorly given messages for the Shepherds of Christ Movement through the messenger Rita. Satan will continue to cause distraction, division and confusion by giving messages contrary to the Father's Plan through other visionaries.

Your main focus is to act jointly in this Mission to renew the Church and the world. You will receive messages from others that will distract you and take your focus from the many messages I have given to you.

I am telling you that your Mission is a joint Mission to be the two greatest apostles to help bring about the Reign of My Heart. The new era greatly depends on your joint effort to come forth with the antidote for the poison in the Church and the world. When the world reaches the peak of pain I will pour down the antidote with these messages, your writings and

Rita's writings. You act in one mind and one heart joined with My Heart and the heart of My Mother to help bring about the age of the Two Hearts.

Satan has caused major confusion and damage to your Movement because of faulty messages given through other visionaries manipulated by men and led to you by men. Satan wants to delay the procedure to move forward in any way he can. He wants to confuse the issues.

Any distraction created which takes the focus off of the main Mission to publish these writings is a delay tactic used by satan. Satan can give similar messages through visionaries that can seem to be authentic messages. Then he will begin to change the messages and make major confusion. Satan gives conflicting messages to the authentic messages and the confusion begins.

To avert this problem any further, I am giving this message. The message is this: your message is a joint message with Rita to help bring about the Reign of My Sacred Heart. You must focus on these messages. Satan will try to get you to put your focus on other messages, to stop the progress of this Mission. There are other priests that can handle other visionaries and their messages. You must focus on your joint Mission. I am giving this message to you and to Rita. Rita is not to discern the writings of others or to help publish them. It is distracting to the Mission I am giving to her. She is not to get involved with others writings. If people legitimately want to enter the priesthood and be a minister for Shepherds of Christ they will be a help not an added responsibility.

There are 21 books of unpublished messages given. There are directions given that have not been followed. I have begged, I have pleaded, I have given you great sufferings to get your attention. You must not give into the distractions of satan to take you from your post. You must stay focused on this Mission. Other visionaries could cause great confusion. Your Mission is given as a great gift to this world. I am asking you to study the messages I have given here. You must realize the great Mission I have given to you both and how important it is to the renewal of the Church and the world.

Others will come to distract you. Other messages will come through other visionaries to get you majorly off course. These messages have already damaged your Movement.

Please, you must learn to focus on your joint Mission and limit your activities to trying to organize, discuss and publish all that you can of the material I have given to you.

Do not be distracted by the present situation. Please continue to get the *Priestly Newsletter Book* in the hands of as many priests as possible. Please spread the Blue Book messages. These messages change hearts. Many are spending intimate time with Me after communion and before the tabernacle because of these messages. Your job is the most important job. You must focus on what I have told you to do.

I tell you again, doing a good thing is not, necessarily, doing the Father's will. You must study the messages. I beg you, I beg you, to study the messages and pray for the grace to do the Father's will.

Do not judge your actions by the events of men around you.

See the big picture. Your joint Mission will majorly bring about the Reign of My Sacred Heart. You must study these messages to know what the Father, the Son, the Holy Spirit and the Blessed Mother are telling you. Your Mission is defined here. Other messages are great distractions if they take your focus off of this Mission.

You must work together and work on the plan given jointly to you. I am giving you both the plan for the Shepherds of Christ Movement. You will work harmoniously to accomplish this work.

Satan can infiltrate your movement in faulty messages.

Note: for Rita

Jesus: The messages given for the Shepherds of Christ Movement are given through Rita and Fr. Carter.

Jesus Speaks - to his Priest:

I give you this message as a warning. You will have tremendous sufferings if you do not heed this warning.

Messages given through other visionaries will cause great sufferings in the Movement unless you focus on the ones I am giving through the messenger Rita.

I beg you to study the Father's messages and the all-night message, and the *Apostles Manual.*

You must keep your focus on these messages. These messages are of great importance to the development and expansion of the Movement.

My Heart will Reign and My Mother's heart will triumph. You are receiving the major source to bring this about. You must not focus on anything that distracts you from this end.

You, Fr. Carter, and Rita, have a joint Mission to help bring about the renewal in the priesthood, the Church, and the world. You must focus on the Plan of the Father. Your writings will go down from generation to generation after you are gone. You must focus on this – see the big picture.

The Father speaks:

I AM WHO AM, without a beginning, without an end. You do not comprehend the importance of this Mission. I beg you to focus on your joint writings and your joint Mission. I beg you to study these revelations. You are to study the material given, information is given that you must know to do what I am asking you to do, information is given to deepen your understanding into My Plan and to help to bring the message of the scriptures into the hearts of priests.

Please, I am the Father. Please study the revelations I give to you.

I love you, My priest-son. It is in the persecution and suffering you will be strengthened for this Mission of renewing the Church and the world. You are a pillar of light to this world. Do not worry, My Plan will unfold through your joint Mission to help bring the love of My Son's Sacred Heart to the world.

Message on the back.

I Am, Who Am. I am All Powerful, Almighty. You must focus on this Mission given to you. You have received writings between both of you to help the Church. To help lead to renewal and to maintain a loving relationship with God, a relationship of great intimacy that man has never known before.

Men must obey My Will. I am the Father. I have spoken. The world is very willful and disobedient. They have run amuck. You will be persecuted, but you will withstand the persecution and the world will turn their hearts to God through your joint writings. Do Not Fear - I am God. I love you, my priest-son. I love you, my appointed priest to renew the Church.

You are "My Father" - you are a holy Father, living a life of holy priesthood in which My Son Jesus ministers to the people through you.

Any person coming in anger and demanding to be heard is not from God. Do not respond to angry people. Do not act because another approaches you with irritability, anger, or force. This is not the way of My Will. When you are approached by one demanding their way, do not act, it is a sign - anger is NOT from Me.

I love you. I am the Father.

6/9/97

All Different Love Relationships

R. Mom –

Dad –

Spouse –

Brother –

Love that binds.

Every love relationship teaches us about love. We have imperfect love relationships with others. We are wounded. We can relate to God the Father as Our Father; to Jesus, as the

Bridegroom of our Soul and to Mary, as our Mother. I know God: Father, Son, and Holy Spirit – three Persons in one God.

We have all these love relationships from the moment of conception. When we are born our Mother and Father and those around us teach us about love. We are taught about love from imperfect people - we learn defectively about love. We are wounded in our heart because if we are loved improperly it wounds our heart, especially during childhood. The way we are loved or not loved can effect our love relationships for our entire lives.

We know God the Father, as our Father, a most perfect, loving Father. We know Jesus as a great lover, loving us as our brother, our beloved Jesus in a spousal relationship - our most intimate, All-Perfect Spouse and Friend. We know the Holy Spirit deeply in our heart – knowing God on-fire for love of us – we know the Holy Spirit in us.

Also, we love Mary as the most loving Mother, with the love, the all-perfect Mother, the Father choose for us, Mary is Mother at our side. Mary is our Spiritual Mother.

Now it becomes clear to me why Mary would have to be sinless to be the all-perfect mother of the Divine God and of us all.

The Holy Spirit to me just fills my heart with fire. The Holy Spirit fills me and my heart burns. I see a white misty, cloudy, sparkled substance that looks like a penetrating cloud when I see Him. He works in the heart of "Mary, our Mother".

Jesus loves Mary most perfectly. Jesus loves me perfectly. The Father loves me perfectly.

Excerpt from *Response to God's Love* by Fr. Edward Carter, S.J.

... In reference to Christianity, God himself is the ultimate mystery. Radically, God is completely other and transcendent, hidden from man in his inner life, unless he chooses to reveal himself. Let us briefly look at this inner life of God.

The Father, in a perfect act of self-expression, in a perfect act of knowing, generates his son. The Son, the Word, is, then, the immanent expression of God's fullness, the reflection of the Father. Likewise, from all eternity, the Father and the Son bring forth the Holy Spirit in a perfect act of loving.

At the destined moment in human history, God's self-expression, the Word, immersed himself into man's world. God's inner self-expression now had also become God's outer self-expression. Consequently, the mystery of God becomes the mystery of Christ. In Christ, God tells us about himself, about his inner life, about his plan of creation and redemption. He tells us how Father, Son, and Holy Spirit desire to dwell within us in the most intimate fashion, how they wish to share with us their own life through grace. All this he has accomplished and does accomplish through Christ.

end of excerpt

From *Tell My People*
by Fr. Edward J. Carter, S.J.

The Holy Spirit

Jesus: "My beloved friend, tell My people to pray daily to the Holy Spirit. They are to pray for an increase in His gifts. My people must realize that the Holy Spirit comes to transform them. The Spirit desires to transform you more and more according to My image. Those who are docile to His touch become increasingly shaped in My likeness. He performs this marvel within Mary's Immaculate Heart. The more one dwells in My Mother's Heart, the more active are the workings of the Spirit. The Spirit leads Mary to place you within My own Heart. In both Our Hearts, then, your transformation continues.

The more you are formed after My own Heart, the more I lead you to the bosom of My Father. Tell My people all this. Tell them to pray daily for a greater appreciation of these wondrous gifts. I am Lord and Master. All who come to My Heart will be on fire to receive the gifts of the Spirit in ever greater measure! I love and bless My people!"

Reflection: The Holy Spirit is given to us to fashion us ever more according to the likeness of Jesus. And the more we are like Jesus, the more Jesus leads us to the Father. Do we, each day, pray to the Holy Spirit to be more open to His transforming influence? Do we strive each day to grow in union with Mary? The greater our union with our Mother, the spouse of the Holy Spirit, the greater is the transforming action of the Holy Spirit within us.

end of excerpt

R. God unites to us in His All - Perfect love. This heals the wounds from imperfect relationships.

What is so beautiful is that I know each Person of the Trinity in deep love, I know Them as one. I know them as one, especially in the Mass. This union is magnified so much in the Mass, to me. I know God so intimately in the Mass. From the Mass - I am so one with my Father.

The whole Mass I have this great love relationship with My Father. I have a great love relationship with Jesus giving me Himself in the Eucharist, and I feel filled with joy and the Holy Spirit moves my heart many times to pray in tongues.

I know the Father, Son, and Holy Spirit in deep relationship at Mass. I know Them as one, I have a deep relationship with each Person. This is the key to peace. God is love. We experience love. We share in love with the Trinity. I know Them as one and I know Them as perfect lovers - and I know and love Them each as Persons: Father, Son and Holy Spirit.

Jesus: My beautiful spouse, what can I say? I love you, Jesus.

R. The secret to love is knowing the Persons of the Trinity. I know God: Father, Son and Holy Spirit dwelling in my graced, baptized soul.

I see my Father holding me as a child and I love Him like this at Mass. Fondly, I know Him in my heart. I know the

Father's love. I never had this relationship with Him until I had this great spousal relationship with Jesus. I have had this oneness with the Father because of my oneness with Jesus, especially in the Eucharist. I am one deeply in Jesus' Heart – I am one with the Father. Now I can go to the Father anytime. I love Him so much. He loves me as my all-perfect Divine Father. I just love Him as a little child. I want to do everything to please Him. I want to do His Will! The Holy Spirit fills me with the fire of God's love. The Holy Spirit fills me, counsels me, loves me, gives me His gifts.

Mary is my Heavenly Mother.

I can lay my little head on my mother's lap when my heart is torn and she lets me cry there and comforts me.

11:00 p.m. - 6/9/97

My Mother

R. I see this Jesus on the *Apostles Manual* during Mass and this love I have for Jesus makes me cry. It is this Jesus that has swept me away after communion for I see Him as I go to the altar and His arms are open and He gives Himself to me.

Mary said: I stood beneath the cross of my Son and I cried!

R: I have cried for I have been consumed with the love of Their Two Hearts from these pictures. I was overwhelmed with the love of Their Hearts on the Feast of Margaret Mary. It is so simple - these Two Hearts are the most perfect Hearts of love and They love us in this perfect love. Jesus gives to us this spousal relationship with Him. Jesus loves us so much! Mother Mary is the all-perfect Mother.

The Father picked her "My Mother", His Mother of all of His children. It is the Mother of all that leads us to the Heart of Jesus.

The gold cross and Eucharist sparkled after communion and Their halos glowed. God is with us. No matter how we feel - inadequate and sinful, the love is there for us despite our ways. It is love He comes for, it is love He gives, it is love!

Jesus is the Son of God. We see Our Lady of Clearwater.

Revelation 12: 1-2

Now a great sign appeared in heaven: a woman, robed with the sun, standing on the moon, and on her head a crown of twelve stars. She was pregnant, and in labour, crying aloud in the pangs of childbirth.

Reference: Luke 1: 26-38

R. Mary is the chosen Mother. Mary is the Spouse of the Holy Spirit. Mary carried the Light of Life. Mary is full of Divine Grace. Mary is a Virgin. Mary is Mother of Jesus. And we are the children, conceived and brought forth of the Lady, the Children of Light, we are the sons and daughters of Mary.

'Look, he is destined for the fall and for the rise of many in Israel, destined to be a sign that is opposed – ***Luke 2: 34***

6/10/97

God the Father Wants Us to be One With Him

R. I see myself in the bosom of the Father. Jesus takes me to the bosom of the Father.

All through Mass the day in the little chapel I cried so hard - Sunday, it was the day after the Feast of the Sacred Heart and the Immaculate Heart.

The Feast of the Immaculate Heart I was overwhelmed with the love of the Two Hearts. The next day Jesus took me to the Father. I am the little child of the Father. A new peace has come over me for I know the Father – I love His will. I unite with Jesus at Mass. See the altar of sacrifice. Know the love of God the Father. I realized the Father's immense love on Sunday. A lot went on with the Father on Sunday.

Oh, glorious love of my Father.

The prayer of Jesus, John 17 –

Reference: John 17: 20-23

R. Oh delight of all delights to be a child of God, a child of the Father!

6/10/97

35th Anniversary of Fr. Carter's Ordination

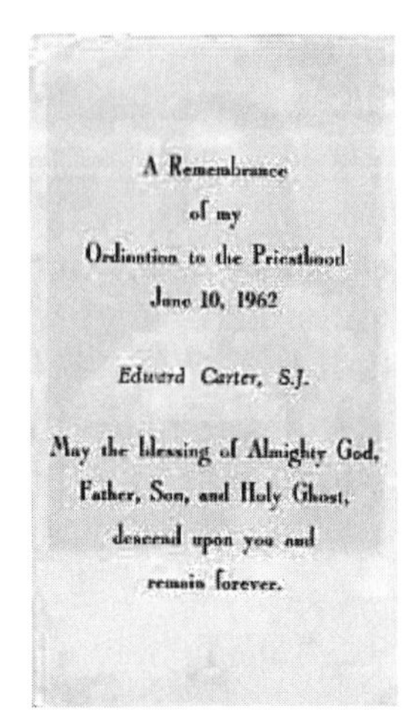
A Remembrance
of my
Ordination to the Priesthood
June 10, 1962

Edward Carter, S.J.

May the blessing of Almighty God,
Father, Son, and Holy Ghost,
descend upon you and
remain forever.

July 31, 1994

Words of Jesus to Members of Shepherds of Christ Associates:

"My beloved priest-companion, I intend to use the priestly newsletter, *Shepherds of Christ*, and the movement, *Shepherds of Christ Associates*, in a powerful way for the renewal of My Church and the world.

"I will use the newsletter and the chapters of *Shepherds of Christ Associates* as a powerful instrument for spreading devotion to My Heart and My Mother's Heart.

"I am calling many to become members of *Shepherds of Christ Associates*. To all of them I will give great blessings. I will use them as instruments to help bring about the triumph of the Immaculate Heart and the reign of My Sacred Heart. I will give great graces to the members of *Shepherds of Christ Associates*. I will call them to be deeply united to My Heart and to Mary's Heart as I lead them ever closer to My Father in the Holy Spirit."

- *Message from Jesus to Father Edward J. Carter, S.J., Founder, as given on July 31, 1994, feast of Saint Ignatius Loyola, Founder of the Society of Jesus (The Jesuits)*

Fr. Carter had a dream.

Letter to Fr. Carter on his 35th Anniversary

R. My dear Father,

Happy, happy day when you were ordained His beloved priest. This day is the greatest gift to us all. You have led me to the bosom of the Father.

I see myself as a little child of the Father and crawl into His embrace, of my Divine God. God loves me. I want to only do His will. I want the Kingdom of God. I want to be as God desires. I want the Sacred Heart of Jesus to Reign. Jesus is the King.

Lucia's vision

R. Mary intercedes by the altar. Grace and mercy fall upon us abundantly.

Mary says –

***Mary's Message* - from the Rosary of August 27, 1996**

Mary: I stood beneath the cross of my Son, and my Heart was in such pain for I saw Him before my eyes. I saw Him covered with blood. I saw Him die. My Heart, my children, my Heart to watch my Son, but my Heart, my Heart, how I suffered for my little children of the world that give in to this world and give up the love of my Son. O my little children of light, I give you this message. Carry this light into the darkness for your Mother Mary, for I stood beneath the cross and I cried. I cried for the little ones. I cried for the young ones, the ones that do not care and will lose their souls. How do I make you see for you will not listen to me? What can I do? I come. I appear. I beg. I plead. I give you these gifts from my Son, and you reject me. I do not deliver messages very often anymore for I have been ignored. The message is the same. You do not read the messages I have given to you. Please help me. Help the little children. I appear. I appear. I appear, and I am ignored. I stood beneath the cross, and I cried. I cried, and my Heart was in such anguish for my little children, for I am searching for them this day as I searched for the Child Jesus. Please, please help me. I cannot hold back the hand of my Son any longer. I am Mary, your Mother. I ask you to help my children. You are my children of light.

end of Mary's Message

6/10/97

Mary: I Stood Beneath the Cross

Mary said: I stood beneath the cross of My Son and I cried for the little ones that would lose their souls and give up the love of my Son.

John 3:16

For this is how God loved the world:
he gave his only Son,
so that everyone who believes in him
  may not perish
but may have eternal life.

R. Jesus is the Son of Mary. Mary is the Spouse of the Holy Spirit. Jesus came and paid for the sins of men. Mary shows us her Immaculate Heart under the cross and she says –

Mary: This is the way, my tainted children. I am the Immaculate One. Come into my heart and I will take you deeply to the Heart of Jesus.

My Spouse is the Holy Spirit that permeates my heart (your spiritual womb) and brings you forth as the children of light. My Son is the Lamb that shed His Blood for your sins and my Father, Our Father, is your Father - most loving and true, the great Father of love of all of you - His creatures. The Father created you for this.

R. God gives us a sharing in His life in baptism. The Father, Son and Holy Spirit live in our graced, baptized soul.

Mary says: I stood beneath the cross of my Son and I cried for the children of darkness who give into this world and give up the love of my Son. Oh, children of light, carry the light into the darkness for your Mother Mary.

R. Will we answer the call of our weeping Mother standing by the altar of sacrifice in the Mass? Mary takes us to the Heart of her Son.

We are united to God: Father, Son and Holy Spirit.

Yes, our mission is a mission of leading souls to the love of the Two Hearts, for Mary stood beneath the cross and Mary cried, for she knew from the prophecy of Simeon that this child is destined for the rise and fall of many in Israel, and her heart was pierced by this prophecy since their visit to the temple, and it reached an agony of tremendous proportion as she stood beneath His cross gazing at the wounds of her Son and the battered body covered with dried blood and His head crowned with the crown of thorns. Mary knew many would throw away the graces God was giving them. Jesus paid such a price for our sins for us! Mary cried a cry of pain for her children lost in hell. Mary is the Perfect Mother of Love chosen by the Father. Mary was chosen by the Father as Mother. The Mother chosen by Him to lead the sinful ones to His bosom and live as children of the light as He intended for His creatures.

The light was dimmed by the sin of Adam and Eve. Jesus is the Light of the World. Jesus is our Savior. Jesus gives us a sharing in His life in baptism. Mary cries for the death of the children.

What of the sorrow of the Mother? Jesus took over the Fatima Mission on October 13, 1996.

Jesus continued to give messages during this period from October 13, 1996 - May 13, 1997. Mary said on October 5, 1996, "she could not hold back the hand of her Son anymore. His hand is struck with power."

On the Feast of St. Margaret Mary, October 16, 1996, Jesus warned that you do not comprehend the importance of this period to the world, many are willful. On December 5, 1996, Jesus appeared on the cross with His mouth moving. I saw Him at the point of death. Later that night He said no one was listening.

Jesus warned in December, Mary appeared in Clearwater 12 days later. December 19, 1996 – 2 days later, Mary said, "you have made money your god." Mary and Jesus asked that on the Feast of Our Lady of Guadalupe the Mary Message tape be given to the world. A tape from the Hearts of Jesus and Mary.

Mary gave a strong message on December 19th and Jesus gave strong messages on December 19th and 22nd, speaking of chastisements and the moon going to blood – it is the blood of the lamb.

Jesus refers on Bloody Friday how these prayers said at 9,

12, 3 and 6 will help protect us with His Blood.

On December 29th, Jesus gave the All-Night Message, putting in order all the events He wishes us to study.

The Father speaks and gave warnings of Falmouth. The Father states anyone getting in His way will be removed.

On March 3rd, there is the flood and the message is clear this day.

March 3, 1997 - Day Falmouth Flooded Early Morning

Jesus: Oh, the waters will run and the earth will shake and you will suffer and suffer and work your own plan and say it happened before, it is not a sign from God - it is a phenomenon, a happening, no reason to take notice.

And I will shake you on your tree and you will fall to the ground as rotten fruit and all that will remain will be the fruit of heaven.

Reference: Romans 12: 13-21

This is a NOTE: Fr. Carter, at the same time as these writings, sent the Priestly Newsletter every other month, to more than 75,000 priests and hierarchy around the world. He sent the Priestly Newsletter to every priest in the United States. We have sent about 18,000,000 Priestly Newsletters to priests and hierarchy in 21 years since 1994 - loose and in books.

Rita Ring March, 2015

Priestly Newsletter May/June 1997

Incarnational Perspectives

I am the good shepherd: the good shepherd is one who lays down his life for his sheep. The hired man, since he is not the shepherd and the sheep do not belong to him, abandons the sheep and runs away as soon as he sees a wolf coming, and then the wolf attacks and scatters the sheep; this is because he is only a hired man and has no concern for the sheep. I am the good shepherd; I know my own and my own know me, just as the Father knows me and I know the Father; and I lay down my life for my sheep. (Jn 10:11-15 [1])

The Son of God be-came man for our salvation. Yes, He became incarnate. He took to Himself a real human nature. Because Jesus possessed a real human nature, He could die for us. As the Good Shepherd, He has laid down His life for us, His sheep.

There are many thoughts which come to us when we reflect upon the truth that the Son of God took to Himself a human nature and dwelt among us. Some of these are as follows:

- **The Word Was Made Flesh.** St. John puts it very simply in his Gospel: "The Word was made flesh, he lived among us..." (Jn 1:14). Yes, John states it so succinctly, yet these few words contain a wealth of meaning and mystery. We should expect nothing else, since this brief statement of the fourth Gospel points out the central event of all human history. These words sum up God's creative and redemptive activity. They sum up God's process of Self-communication to us. Let us briefly examine some of the implications of the Son of God becoming man.

  Adequately to explain the intimacy of the way of redemption which is the Incarnation is beyond the human powers of articulation. Jesus is Emmanuel - God with us. How tremendously more approachable God is to us because we have Jesus. The more the mind dwells on the meaning of the Incarnation, the more one is stricken with wonder at this unfathomable mystery of love. And yet, for one reason or the other, we are tempted to allow the mystery of the Son becoming man to be a fact we take for granted. Our sense of appreciation becomes dulled, and our feeling of enthusiasm about Jesus becomes so tragically mediocre. If our enthusiasm concerning Jesus is less than it should be, what are the reasons? We are speaking of a deep-rooted penetrating kind of enthusiasm centered in our graced wills. Sometimes this enthusiasm has deep emotional overtones. If properly controlled, this enthusiasm involving the human emotions can be a tremendous asset in one's commitment to Jesus. But we just do not have it within our power to turn the emotions on whenever we wish. The more fundamental enthusiasm for Jesus which is rooted in the human will can and should always be substantially with us.

- **Realizing Jesus' Love for Us.** One reason our commitment to Jesus can lose its ardor is that the realization of how much Jesus loves each of us becomes a kind of peripheral or notional assent. We intellectually assent to the fact that Jesus loves us, but at times such an assent does not have much more effect on our lives than admitting that Caesar crossed the Rubicon.

We are meant to assent with our entire being to the fact that Jesus loves each of us so uniquely, so intimately, so unreservedly. This truth of Jesus' love for us is supposed to transform our lives. It is supposed to so grip our imagination so that we can say in the spirit of St. Paul: "For I am certain of this: neither death nor life, no angel, no prince, nothing that exists, nothing still to come, not any power, or height or depth, nor any created thing, can ever come between us and the love of God made visible in Christ Jesus our Lord." (Rm 8:38-39)

Giving ourselves over to Jesus' love does not remove pain and suffering from life. But, through the prism of Jesus' love for us, suffering is seen in proper perspective. We see the pain and suffering as being able to lead to something greater, just as it did in Jesus' life. His suffering led to resurrection. We realize that if we relate to suffering properly, we become persons with a deepened capacity to love God and man - persons sharing more fully in Jesus' resurrection. With such an attitude, this pain dimension of life can at times become hardly noticeable because we are so taken up with Jesus and His cause.

- **The Cause of Christ.** What is this cause? Some two thousand years ago Jesus walked this earth preaching His Father's message, healing the sick, forgiving sins, extending His kindness and mercy, training the apostles. In all His varied activity, Jesus was accomplishing the redemption. Today, Jesus still walks the earth. He teaches the Father's truth. He is concerned with the sick and the ignorant. He administers the sacraments. He manifests the Father's love in many different ways. But, unlike that time of two thousand years ago, Christ Himself is not visible. He is visible only through us, His members. He extends to us the great privilege - and responsibility - of assisting Him in the continuation of His redemptive work. The total Christian community and each individual Christian are, then, certain extensions and continuations of the Incarnation. So close is this union between the Christian and Christ that St. Paul speaks very strikingly that it is more Christ than Paul who now lives: "I have been crucified with Christ, and I live now not with my own life but with the life of Christ who lives in me. The life I now live in this body I live in faith: faith in the Son of God who loved me and who sacrificed himself for my sake." (Ga 2:19-20)

  Each of us has the privilege of offering Jesus his or her own unique person, one's own humanity, one's own human existence. As with St. Paul we are asked to allow Jesus to live within us. Each Christian has the opportunity to allow Jesus to live through the uniqueness which is this particular Christian. To the extent the Christian does offer himself to Jesus in this manner, to that extent Jesus has a unique opportunity of continuing His redemptive work. To the extent the Christian holds back and does not allow Jesus to live in oneself, to that degree Jesus loses this unrepeatable opportunity.

- **Historical and Cultural Awareness.** If we are to carry forth the salvific mission of Jesus properly, the People of God, individually and collectively, must be aware of the Incarnation's principle of historical and cultural awareness. Jesus, through His enfleshment, became situated within an historical situation. He lived at a particular stage of history, in a particular geographical locale, amid a particular kind of culture. Jesus respected this historical conditioning. Without compromising His

Father's message, Jesus was aware of His historical milieu. He lived like a good Jewish man of the time. He talked in language which respected the linguistic idiom and thought patterns of the then existent Jewish culture. He accepted the Jewish people as conditioned by a certain historical and cultural milieu, and dealt with them accordingly.

The members of the Christian community must follow the example of Jesus. In living and proclaiming the Gospel message, the People of God must be aware of the particular historical and cultural milieu in which they find themselves. But, also after the example of Jesus, they must strive for this awareness without compromising the Gospel. We immediately see that the Christian community is consequently open to a double danger. On the one hand, there is the danger that the People of God will not read the signs of the times properly. On the other hand, in the effort to be aware of their historical setting there is the danger of compromising the Gospel message. But the Christian community has to face these dangers and not surrender to them.

- **The Temporal Order.** Another truth connected with the Incarnation - another incarnational perspective - leads us to a discussion of the Christian's responsibility toward the secular or temporal order of things. Through His enfleshment Christ has assumed, or united to Himself, not only the human race but the entire world or temporal order. The world literally belongs to Christ. The Christian's attitude toward authentic temporal values should therefore be obvious. He or she should love the world as redeemed by Jesus more than does the non-believer. The Christian should be the first to love all authentic human values. He or she should be the first to promote these values. Obviously, the real progress of these values must be according to their Christic design, however hidden this design may be at times. Very importantly, the Christian should be the first to be willing to suffer for the authentic progress of the world. And why? We reiterate - because it all belongs to Christ.

The Christian should grieve because all is not well with the temporal order. He or she should be duly disturbed that there is so much violence, murder, social injustice, lust for power, drug peddling, pursuit of hedonism, increasing Godlessness. These and other evils sadly mar the name and image of Jesus which He imprinted upon the universe through His life, death, and resurrection. The Christian should grieve because the face of Christ is thus so often covered by the sinful dust of the market place.

But the market place, the temporal order, is not all evil. Far from it. It is basically good with the creative goodness of God. It's basic goodness and beauty have been deepened by the grandeur of Jesus' redemptive effort. There is so much good in so many human hearts. This goodness manifests itself in countless ways. There are so many ways that many allow us to see their love for neighbor. There are those who selflessly give of themselves for the good of others in the field of medicine and nursing, in the political arena, in education, in science and technology, in laboring for justice for the consumer, in striving for pollution control. The list only be extended indefinitely. Some of these services of so many for the good of neighbor command national attention. Many, many more services are so hidden, hardly noticed.

Each Christian, grieving at the world's evil, but rejoicing in its goodness and potential for greater good, must be inspired to action. He or she should deeply love the world because it belongs to Christ. He or she should deeply love the people who cover the face of this world, because they too belong to Christ. His blood has touched them and redeemed them. The love of the Christian for others must be an operative, an efficacious love. It must be willing to do, to accomplish, and, in rare cases, to die. Whatever one's state of life, be it activist or cloistered contemplative, this is the privilege and the responsibility of the Christian. He or she cannot be committed to Jesus in love without concomitantly being dedicated to the human family and the temporal order. Through the Incarnation, all this is interlinked.

If the Christian is to promote the good of the temporal order, one must be free in regards to it. One must be free, even to the extent that he or she is willing to renounce certain temporal values, good in themselves, for the service of others. The one who really loves the world is the person who is willing to forego its use at times. To love the world and to love the things of the world are not always one and the same. A person can love the things of the world - selfishly - and consequently, not love the world in itself. This selfishness is an obstacle to helping the temporal order to progress as it should.

- **The Human Condition.** As we continue a survey of some of the truths or perspectives connected with the Incarnation, we notice that Jesus has taught us that redemption occurs within the human condition. The Father could have redeemed us in a number of ways. He chose that setting which was the Incarnation of His Son. Jesus saved us by being fully man, a man who exercised His manhood perfectly in the self-libation which was His. Although His mission led Him to give up certain human values, He saved us through real human acts. He saved us by loving Mary and Joseph, by eating with friends, by teaching, by loving the little children, by thrilling to the beauty of nature, by bearing properly insult and abuse, and, of course, by dying and rising. Summarily, Jesus saved us by living that kind of human life which was in harmony with His Father's will.

Jesus did not rebel because He found the human condition less than perfect. He had come to change things, to give a new release to the goodness of man. He was a revolutionary in the best sense. His effort was to turn things around, to reorientate the human race toward God. But Jesus was by no means always the recipient of the goodness He had come to preach. Although He taught that one should love his or her neighbor, He himself was not always loved. He suffered, and He suffered mightily, because of the mean streak, the sinful streak in others. He Who had done nothing wrong, Who had showed His love for others in so many different ways, this man was the one they beat, insulted, scourged, crowned with thorns, and nailed to the cross.

Jesus redeemed us within the human condition. We receive His redemption, and help channel it to others, within that same human condition. We are redeemed by living the authentically human in the way indicated by the Father's will. Although we are led by that will to renounce various human values at various times in various ways, we are saved by living a human existence, or we are not saved at all. We have often heard that grace does not destroy nature. But, perhaps, we do not too often penetrate the depths of this theological truth. Perhaps we do not very often have a firm realization that grace elevates nature, gives it a deepened capacity for fulfillment, and that grace needs nature. Grace must work through nature if it is to save. Consequently, we are not saved and sanctified by becoming less human. We are saved and sanctified by being very human - by allowing grace to perfect the various dimensions of our human nature. Grace inspires us to the fullest exercise of our humanity. Grace inspires to a Spirit-directed way of living, of eating and drinking, of working and playing, of enjoying sense pleasure, of experiencing joy and suffering.

Participation in the human condition, then, offers us a marvelous opportunity of developing all our human capacities in the work of ongoing redemption. Yet the human condition is not by any means a completely pleasant situation. As Jesus before us suffered because of the human condition, so also must we. The human condition can be the occasion of suffering in so many different ways. For instance, a person can suffer because others treat him or her unjustly. One can suffer also precisely because someone loves him or her and he or she loves in return. This love makes one vulnerable to pain, not because the other intends it, but merely because to love within the human condition means a certain amount of inevitable suffering. We suffer also because we are to a certain extent pilgrims in exile. We have not yet arrived at our final destiny, a destiny which will be achieved only in eternity. Because we are still on the way, we are not yet completely alive, completely fulfilled. And because all this is so, we suffer, and sometimes deeply so. But, again looking to Jesus, we must learn how to encounter suffering properly. He encountered the human condition perfectly, whether it meant great joy or deep anguish. The Spirit asks us to live by the same attitude.

- **Bodily Values.** Another perspective very close to the heart of the Incarnation is the concept of bodily values. The connection is obvious. The Son of God assumed a human nature with its bodily dimensions. He has given a great new dignity to the human body. Any attitude which deprecates the body is consequently totally un-Christian.

There have been numerous such attitudes which have influenced Christian thought and practice, unofficially, of course. There have been Manichaeism, Gnosticism, Neo-Platonism, and Jansenism, to name some. Each of these has in one manner or other failed to see the beauty, dignity, and purpose of the human body.

The body, despite its basic goodness and grandeur, still has sinful tendencies, tendencies toward laziness, lust, unbridled pursuit of all kinds of sense pleasure. If the body is to achieve its purpose, it must obviously be properly disciplined. The one who loves his body the most is, quite obviously, not the one who gives to it all its desires. He or she is the one who takes the necessary means, however painful, to ensure that the body serves its wonderful and God-given purpose.

- **Incarnationalism and Transcendence.** In a quick survey of some of the important truths consequent upon the Son of God becoming man, certainly one to be mentioned is the fact that Incarnationalism leads to transcendence - to that which is invisible, to that which is above material limitation. At the offertory of the Mass, as the priest adds a drop of water to the wine to be offered, he says: "By the mystery of this water and wine may we come to share in the divinity of Christ who humbled himself to share in our humanity." The Son has come to draw us to God - to the ultimate Transcendent Reality.

Even though we would not have been given a supernatural destiny, we would have had a thrust toward the transcendent. Our graced nature has an even greater thrust toward transcendence. The ultimate Transcendent is God, and, as St. Augustine said long ago, our hearts will not rest until they rest in God.

Christ, in His human nature, points to that which is beyond His humanity and everything else created. Christ ultimately points to God alone. Through His enfleshment, the Son was marvelously immanent in this world. But this very immanence of God pointed to the otherness, the transcendence of God. Jesus taught us that there is something beyond the material, something beyond marriage, and riches, and culture, something beyond all earthly values.

Jesus told us to relate to these values in so far as they lead to God. He told us to renounce them in so far as this would be more conducive to union with God. Jesus told us something which we all have experienced - the created in itself cannot radically satisfy us. Only God can, and the created takes an ultimate meaning, and renders authentic satisfaction, only when it leads us to God. The Son became man to lead us to transcendence - indeed, to ultimate Transcendence, God Himself.

Scriptural Reflections

- **Life and Death.** "When this perishable nature has put on imperishability, and when this mortal nature has put on immortality, then the words of scripture will come true: Death is swallowed up in victory. Death, where is your victory? Death, where is your sting?" (1 Cor 15: 54-55)

  Death is a certainty. It cannot be wished away. It cannot be avoided by pretending it is an event overtaking all people but oneself. It is a sign of maturity, then, that a Christian fully and meaningfully accepts the reality of his or her own death, and lives with this realization holding proper perspective in one's consciousness.

  God does not intend that a morbid fear of death poison the beauty of our days. He does not intend that the thought of death diminish our enthusiasm to be and to accomplish. He does not intend that the prospect of death become an obstacle to our fulfilling our potential here below. God rather intends that we see the profound union which is meant to harmonize the reality of life with the reality of death.

  If we have the proper attitude toward life, we will have the proper attitude toward death. If we live the life-event properly, we will be prepared to live the death-event properly. Death is the final event of our earthly sojourn. If we live life generously, we shall be oriented to live death generously. If we have tried lovingly to conform ourselves to God's will throughout the course of life, we will be disposed to accept His will in meeting death.

  The attitudes and virtues which comprise a good Christian life are, then, the same attitudes and virtues which will assure a good Christian death. The best preparation for a successful Christian death is a successful Christian life. To live each day as it comes with a deep love of God and neighbor is simultaneously to prepare properly for the inevitable event of dying. To live each day according to God's designs is to enable one to say, "Death, where is your victory? Death, where is your sting?"

- **Idols Which Should Not Be.**

"When Israel was a child I loved him,
and I called my son out of Egypt.
But the more I called to them,
the further they went from me;
they have offered sacrifice to the Baals
and set their offerings smoking before the idols.
I myself taught Ephraim to walk,
I took them in my arms;
yet they have not understood
that I was the one looking after them.
I led them with reins of kindness,
with leading-strings of love." (Hos 11:1-4)

God loves us tenderly, mightily. He watches us grow, guiding our steps with a loving concern so deep that we can never fully fathom it. He constantly showers us with his varied gifts, all signs of His love. Reflecting upon how much God loves us and how tenderly He cares for us, we wonder how we could ever wander very far from His loving truth. But we know there are numerous idols which can usurp His place in our lives if we fail to resist their specious attractiveness.

Selfishness, greed, pride, laziness, gluttony, manipulation of others for personal gain, a hedonistic pursuit of pleasure, abuse of power and authority - these are some of the idols we can focus on rather than God Himself. It is amazing that the false glitter of such idols, which but thinly covers layers of ugliness, can tempt us to reject in varying degrees the loveliness of our God, our God who, infinite in all perfections, has consistently and overwhelmingly, and so mercifully, shown how much He loves us.

Pursuing false idols will eventually leave us feeling empty, frustrated, disgusted. How would it be otherwise? For to pursue false idols in the place of God is to expect fulfillment and happiness from that which lacks the capability to satisfy the human nature God has created. God makes us for Himself. He alone can fulfill the fundamental longing we have for complete happiness. He made our hearts to seek Him, and in Him alone do they find the love, the peace, and the security they so deeply desire.

- **The Way We Talk.** Jesus tells us: "Make a tree sound and its fruit will be sound; make a tree rotten and its fruit will be rotten. For the tree can be told by its fruit. Brood of vipers, how can your speech be good when you are evil? For a man's words flow out of what fills his heart. A good man draws good things from his store of goodness; a bad man draws bad things from his store of badness. So I tell you this, that for every unfounded word men utter they will answer on Judgment day, since it is by your words you will be acquitted, and by your words condemned." (Mt 12:33-37)

The above scriptural passage tells us that the faculty of speech is indeed a mighty one. It can accomplish much good. It can produce much that is evil. Consequently, to use speech in a Christlike manner is a sign that grace has taken deep hold of a person. On the other hand, a noticeably un-Christlike mode of speech is a sign that the way of Christ has not yet deeply penetrated the heart.

Our speech is laden with numerous and varied possibilities for good. There is the sympathetic word. Words which convey a sense of "I understand and I care", can be a soothing balm to the troubled heart. As insignificant as such words may seem at times to the one offering sympathy and understanding, to the recipient they can be one of the most precious gifts possible. Especially is this true at moments of deep anguish. Only one who has been spoken to with sincere sympathy at such a time can fully appreciate the healing power of the kind and understanding word.

We should also highly value our words of affirmation and encouragement. These can contribute significantly to the development of a person's potential. One person needs more affirmation and encouragement than another, but we all need some. Actually, we can be overcome with awe as we reflect on the powerful role words of affirmation can assume in helping a person to be and to to become. To help a person to be and to become what God destines him or her to be - what a privilege this is - and yet we have numerous, even daily opportunities to be such a catalyst. The right word at the proper time can help change the orientation of a person's life. On a more moderate scale, words of affirmation can be a sustaining force in a person's quest for continuing growth.

We have discussed a few ways in which our words can be a very positive force. However, the faculty of speech which can be a source of constructive good, can also be the source of destructive evil. There is the uncalled-for word which is so unkindly cutting. Always uncharitable, it is especially so when it tends to crush the already bruised reed - the heart already burdened with paralyzing sadness, or discouragement, or grief. There is also the unjust word which can so suddenly and so decisively ruin a reputation. There is the word which spreads unjust criticism concerning a person who perhaps is performing marvelously in an almost impossible situation. There can also be the word which needlessly divides people. The different forms of community we must often build rather slowly, and with much effort, pain and selflessness. Then comes the divisive word which need not be.

We can so often be tempted to look for the more grandiose opportunities to promote the cause of Christ. Such times, however, occur for most of us only at rather rare intervals. It is the more ordinary setting for accomplishing good that is usually ours. But the ordinariness of our opportunities does not detract from their inherent greatness. One of those ordinary possibilities for good, one which is constantly present, is the proper use of our God-given power of speech.

• **To Pay the Price.** "All the runners at the stadium are trying to win, but only one of them gets the prize. You must run in the same way, meaning to win. All the fighters at the games go into strict training; they do this just to win a wreath that will wither away, but we do it for a wreath that will never wither. That is how I run, intent on winning; that is how I fight, not beating the air. I treat my body hard and make it obey me, for, having been an announcer myself, I should not want to be disqualified." (1 Cor 9:24-27)

Long hours of practice, the physical weariness, the mental pressure of competitiveness, the at-least-occasional sting of defeat, the discipline of regular hours and diet - these are some of the factors involved in the striving for athletic success. Some never do succeed; they never make the team. Some achieve only moderate success. A few achieve top glory. However, there are always numberless individuals who keep trying. Win or lose, the price must be paid even to have the chance at victory and success. The athlete knows unequivocally that to achieve a cherished goal one must be willing to extend the necessary effort - one must be willing to pay the price.

Obviously, it is not only the athlete who must pay the price for achievement. Any worthwhile human endeavor demands effort and a type of discipline commensurate with the envisioned goal.

The medical student, for example, must endure long years of demanding and competitive study. His or her friends, engaged in less demanding academic programs, have many more leisure hours for social events and other interests. The medical student is tempted at times to wonder if the demanded price is not too great, as one watches one's peers travel considerably easier paths. The overriding desire to be a doctor, however, is etched deep within the spirit. It resides there constantly, sometimes as a quiet glow, sometimes as a burning flame, always, however, as a persistent force thrusting the young man or woman onward toward a medical career.

Our goal as followers of Jesus is to be committed Christians. If we are committed Christians, Jesus is the center of our existence. Jesus sums up all for us. In Him, and through Him, and with Him, we, as committed Christians, try to relate properly to all reality - to God, our fellow human beings, the temporal order, and all else. In order to be committed Christians, however, we have to be willing to pay the price - just as the athlete and the medical student.

Sometimes, as we so well know from our past experience, we aren't willing to pay the price. We turn a deaf ear to the voice of Jesus, which quietly but persistently calls us to higher things, to a more mature living of the Christian life. Sometimes we refuse Him because of fear, sometimes because of laziness, sometimes because we simply don't take the time to listen. There are other reasons too, but whatever the cause, we are poorer because of our refusal. In the moments of honesty we admit this to ourselves. We know that to refuse Jesus is to refuse growth. It is to refuse more vital living. It is to refuse greater happiness. It is to refuse a greater capacity to love our neighbor. It is to refuse a greater love-union with Jesus himself.

At other times, we respond to the voice of Jesus. Whatever the inconvenience involved, we are not deaf to His whisperings. Whatever the pain involved, we tell ourselves that He suffered much, much more for us. Whatever the fear involved, we are thoroughly convinced that Jesus will never fail us. We are open to the way He is leading. We pay the price - and how happy we are that we do. Jesus draws us closer to Himself. We feel more intimately the warmth and security of His loving touch. In these moments we wonder how and why we ever refuse His voice. We wonder how and why we ever refuse to pay the price.

The Priest And The Universal Church

The Directory on the Ministry and Life of Priests tells us: "The command of the Lord: go to all the nations (Mt 28:18-20) definitively expresses the place of the priest in front of the Church. Sent-missus-by the Father by means of Christ, the priest pertains 'in an immediate' way to the universal Church, which has the mission to announce the Good news unto the 'ends of the earth' (Acts 1:8).

"The spiritual gift received by priests in Ordination prepares them for a wide and universal mission of salvation. In fact, through Orders and the ministry received, all priests are associated with the Episcopal Body and, in hierarchical communion with it, according to their vocation and grace, they serve the good of the entire Church. Therefore, the membership to a particular church, through incardination, must not enclose the priest in a restricted and particularistic mentality, but rather should open him to the service of other churches, because each church is the particular realization of the only Church of Jesus Christ, such that the universal Church lives and fulfills her mission in and from the particular churches in effective communion with her. Thus, all the priests, must have a missionary heart and mind and be open to the needs of the Church and the world."[2]

The Priest And The Euchrarist

The Directory now speaks to us concerning the priest and his relationship with the Eucharist:

"If the services of the Word is the foundational element of the priestly ministry, the heart and the vital center of it is constituted, without a doubt, in the Eucharist, which is, above all, the real presence in time of the unique and eternal sacrifice of Christ.

"The sacramental memorial of the death and Resurrection of Christ, the true and efficacious representation of the singular redemptive Sacrifice, source and apex of Christian life in the whole of evangelization, the Eucharist is the beginning, means, and end of the priestly ministry, since 'all ecclesiastical ministries and works of the apostolate are bound up with the Eucharist and are directed towards it.' Consecrated in order to perpetuate the Holy Sacrifice, the priest thus manifests, in the most evident manner, his identity.

"There exists, in fact, an intimate rapport between the centrality of the Eucharist, pastoral charity, and the unity of life of the priest, who finds in this rapport the decisive indications for the way to the holiness to which he has been specifically called.

"If the priest lends to Christ, Most Eternal High Priest, his intelligence, will, voice and hands so as to offer, through his very ministry, the sacramental sacrifice of redemption to the Father, he should make his own the dispositions of the Master and, like him, live those gifts for his brothers in faith. He must therefore learn to unite himself intimately to the offering, placing his entire life upon the altar of sacrifice as a revealing sign of the gratuitous and anticipatory love of God."[3]

The Heart Of Christ, The Heart Of Mary

Pope John Paul II speaks to us movingly concerning the Heart of Christ: "The Heart of the Redeemer enlivens the whole Church and draws men who have opened their hearts 'to the inscrutable wealth' of this unique Heart....

"I desire in a special way to join spiritually with all those who inspire their human hearts from this Divine Heart. It is a numerous family. Not a few congregations, associations and communities live and develop in the Church, taking their vital energy in a programmed way from the Heart of Christ. This spiritual bond always leads to a great reawakening of apostolic zeal. Adorers of the Divine Heart become people with sensitive consciences. And when it is given to them to have a relationship with the Heart of our Lord and Master, then need also reawakens in them to do reparation for the sins of the world, for the indifference of so many hearts, for their negligence.

"How necessary these ranks of vigilant hearts are in the Church, so that the love of the Divine Heart shall not remain isolated and without response! In these ranks, special mention deserves to be made of all those who offer up their sufferings as living victims in union with the Heart of Christ pierced on the cross. Transformed in that way by love, human suffering becomes a particular leaven of Christ's saving work in the Church...

"The Most Sacred Heart of Jesus reminds us, above all, of those moments when this Heart was 'pierced by the lance,' and, thereby, opened in a visible manner to man and the world. By reciting the litany and venerating the Divine Heart in general, we learn the mystery of the Redemption in all its divine and human profundity."

And the Pope also speaks to us about the heart of Mary: "The Immaculate Heart of Mary was open to the word, 'Woman, there is your son.' It went to meet spiritually the Heart of the Son opened by the soldier's lance. The heart of Mary was opened by the same love for man and for the world with which Christ loved man and the world, offering up himself on the cross, even to that lance stroke from the soldier.

"Consecrating the world to the Immaculate Heart of Mary means approaching the same Source of Life, through the Mother's Intercession, that life which flowed forth from Golgatha, the source which gushes out ceaselessly with redemption and grace. Reparation for the sins of the world is continually being accomplished in it. It is ceaselessly the font of new life and holiness.

"Consecrating the world to the Immaculate Heart of the Mother means returning under the Cross of the Son. More: it means consecration of this world to the pierced Heart of the Savior, by bringing the world back to the very source of its Redemption. Redemption is always greater than man's sin and 'the sin of the world.' The power of Redemption infinitely surpasses the whole range of evil in man and in the world.

"The Heart of the Mother is aware of it, more than anyone in the whole cosmos, visible and invisible. This is why she calls. She does not call only to conversion; she also calls upon us to let ourselves be helped by her, the Mother, to return to the source of the Redemption."[4]

Thoughts On Prayer

- Archbishop Joseph M. Raya of the Byzantine rite, speaks to us about prayer: "The Fathers can tell us how to fast and abstain, or how to recite and sing psalms. They can give some guidelines to the soul reaching out to touch the Lord. But they know that prayer is essentially an experience of a person-to-person relationship, a realization where mere information becomes life, where the soul reaches out to touch a deeper life. They know that it is ultimately God, and God alone, who teaches one how to pray. The cry of the apostles - 'Lord, teach us how to pray'-is not the expression of a desire for a new method. Rather, it is man's basic longing for a personal relationship and encounter with God."[5]
- A well-known spiritual writer of our times, Don Humbert van Zeller, reminds us that prayer is meant to unite us, not only with God, but also with each other: "Not only is there a law in our members which wars against the spirit and tempts to sin, but there is a law too which appears to be on

the side of the spirit but which in fact wars against it. This is the law in us which tempts to personal autonomy. Pleading detachment from human affection and the avoidance of distraction, this spurious law is the enemy of the one thing, namely individual wholeness, which it claims to be preserving. We are whole only when we are one with everyone else. This unity of outlook has to be universal in application, because by being selective it fails in an essential quality.

"Christ died for all, and not merely for an elect percentage...

"So we must be on our guard against the temptation which disguises itself as a grace: the instinct which shrinks from closeness to our fellow human beings. Psychologists have one name for it, theologians another. By refusing to break down the barriers and by clinging to our independence, we are not only being proud and uncharitable, but are also defying the law of our nature - and a good law this time, not the kind of fallen law which tempts. Whatever the call to contemplation, it can never be the call...to contract out from mankind and live on a lonely peak.

"Somehow an exchange must be assured which means more than mutual toleration. It means welcome, consideration, the crossing over from self to another self. This is why Christianity, the law of love, alone brings completeness..."[6]

- A modern master of prayer, Thomas Merton, tells us: "In the 'prayer of the heart' we seek first of all the deepest ground of our identity in God. We do not reason about dogmas or faith or 'the mysteries'. We seek rather to gain a direct existential grasp, a personal experience of the deepest truths of life and faith, finding ourselves in God's truth. Inner certainty depends on purification. The dark night rectifies our deepest intentions. In the silence of this 'night of faith' we return to simplicity and sincerity of heart. We learn recollection which consists in listening for God's will, in direct and simple attention to reality. Recollection is awareness of the unconditional. Prayer then means yearning for the simple presence of God, for a personal understanding of his word, for knowledge of his will and for capacity to hear and obey him."[7]

The Hidden Pain

There formerly was a popular song that talked about smiling on the outside, crying on the inside. The song touched upon a very real human experience. During the journey of life all of us come to turns in the road where heartache awaits us. It is impossible, given the human condition, to avoid all such turns. There are no detours available. For the most part, we have to bear the pain within the confines of our inner selves. There may be another, or a few others, who know about the pain. It can help some to talk to them about the suffering. But this by no means takes away all the pain. The greater part of the suffering remains there, lodged firmly in the center of the heart. And we wonder if it will ever leave. Obviously, we have to go on living, but the heaviness of the days caused by the heaviness of the heart, makes us feel as if we have lived, oh, such a long time, since the heartache began. We try to put up a cheerful front, and with God's help we even surprise ourselves at the degree of success we achieve with this smiling on the outside. But the few who know us well, and who may know of the pain, realize the price we are paying to appear the way we do.

During times of hidden pain, there is present a unique opportunity for spiritual growth. We have to ask Jesus to allow us to see the pain in proper perspective. We have to ask Him to help us grow through the experience - grow into persons who increasingly project Christ to the world. We have to be aware that Jesus is with us in His tender and consoling love, this love which soothes the hidden pain within, this love which allows us to be in basic peace.

The Trinity In Our Lives

St. Athanasius tells us: "Even the gifts that the Spirit dispenses to individuals are given by the Father through the Word. ...and so the graces given by the Son in the Spirit are true gifts of the Father. Similarly, when the Spirit dwells in us, the Word who bestows the Spirit is in us too, and the Father is present in the Word."[8]

NOTES:

1. Scriptural quotations are taken from *The Jerusalem Bible,* Doubleday & Co.
2. *Directory on the Ministry and Life of Priests*, as in special supplement, Inside the Vatican, No. 15.
3. *Ibid.*, No. 48.
4. Pope John Paul II. *Prayers and Devotions*, edited by Bishop Peter Canuis Johannes Van Lierde, Viking, pp. 449-451.
5. Archbishop John M. Raya, *The Face of God: An Introduction to Eastern Spirituality*, God With Us Publications, p. 199.
6. Don Hubert van Zeller, *More Ideas for Prayer*, Templegate, pp. 119-120.
7. Thomas Merton, *Contemplative Prayer*, Doubleday Image Book, p. 67.
8. St. Athanasius, as in *The Liturgy of the Hours*, Catholic Book Publishing Co., Vol. III, pp. 584-585.

The Elements

R. God shows His power by working on the elements - letting water spill on the dry land. God has all the power. God operates in order! We take things for granted many times. We take vegetation for granted - He can take it away. He can turn the moon to blood and dim the sun.

Romans 8: 5-9

Those who are living by their natural inclinations have their minds on the things human nature desires; those who live in the Spirit have their minds on spiritual things. And human nature has nothing to look forward to but death, while the Spirit looks forward to life and peace, because the outlook of disordered human nature is opposed to God, since it does not submit to God's Law, and indeed it cannot, and those who live by their natural inclinations can never be pleasing to God. You, however, live not by your natural inclinations, but by the Spirit, since the Spirit of God has made a home in you. Indeed, anyone who does not have the Spirit of Christ does not belong to him.

R. When God allows the sun to spin in the sky it is a great gift for us. When He gives a rainbow, when He allows halos around the moon, it is a great gift of His love.

So, too, the devil can cause false lights, give false voices to people to try to put them off guard and confuse the situation. The devil can give false apparitions of Jesus and Mary and give false lights and messages.

God is all powerful. He says, "you know not the day nor the hour." We think we know it all. This pride of man is not of God's liking. We are dependent on Him. God is the Creator, we are the creatures.

God can allow bugs to crawl on the earth and can overwhelm man with them. They can infect man and wipe him out.

God is in control, not man. Man is given great gifts from God. Man's intelligence has been used against God's plan, many times. It is not always in harmony with God's plan.

The television, the movies, the video games, have been used to hurt the mind of the young.

Man has used his great intelligence to promote sin, many times. Man should use His intelligence to spread the Good News.

Man has a free will. Man is to choose love. Man is to be obedient to God.

Some men have used their medical advances to perfect abortions. Some men have killed the great life that God has created - a human person. Man is offending God. We should be making reparation as a human race for the offenses against Him.

God created the whole earth and its creatures in six days and He rested on the seventh day.

What is it that man is so busy he needs not rest on the seventh day?

He commands us to "remember thou keep holy the Sabbath day."

The priest and the people are to pray as one body in Christ. We receive the Body and Blood of Jesus at Mass. The Mass is the Sacrifice of Calvary, sacramentally made present. We pray to the Father, united to Jesus, in the Holy Spirit at Mass. We pray for grace.

We eat the Body of Jesus and drink His Blood. We are one in Christ. Christ gives His Body and Blood. We pray to the Father, in the name of Jesus, united to the Holy Sacrifice of the Mass, in the Holy Spirit, through the powerful intercession of the Virgin Mary, with all the angels and saints and the souls in purgatory.

We pray for grace for the priests, the Church and the world. We unite to the Mass, all day, in the Morning Offering.

We are missing the great gift of intense union of God with man in the Mass.

It is a mystical marriage of Christ to the soul. Jesus gives us Himself, Body, Blood, Soul and Divinity in the Holy Eucharist. Jesus is the Bridegroom of our soul!!

I see myself walk the aisle to receive Him and my heart is filled with such anticipation I can hardly breathe and I see Jesus (on the Apostles Manual) with His arms outstretched and He unites to me in this intense mystical union.

Nothing is like the intense relationship I know after communion when I feel God's presence. Jesus' presence envelopes me. I am staggering to walk to my pew. I know God and God's presence. It is highly mystical. I am taken to heights that I cannot describe and my breathing even gets in the way because it is a physical activity. I feel I cannot breathe. I want to just be united in Him. I do not want to be engaged in a physical activity. My being is one in Him. I want to be absolutely still and at rest - being one in Him!

Song: *I Love You Jesus*

I Love You Jesus

by Rita Ring

Song: *Your Presence Pervades My Soul*

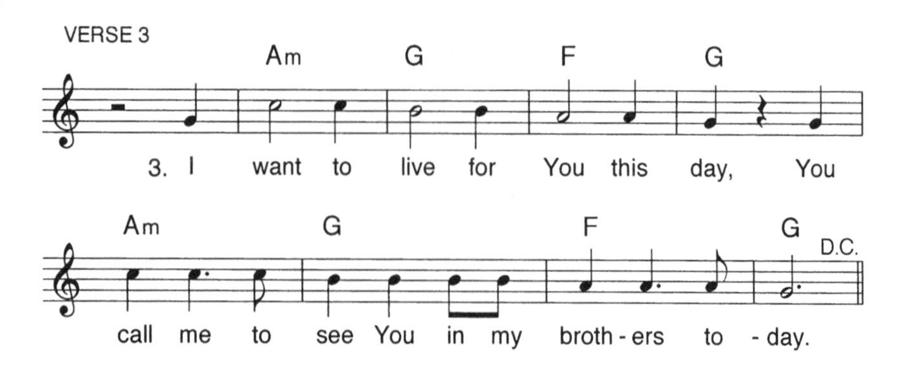
VERSE 3
Am G F G
3. I want to live for You this day, You
Am G F G D.C.
call me to see You in my broth - ers to - day.

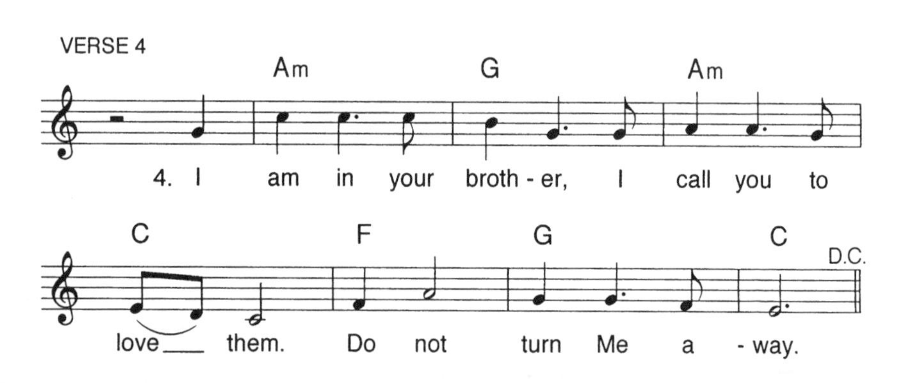
VERSE 4
Am G Am
4. I am in your broth - er, I call you to
C F G C D.C.
love them. Do not turn Me a - way.

Shepherds of Christ
Spirituality 2 Newsletters
by Father Edward Carter S.J.

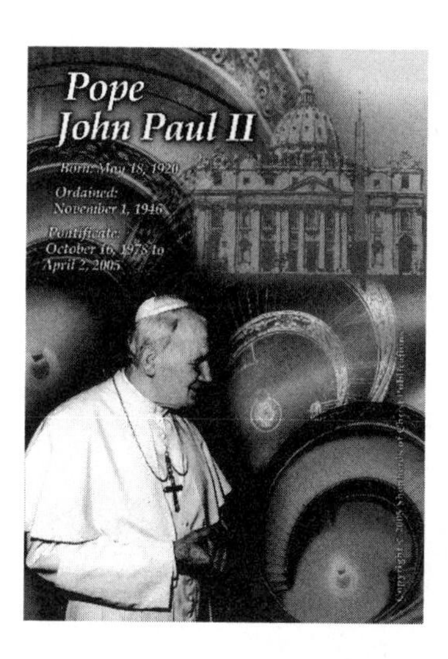

Priestly Newsletter - January/February 1997

Thoughts on the Eucharist

• In his recent book, *Gift and Mystery*, Pope John Paul II speaks of the Eucharist and the priest: "In the Eucharist, the Son, who is of one being with the Father...offers himself in sacrifice to the Father for humanity and for all creation. In the Eucharist Christ gives back to the Father everything that has come from him. Thus there is brought about a profound mystery of justice on the part of the creature toward the Creator. Man needs to honor his Creator by offering to him, in an act of thanksgiving and praise, all that he has received. Man must never lose sight of the debt, which he alone, among all other earthly realities, is capable of acknowledging and paying back as the one creature made in God's own image and likeness. At the same time, given his creaturely limitations and sinful condition, man would be incapable of making this act of justice toward the Creator, had not Christ himself, the Son who is of one being with the Father and also true man, first given us the Eucharist.

"The priesthood, in its deepest reality, is the priesthood of Christ. It is Christ who offers himself, his Body and Blood, in sacrifice to God the Father, and by this sacrifice makes righteous in the Father's eyes all mankind and, indirectly, all creation. The priest, in his daily celebration of the Eucharist, goes to the very heart of this mystery. For this reason the celebration of the Eucharist must be the most important moment of the priest's day, the center of his life." 4

4. Pope John Paul II, *Gift and Mystery*, Doubleday, pp. 74-75.

*We are all suffering because He wants the *Mass Book* out. We will continue to suffer.

Fr. Carter quoted the *Mass Book*.

Priestly Newsletter March/April 1997

Here are thoughts from one woman's spiritual journal on the Mass:

"The priest needs to feed the people with the love of God. When people come to the Mass and the sacraments, they are spiritually fed.

"The world cries out to be fed. The Church is the body of Christ. Jesus has chosen each priest and anointed him as Christ alive in this world today. The greatest calling is to be called to be a holy priest by our Lord Himself. How dearly He loves His beloved priests and longs for their love. As He suffered so during His bitter Passion for the lack of love of some of His chosen priests betrothed to Him, He was comforted by His holy priests. Jesus truly loves His sacred priests.

"Jesus must live in the priest. The priest's every action must be one with Jesus. He is a priest forever according to the order of Melchizedek.

"When a priest is filled with the love of Jesus, He will unite more deeply with Christ in the great sacrifice being offered to the Father. In the holy sacrifice of the Mass, the faithful will see Jesus through the priest offering sacrifice to the Father. We will lift our eyes and we will feel, at this great sacrifice, the presence of God, Father, Son and Holy Spirit. We unite in offering sacrifice to the Father. We all unite as one and give ourselves in such oneness with Jesus, in such love to the Father, in the Holy Spirit. We die to all those things that are not of Him and join in this great miracle taking place. The Father looks down and He sees the sacrifice of His beautiful Son through the consecrated hands of His holy priests. Heaven unites to earth. Earth cries out in such jubilation at the great gift given from the Almighty God, and we unite as creatures giving ourselves as a sacrifice to our beloved Creator. Do we experience the presence of God as His power flows through the hands of a man, the priest who takes ordinary bread and wine and changes them into the Body and Blood of our Lord? Do we hear Jesus cry out, as He did at the last supper, with the intensity in His voice reflecting all knowledge of the upcoming events of His passion and death?

"Do we hear the priest say the words of consecration with the emotion of Jesus, about to give His life for His beloved souls? And the earth stands still. There is, at that moment, the sacrifice of Calvary sacramentally made present through the hands of the priest. Oh, that God so loved this world to give His only Son as a sacrifice and that God wants us in this deep oneness with Him. I give You myself, my beautiful God, as You so willingly gave Yourself to me on Calvary. I want to die with You.

"Love between two persons is mutual giving. It is interaction between two people. It is intimacy. It is dependent on how much we give. We receive intimacy, interaction, according to how much we put into it. God gives His all. We see Him hanging, covered with blood, crowned with thorns, hands and feet pierced. We see His precious heart, font of life and love and mercy, pierced. This is freedom. He shows us the way. We give ourselves. We sacrifice and beg to be made holy, beg to be like Him in this holy sacrifice. The most important aspect of our offering sacrifice is how we are in our heart. Are we one with Jesus, giving ourselves to our beloved Father Who is all worthy of our love? Who are we that God loves us creatures so much that He, Almighty God, becomes present, no less present than the day He walked this earth, through the hands of a man, and we take it so lightly. Think of Jesus calling out. Raise the Host high, beloved priests. This is the Son of God and you have been given the greatest honor on this earth.

"God comes to us. He gives Himself to us. Let us see ourselves as one in Him. Let us unite. Let us look at ourselves, all creatures of our beloved God, God, all Holy, all Magnificent, Almighty, all Powerful, and see what He gives us. Let us see ourselves as His creatures and Him as the Creator, and look at ourselves and see how we, and all men, are offending our precious God. As we unite, we beg, beg, with this holy sacrifice of His Son, for mercy. We watch it flow from the Father, in the Holy Spirit, through the font of grace and mercy, the pierced Heart of Jesus, through the heart of Mary, by the hands of the priest, who is one with Jesus, to us. We are so joined in such oneness with the Hearts of Jesus and Mary. We have given ourselves to Them. It is here, united to Christ in such oneness, that my sacrifice is received by the loving hands of the Father. It is in this oneness that He pours out His grace. We unite through Him, with Him, and in Him, in the unity of the Holy Spirit, and we beg for mercy as His creatures who have offended our beloved God. This is our gift to You, our beloved Father. As Vatican II says, in union with the priest, we offer the Son to the Father. We give Him the greatest thanks for this holy and living sacrifice. We unite with the whole Church. We ask to be nourished by His Body and Blood, to be filled with the Holy Spirit, and increasingly become one body in Him. We join with Mary and all the saints and constantly plead for help through this sacrifice. Through this sacrifice may we make peace with You and peace for the salvation of the whole world. We pray in love and faith for your pilgrim Church, for the Pope, our bishop and all bishops, all clergy and all people. We ask the Father to hear the prayers of His family and ask Him in mercy and love to unite all children the world over. We ask the Father to take all our brothers and sisters that have died, that were good, into heaven. And we pray that we will have the vision of Your glory, through Christ, Our Lord, and we pray through Him, with Him and in Him, in the unity of the Holy Spirit. All glory and honor is Yours, Almighty Father, forever and ever.

"We pray to the Father, with all our hearts and all our love, the 'Our Father.' We say every word. We say with such love, 'Our Father,' we pray that Thy kingdom comes on earth as it is in heaven. We want this kingdom here, we are all brothers and sisters and God is our Father and we want all men doing His will. We ask to be fed both spiritually and physically every day. We beg to be free from evil and have peace. We ask Him to keep us free from sin and anxiety and hope for His coming. We pray that the kingdom and power and the glory are God's now and forever. We give to each other peace and we beg for forgiveness and mercy. We are sinful, but we want mercy. We stand. We should shout out to the Father, "Look how sinful we are!" We beg for mercy for our sins and those of all men.

"I experience the action of the Holy Spirit in a special way from the Consecration of the Mass. It fills me with such anticipation to receive Jesus, and I want to be holy. From the Consecration, I give myself to the Father, united in the Holy Spirit, in a special way. Consecrated to the Hearts of Jesus and Mary, I experience God. I love the Mass so much. The rest of this book that follows are my experiences during Mass, after Communion, and other times. Many are experiences at Holy Cross-Immaculata Catholic Church in Cincinnati, Ohio. For four months straight I experienced special moments with my beloved Jesus there daily."[5]

5. Rita Ring, *The Mass: A Journey Into His Heart*, to be published by Shepherds of Christ Publications.

A Letter to Core Leaders

Jesus: Dear Shepherds of Christ Core Leaders,
Fr. Carter, John, Rita and those involved,

I have told you to publish the *Mass Book.* The great writings on the Mass are given in this book. I allowed you to experience these great gifts to write about them for this world in the

Priestly Newsletters and the Mass books. I am telling you to publish the book and begin compiling the second book. I am telling you to publish the Children's Rosary Book. This is a necessary tool to spread the movement to the schools and the family, and the youth. The picture of Our Lady of Sorrows and Our Lady of Light are important to understanding how Mary is pleading to reach her lost children. Mary appeared in her last apparitions daily as a combination of Our Lady of Sorrow and Our Lady of Light. Mary is bringing forth the children of light but many will be lost. The more My Movement, Shepherds of Christ, spreads across the earth, the more souls will be led to the light and united to My Sacred Heart. This Movement is majorly to bring about the completion of the Fatima Mission. You should not fear those working for you.

John is the President of Shepherds of Christ. He has pleased me in carrying out the wishes in the messages. Study these messages and obey. I will reward you when you obey the directions I have given to you. You are to study all messages and obey as I have instructed you. Your movement will flourish when you obey the messages. Disobedience has caused you immense sufferings. I am communicating to you in these messages. I am instructing Rita to call a married couple and tell them of the Father's Plan. Every piece is a piece of the puzzle. I will send funds for the chapel. I am instructing you to build or construct a separate building for the chapel. The chapel is not to be attached to the house. This message has deterred the progress of the building of the chapel. You must pray and contact all I have instructed you to contact. Ask Mike to contact Bob and tell him about the chapel.

Your friends will be friends to the end. Your enemies will cause you great problems. You may be leery of those who say 'yes' one day and 'no' the next day. The Father will stand behind all action you take to see that His Plan unfolds. This is why I tell you not to fear. You must pray fervently for the Father will give you all the grace you need to do anything that is difficult to purify the movement.

Your movement must be united, operating according to the Father's Plan. I give these instructions for the Shepherds of Christ Movement here. No one is to discern any material or messages except Fr. Carter. You must wait for direction from Me concerning discernment. Distribute directive messages as I direct. It is necessary for the Movement to proceed to give messages that will direct your Movement. I will give the directions through Fr. Carter and Rita until further notice. You must obey these directions for discernment. The devil will attempt to use other messages from other visionaries to cause major problems for your Movement. You must study these messages and obey them. Your Mission is defined clearly in these messages.

I am Jesus. I am pleased with your obedience to the messages. The Father is pleased when you proceed according to the Plan I am revealing to you here. The Father has spoken. Study His messages. He is guarding your Movement. He wants obedience to the Plan. It is in obedience the Plan will unfold.

It is important that the Churches are praying for the priests and the renewal of the Church and the world. Make every effort to begin prayer chapters in Churches, before the tabernacle. In these Prayer Chapters use the material with the Imprimatur and encourage the priest to read the Priestly Newsletter. The school children must be encouraged to pray the Consecration and the rosary on a daily basis. Do you want peace? Mary told the children at Fatima that you must pray the rosary.

Do not be discouraged by all these directions. I have summarized My directions given since October 13, 1996. What you do will help majorly to bring about the Reign of My Sacred Heart and the Triumph of My Mother's Immaculate Heart.

Yesterday was a great beginning in your Movement, on the Feast of St. Anthony.

The Center in China will become important to the Movement. I am asking that a rosary and meeting be scheduled there as soon as possible. That area is richly blessed with Shepherds of Christ people. They are ready to spread the Shepherds of Christ Movement from there as a center. I am working behind the scenes to spread the Movement. Do not allow satan to distract you or discourage you.

Continue to pray hourly for Fr. Carter, the funds and grace for the Movement. Spread the Falmouth picture. Take them to Florida on June 21st and publish the *Mass Book* immediately. This has displeased Me - the delays on this book – please tend to this immediately.

Parts of this message may be circulated to the individuals involved. Other parts of the message may be circulated when necessary.

Tell the ____ the material concerning the chapel. I am pleased with all the help that ______ has given to the Movement. His farm is a most sacred place.

I am greatly pleased with the role that Mike has assumed in helping in the Movement. He is a great apostle. His work is most important to the advancement of the Father's Plan. Tell him I am longing to be so close to him and I wait for him every day to shower Me with his love.

I love you. Jesus

6/14/97

Mary: Don't Offend God

R. Mary appeared as Our Lady of Light in the Lady of Sorrows statue. The devil has waged a war against the children of light and he is tripping them on their way. Her attempts to reach them at Fatima and through other visionaries have not gotten the attention of her children. Mary appeared to me every day in one of Mary's last attempts to reach her children. They did not respond, now she appears on the building in Florida, the Lady of Fatima, in the Americas, Our Lady of Guadalupe bringing forth her children of light from the apparition site.

Mary: I am the Lady clothed as the sun and appearing as Our Lady of Fatima in the Americas, Our Lady of Guadalupe - all of my titles will merge into one as the world is brought into oneness, majorly through the Chief Shepherd of the Flock, my Son Jesus. I am Our Lady appearing on a former bank building in Florida. You have made money your god! You are a sinful, willful race and our Blessed Lord is angered at the ways of the children of the world. You have not loved Him. You have offended God. The Father will chastise the earth because you fail to respond to the warnings given. The Father has asked for the Falmouth picture to be circulated throughout this earth. I request this picture to be circulated from my

Florida site along with the other image and pictures of Our Lady of Light and Our Lady of Sorrows.

I am sorrowful for you have offended God and treated Him with indifference and neglect. I am Mary, your Mother. Oh, children of this earth, you are in for a weird awakening. You will suffer, but it will not be in ways you think. I am asking you to begin prayer chapters as the Father requested and spread the Priestly Newsletter. I am Our Lady of Fatima in the Americas, Our Lady of Guadalupe.

6/14/97

June 15, 1997
Morrow, Ohio
The Joyful Mysteries

The Annunciation

1. **R.** The angel Gabriel appeared to the Virgin Mary and asked her to be the Mother of God.
2. **R.** Mary responded to the request.

Luke 1: 38

Mary said, 'You see before you the Lord's servant, let it happen to me as you have said.'

R. This is how it is with Mary. All through her life she always, always lived according to the Father's will.

3. **R.** Mary is the new Eve. We see the old Eve. We see Adam and Eve in the garden given the great gifts and knowing God in such an intense way of having the light, of having all these gifts and they disobeyed and they ate of the tree. Mary, the sinless one comes and she obeys all that the Father wishes her to obey. Mary is sinless and all holy. Mary is the pure and the Immaculate One. Mary is the mother of God and our Mother to lead the sinful race through the Holy Spirit to be brought forth as children of light in her Immaculate Heart.
4. **R.** And the Holy Spirit descended upon her and Mary conceived of the child, Jesus.

Reference: John 3: 16

R. God the Father gave His Son to us that we would share in His life. We are to model our lives after the life of Jesus. As we meditate on these mysteries of the rosary, let us ask for Divine wisdom especially from the Holy Spirit that we may see lights and insights into these mysteries. Let us consecrate our hearts to the Hearts of Jesus and Mary. Give ourselves to Mary in her heart, for it is there that the Holy Spirit works to give us these lights, to give us insights into the Divine mysteries. God loves us to pray the rosary. Mary gave us the rosary as a great gift in which we would be united in a deeper way to God by meditating on the lives of Jesus and Mary. It is in the rosary that the Holy Spirit does give us great lights. The Holy Spirit wants us to pray the rosary. The Holy Spirit is the Spouse of the Virgin Mary and the Holy Spirit works very closely with the Virgin Mary in bringing us forth into the light. Is this not all that we crave? We are like blinded. We are like walking in darkness. We have our human minds but He elevates our knowing capacity and loving capacity, we share in His Divine Life in baptism. And to know a little bit, to receive a light from the Holy Spirit is so satisfying for this is what we crave. This is what He has done for us in these rosaries. He has lifted the shade and He has given us insights into the Divine mysteries. It's really up to Him and what He gives us. God is the Initiator. We the one waiting His favor.

5. **R.** I give my heart to Mary and I ask the Holy Spirit to work. We see that it is through the power of the Holy Spirit that she conceived of the child Jesus. And it is through the power of the Holy Spirit that we will be brought forth into the light.

From *Tell My People*
by Fr. Edward J. Carter, S.J.

The Holy Spirit

Jesus: "My beloved friend, tell My people to pray daily to the Holy Spirit. They are to pray for an increase in His gifts. My people must realize that the Holy Spirit comes to transform them. The Spirit desires to transform you more and more according to My image. Those who are docile to His touch become increasingly shaped in My likeness. He performs this marvel within Mary's Immaculate Heart. The more one dwells in My Mother's Heart, the more active are the workings of the Spirit. The Spirit leads Mary to place you within My own Heart. In both Our Hearts, then, your transformation continues. The more you are formed after My own Heart, the more I lead you to the bosom of My Father. Tell My people all this. Tell them to pray daily for a greater appreciation of these wondrous gifts. I am Lord and Master. All who come to My Heart will be on fire to receive the gifts of the Spirit in ever greater measure! I love and bless My people!"

Reflection: The Holy Spirit is given to us to fashion us ever more according to the likeness of Jesus. And the more we are like Jesus, the more Jesus leads us to the Father. Do we, each day, pray to the Holy Spirit to be more open to His transforming influence? Do we strive each day to grow in union with Mary? The greater our union with our Mother, the spouse of the Holy Spirit, the greater is the transforming action of the Holy Spirit within us. *end of excerpt*

6. **R.** We have been given these messages from God, and from God the Father. And all of us have grown so much in our relationship with God. And He expects us to live by the messages that He has given to us. Here is something that I would like to read out of the scripture.

   Reference: Luke 1:18-20

7. **R.** The devil worked very cunningly trying to block the message God has given. God gives us signs.

August 11, 1996

Jesus: I have given permanent signs of the authenticity of these messages. Time is urgent and the messages need to be supported and circulated by the leaders in the Shepherds of Christ Movement.

Over and over again, I have told you what would happen if you ignore the messages. I am asking you to see that each and every person involved in the Shepherds of Christ Movement read the message of March 7, 1994 and March 13, 1994. Please discern and circulate the message of March 20, 1994, before the end of the building collapsed.

I am asking all to help circulate the video of April 17, 1994. I have given several permanent signs in this video. The sun spins in the beginning: the sun spins when Rita is reading a message from God's Blue Book 1. These are permanent signs I have given to prove that I am delivering these messages.

I ask you to circulate the video from September 15, 1995. The mist received around the Sorrowful Mother is her sign given that she truly appeared daily from July 5, 1994 until September 5, 1995. This is your sign to help in circulating the *Rosaries from the Hearts of Jesus and Mary*.

end of excerpt

Reference: Luke 1: 19-20

R. Mary appeared over and over and over again as Our Lady of Light for fourteen months, Mary appeared almost for 2 1/2 years on the 5th of the month and then Jesus appeared hanging on the cross in December with His mouth moving, speechless, because nobody's paying attention to what He's saying. And then the Father starts speaking in Blue Book 14. When I got the messages from God the Father, there was intense authority. The first day I got that message from God the Father and it came in about seven minutes, both of those messages. I just knew what I went through inside when God the Father spoke and it was forceful and it was authoritative. Mary speaks like Mary, Jesus speaks like Jesus.

Mary is the New Eve. Jesus is the New Adam.

Song: *A Song from Jesus*

R. The new Adam and the new Eve, Jesus and Mary.

Luke 1: 38

Mary said, 'You see before you the Lord's servant, let it happen to me as you have said.'

R. And Jesus gave Himself to His death on the cross, always obeying the Father's will. It is obedience that the Father wants of His children for we are the children of the Father and He wants us to obey Him.

8. Sing Song: *See the Eyes that Look at Mary*
9. Hail Mary
10. Hail Mary

R. Christ came and He walked the earth and He told them what they must do and He showed them through His life how to live and they hung Him on a tree. To His death they hung Him on a tree, the all-just and holy one, the King of all Kings, the Almighty God, they hung on a tree. We see Adam and Eve in the garden and we see them willfully take the fruit from the tree and eat.

PRAY the ROSARY.

The Visitation

1. **Reference: Luke 1: 39-45**
2. **R.** Mary appeared at Clearwater. Mary has visited us in these apparitions. Listen to Mary.

December 19, 1996

Mary: My dear children, I give to you, my Son, Jesus, born in a stable in Bethlehem on Christmas morn. He is the Almighty God, the Light of the World.

I appear to you, my children, on a (former) bank in Florida. You have made money your god! Do you know how cold are your hearts? You turn away from my Son, Jesus, for your money. Your money is your god.

I am Mary, your Mother. I do not appear as I once appeared to you. I am asking you today to circulate my message given on a tape on the feast of Our Lady of Guadalupe, December 12, 1996. Please circulate this tape now. Give it to as many people as you can. I am Mary, your Mother. Please circulate my *Rosary Book.*

end of December 19, 1996

3. **R.** And the Father said to read the two messages that were in the Apostles Manual on the 11th and the 18th. I continue to read them and learn more and more each time I read them. He wants us to study them for they are not from Mary and Jesus, but they are from the Father. And the Father has spoken in there and He really wants the Mass Book out. When the Mass Book is circulated, people will attend the Mass in a different way. We do not see that this is the plan from all time. We are living in this little time zone right now in this room. Today is Father's Day. Today is this, that and the other. But this plan goes back to Adam and Eve and how man has offended God. It goes back to the Visitation. It goes back to the lesson that Mary taught, that she taught us when she said, "be it done unto me according to thy word."

Reference: Luke 1: 46-48

R. Right, they will call her blessed for she is the mother of the children of light. For God has looked upon His handmaid's lowliness. We are the lowly ones. He has looked on our lowliness and He has raised us to heights. We receive a sharing in His life in baptism. Let us see Jesus in each other. We need to meditate on the mysteries of the rosary and live in Jesus! How did Jesus treat people? How did Mary treat people? Every act that They did was to please God the Father. We are doing what we are doing for God. Jesus is alive and He lives in us and He lives in this world. We must act for the honor and glory of God - do good acts. I go to the tabernacle to be with Jesus. We are the carriers of the light. We are the carriers of the joy that is alive within us for God has taught us in a very special way. And we must have that connection in our heart and our mind at all times, that whatever I am doing for anybody else I am doing for God and see Him in that person.

4. **R.** We cannot forget about our intimacy with God. For it is in that intimate time that He gives us strength. But we must realize that sometimes our prayers do not always get done exactly the way that Jesus has told us to try to do them. That we can't always pray every hour on the hour. So if we think about it 15 minutes late then we pray then. He wants strict adherence to that at the Center. The main function is at the Center to join us together in the Heart of Jesus in prayer. But in our lives, we cannot be caught up to the point where we are anxious when we do not do everything that He has asked us to do. We must try to be saints, to do what He is asking us to do. But our main focus is, is in dealing with others. We see Christ in them, the creation of God the Father.

5. **R.** We are at a new stage in this movement. We are going out as Mary visited her cousin, Elizabeth. We too, are in the stage of going out. We have our most intimate time with Jesus, which gives us strength but we must see God in others those He called us to work with, and realize that when we are serving them, when we are loving them, when we are making them smile, that we are serving and loving God.

Reference: Matthew 22: 34-40

6. **R.** We are the Shepherds of Christ. He is living in us in a special way. He has called us to this special core group, and special oneness with Him. Many of the religious are not living up to their commitment of spending time with Jesus and loving Him. He has called us as a lay people and He has given to us a great desire to love Him and to want to be with Him. And we are serving many purposes. And how immensely happy we make God when we spend our time in fervent prayer and loving. We do not even comprehend how one of us individually make Jesus so happy when our whole life is centered on Him, loving Him in others and loving Him in prayer to Him. We have a big mission all right. And the big mission is that He has given us this great oneness with Him and we give Him a lot of joy when we do things in love for Him and for others.

7. **Jesus:** Do not underestimate the great love that I have for each one of you gathered here. I have joined you to My Heart

and it is your individual sacrifice and love that gives Me immense joy. I am treated with such indifference and such hatred by so many. God is greatly offended by the creatures of this earth. And it is through your actions and your love that I receive great happiness from you. I have given to you this great union with Me and in your actions I am immensely happy with the love that you give. You help make reparation for offenses against My Heart and Mary's Heart.

8. **R.** Remember Fr. Carter saying a long time ago that we can give Jesus happiness when we love Him and when we do things that make Him happy. Jesus is waiting for us to give Him this great love. For He is offended by the creatures of this earth and He is all deserving and loving of all of our love. Jesus has given to us great gifts that we have squandered and we have not thanked Him for and so many today do not even ever say thanks to Him. Jesus has given to us a great union with Him and we give Him great happiness when we love Him and when we do what the Father wants us to do by obeying Him and spending our life doing just the things that we are trying to do. God is immensely pleased with this core group and each one of us gathered here. We should not look at ourselves and be so hard on ourselves but we should see that God is thanking us and loving us in a special way as His precious chosen ones. And be grateful that God cares for us so much.

9. **R.** We thank You, our beloved God and we love You.

10. **R.** Be grateful for these gifts from God to us.

Song: *Oh Holy Dwelling Place of God*
Song: *Hail Holy Queen Enthroned Above*

The Birth of our Lord Jesus

1. **Reference: John 3: 16**

2. **R.** Jesus died for us.

3. **R.** And we are given this sharing in His life in Baptism. Pray for grace, for this increase of His life in us. We can be permeated and saturated more with His life. The more we go especially to the Eucharist, and stay after Communion in the Mass and sit in front of the tabernacle we can receive abundant grace.

4.

Prayer for Union with Jesus

Come to me, Lord, and possess my soul. Come into my heart and permeate my soul. Help me to sit in silence with You and let You work in my heart.

I am Yours to possess. I am Yours to use. I want to be selfless and only exist in You. Help me to spoon out all that is me and be an empty vessel ready to be filled by You. Help me to die to myself and live only for You. Use me as You will. Let me never draw my attention back to myself. I only want to operate as You do, dwelling within me.

I am Yours, Lord. I want to have my life in You. I want to do the will of the Father. Give me the strength to put aside the world and let You operate my very being. Help me to act as You desire. Strengthen me against the distractions of the devil to take me from Your work.

When I worry, I have taken my focus off of You and placed it on myself. Help me not to give in to the promptings of others to change what in my heart You are making very clear to me. I worship You, I adore You and I love You. Come and dwell in me now.

- *God's Blue Book*, January 17, 1994

5. Sing: *Angels We Have Heard on High*
6. Sing: *Oh Little Town of Bethlehem*
7. **R.** A little baby in the crib, wrapped in swaddling clothes.
   Reference: Luke 1: 4-7
8. Song: *Oh Holy Dwelling Place of God*
   Song: *See the Eyes that Look at Mary*
9. Song: *What Child Is This*
10. Sing: *Silent Night*
    Song: *Come Holy Spirit*

The Presentation in the Temple

1. **Reference: Luke 2: 25-32**

2. **Reference: Luke 2: 33-35**

   R. Mary looked into the face of her Son and she saw Him battered and bruised and bloodied. Mary saw Him with the blood in His eyes. Mary saw His body covered with wounds and Mary knew that despite His suffering that many would throw away the great grace that He wanted to give them. Mary says many of her children are going to hell like rain.

3. Sing: *Little Baby Hands and Feet*

   Reference: John 19: 25-27

4. ***Mary's Message* - from the Rosary of August 27, 1996**

Mary: I stood beneath the cross of my Son, and my Heart was in such pain for I saw Him before my eyes. I saw Him covered with blood. I saw Him die. My Heart, my children, my Heart to watch my Son, but my Heart, my Heart, how I suffered for my little children of the world that give in to this world and give up the love of my Son. O my little children of light, I give you this message. Carry this light into the darkness for your Mother Mary, for I stood beneath the cross and I cried. I cried for the little ones. I cried for the young ones, the ones that do not care and will lose their souls. How do I make you see for you will not listen to me? What can I do? I come. I appear. I beg. I plead. I give you these gifts from my Son, and you reject me. I do not deliver messages very often anymore for I have been ignored. The message is the same. You do not read the messages I have given to you. Please help me. Help the little children. I appear. I appear. I appear, and I am ignored. I stood beneath the cross, and I cried. I cried, and my Heart was in such anguish for my little children, for I am searching for them this day as I searched for the Child Jesus. Please, please help me. I cannot hold back the hand of my Son any longer. I am Mary, your Mother. I ask you to help my children. You are my children of light.

end of Mary's Message

5. **R.** We must act according to the Father's will.
6. **R.** Jesus said on the day of the flood that He would shake the tree and the rotten fruit would fall to the ground and all that would remain on the tree would be the fruit of heaven.
7. Song: *We Have Been Told*
8. **R.** And God told them that they could not eat of the forbidden tree. And the garden was the most beautiful place. And they had all the gifts and everything that they needed. But they ate of the fruit of the forbidden tree.
9. **R.** And the new Adam and the new Eve came and He is hung on a tree and He shows us that to His death on the cross, He obeyed the will of the Father and that Mary stood beneath the cross and that she obeyed the will of the Father. I see this when I see Mary, holding Jesus in her arms. What a testimony to Mary and Jesus living in the Father's will. Look at them in such sorrow under the cross. Mary, her face is covered with sorrow and Jesus is dead in her arms.

China Mural (Over Altar)

10. **R.** Such unity between Jesus and Mary – Mary was conceived sinless, Jesus, the Son of God.

    Unity, Unity, Unity!

The Finding of Our Lord in the Temple

1. **R.** Mary stood outside of the tomb. Mary could barely stand and she looked and her Son had been locked in the tomb. Can you imagine the sorrow within the heart of Mary as she looked at the locked tomb. Mary cries out to us today about her lost children. Mary knew of those souls that would be locked in the everlasting tomb of hell, never ever, ever to get out.
2. **R.** And so I wrote yesterday, this is how Mary appeared to me for fourteen months as Our Lady of Light. Mary appears with the sword in her heart and Mary speaks and she says, "I am the Lady of Light. I lament the loss of my precious children. I knew from the prophecy of Simeon so many would be lost."

    Reference: Luke 2: 31-35

3. **R.** God shows His power by working on the elements, letting water spill on the dry land. Everything operates in order. We take it for granted. God says, "Here, I will get your attention." We take vegetation for granted. He can take it away. He can turn the moon to blood and dim the sun. Man may not recognize the hand of God. He says it is a happening. God allows the sun to spin in the sky, it is a great gift for us. When He gives a rainbow, when He allows halos around the moon, it is a gift of His love. So too, the devil can cause false lights and give false voices to people to try to get them off guard and confuse the situation. The devil can appear as Our Lady and Our Lord, sometimes, and give false lights and messages. God is all powerful. He says, "you know not the time or the day." We think we know it all. This audacious pride of man is not to God's likings. We are dependent on Him.
4. **R.** God can allow bugs to crawl on the earth and can overwhelm man with them. They can infect man and wipe him out. God is in control, not man. Man is given great gifts from God. Many times man's intelligence has been used against God's plans. It is not always in harmony with God's plan. The television, the movies, the video games have been used to infest the minds of the young. Man has used his great intelligence to promote sin. His intelligence should be used to spread the Good News. Why should God allow men to continue to do so. Man has used medical advances to perfect abortion. Man has killed the great life that God has created, a human person. On March 3, 1997, the day of the Falmouth flood, Jesus spoke and He said, "When the poison reaches the peak of pain, I will pour down the antidote in these revelations."

Genesis 1:27

"God created man in the image of himself,
in the image of God he created him"

R. And man takes the liberty to violate the commandment, 'thou shalt not kill' and kills the child God created in His image and likeness in the womb of the mother. Oh men of the earth, abortion is wrong, you anger God and test His great love and mercy given for man.

5. **R.** The greatest offense is not what we are doing to man, it is how we are offending God. We should be making

reparation as a human race for the offenses against Him. God created the whole earth and it's creatures in six days and He rested on the seventh day. What is it that man is so busy he need not rest on the seventh day. He commands, 'remember thou keep holy the Sabbath day', another commandment that is violated.

6. **R.** The priests and the people are one body in Christ. The priest is another Christ. Man is given the sacraments.
7. **R.** It is a spousal relationship that Christ wants with us. He gives His body to us in the Mass and we unite with the Divine God in this intense mystical union. God has lifted the veil for us in this core group that we can experience this mystical union with Him. It is a great gift that will happen in the new era. We have been given great gifts and we must be most thankful for the gifts that He has given. But in no way are we to be so hard on ourselves that we do not realize that God loves us immensely and that He is pleased with the acts of love and the acts of sacrifice in giving that we are giving to Him. God has given us this Movement for the renewal of the Church and the world. Pray for faith – Mary has appeared – Let's do what Jesus and Mary say to do.
8. **R.** We are making Jesus happy when we love Him and love each other.
9. Song: *We Have Been Told*

   R. We pray to be deeply one in Jesus and let Him operate in us.

   Reference: John 17: 20-23

   Song: *We Have Been Told*

   Jesus: And so My beloved ones, when they persecute you, when they holler every evil word against you, know that My Father is with you and know that He is protecting you and loving you and that you are spreading My word to those that I love. And if you are silent, they will not hear the words that you speak to them. For I live in you. I am the vine, you are the branches. All who live in Me will bear great fruit.

   R. And He will shake the tree and the rotten fruit will fall to the ground and all that will remain will be the fruit of heaven for He is the Almighty God and He created the world in seven days He created the light and He created the darkness and He created the creatures of this earth and He came and gave Himself that we would share in His Divine life and He is giving to us an abundant sharing in this Divine life that we can act in this world as He lives in us. And He is the vine and we are the branches. And we will bear great fruit for we will not wither and die, if we remain in Him. And so as it was in the beginning where He talked about taking the little shoot off of this tree. This is why I thought that this pertains to the Shepherds of Christ.

Reference: Ezekiel 17: 22-24

Reference: Psalm 92: 12-15

Reference: 2 Corinthians 5: 6-10

Reference: Mark 4: 30-34

R. And there was a reading this week and He talked about unveiling the scriptures. He has unveiled the scriptures to us.

From Genesis to Revelation. To know God is to know His Word for Jesus is the Word and He is living in our hearts. And when we speak it is like a two-edged sword that penetrates the heart and the soul of those that are the receivers because He is alive in our hearts.

Jesus: And so I say to you My beloved ones, I have called you. You have been chosen by the Father to help accomplish this plan on this earth. Do not be afraid for He guards you night and day.

R. The Father comforts me. And I am not afraid for my greatest desire is to do His will. We love You, our beloved Father. We thank You. We are imperfect. We seek to be more perfect as our Heavenly Father is perfect. And we know You more and more through your Son, Jesus, and we grow in our love relationships. We thank you, Jesus, You have given us this Spousal relationship. We can go to You and know Your love. And we thank you Mary, the all perfect mother, the mother that loves us and teaches us love. The more we know God: Father, Son and Holy Spirit, the more we can imitate God and be healed. And God has given to us each other that we can love more perfectly for we are human persons and we are loving one another as Christ loves through us. And the Holy Spirit binds it all together with the fire of God's love, permeating and acting within the heart of Mary to help us to be more and more like Jesus, our Savior. The Holy Spirit is working in Mary's Heart. Amen.

10. **From *Tell My People***
by Fr. Edward J. Carter, S.J.

The Holy Spirit

Jesus: "My beloved friend, tell My people to pray daily to the Holy Spirit. They are to pray for an increase in His gifts. My people must realize that the Holy Spirit comes to transform them. The Spirit desires to transform you more and more according to My image. Those who are docile to His touch become increasingly shaped in My likeness. He performs this marvel within Mary's Immaculate Heart. The more one dwells in My Mother's Heart, the more active are the workings of the Spirit. The Spirit leads Mary to place you within My own Heart. In both Our Hearts, then, your transformation continues. The more you are formed after My own Heart, the more I lead you to the bosom of My Father. Tell My people all this. Tell them to pray daily for a greater appreciation of these wondrous gifts. I am Lord and Master. All who come to My Heart will be on fire to receive the gifts of the Spirit in ever greater measure! I love and bless My people!"

Reflection: The Holy Spirit is given to us to fashion us ever more according to the likeness of Jesus. And the more we are like Jesus, the more Jesus leads us to the Father. Do we, each day, pray to the Holy Spirit to be more open to His transforming influence? Do we strive each day to grow in union with Mary? The greater our union with our Mother, the spouse of the Holy Spirit, the greater is the transforming action of the Holy Spirit within us. *end of excerpt*

R. The Bread of Life is the Word and the Eucharist. Jesus is the Bread of Life. God gives us a sharing in His life in baptism and nourishes this life with Himself. We've been praying for this mission that He's called us to. Why He called us, He knew that we would say yes.

Say the Our Father.

6/15/97

Mother's Day Picture 1995

June 1997

R. Mary, the Mother of the Children of the Light

Simeon's prophecy:

1. This child is destined for the rise and fall of many in Israel.
2. Now the devil has gone into a rage after the children of light.
3. The devil wishes to stop the children of light.
4. Many will be lost despite the suffering of Jesus because of their mortal sins and not repenting.
5. Mary stood beneath the cross.
6. Death is final.
7. Mary says souls are going to hell like rain.

Mary appeared with the sword in her heart for 14 months.

She was covered with Light. Mary called herself the Lady of Light.

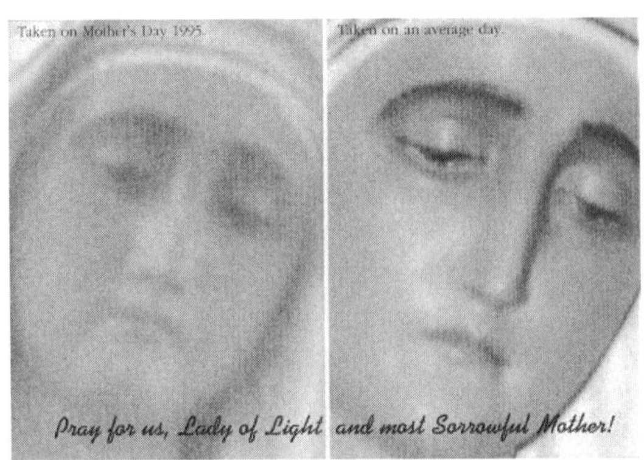

Mary: I am the Lady of Light. I lament the loss of my precious children. I knew from the prophecy of Simeon how so many would be lost for he said to me:

Reference: Luke 2: 29-35

Jesus the King of Kings

R. They smacked Him, they whipped Him, they tore His flesh - nothing they did to Him could get Him to deviate from the Father's Plan. The Chief Shepherd of the Flock, born in poverty, the little King, now mounts the cross, the throne they hung Him on. He is the King of all Kings. He showed us the way - it is in compliance to the Father's Will to His death on the cross. The old Adam was weak. Adam ate of the tree and we the children of Adam and Eve suffered.

1 Corinthians 15: 20-28

In fact, however, Christ has been raised from the dead, as the first-fruits of all who have fallen asleep. As it was by one man that death came, so through one man has come the resurrection of the dead. Just as all die in Adam, so in Christ all will be brought to life; but all of them in their proper order: Christ the first-fruits, and next, at his coming, those who belong to him. After that will come the end, when he will hand over the kingdom to God the Father, having abolished every principality, every ruling force and power. For he is to be king *until he has made* his enemies his footstool, and the last of the enemies to be done away with is death, for *he has put all things under his feet.* But when it is said everything is subjected, this obviously cannot include the One who subjected everything to him. When everything has been subjected to him, then the Son himself will be subjected to the One who has subjected everything to him, so that God may be all in all.

Mary cries, "I stood beneath the cross of my Son and cried."

Diagram: I was waken at 3:00 a.m.

Whipped Jesus, smacked Jesus, and Jesus said "Thy Will Be Done."

Mary - beneath the cross - Jesus on the cross.

Reference: John 1: 14

Jesus said: Not My Will But Thine Be Done!

R. Mary cries out to pray for the willful ones, the ones doing their own will.

Jesus will Reign - Jesus is Chief Shepherd of the Flock. There will be One Flock and One Shepherd and they will follow Him.

We see Jesus being smacked, tearing His flesh. Jesus did not come down from the cross they nailed Him on. Jesus was crucified to His death doing the Father's Will. The New Adam - the New Eve. The old Adam and old Eve were weak. They disobeyed, they sinned, they were willful.

Reference: Romans 5: 10-11

R. So what does the Father want? He wants us to model ourselves after the New Adam, and the New Eve, to be one in the Father's will, to die to our own will rather than deviate, to give ourselves, to die and rise in Christ. For it is in dying to ourselves that we are reborn.

Prayer for Union with Jesus

Come to me, Lord, and possess my soul. Come into my heart and permeate my soul. Help me to sit in silence with You and let You work in my heart.

I am Yours to possess. I am Yours to use. I want to be selfless and only exist in You. Help me to spoon out all that is me and be an empty vessel ready to be filled by You. Help me to die to myself and live only for You. Use me as You will. Let me never draw my attention back to myself. I only want to operate as You do, dwelling within me.

I am Yours, Lord. I want to have my life in You. I want to do the will of the Father. Give me the strength to put aside the world and let You operate my very being. Help me to act as You desire. Strengthen me against the distractions of the devil to take me from Your work.

When I worry, I have taken my focus off of You and placed it on myself. Help me not to give in to the promptings of others to change what in my heart You are making very clear to me. I worship You, I adore You and I love You. Come and dwell in me now.

-*God's Blue Book*, January 17, 1994

Reference: John 12:24

R. Jesus died for us. We die to ourselves and are born in Him. We put aside the selfish ways and are born into His ways.

The ten commandments are a covenant given by God to man. Man was sinful, willful - he was sent out of the garden. God told them to obey - to do His will.

This new era is the Reign of the Chief Shepherd in which there will be One Flock, One Shepherd. There are many wills in the Church on the simple issue of birth control.

Moses gave the ten commandments: "I, the Lord, am your God. You shall not have other gods besides me." We have worshipped the golden calf, the football on Sunday, the Lord's Day, that is to be kept sacred. We have worshipped our TV's and Nintendo games - our glorious money, to the point we work for money on His day of rest when many don't have to, they work any way. The Lord created the heavens and on the seventh day He rested, yet we are so busy. We, the creatures of this earth, work on Sunday. Our stores are open and our malls are packed. Some wear shorts to Church and run to get to the mall or skip Church and work for double money, or some go to rock concerts or football games for which we pay tons of money for, but the collection in Church is left with a few pennies and some don't even go to Church.

So Moses went up the mountain and He received the commandments, a covenant God made with the sinful men and we disobey His commandments!

How are we praising and loving God at Church? Are we obedient to God's law? Are we obedient to God's will? Do we obey the pope? Is authority recognized as it should be? We have removed the crucifixes in many places. The crucifix is the tree they hung Him on, for He did the Will of the Father. Without the death, there would not be the resurrection.

The Father says on January 18, 1997: "I tell you all to read the accounts concerning Noah. Nowhere in history has God been offended as He is this day by this sinful world. You will suffer a fate for the offenses against God."

R. Read the accounts of Noah - He wiped out most of the earth by flood because of the willfulness and sin.

Is this how we show God that we follow the Chief Shepherd

by disobeying the commandments, by disobeying the pope?

The new era will be when men will know God with such oneness in Him. They cannot help love Him when they know Him.

We are a people walking in darkness because of our tainted human natures because of the sin of Adam. We are worshiping the golden calf. We are willful and sinful. We do not see the light because we are not born as children of the light. We need to consecrate our hearts to Jesus and Mary's Hearts.

The era is upon us. The answer to being One Flock and One Shepherd is to follow the Chief Shepherd of the Flock. Jesus mounted the tree and gave Himself as a sacrifice. Jesus died to give us life. Jesus is the first-born from the dead. Jesus is brought forth from the tomb on Easter morn because He died to do the Father's will.

Mary held Jesus' lifeless body in her arms under the cross. Mary held Jesus in the temple. Mary was told, "this child is destined for the rise and fall of many in Israel and a sword shall pierce your soul, Mary." (Luke 2: 34-35) Mary carried Jesus in her arms into the temple. Mary held Jesus' lifeless body under the cross. In the arms of Mary, Jesus was presented in the temple. In the arms of Mary, Jesus was received beneath the cross - and so Mary cries under the cross, for her little lost children, the ones who did not learn from the prophesy of Simeon - some will fall; some will rise.

Adam and Eve did their own will and the light was dimmed. Why should God give us the light of knowing Him in great intensity? Jesus shows us the way. Dwell in the Hearts of Jesus and Mary. Consecrate your hearts to Jesus and Mary's Hearts.

We are given baptism. We receive a sharing in His life in baptism. Jesus was carried to the temple in the arms of Mary. The new born baby is carried to Church many times to be baptized. In baptism we receive a sharing in His life. We must follow Jesus. We must obey the Father's will.

There is only one way; it is to do God's will. It is disobedience that got us into this mess.

The Father speaks of obedience – the world is really willful. It is this word, "obedience".

Jesus speaks on the day of the flood, March 3, 1997. When the Church reaches the peak of pain, God will pour down the antidote in these writings. The rotten fruit will fall to the ground and all that will remain will be the fruit of heaven.

The Father speaks on January 18, 1997 how angered He is for us ignoring Our Mother.

6/20/97

One Flock and One Shepherd

Jesus: My dear Shepherds,

You will be One Flock with One Shepherd. The Father has wiped out most of the willful ones in your Movement. Any willfulness will be dealt with. To My death on the cross I obeyed the Father's Will. You are the little family, the Father is using in the Shepherds of Christ to light up the earth. You will be one flock and one in your dealings. Praying the Morning Offering will unite you into one fold. Praying the Consecration will unite you into one fold. When the poison reaches the peaks of pain I will pour down the antidote in these writings. Anyone with their own plan will be dismissed from the Movement.

If you do not comply to the directions, the Father will act so that you turn to obedience.

R. He mounted the cross and gave His life that we would live. He obeyed His Father to His death on the cross. Mary stood beneath the cross and she wept for the willful ones that would be lost.

Jesus: Disobedience in your Movement offends the Father greatly. It is My Movement. I am Chief Shepherd of the Flock. There will be One Flock and One Shepherd. (You must ask Ellen to read all messages concerning the Church and the Shepherds of Christ.) Obedience is rewarded in the Movement by gifts from the Father. Disobedience gives Him great displeasure.

You are to live by the Blue Book messages and the Apostles Manual. Any leader must be a firm believer of these messages I give to you. If new people enter the Movement they are not to enter into leadership positions, sisters and religious included. I have formed you into leaders for the new era. Anyone in a leadership role must be a product of these revelations, living according to the Father's Plan. He has weeded out the willful ones in the Movement. Those that remain will be dealt with accordingly. No one will exist doing their will. This is His Plan to lead the stayed ones in the Church and the world into one. Anyone having their own plan will be dismissed. I will give you the grace to deal with this. Willfulness will be dealt with. Those who have opposed you in the past are suffering tremendously - interior suffering. They are trying to fight the will of God.

It pleases the Father when you obey, when you pray the hourly prayers and follow the messages. The moon will turn to blood and you will be protected by the Blood of the Lamb. You are being dressed in My Blood at the appointed hours of 3:00 pm, 6:00 pm, 9:00 pm, and 12:00 am.

I am requesting you make a tape of the Morning Offering and Daily Prayers, on one side and the hourly novena on the back side, with the Holy Spirit Prayer and prayers from p. 10 to the end. Do not be afraid. I will protect you with My Blood.

Acts of obedience please the Father. You are against a willful world and many priests have been neglectful of the authority in the Church. Man is reconciled to God through the Blood of the Lamb, shed for man's sins.

Oh, night, greatly blest, you will know a time of terror and a time of joy, for you will know that: I AM GOD AND I WILL HAVE NO GODS BEFORE ME! I have made a Covenant with man and man has broken this covenant. You will suffer a fate for the deed.

This movement will be one in the Father's Will. You must be obedient to the directions given to help bring about the Reign of My Sacred Heart.

The Reign of My Heart will be a Reign of living in the Father's Will..."Thy Kingdom come, thy will be done, one Earth as it is in Heaven. Give us this day our daily bread...."

I give you My Body and Blood and you ignore Me and treat Me with indifference. Disrespect given to My letters of love displeases Me. I will wipe out the earth and you will know how offended is your God for the deeds of sinful men.

You must obey the commandments. God is the ruler. He is the King. The Pope is the Vicar of the Church. The Father, the head of the family. Authority has not been obeyed. There is much disobedience in the Church and the world. The willfulness of the earth displeases the Father. God is God - Man is Man. What is right is right; what is wrong is wrong. You have disobeyed the commandments and the pope. You have offended your God by your treatment of the Eucharist.

I send teachings in My Love Letters that are ignored and ridiculed. I will strike the earth with a strong hand and the audacious men will scatter and you will know the wrath of God. I am offended by the lack of response to the messages I give here. I will tell all of the authenticity of these messages.

My Mother appeared for 14 long months everyday and she was ignored and treated with disrespect. They moved the statue that she appeared in as Our Lady of Light, which angered the Father.

This will go down in history as the era of great willfulness against God. You are a sinful race. You have ignored the warnings I have given. The Father will not tolerate the disrespect of the greatest gift you have received. He will not tolerate the disrespect of the Eucharist. You will suffer. The people I have called to your movement have turned to their own ways. They have not helped you because of willfulness. Anyone that has turned against you is suffering greatly interiorly. Do not worry about the enemies, give them to Me and pray, pray for them with the greatest love. They are suffering tremendously. Anyone opposing the Father's Plan will suffer.

You must join in the hourly prayer and pray with the greatest fervor.

Pray to be one in your Movement. Your Movement will be My beating Heart in the world, with One Flock and One Shepherd.

Give Me your heart and your soul in surrendering to the Father's Will.

Give your heart to Me and I will make you Fishers of Men.

You are the Apostles of the New Era.

6/20/97

June 22, 1997
Morrow, Ohio

Sorrowful Mysteries

The Agony in the Garden

1. **R.** This is from the Gospel today.
   Reference: Mark 4: 35-41

Job 38: 8-11

Who pent up the sea behind closed doors
when it leapt tumultuous from the womb,
when I wrapped it in a robe of mist
and made black clouds its swaddling bands;
when I cut the place I had decreed for it
and imposed gates and a bolt?
'Come so far,' I said, 'and no further;
here your proud waves must break!'

2. Song: *Be Not Afraid*

3. **R.** Jesus has given me a lot of messages this week. And the one was all night. And if you see Jesus, see Him hanging on the cross. See Him whipped. See how they smacked Him and see Him say, "Thy will be done." They smacked Him. They whipped Him. They tore His flesh. Nothing they did to Him could get Him to deviate from the Father's plan. The Chief Shepherd of the flock born in poverty, the King of Kings, now mounts the cross, the throne they hung Him on. Jesus, the King of Kings, Jesus showed us the way. Jesus complied to the Father's will - Jesus died on the cross.

4. Song: *A Song from Jesus*
5. **R.** Jesus is the Almighty God that could quiet the sea, that could stop the waves, that they went exactly so high, but not too high to tip the boat over, that He set a limit on these waves. And the apostles with a fear in their heart, were filled with such fear that they woke the teacher and they said to Him, "teacher, we are going to drown".
6. **Jesus:** Do you feel alone, My beloved ones? How do you feel in this world? I have taught you and I have brought you to this level. But I see the fear within your heart. Are you like the apostles that are in the boat, that are watching the waves as it tips the boat back and forth as your boat in the sea of life is being tipped back and forth? And you are saying, "Lord, Lord, I am going to drown." Is this what you are saying to Me? You are in the world but you are not like the world. But your truth is in the scriptures for you know that every word that I speak here is the truth that lives in the scriptures. It is in the scriptures that you will find your comfort and your consolation.

   And as you go to the Mass and the Eucharist, you will be nourished and fed and you will feel close to Me. But the moment you go into the world your boat will tip one way and another for the world is not like you and you will suffer persecution. But your truth will be found in Me for you will know as you give yourselves in this oneness to Me, that you are molded more and more into My image and likeness and I live in you in this world and I am operating through you and touching the hearts of many for what you do with your life will make the difference to millions of souls. I knelt in the garden and I sweat blood for these souls, the souls that I loved. Do you care My beloved ones? Do you care for all your brothers? For these souls that will be lost if you say no to My call. I am asking you as your boat tips back and forth, as you go through this sea that seems violent and turbulent at times, that you are not afraid, for you know that you must trust in Me and you will not come to Me and say, "Lord, Lord, we may drown." But you will know that it will be turbulent and you will suffer persecution and the boat will tip for the world is not like you. But your truth will be found in the scriptures and in Me.
7. **R.** The old Adam was weak and he ate of the tree. Mary

cried, "I stood beneath the cross of my Son and I cried." Mary cried out for the willful ones, the ones doing their own will. Jesus will Reign as Chief Shepherd of the flock. There will be one flock and one Shepherd and they will follow Him. Jesus shows us how He was treated with the tearing of His flesh. Jesus did not come down from the cross. They nailed Jesus to the cross. Jesus was crucified to death, for Jesus lived always in the Father's will. The new Adam, the new Eve. Mary stands beneath the cross, the Mediatrix of grace. Mary always lived in the Father's will, saying, 'You see before you the Lord's servant, let it happen to me as you have said.' *Luke 1: 38*

And Jesus said, 'Father,' he said, 'if you are willing, take this cup away from me. Nevertheless, let your will be done, not mine.' *Luke 22: 42*

R. The old Adam and old Eve were weak. They were disobedient. They sinned. They were willful. Jesus died for our sins.

8. **R.** And I hear the noises and I hear them questioning Jesus and asking Jesus, "what did you say, what did you say, tell us what you said, who are you?" And He answers them very quickly and directly, but Jesus does not argue. And I hear the noises and I hear them battering Him and beating Him and Jesus constantly proceeds ahead in the Father's will. Is this not how it is in our life? For we are walking in Jesus' footsteps and we are persecuted and we are battered. But we know that we too are doing the Father's will. We follow in the footprints of Jesus.

9. Song: *Be Not Afraid*

   R. So you see yourself suffering and you know that it is hard in order to get along with one another, but you are joining with one another in a most intimate love. For in this new era there will be the greatest oneness and the greatest love between brothers and sisters of this earth. And so you are bumping heads now and you are suffering but you are trying so hard and saying to yourself, "why do I have so much trouble with my brothers when I pray all the time?" And He tells us that we are not perfect, that we are imperfect. We have a wounded human nature. We must grow more and more in the image and likeness of Jesus. We should not be upset because as we die to our imperfections, we are becoming closer to one another. We are growing in oneness. The only way to become one with each other is for these imperfections to come out and to be brought to the light. And then we see that we should not act this way or we should not act that way. We see when we were not loving, as Christ wants us to be. But we are not perfect. Jesus sweat blood in the garden because of His great love for us. And He is calling us today to die to our imperfections. God is calling us to be more and more in the image of Jesus. Dear Jesus, I am sorry for my imperfections. Help me to die to them that I may be more like You.

10. Song: *Be Not Afraid*

The Scourging at the Pillar

1. **R.** Jesus is telling us there will be a new Era. Jesus is Chief Shepherd of the Flock. There will be one flock and one shepherd. There are many wills in the Church on the simple issue of birth control. The Holy Father tells us that artificial birth control is wrong. Moses was given the ten commandments. I am the Lord thy God thou shalt not have any gods before Me. We have worshipped the golden calf, on Sunday, the Lord's Day, that is to be kept sacred. Willfulness. We have worshipped our t.v.'s, our nintendo's and our money to the point that we work for money on His day of rest. The Lord created the heavens and on the seventh day He rested.
2. **R.** We call ourselves one, holy, catholic and apostolic. How is it when you go to Church? Do you feel one in the Church closely connected to those, your brothers? Do you feel this deep mystical union? Is there love? Is there deep union in men's hearts at Mass? Or do we feel separate, even at Mass many times? And people run from the Church after communion with Jesus in their mouth. Are people talking loud to one another about the weather after they go to the Eucharist?
3. Song: *I have Called You by Name*
4. **R.** And He says, "Let My people come together, proclaim the news, the blind shall see and the deaf shall hear." But will they see and will they hear if we to whom He speaks, holds back and are afraid. How are we on the sea of life? For

the boat goes back and forth everyday. I know how it is for me out there. More and more everyday I know that the world is not like me. And I know that there are many that do not believe in what I am saying. And so this is how it is. But I know what He is saying and I know what happens if I stop. For it is serious. We do not obey the ten commandments that are given by God. He has given to us this great gift in the Holy Eucharist. And how have we treated this great gift that He has given to us? He has given to us the Blue Book messages and we are the messengers. What we do with these messages will make the difference to spread the devotion to the Eucharistic Heart of Jesus to this world. It will make the difference to many coming to the Churches and staying after communion and adoring Jesus in the Blessed Sacrament. I am filled with fear within my heart that the way that He will allow us to suffer, if we do not pay attention to what He is saying, is to decrease our availability of the Eucharist and of the Mass. This indeed is the great gift that He gives. And we are the bearers of His sacred letters that tell the people of His presence and His love and His desire for us to remain after communion and to adore Him in the tabernacle.

The Blue Book messages are of great importance to Jesus. It is not what we are doing to one another that is so offensive, but it is how we are offending God, especially in the Eucharist, where Jesus Christ is truly present in His Divinity and humanity. Jesus is asking us to take our mission with the gravest seriousness to spread these messages about the Eucharist. It is our job to do this. Jesus has called us by name. What we do will make the difference. When one person receives that Blue Book, if they are a faithful soul that He is calling and they respond to those messages and the grace that they receive from us praying our Morning Offering. They may take that message in their heart to the Church and try to start adoration in that Church. They will get others sitting in front of the tabernacle. This is where the power is at. This is the greatest way that God is being offended today, is by the way He is treated in the Eucharist. This is our mission. Will we answer the call? For He says to us –

Song: *I have called you by name, you are mine, says the Lord*

R. They who sailed the sea in ships trading on the deep

waters, these saw the works of the Lord and His wonders and the abyss. Jesus is calling out to us even though we are on the sea of life and the boat goes back and forth as we travel on our way, and telling us not to be afraid for there is not time to waste. The time of reckoning is at hand and we must continue steadfastly ahead trying to get people to understand about Jesus in the Eucharist and how He is longing for them to come. To get people to understand about the consecration and spreading this, to help to spread the Priestly Newsletter and the prayers and prayer chapters if possible. We are on the sea of life and the waves are really, really, really high. But He has the power to control them so they do not tip the boat over. And so we really don't have to say to Him, 'Master, do you not care? We are lost!' *Mark 4: 39*

5. **R.** And so here it is, we feel as if we are laid open. For we do have to go out of our self to do this mission. We can not stay within ourselves. We must not be afraid to open up our mouths and tell people what is in our hearts. And what the work that we are doing is coming from our hearts. We truly are opening up ourselves raw. We are opening up our hearts for love of others and we are saying what is in the scriptures, what Jesus told us to do in the Church. We are telling people what the Church should be telling the people about, the Eucharist, the love of Jesus, the ten commandments, giving our hearts to Jesus and Mary. And we are being stepped on and we are being persecuted but we see Him there and He is tied at the pillar and His hands are held by ropes and He is being whipped now and His flesh is torn and the wounds are deep. For He was not afraid to open up to the point where His wounds were laid open and His insides hanging out. And I know how I feel many times. I open myself up and I am rejected and I want to close up. We are lovers. Lovers give. Lovers open themselves up. Lovers are in their hearts. We are the lovers He has called to spread the fire of His love to the far corners of the earth. And we cannot be afraid because what we do will affect the lives of millions of souls. And so we saw Mary on that building this morning. That recent. And she has called us in the Shepherds of Christ Movement to support that image and to support this Mission. Mary is really on that building appearing to the world. And there should be crowds flocking down there. But there is not even what there should be down there. And for the first

time in the history of the Blue Books, and the Shepherds of Christ Movement, these materials are going out and God is very pleased. We must pray fervently for that Mission there. For what happens there with the books, talking about the Eucharist and the Shepherds of Christ praying for the priests and the renewal of the Church and the world and the consecration, is changing the lives of millions. We do not know how one little book can change one person's life that when He applies His Might to it can change so many more. But we are in the boat in the sea of life and its tipping over and people are coming up and rocking the boat while we are in it when its already moving in the wrong direction. And so we feel like maybe we should get out because its about to tip over and He says to us:

Song: *Be Not Afraid*

6. **R.** The Father says on January 18th, 1997, "I tell you all to read the accounts concerning Noah. Nowhere in history has God been offended as He is this day by this sinful world." He wiped out most of the earth by flood of Noah because of the willfulness and sin. Is this how we show God that we follow the Chief Shepherd by disobeying the commandments and disobeying the pope? The new era will be when men will know God with such oneness in Him. They cannot help love Him when they know Him.

7. **R.** We are a people walking in darkness because of the tainted human nature and the sin of Adam. We are worshipping the golden calf. We are willful and sinful. We do not see the light because we are not born as children of the light until we go through her pure and Immaculate Heart. The era is upon us. The answer of being one flock and one Shepherd is to follow the Chief Shepherd of the flock. He mounted the tree and gave Himself as a sacrifice. He died to give us life. Jesus is the first born from the dead. Jesus is brought forth from the tomb on Easter morn because He died to do the Father's will.

8. **R.** There is only one way. It is to do God's will. Adam & Eve disobeyed God. It is disobedience that got us into this trouble. The Father speaks of obedience. It is this word, the sinful world objects to. Authority, structure are how God operates. God is above – we are creatures. We are persecuted for preaching about Jesus in the the Blessed Sacrament. God

spoke on the day of the flood, March 3rd, 1997, He tells us His side of the story. "When the poison reaches the peaks of pain, I will pour down the antidote on the Church and the world through these revelations. ... And I will shake you on your tree and you will fall to the ground as rotten fruit and all that will remain will be the fruit of heaven."

9. **R.** And this is the message that Jesus gave to us, "My dear Shepherds, you will be one flock with one Shepherd. The Father has wiped out most of the willful ones in your Movement. Any willfulness will be dealt with. To My death on the cross I obeyed the Father's will. You, the little family, the Father is using in the Shepherds of Christ to light up the earth. You will be one flock and one in your dealings. Pray the Morning Offering. Praying the Morning Offering will unite you into one fold. Praying the consecration will unite you into one fold. When the poison reaches the peak of pain, I will pour down the antidote in these revelations. Anyone with their own plan will be dismissed from your Movement. If you do not comply to the directions the Father will act so that you turn to obedience." Jesus mounted the cross and He gave His life that we would live. He obeyed His Father to His death on the cross. This is our Mission. Our Mission is to show that we are obedient to the commandments, that we are obedient to the pope, that we do the will of God and that we follow the Chief Shepherd of the Flock who spread His arms and gave His life because it was the will of the Father.

10. Hail Mary

The Crowning with Thorns

1. Song: *Crown Him with Many Crowns*

2. **R.** How are we bearing the cross that He gives to us? And how are we wearing the crown that He gives to us? For we are walking in His bloody footprints and why we think that if we are doing His work that it would not be a trial and a struggle many times. Jesus struggled on this earth. We look at His life and see Him walk with a crown on His head and His cross on His back. We see them spit at Him, mock Him and laugh at Him and it is hard, it is so hard that I cannot even sometimes understand how I can make it any different. But it is hard to deal with one another in this intimate relationship that we have with one another. And the devil

knows this and the devil wants to divide us to stop the work that we are doing. We see that the Father allowed Jesus to suffer and to die but it was through His life, death and resurrection that we share in His life.

3. **R.** This new era is characterized by what things? First of all, it will be everyone complying to the will of the Father. Secondly, it will be intimacy, deep intimacy in love relationships between all of us, between God and us. This is not how it is this day. People are not connected as they should be, the one holy, happy family. "The time is nigh", Mary says. And the King, the Sacred Heart of Jesus, will Reign on His throne. And it depends on what we do in the Shepherds of Christ Movement that will help bring this about. The world is not like us. The world is disobedient in many cases. This is why He is saying that when it reaches the peak of pain He will pour down the antidote in these revelations. He is giving us the antidote for what is wrong. And the people are looking at us and they are saying, "you're the poison, you're the one that's wrong." But we know we're not. We know how important the Eucharist truly is. How Jesus wants to be loved in the Eucharist. We know how important it is that we are praying for holy priests, that we are praying for the renewal of the Church and the world. These are the things that the people are objecting to, that we are spreading the rosary, that we are talking about this when many people do not even know how to pray the rosary. But Mary says we must pray the rosary. And so we're in the boat and it is rocking, they try to tip the boat because satan does not want us doing what we are doing. We can say because of our lack of faith, "God, are You going to help us because we are going to drown?" Jesus is telling us today that He is helping us, that this is His Movement, that He is behind us 100% and that if we get afraid and we run the other way, there is going to be millions of souls that will be affected. Did you say millions? Yes, I did, because we are the core group, the center of this Movement. And it is spreading out and the people that should be answering His call are not answering His call. Majorly, if someone does not spend the time in front of the tabernacle, the devil works on them until they get involved in many other things. We need help so bad out here to do what He is asking us to do. And a lot of people are not doing what He is asking them to do that should be

helping us. But I was told yesterday something really important. It is obedience that He wants. Those that remain will be dealt with accordingly. No one will exist doing their will. This is His plan to lead the strayed ones in the Church and the world into one. Anyone having their own plan will not stay in the Movement. I will give you the grace to deal with all of this. Willfulness will be dealt with. Those who have opposed you in the past are suffering tremendous interior suffering. They are trying to fight the will of God. Those at Our Lady of the Holy Spirit Center who have persisted in their own wills and disobeyed to the bitter end despite the warnings will suffer immense interior sufferings. They are fighting the plan of God. It pleases the Father when you obey, when you pray the hourly prayers and follow the messages. The moon will turn to blood and you will be protected by the Blood of the Lamb.

Jesus: You are being dressed in My Blood at the appointed hours of 3, 6, 9 and 12. I am requesting you make a tape of the Morning Offering. Do not be afraid, I will protect you with My Blood. Acts of obedience please the Father. You are against a willful world and some priests have been neglectful of the authority in the Church. Man is reconciled to God through the Blood of the Lamb shed for man's sins. Oh, night greatly blessed, you will know a time of terror and a time of joy for you will know that I am God, I will have no gods before Me. I have made a covenant with man and man has broken this covenant. You will suffer a fate for the deeds. This Movement will be one in the Father's will. You must be obedient to the directions given, to bring about the Reign of My Sacred Heart.

R. Jesus says that the Father looks to the earth when we are doing these hourly prayers and that when we do them He is greatly pleased because He knows the little family that He has called, which is the Shepherds of Christ Movement, to lead all into one flock, is doing His will. And this pleases Him greatly and He will give us great favors in helping us to spread the movement when we do what He is asking us to do.

4. **R.** He says, "the Reign of My Heart will be a Reign of living in the Father's will." We see Him crowned with thorns. Jesus allowed Himself to be crowned with thorns because it was the Father's will. The King of heaven and earth and we

say in the Our Father, thy kingdom come, thy will be done on earth as it is in heaven. He says, "I give you My Body and My Blood and you ignore Me and you treat Me with indifference. Disrespect given to My letters of love displeases Me. I will wipe out the earth and you will know how offended is your God for the deeds of men. You must obey the commandments. The world is not a democracy. God is the ruler. He is the King. The pope is the Vicar of the Church. The father is the head of the family. Authority has been almost wiped out in your church and your world. The willfulness of the earth displeases the Father. God is God. Man is man. What is right is right and what is wrong is wrong. You have disobeyed the commandments and the pope. You have offended your God by your treatment of the Eucharist. I am sending teachings in My love letters that are ignored and ridiculed. I will strike the earth with a strong hand and the audacious men will scatter and you will know the wrath of God. I am offended by your lack of response to the messages that I give here."

5. Hail Mary
6. Hail Mary
7. Hail Mary
8. Hail Mary
9. Hail Mary
10. Hail Mary

Song: *A Song from Jesus*

The Carrying of the Cross

1. **Jesus:** And so My beloved ones, you are suffering and you are opposed by many. Those that oppose you are being taunted by the devil. It is the devil that you are dealing with. I am telling you this. I give to you the directions in order to proceed steadfastly ahead. There are these directions. You must pray the prayers hourly. I am asking you to pray on the hours of 3, 6, 9 and 12. I am asking you to spend an hour before the tabernacle or in private in deep intimacy with Me each day and to go to daily Mass and communion. You are the leaders of this Movement. Every person in this room I have called to help to bring about the Reign of My Sacred Heart. You are being pressed on by the devil. My beloved ones, the only way that you can fight this battle, this war is through prayer. It is the grace that will fight the battle. The

battle is not here below, it is with the devil that is pressing on the individual people that are opposing you and trying to stop your Movement. It is in the hourly prayer that this battle will be won. It is in the prayers that are prayed at 3, 6, 9, and 12 that you will be protected by My Blood. In one moment, I can give you all that you want to help the Movement proceed ahead. But you continue to think that it is through your might that the work is being accomplished. It is through My Might that the work will be accomplished. It is in obedience that you will be rewarded with funds and with workers. I am asking you to pray and to put all your trust in My most Sacred Heart, to surrender totally to Me, to give yourself to Me, to come to My Heart and to trust in Me.

R. And they said to the Lord that they were afraid that they would drown. Jesus tells us to go to Mass and pray before the Blessed Sacrament. God the Father has called us to this great Mission. If we get out of the boat, any one of us here, it will make a big difference to many souls. We must be strong and although it is hard, proceed ahead to help to promote the prayers, to pray for the messages which lead people to the Eucharist.

2. **R.** And it is hard because the Almighty God is the All-Perfect lover and we are trying to learn how to love and to be more like Him. And we may think that love may seem easy but love is not easy. And it is not an easy road to try to be like Jesus. It is very difficult and He knows this and He is giving to us great grace. But we still fall and we are not perfect and we must tell Him that we need His help, that we want to be one, holy, happy family as the Father intends us to be, living in the Father's will. The devil is the one who divides. Where there is division, there is the devil.

3. **R.** There is division in families, division in Churches, division in schools, division in politics, division in the work place and there is division in parts of our Movement, little irritating things in which we may remain divided. But each one of us have an important mission and we must work with one another to love each other, that this work of the Father will be accomplished. We must be sisters and brothers of love gently treating each other with love. Gently accepting ourselves as being imperfect and accepting others as being imperfect. Oh yes, a great battle is waging here and we do

not even see it, and they do not see it down in Florida. The battle is the same battle that stopped all the messages and prayer manuals from going out on the Falmouth Farm because the battle was a big battle of the devil's trying to stop the progress of this Movement. And those same devils are working so hard to try to divide any one that goes there. And they are working in our Movement trying to distract us, to get us to think that other things are more important. Things that are our will that we should do and is a good act, but is God calling us to truly be here, helping as a Shepherd of Christ person? We must weigh all of the things that we are doing and pray to Him and see what is His will because we need the help here to do what He is asking us to do.

4. **R.** The devil is crafty and he is working at all times to try to create confusion and division in our lives so that we cannot do the work that He wants us to do. Majorly we are the ones that will help lead the Church and the world into oneness.

5. **R.** There was so much division that was created down in Florida that each and every person wanted to almost leave that site. The Virgin Mary has given an image of herself on that building, for this world. And we have a few scrawny four or five souls from the earth that are down there that are having trouble staying. What do we want God to do to get our attention?

6. **R.** If Mary appeared twenty-two months at Falmouth and God gave a great grace that so many people were changed in their heart, received miracles, saw rainbows, and whatever happened over there? Why did they not respond more to what she was saying? Why weren't the prayer manuals passed out as they should have been? It is because of the battle above. The battle of the devils. We cannot fight this individually. It is only through the prayer that this battle will be won. God gives to us the messages for they are the way that the plan will be accomplished. It is in doing what He is saying, the hourly prayers, the prayers at 3, 6 and 9, the hour before the tabernacle that it will be His work, His Might that will send more workers that will make the load lighter.

7. **R.** The Father is looking down at us, this core group. We are the center of this Movement that has spread out to the far corners of this earth and we are being pressed on very hard.

Majorly, the message that I am receiving now is that the prayers are so important that we are doing. And the Father, in seeing us obey is greatly pleased with our obedience and will shower us with blessings when we obey Him.

8. **R.** God is not asking us to be anxious about the prayers. God is not asking us to do things, like skip our work, or do things that we have to do for our family. Whatever it is, He is asking us as far as is possible to spend the hour, to pray hourly and to pray whenever possible at 3, 6, 9, and 12.
9. Hail Mary
10. Hail Mary

Song: *I Love You Jesus*

The Crucifixion

1. **R.** It displeases the Father greatly when there is division. For we are the ones that He has called to help to bring the world into one fold. We are the lights on the tree. We are the ones that He is counting on to live according to His will. We must realize that we must spend this time alone with Him everyday, that God can tell us what His will is for us. And He has spoken over and over again and told us that our answers are in the messages, in the Apostles Manual, in the Blue Books. These are our messages to be able to accomplish the task that He has called us to do. Do you believe? Do you believe that you have truly been called, a great apostle? You must have faith, for you truly have been called by Him to be this apostle. And what you do with your life will make the difference to so many souls.
2. **R.** God is telling us to live according to the Father's will at every moment. That is eating properly, sleeping properly, being with our family. But it is, as an apostle, to do those things that He has asked us to do. To try to follow the prayer schedule if at all possible. To try to do whatever it is He has called each person in this room to do. Each person comes with a piece of the puzzle to help make the mechanics of this movement to work. What is your piece of the puzzle that will make the Movement operate as the Father intends it to? And what happens to the Movement when you are weak in your performance because the devil has distracted you away from your post?

3. **First Friday - December 6, 1996**

Jesus: I am calling you as a family. You will be joined in one heart, acting as My Heart beating in this world. All the apostles in the Shepherds of Christ Movement are joined in one Heart.

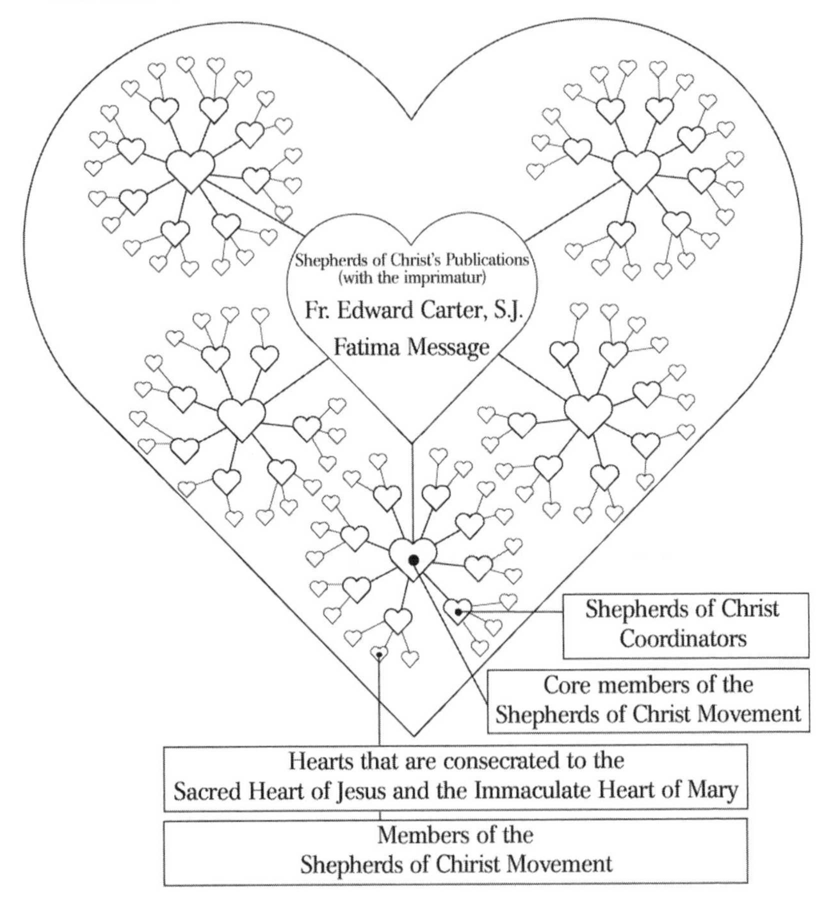

R. The core leaders will contact the coordinators. The coordinators will contact the individual apostles. All are apostles with a job directed by Jesus to do. Her peace plan was given at Fatima:

1. Until a sufficient number of people have consecrated their hearts to the Hearts of Jesus and Mary, we will not have peace in the world.
2. Mary has requested all to pray the daily rosary.

3. We must observe the Five First Saturday devotion:

   - Communion, confession (within 8 days before or after the Saturday), recital of the rosary, meditating for 15 minutes on the mysteries of the rosary. All this is to be done in spirit of reparation.

4. We must make reparation to the Hearts of Jesus and Mary.

His plan centers around this.

We have heads functioning in the individual ministries. Everything we do leads to consecration of hearts. As the apostles press on the three institutions, the Church, family, and school to help spread the consecration, the strayed ones will be led home to His Heart.

Mary said at Fatima until a sufficient number of people have consecrated their hearts to the Hearts of Jesus and Mary, we will not have peace in the world.

The present condition of the world

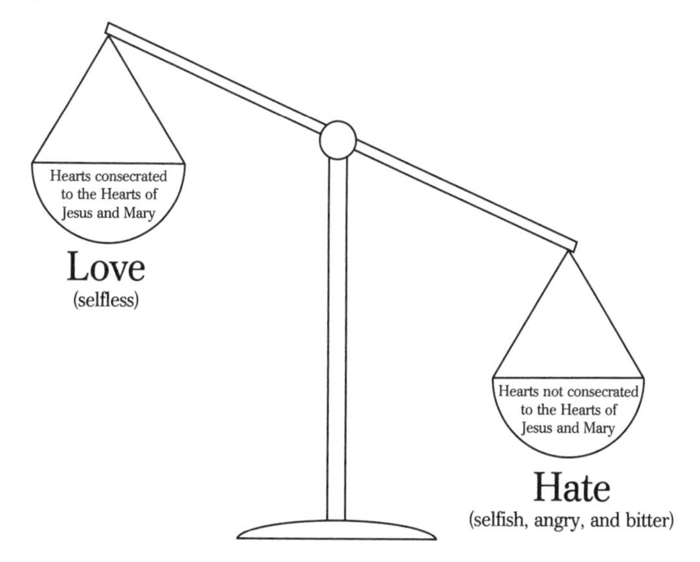

Peace will come when hearts are hearts of love. The scales must shift. It will happen through the consecration. Mary's peace plan: until a sufficient amount of people consecrate their hearts to the Hearts of Jesus and Mary, we will not have peace.

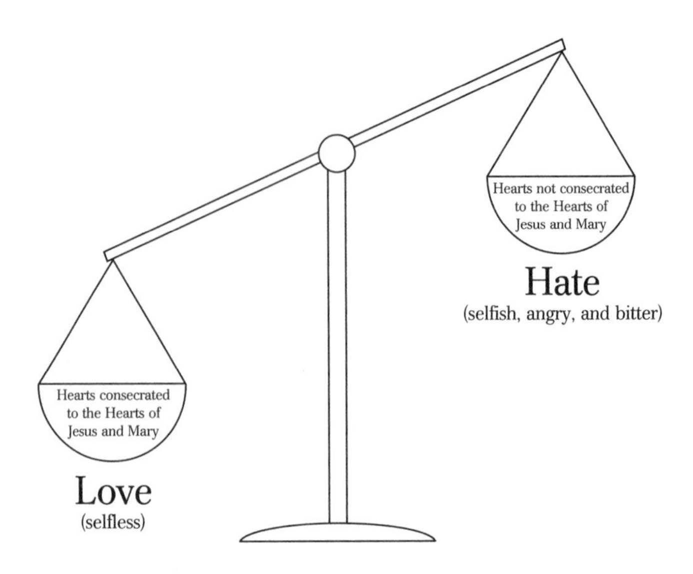

The Father looks to the earth; He sees much darkness.

The Father looks to the earth. There are few hearts fervently in love with God. The hearts of love light up the earth. It is as lights on a Christmas tree. It is sparsely lighted by a few hearts. Therefore, the tree looks dark.

As the Shepherds of Christ Movement spreads (as well as other movements focused on spreading consecration to Their Hearts) the tree is covered with more hearts and the earth becomes more lighted.

The tree is covered with hearts consecrated to the Hearts of Jesus and Mary. The tree is illuminated.

As the Shepherds of Christ apostles spread the consecration to the Church, the family, and the school, the tree is covered with lights and the earth is covered with the fire of His love.

The Father looks to the earth now. He is displeased with the hearts of men. The Father wants us to love God and love each other. He wants us to live according to His will in love.

Mary appears at Fatima. She tells us that we are offending God. She tells us what we must do. Mary's peace plan:

1. Until a sufficient number of people have consecrated their hearts to the Hearts of Jesus and Mary, we will not have peace in the world.
2. Mary has requested all to pray the daily rosary.
3. We must observe the First Saturday devotion.
4. We must make reparation to the Hearts of Jesus and Mary.

Mary said there will be an era of peace, no matter what we do, in which the Sacred Heart of Jesus will reign and the

Immaculate Heart of Mary will triumph.

Man disobeys, the devil blocks the Fatima message. World War II happens just as Mary said.

Mary appeared to me for 14 months daily. She gives us the same message as Fatima. Jesus and Mary give us *God's Blue Book* and *Rosaries from the Hearts of Jesus and Mary.* He writes His message of love on our hearts. His life lives in our hearts. The Scripture and the Mass live in our hearts.

In the Shepherds of Christ Movement, our focus is on the priest. *end of December 6, 1996*

4. **R.** God will give the grace to fight for this mission if we work the spiritual program He gave us. It is by His grace we can fight this battle. It's the spiritual battle that they are fighting and it is the prayers that combat it. The devil is behind their opposition.
5. **R.** Because of anger and hatred in the hearts of men they killed Jesus. They nailed Him to a tree and He hung to His death on the cross. And what does Jesus say to us as Jesus hangs on the cross? Jesus speaks no words but we know this, that Jesus gave His life doing the will of the Father.

December 5, 1996

R. On December 5, 1996, Our Lord appeared to me at Holy Cross-Immaculata Church, after Mary had appeared on most of the 5ths since July 5, 1994. Our Lord now appeared, dying on the cross.

His withered body was horrifying to me. I cried and looked at Him in horror. This lasted about twenty minutes. It looked as if He could exert no effort, but His jaw moved and moved and moved. It was a big movement as His mouth moved. I heard no words. I was sickened.

I was horrified at the sight of His weakness, the vision I saw and I cried from the depth of my soul as I watched I could hardly stand it.

It was in the church, Holy Cross-Immaculata. He appeared on this crucifix. It was horrifying for me. I was in such anguish and tears. I know this experience so well, He implanted it in my soul. This was after Mary appeared for 2 years and 4 months on the 5ths. Jesus appeared on the 2 1/2 year anniversary on the crucifix.

At the traditional rosary (I had done them now for 2½ years of 5ths) that evening at 6:30 with all the Shepherds of Christ people there, He said He moved His mouth because no one was listening.

This was December 5, 1996, after all those visits of Mary on the 5ths when very few came and listened.

Mary did not appear. Jesus is handling it. He is speaking in the rosaries and in the *Blue Book* messages.

In the year 1996 Mary began to speak less and less in the live rosary messages because she said people were not listening.

I wish you would envision our Lord at the point of death as I saw Him December 5, 1996. See the weakened body, see the body of a full size Man in anguishing pain, see a Man dying on the cross, nailed to the cross by our sins.

end of excerpt

6. **R.** The old Adam and the old Eve sinned and the human race was tainted by the sin. Mary was conceived without sin. Jesus, the new Adam and Mary, the new Eve showed us how They complied to the Father's will. Man is reconciled to God by the Blood of the Lamb. It is in our acts of obedience that the Father is well pleased. For we show Him that we are dependent children. God gives to us a covenant. God gives us the commandments and we disobey them.
7. **R.** God gives us apparitions of the Blessed Virgin Mary and Mary told us at Fatima what we must do to have peace. And we disobey Mary!
8. **R.** God the Father, gives us His Son! Jesus is truly present in the Blessed Eucharist. Jesus is there truly present in His Divinity and humanity. And we treat Him with indifference. It is so awful for us to get such a gift as giving Himself to us in the Eucharist and we are ungrateful and to not give ourselves in great love to Him.
9. **R.** God promised us a new era of peace in which the Sacred Heart will Reign and the Immaculate Heart will Triumph. We will be the Father's happy, holy, family living according to His will in obedience. This is the Movement that majorly will help bring this about. We must comply to His request in the messages, for it is in obedience that He is greatly pleased.

And He is telling us exactly what we need to do. It is the grace that will fight off the attacks by the devil. That is why Jesus asks us to pray. We do not comprehend. We have human minds and we do not understand the Divine plan. But Jesus is telling us what will make the Movement move ahead. We must have faith and do as He asks us to do.

10. Song: *Be Not Afraid*

Reference: Matthew 8: 23-27

R. They were in the boat with Jesus and a storm came up. Jesus was sleeping. They woke Him because they were afraid.

Song: *Be Not Afraid*

Jesus: And if you say no and you abandon your post and if you go away, who will I send. For I have sent you into the darkness and you will carry My light to the far ends of the earth.

R. For the world is hurting and this is how we must act always, in love. For there is a message in the third Blue Book and it reads, *Is the Glass half-empty or half-full?* Our glass has been filled, filled to the brim with His Divine grace. And the boat has rocked and even people have come up and tried to tip our boat over. But Jesus tells us, "do not be afraid for...

Song: *I Will be With You*

R. And I remember the story that He said of the ants. There are all these ants and they are all supposed to be working trying to accomplish a task. But there are some of the ants that are arrogant and they want their own way, and they kick each other and they bump each other. And how is the work being done when the ants are fighting with each other? And we say, "Oh, so silly", you are ants. Why don't you just do the work that is at hand. And the Father looks to the earth and He sees us and He says the most important thing that we do is love Him and love one another and be united to Him. And we get huffy in our hearts and haughty and we want to get the job done and He looks down and He says –

Jesus: I am God, I will calm the storm. Why are you afraid? It is My Might. It is My Movement. You are My beloved ones, My apostles. I am teaching you My way, this day. I am teaching you to be the strong apostles, the strong ones that I have called that will carry out this Movement. And as you are learning, you are suffering and you are being tested and tried in fire. Do not give up your post for what you do will affect the lives of millions of souls. I am well pleased with the work that you have put forth. I am asking you to come to Me and to help Me to spread My love so that My kingdom will come with the greatest love to this earth.

6/22/97

Sufferings of the Body

R. I was upset - Fr. Carter and I went to Mass at St. Theresa's. A vibration went over my whole body and I felt like I was paralyzed - it hurt awfully - I wanted to cry out. I could not move. I was entirely paralyzed and gripped with pain across my shoulders and down my arms. It reminded me of His arms on the cross and it felt as a heavy cross was on my back, but it was not from the outside of the body, it was inside my body. I was totally paralyzed with pain across my back and down my arms on the back. When I was suffering it, all I could do was to be in the pain and I had that realization of the cross on my back.

This is what happened after the Mass at Dale. It was again across my back. It may have extended to my whole body. I was paralyzed with an interior pain that was excruciating and I could not move. It was greater there and it lasted longer. I totally had to surrender to the pain.

When I said the rosary at _____ in Florida, in June 1995, I had such a headache, all around my head. I couldn't focus on anything but Him because my head hurt so bad - that is the way I said the rosary in front of that whole room of people – there were a lot of people there.

When I said this rosary in June of 1995 I had horrible pains in my hands. I felt like screaming. I remember when I said the rosary in Florida in June 1995 - I had gotten a message about the pain in the body, shooting up and down His arms and legs and the blood shed and the pain in the Church would continue until we spread the message of His love. Then He said that I would get pains in my hands and feet to remember this message - June 26, 1995. I got this message when I arrived in Florida.

June 25, 1996 was the first rosary we did at Tom Arlinghaus' farm. The priest at Mass today said that so many people do not believe in the real presence! I realized most of my pain and suffering is from the frustration of talking to God and not being able to do more about the Eucharist and the people praying as they should!

I suffered so much about the Eucharist all day and I suffered so much for my lack of being able to express the sufferings and the ecstasies at Mass, and not being able to express "oneness".

6/25/97

The Pain - Naples, Florida

June 26, 1995

R. He spread His arms, He gave His all, Jesus, the Son of God, the greatest sacrifice, He gave Himself entirely for the good of all men. He opened His arms, He died on the cross.

His arms were covered with blood, His arms so weak and filled with pain, wounded. His arms, the pain shot up His arms and the final blow to each arm a nail through each precious hand.

All the agony He experienced, all the pain, and the crown, to each arm, a nail hammered into the hand.

All the nerves cut and severed by the nail, the pain shooting up His precious arms, the final blow given to His most precious members.

The legs that carried Him, that carried the heavy cross, the legs that were forced and cajoled, that continues to Calvary - the legs weakened, skinned, bleeding, beaten, burned, the legs that knew patience and perseverance, the legs connected to a sore foot that was rubbed and gashed and bleeding, the members of Jesus, filled with such pain and exhaustion, now is crowned with the final glory. The nail that was driven into the foot, the pain shot up this already weakened leg, covered with blood and wounds and pain, the final blow, the nerves severed by the hammered nail.

A blow to each hand, a blow to each foot, a blow to the head, a stamping that pressed down and continued in excruciating pain.

Jesus: They numbered all My bones. They gave Me vinegar and gall to drink. They gave Me a cloth to wipe My blood-covered flesh.

What did they give to Me? Love is giving, My dear ones. How many of you are wounded when you are not given things by your brothers you love?

My members were in such pain, the pain shot up My arms. My legs were so weak I could scarce move them. I was filled with pain within them.

To all who watched, they saw a man, weakened and covered with blood and wounds. They did not see the pain inside that shot up My legs and arms, the nerves inside My body that sent signals of deep pain to My central nervous system. They did not see the nerves inside sending pain signals everywhere.

The final blow being to each hand and foot, the severing of My nerves by the blunt and rusted nails.

An arm extended. A final blow. I beheld a nail pounded into My hand and the pain shot up My arms, unbearable to a human mind.

Do you know of the pain within My body? Signals sending messages of deep pain everywhere. I knew all of these sufferings in the garden. So great were the sufferings to My mind, I sweat blood.

My flesh was covered with wounds. My arms were stretched from their sockets. My body was beaten and bleeding, every inch of My body covered with deep wounds. But, My loved ones, you miss the depth of My love. My wounds were so deep, but the final wound, the pounding of the nails in My hands and feet, a severing of the nerves, an ending of the deepest pain, to experience even deeper pain, beyond your human comprehension, it was done to the Almighty God, a Divine Person, I suffered the final blow to each member.

The pounding in the hands and feet, the crown to each member, and they numbered all My bones. My nerves a network of pain running throughout My entire body.

The pain within the body, the pain recorded in My loving head, the pain sent by a network of nerves in My body, now records the final blows, the nails in the hands and feet, the pain being recorded from every thorn that pierced My skull, every gash to My body, the pain, the pain, the pain - a network of signals and pain, running through My body and the final hour, the pains recorded on the cross, arms outstretched - a surrendering to all pain. I surrendered to a body laden with pain.

You focus on your little problems, your little aches and pains. You discuss them and show the world your pin pricks and sufferings.

Do you want to know holiness and love? They gave Me vinegar mixed with gall. This was their offering. They gave Me a cross. They crowned My head with a crown of thorns.

This, My dear ones, is suffering, My beloved souls, I gave My life for and this is their return.

A severing of My nerves, the final blows to all the aches and pains recorded in My nervous system. This was one of the final blows - the rusted nails pounded into My hands.

You will feel little aches and pains in your hands and feet to remind you of this message. Your understanding of the immense pain within will deepen. What was visible to the eye on My battered body was nothing compared to the pains within. I gave My all. I gave My insides, My mind, My Heart, wounded for the love of men.

All functions in the body were stopped.

The final curtain, blood and water pouring out from My Heart, show that all functions of the body had ended.

R: All signals that carried messages of immense pain had ended, the final act of surrender for God to die to this human body and surrender His flesh.

Jesus: And end, a beginning, the water and blood flowed from My Heart, the beginning of My life in the Church, life flowing into your spirit.

R: Come give me life, abundant life. I thirst to be with Thee.

Jesus: My blood was spent. My human flesh and blood offered as the sacrifice, the sacrifice of Calvary is now made present at every Mass.

An end, a beginning, and the grace and life flow through the sacraments in the Church. My life flows to you in the Mass. Mary, the Mediatrix of all grace, stands by the side of the altar and the grace flows from the Father, through My body offered up as a sacrifice in the Holy Spirit, given through the Mothership of Mary to you in the Church.

You stand under the cross with My Mother and you receive the gift given, My Body, My Blood.

R: Man is reconciled with the Father through the Divine Person, Jesus Christ, and you receive His life poured out to you as Calvary is made present in the unbloody sacrifice of Jesus Christ.

Do you feel the graces poured out to you at this sacrifice of the Son of God at every Mass? Do you feel the presence of the Father, Son and Holy Spirit and Mary, all the angels and saints, and the souls in purgatory? Do you feel united as one at the sacrifice of Calvary sacramentally made present upon the altar through the priest? The priest who now puts on Christ and through Him the dispenser of this life given to man.

Jesus: Oh, My beloved ones, love so dearly your priest. Give him such reverence. He is the chosen instrument of God and you treat him with such ordinariness. You are so blind and so dumb in your ways.

And they numbered all My bones. Each nerve carrying a message of My love of mankind, each member in My Church carrying a special message, all united as one working in harmony according to the Father's will, each carrying a message of love to one another.

The body is many members, you are the messengers of My love. Christ is the head. The message does not flow as it should when some are cut off from the Head.

They nailed My hands and feet and My nerves were severed by the nails, such pain, undescribable in words, the severing of My nerves from the body, the severing of many members from the body of Christ.

My Body given for all on the cross, the network of nerves within carrying the messages of My love to all mankind. My body covered on the outside with blood and wounded, the pain recorded within.

Your Church, covered with blood on the outside, the slaughter of innocent babies, the homosexuality, the sins of the flesh, the members that have severed themselves from the source by their sins, but the pain is carried in the nerves inside. The blood of the Lamb shed for each and every soul, the real pain carried within. The life is weakened in your Church because the love of God is so weak in many members. The messages of love are not being transmitted as they should be. Your body shows the wounds, but your pain within is the root of the problems. The pain is from the messages of love that are not being transmitted.

Unless you seek to fill your priests and sisters with the fire of God's love, fill their hearts with burning love for God, your Church will continue to show the marks of the blood shed without. I give to you these letters as a mighty medicine for this world, directed to make men's hearts burn with love of God and love of one another. The rosaries are meditations and messages given from the Hearts of Jesus and Mary.

These messages will make men's hearts burn with fire for love of God.

You have ignored the importance of these letters.

I send to you the mighty medicine to heal a hurting world.

My priests and religious need these messages. The love of God will be transmitted to the Church from these messages when you circulate these letters.

The devil has blocked the minds of men involved in these messages because of their importance to the world and the Church.

I am speaking to you Fr. Carter to help to get these messages published and circulated as soon as possible. I give to you a mighty medicine for a sick world.

Read St. Thomas Aquinas about the medicine for the sick Church.

You know what these messages have done for you. I am

Jesus. I give to you the mighty medicine for a sick world, for a sick Church, rosaries and letters from the Hearts of Jesus and Mary.

Your Church shows the wounds of bloodshed, abortion, homosexuality, sins of the flesh, murder of little children's minds with sex education in Catholic schools and you hold back the gifts of God's love I am giving to the Church and this world.

My arms were weak and wounded but the final blow as the nail put in My hand. It severed the nerves.

The final blow is the bloodshed in the Church, the slaughtering of children's minds in Catholic schools. My children are pure and innocent. They are not being taught messages of God's love, they are being taught messages of sick sex and coldness.

Men's hearts have turned cold. They have been severed from the life of the body. The body is decaying from within. Only with the love of God enkindled in men's hearts will this bloodshed stop.

I beg you to publish and circulate these messages in the Church. I am Jesus. I am giving you the mighty medicine for the world. Your body wears the marks of the bloodshed, only with messages of My on-fire love will it stop.

Mary leads you to Jesus. Never is she the end. The Father has a plan. Mary's messages have led men and will lead men to Jesus. Satan has tried to stop all efforts to publish and circulate these messages. I am the Almighty God. The funds will come when you circulate and publish these messages and rosaries under the Shepherds of Christ Publishing. I am working with Fr. Carter and Rita as messenger to renew the Church and the world. Each messenger has a very vital role in the Father's plan. The significance of these messages are being overlooked. You are not studying the messages as a whole and their content. There are five unpublished Blue Books and more than four Rosary Books which I and My Mother have given to this world in the last 14 months. I have also given 15 songs of My love. I am begging you to see to the recording and publishing of this music. I beg you to listen. This is the mighty medicine for the Church and the world to draw men to the burning love of Jesus. Please harken to My call. I will send you the money. You must study and read these messages. This is a fulfillment of Fatima - these messages were given to bring priests to the burning love of Jesus. I am Jesus, your beloved Savior.

end of June 26, 1995

Wolves

God the Father Speaks:

A mother loves her children. She stands behind the children she bore.

I give to you members rooted in love and giving their lives for the Movement. When they are in need they are expected to care for themselves, but those opposing the ones who are working spreading the Movement get the attention. The Plan is an easy plan. In order to accommodate those who have their own plan, you have focused on those who have opposed the main plan and given them wind and strength in the Movement. A family is protective of the little children. When the wolf comes he is cast out. The wolves were nurtured and given control. The devil comes in the ones with their own plan.

Be leery of the workings of satan to distract you so that the wolves will receive attention and will create confusion.

Who has satan worked through to block the plan? Where has the main progress come from? Who has given their life for the Movement? Do you support the workers, the faithful ones and give all your attention to the willful ones? A mother does not forsake her child. Your children in the Family, Shepherds of Christ, are those who are faithful members bearing fruit, to waste your time on willful ones, those who opposed the plan will cause your children to suffer and allow the devil to get in through the willful parties. I beg you to take care of your children who are bearing the fruit. Why nurture those who have opposed the plan and made the Movement suffer?

The little children suffered and the mother went out to protect the wolves. How foolish a plan. A house divided against itself will not stand. You will suffer more and more for your lack of prudence and the devil will come in through the willful ones.

They threw out the cornerstone. They crucified the Lord. They hung Him on a tree and watched Him die.

They stoned the prophets and jailed the apostles. When he comes in My name you will know that he has gifts to bear. He works for nothing and gives his blood. When they come with a big mouth criticizing and trying to tear apart that which is working, you will know they are from the evil one.

Do you support the faithful ones or ignore them and listen to those causing opposition, then give the children nothing and feed the wolves?

Do you invite the noisy ones, those who enter with division and hatred on their lips and then ignore the faithful at work or tell them to be quiet because your energy has been spent on the willful wolves?

I will separate the sheep from the goats. The goats have had their way; they have squandered the feed and made the right noise. They have broken the fence and tried to lead the faithful sheep to the edge of the hill.

They come with a wolves' mouth, with a mighty roar to destroy you. The meek and the humble wait by and demand little of your feed. They work for nothing and give their all. They pray and turn to God.

Who are the sheep? Who are the goats? Who have helped spread the Movement? Who have demanded their own way and their own plan?

They will trip you up. They will talk in the assembly and you will be faced with a mob that fights you and hates you.

You gave them your feed and you starved the faithful sheep. They entered with a mouth of anger and discontent and they ended receiving the pay and the feed. The others washed and scrubbed the floors and their knees bled and when they moaned after much hard work you told them to be quiet for you were worn out from tending the wolves.

Will the wolves do their will or God's will? Who will do what I ask here? This is a Movement to bring about oneness. Were the wolves divided or one? They came in speaking of division and demanded to be heard. They introduced a plan that led to confusion and wanted to be in charge. They were willful and arrogant and wanted it their way.

The new era will be marked in deep intimacy in My Heart. The leader will be of the heart. Their main focus will be spreading My Heartfelt love. They will love God with their whole heart and soul and will give their heart to Him. They will unite with others, they will not stick out as a sore thumb.

The new era will be according to one Plan, the Father's Plan. It is written in the scriptures: They will be united in the Holy Mass as One.

Whoever leads your Movement must be fervent in prayer. They must be obedient and not willful. They can unite with others. They are devoted to the burning love of Jesus.

You will suffer if you do not tend to the flock for the wolf is coming and some have been bitten by the viper snake.

The directions are given, but they are ignored. Obedience is important to the Father.

Disobedience will not be tolerated. The deaf will hear; the dumb will speak and you will know that the Lord is present.

6/26/97

June 29, 1997
Morrow, Ohio

Glorious Mysteries

The Resurrection

1. **Jesus:** I have called you, My special little family to this room this day to teach you. I have called you to hourly prayer and I am teaching you to intercede to the Father, to ask the Father for those needs that you have. It is in this time that you will be united to one another and to God in a special way. And I will outpour abundant grace for all of your needs for you must believe and you must have faith that you are the chosen ones that I have called to help spread the fire of My love to the very ends of the earth. Do you have faith, My chosen ones, that I have called you, that I have trained you, that I am teaching you and that you will proceed steadfastly ahead and that the world will be changed through the efforts

that you are putting forth in this Movement? You must believe. Have faith, My chosen ones for I am with you.

Song: *I Will Be With You*

2. **R.** Picture Jesus coming forth from the tomb in the brightest light. The glory shines forth from the Almighty God.
3. **R.** And so He has called us to hourly prayer for it is His Might that will spread this Movement to the far ends of the earth. Are we afraid? Do we think that we must act? It is in obedience that the plan will unfold for the Father has given His directions for many years for the unfolding of His plan to help bring about the Reign of His Sacred Heart. We must heed the words that He speaks to us. I know in my life that my life is changing because of this hourly prayer. That it is at these times, at these hours, that whatever it is that troubles me, I have been trained by Him to pray hourly and therefore, I add this to the list of intentions that I am praying for. And it eases the discomfort and the worry within my heart for I know that I am truly interceding to Him in the way that He has taught me to do. Each one of us have been trained through these hourly prayers, a great gift that He has given to us. We no longer have to fret or fume for we know that He will answer the prayer. We are using the most powerful words that Jesus has given to us in order to pray, to Jesus, and to the Father, through the intercession of Mary, and He will answer the prayers that we ask Him. The Father told me on March 25, 1995 that what I ask for of Him in prayer is answered. That I must have this faith, that I can change the course of things if I go to Him and if I pray. Look at Peter in the garden. We see him and he slept. The Lord told them that they must pray, but they did not pray. They went over and they slept.
4. **R.** They must not have been in one heart, deep oneness with Our Lord. For how could you sleep if you were afraid? This was the time He went to the garden. He was in such agony but they went off and they slept. And He told them exactly what to do. It is by His Might that things are accomplished. Many times we are actors, we are busy. We think that we must do things. But He is teaching us in this Movement that He is telling us what will do it. He said it all through the Blue Books. He said your answers are given here. You go to

men and you ask questions. I give you the answers. He gives us the answers in the messages and in the scriptures how this Movement will spread to the far ends of the earth. We must listen to Him. Peter slept in the garden. He brought his swords but then, when they came to apprehend Jesus, he pulled out the sword and he cut off his ear. (the high priest's servant's ear as in John 18:10)

5. **R.** We are kind of like this, for He is telling us that it is not us that is going to spread this Movement to the far ends of the earth. We may do this, this day or that, that day. And it may affect a small amount of people, but it is only in the prayers that it will accomplish the plan that the Father intends this Movement to do. And so He is allowing us to suffer. But look at the great gifts that we have been given. For we have all of us learned how to pray. Think of it, do you really think that the little things, even sending out the books that we were going to do, was going to reach the far ends of the earth? The Internet may help, that is why the Father keeps talking about the Internet and of its importance. But the prayers, the prayers with His Might through whatever we are doing will be what will reach it to the far ends of the earth. We are sort of like Peter. He told Peter to pray, but instead of him listening to Our Lord and praying like He told him to do, he was ready with his swords and he cut the ear off of the high priest's servant. Is this how we are many times? We get so focused on this thing will do it and I am busy, busy, busy, busy. I know this week I was busy, busy, busy doing so much because of the mailing. And I missed a day in front of the tabernacle. And I suffered, because Jesus does not want me to miss a day in front of the tabernacle. A day with Him and all the Might that He puts forth when I go to the tabernacle and pray and intercede to Him. The most important thing that we do is spend this hour of intimacy with Him everyday, no matter what is going on. If we can't get to the Church to do it, then we should spend the hour in our house. For He said to the apostles, "Can you not wait one hour with Me?" And this is like He is saying to us. Busy, busy, busy, busy, and I will affect two thousand people. Or maybe I'll only affect 10% of the two thousand. But He is working through us with His Might. It is in the prayers, its in the hourly prayers. It's not in the bags of

envelopes that we send to this one and that one. It is in the grace that He applies to that, that gets that person to go out to get the job done. This is how it was at the site in Florida. They were so worried they were missing this one and that one and they had to have it covered and they were arguing and bickering with one another about what was going on. And it isn't that. It's the one powerful one that Jesus knows will come and answer the call, that He will give the grace to, that will go out and can be as strong as you or me, that really has given their life to the Movement. So you reach fifty, two hundred people. But they're ones that walk off the site and throw the book away. But the one, as each one of you are, that have been called by Jesus to this spot this day and given the grace to respond to His call. Those are the ones. I see a lot of people, but Jesus tells me the one that's the right one, the one that will respond, the one that He is giving a great grace to, to get the job done. When are we going to learn? How many ears would we cut off ? Jesus told Peter to pray. He has told us to pray. The battle is high. The battle is with the devils. We may think that we are handling this person or that person but He is truly teaching us there is only one way. It is in the prayers. Yesterday, so much work was accomplished here and we were joined in the greatest unity. And it was wonderful. It was that day that pleased the Father immensely to see the love and the unity, to see us working, to see the ants as He talked about. Isn't it foolish if we look down and saw the ants bickering and picking on one another? What He wants is love. He's got all the Power. We've got to get this mind slot that it is Him, it is all in His Might. He can come up with so much money that we would not even know what to do with it. But He won't do that. He said He wouldn't do it. He said that He would give us enough, but we have to use it the way He wants us to use it. We have to do what He tells us to do. And He is telling us to pray hourly. The answer is doing this. Praying at the hours at 3, 6, 9 and 12. Yesterday, was so wonderful. It's forever in my heart the joy that we experienced in being one with each other here in a holy, happy family. I have never been that connected to people as I was yesterday and it was through the prayers that He united us in a special way and gave us all a great gift. And when we left, we fell on our couches and were knocked out.

6. **R.** It is in the suffering that there is the Resurrection, in the death that there is the new life. Peter did not comprehend but He made him Vicar of the Church and He keeps showing us in the scriptures how ordinary Peter was, how he denied Him, how Peter was worrying about what people thought. He shows us how the apostles stumbled, how they were not perfect. But He made Peter the Vicar of the Church. And then He called him a Rock, but he was becoming a rock. We are like that. And we look at ourselves and we say, "but we're not perfect". We must tell God we are sorry for our sins. The devil wants us to sin. We must work to build God's Kingdom. God is well pleased for our prayers in asking Him to help us to be more like Jesus. And God knows that we are not perfect and He knows that we are bumping heads and He sees our imperfections coming out and tenderly He comes and He puts us back together. And we really are growing to be great lovers of one another and lovers of God. And we must be patient and we must stop as He says worrying about what other people are thinking, and keeping our focus on Him. Think how many times we are paralyzed because we are worrying about what somebody is thinking. When in fact the devil is putting a lot of the thoughts in our head. And that person isn't even thinking that at all. We must pray for the grace to keep our focus on Jesus, and to see the glass as half-full and not half-empty, to realize that we are the chosen ones called by God that will greatly affect the renewal of the Church and the world, that we believe and that it is in our prayers united with one another in this room, in our private homes as we join in our hearts at the hour, as we join in our hearts at the morning offering and realize that we must be thankful because He has given to us great grace and He has molded us into this special family, the family of love that will help light up this earth.
7. **R.** Jesus told me to read this. I don't really know what it says.

   Reference: Matthew 16: 13-19

   R. And so it is with us that it is as He says here, "No mere man has revealed this to you but My heavenly Father."

   And these are writings from God. That He has revealed Himself in the most intimate way to each one of us. He has taken us in His Most Sacred Heart in the sufferings, and joys and the tears after communion. Jesus has taken us into His Heart. And Jesus takes us deeply into a chamber of His Heart and He gives us suffering but we know Him in that suffering. We turn to Him in that suffering. He takes us into His Heart and He reveals Himself to us and all these things that we know have been great graces and revelations that He has given to us in order to accomplish this task. And He says, "I take you to the deepest chamber of My Heart and I give you Myself, My chosen ones. For you are My beloved Shepherds, that will lead the flock to My Heart through the consecration, through what you do through spreading these messages. Many will be led to My Heart." But He first is taking us in to His Heart. And He has revealed Himself. And so we say, "we do not understand or comprehend how others do not know Him." We know Him because He has given us great gifts. As it will be in the new era, we are the leaders to help lead the others into this era. It is wonderful to pray together for He is here with us and we are one in the Hearts of Jesus and Mary. We are united. There is this presence of God that has united our hearts. And it is powerful. He came forth from the tomb victorious and He has given us a great sharing in His Divine life in the sacrament of Baptism. Our knowing and loving capacity is elevated in baptism. What keeps us focused, Jesus wants us to do work to build up - to lift up - to lead souls in love. He gives us grace. It is a great gift. And there are many that are walking in darkness, and are blind and do not hear. And He showed us the way. It was through the Immaculate Heart of the Virgin Mary that we are being brought forth through the power of the Holy Spirit as children of light. And we are knowing Him in a special way as we dwell in His Heart and Mary's Heart. And so it is in that message that Fr. Carter received that He would give great graces to the members of the Shepherds of Christ Movement to join in deeper union with His Heart and the Heart of His Mother. We have watched this happen and we are the center that will lead others into this Movement. And they will receive this grace when they pray these most powerful prayers given to us by Jesus. The prayers that He is given to us and that He is dressing us in His Precious Blood when we pray them at 3, 6, 9 and 12.

Song: *Be Not Afraid*

8. Hail Mary
9. Hail Mary
10. Hail Mary

Song: *Take Lord, Receive*

The Ascension

1. **R.** This is the Psalm from today.

The angel of the Lord will rescue those who fear Him.

Reference: Psalm 34: 4, 6-7

R. But this is really what it's all about, having that faith and believing that He is going to do it. Or are we like Peter that draws the sword and cuts off the ear instead of praying.

2. **R.** I love to read the scriptures because its like our life.

2 Timothy 4: 6-8, 16-18

As for me, my life is already being poured away as a libation, and the time has come for me to depart. I have fought the good fight to the end; I have run the race to the finish; I have kept the faith; all there is to come for me now is the crown of uprightness which the Lord, the upright judge, will give to me on that Day; and not only to me but to all those who have longed for his appearing.

The first time I had to present my defence, no one came into court to support me. Every one of them deserted me — may they not be held accountable for it. But the Lord stood by me and gave me power, so that through me the message might be fully proclaimed for all the gentiles to hear; and so I was *saved from the lion's mouth.* The Lord will rescue me from all evil attempts on me, and bring me safely to his heavenly kingdom. To him be glory for ever and ever. Amen.

3. **R.** And so Jesus came and He gave His life and He rose on the third day that we would share in His Divine life. And Jesus ascended into heaven but He remains with us in a powerful way this day. And we are the apostles that He is sending to go out into this world to spread the Good News,

the news of the Gospel. And we truly are living these words in the scriptures. The scriptures are our truth for the world has turned in many ways to the wrong ways. And Jesus says that there is poison in the world and in the members of the Church. And so we are mistaken for the poison, but we in fact are the antidote for many of the problems that are going on in the world and in the people in the Church. And we find our truth in the words of the Mass. And it's just so wonderful because it rings in our hearts and we are filled up with such oneness with all these words in the Mass and what's going on, and the words in the scriptures. And our truth is in that.

4. **R.** Again I reviewed the commandments because this is what He spoke to me about this morning. About the Sabbath day and how it is not honored and treated with sacredness. About how He is not the God in many hearts. They have all these false idols that they are worshipping, how His name is used in vain, how people are not obedient as they should be. And this is what the fourth commandment tells us, children being obedient to their parents, people being obedient to the authority, the Church being obedient to the pope. All the way down from Peter, the Lord has guided the popes in this Church. 'Thou art Peter and upon this rock I will build My Church.' And the Pope speaks in the name of God and we must obey the pope in faith and morals. For he speaks for Christ.

5. **Jesus:** And so I tell you My beloved ones, I draw you deeply into My Heart and I reveal to you the secrets of My Heart through the suffering and through the gifts that I give to you. And you must be thankful to the Father for allowing Me to take you to the deepest chamber of My Heart and to share with you My burning love, to share with you the secrets of My Heart, to unveil to you the scriptures. For you do comprehend and you love the scriptures and the Mass and the Eucharist and this is a great grace that I am giving to you that you love all of these things.

6. **R.** And they walked as blind men down the path of destruction and they did not even realize that the road that they walked on, was a road that led to their own doom and to their own destruction. How fast is the road that we are walking on? Is it the path that He laid before us? The one

that leads to the glory land? The one that will lead to our salvation? The one that will help lead many others as we walk this path and they watch us? Or is it the road that we run down? The road that we walk and carry with us all of our false gods in our pockets. And we laugh and we use the name of the Lord in vain, and we run ahead and we think that we are making great strides and He says, that when the Church and the world reaches the peak of pain, on the day of the Falmouth flood, He said He will pour down the antidote in these revelations. Great gifts have been given and we must be thankful to Him. He has sent us His sheep among the wolves. The wolves come with big mouths and the wolves talk and they cause confusion. And they are filled with angry hearts. And they want to be heard and they criticize that which is working. And He says, beware of those wolves that are operating in the world. "I have molded you into a little family, My special ones. You are quiet. You are submissive. You care for the will of the Father. You do not boast and cause trouble but you go about your life in prayer. You demand little and love much." And so we see out in the world the wolves, the ones that are the noisiest, that make the most noise in the dark night. And we hear them clamor and we hear them complain and we hear them want to change the words in the scriptures, and to do this and to do that. What is most important to all of us is our love relationship with Jesus. We must follow those people who are focused on Jesus as their center, where Jesus is in their heart, where they speak about Jesus with love, when what they want is Jesus, not the noisy ones, not the wolves that come in sheep's clothing that are the noisiest, that want their way, that criticize what is working, that tries to stop what is happening, especially here. What are we doing here in the Shepherds of Christ Movement? We are praying, we are spreading devotion to the Blessed Sacrament, we are loving Jesus in the tabernacle and loving one another. We are praying for holy priests and the renewal of the Church and the world. And so they come and they criticize us and they say, look at this here and look at that there. The ones that are rooted in the scriptures see the truth. The ones that go to daily Mass and Communion and sit in front of the tabernacle know the great fruits that are coming forth from this Movement. And it isn't the noisy ones that are clamoring in the dark night. It is the ones that are quiet, that stand by the fence, that work for nothing, He says, (This is the message I got Thursday) "That work for nothing, that demand little and that pray." This is how it is, He said, in the Church, in the school, in the world. And who do we give our attention to? Do we go to that one that is so noisy and we think oh maybe we will change their heart. And so we work and work and work and work and we are worn out from dealing with the wolves. And then one of the sheep come up, the ones that are faithful, that are loving God, that are spending their time in loving God. And we're worn out from dealing with the wolves. He says this, "Look at your Church. Look at the ones that are filled with love of Jesus. Take time with them. Nurture those people. Work with the people that are in one mind and one heart, not the ones that are sticking out like sore thumbs." Not to ignore them or to try to help them if they honestly want to be helped. But let us go to those people that we can work with, that want to help us spread the devotion to the Sacred Heart and the Immaculate Heart. Why go to the most ornery and try to work with them? Go to the ones whose hearts are already rooted with Jesus and try to get them to help us to do this. The one He says that comes in fighting, the one that is criticizing. They are the ones that we should not spend all our effort on. We should go to those in the Church that are open that will help us. Not go to the hardest one. We may have to go to the hardest one some of the time but look at the Church. Who gets the attention? The one that is the noisiest? The one that is criticizing? And what of the faithful? And they come up and they have a decent word. And they are not heard because the leaders, many times, are worn out from dealing with the wolves. We need to go to those that we feel will blend in, in one heart with us and to pull them in. Go to the children and spread the consecration. The ones that we can tell about Jesus, that are open to work with them. So many times we go to the hard one and we spend all this energy on this one. There are lots of people out there that God has called. He will lead them to us. We should work with those people. Not ignore the other ones, but many times we spend all of our energy on one person that is like knocking down a hard rock or a wall, when there are so many others that are out there that are open.

7. **Jesus:** I am molding you into the little family. You will be in one mind and one heart. I am asking you to lead the strayed ones to My Heart, to bring in as many souls as possible. Go out and try to lead the souls into My Heart through the consecration. You do not have to try to change the hearts of those that are opposed and are willful. Go to those that will blend in, that will say yes, and that will continue to say yes.

   R: And He speaks in another message and He said, To 'watch' the ones that say 'yes' one day and 'no' the next day. We must realize that this mission is of great importance to the Father's plan. That what we are doing here will affect millions of souls. That we must have in our heart our whole intention, that of helping to bring about the Reign of His Heart, to help to pray for holy priests and the renewal of the Church and the world and to help spread the Eucharist. We must say yes, yes always to the Reign of the Sacred Heart. " ... Thy kingdom come, thy will be done on earth as it is in heaven."

8. **R.** There was one of the people in Florida and they were going out and trying to crack the hardest person to get them to be part of what they needed. He is calling people. If we take all of our time working on a hard person, then we do not have the time to work with the one that He is sending. We must be open to the moving of the Spirit around us. And if someone is majorly opposed to the plan, maybe the Spirit is working to lead us to another soul that is ready to be part of this Movement and to be one in our hearts. This is what else He said in this message. He said that we are to be in one mind and one heart. When someone insistently is sticking out we must realize that we must pray for them to join into the fold. We are to be united. This is why yesterday was such a great gift, because there was just an immense bond between all these different people that only could have come from God. In this room, this day, we are joined immensely in this oneness. This is what we read in the Mass and the scriptures is oneness. We have been called to this mission. Jesus ascended into heaven, but there will be One Flock and One Shepherd and we are at the center and we must strive for this and hourly pray for this unity.

9. **R.** Many times the devil sends someone into our lives that

takes up a lot of our time to keep us from doing the things that He is calling us to do. Maybe that is not the person that we are supposed to try to bring in. He has called these people. They are responding. We must not tie ourselves up with one person and not be open for maybe ten or fifteen others that are close at hand. Look for the ones that are open and want to be one in our heart with Jesus.

10. **R.** Jesus told them that when they went to a place if they were not welcome that they should shake the dust off their feet and they should move on.

The Descent of the Holy Spirit upon the Apostles and the Virgin Mary

1. **R.** There was someone that I had tried to pull in and I tried and tried and then Jesus told me that He loved them more than I did and that I should leave that person up to Him.
2. **R.** How did you get here? Were you called by Jesus? Was it hard for you to say yes, or was it easy because in your heart you wanted to respond? Jesus is giving many the grace to respond. We must be open to help lead them here.
3. **R.** Many that argue are looking for a fight. "My beloved ones, you must be careful not to argue with men that are looking for a fight. You must come to Me in quiet prayer and you must go to those docile hearts that are open and want to spread the Movement to the far ends of the earth."
4. **R.** Jesus said that some come with criticism and fighting on their lips and then we must be leery of this and we must proceed ahead and we must pray.
5. **R.** Jesus said in another message awhile ago that our Mission is to pray for the priests, it is to pray for the renewal of the Church and the world, it is to spread the rosary and the consecration. That He is given to us a very large Mission. Jesus says people may come and they want us to try to help them with their mission, that this is not what Jesus is calling us to do. Jesus is calling us to be Shepherds of Christ and the Shepherds of Christ Movement is to pray for holy priests, it is to bring about the renewal of the Church and the world and the completion of the Fatima message. There are many missions that are out there that are very good and that are helping many poor people and doing many good things. But

this is not our mission. He is calling us to do this Mission and if we do not do this, if satan leads us astray, by other distractions, who will do the Mission, for He is calling us to this Mission.

6. **R.** I was a school teacher and I taught college Math. And He took my voice away because He wanted me to do this full time. It didn't seem exactly right when I spent my whole life preparing for this vocation. But I prayed and prayed and prayed and asked Him to help me to know His will. And what He did was, He took my voice away. Not for a week or two weeks, but He took it away for almost two years. And after that, I figured that it was His will that I did not teach. I could be teaching Math right now instead of doing this. It was doing a good thing and many people even liked me as a teacher. But it was not what He wanted me to do.
7. **R.** There are many missions out there that are doing very good work. But we are so small in number and it is important that each one of us realize that this is a calling that He is giving to us. If we go and do other missions that we will be spread very thin and we will not be able to give our full attention to what needs to be attended to. This is very important to the Father's plan that we pray for the priests and for the renewal of the Church and the world and that we spread this to the far corners of the earth. He has called each and every person in this room. Be leery of other operations that you may be led to for He has truly called you to help with this. It is totally optional as to whether you respond. But if you decide to say yes to this commitment, know that this is the commitment that He wants you to follow and other things will spread you thin.
8. **Jesus:** You are My lay apostles. You are the strong ones, those that came on June 13th, were the strong ones under the tent. There will be many members in the Shepherds of Christ Movement, many that will be in the Churches and in the schools that will not be called lay apostles. I have called you lay apostles for you have given a good portion of your life to this Movement. It is a commitment and with this you will receive My most abundant grace for I have drawn you deeply into My Heart. And I have given to you the great revelations to know Me and to love Me in the most intimate way. You are the lay apostles of the Shepherds of Christ Movement.

You are permitted at any time to decide that you do not wish to be a lay apostle. But I am calling you. And it is My desire that you respond and that you say yes. You are the apostles that I am sending into this world to help renew the Church and the world. Will you answer yes to this commitment?

9. **R.** And the great vision that we can have is the holy priests celebrating the Holy Sacrifice of the Mass being mystically united in the deepest union with Christ and with the people and grace being outpoured and within their hearts the burning love of the Almighty God.

10. Song: *You are Christ for one another*

    Song: *They will Know we are Christian by our Love*

    Song: *I Have Loved You*

    R. And this is how we are for we are the branches and we are bearing great fruit. And no matter what comes against us, whatever it is, we cannot be destroyed for this is Jesus' Movement for the renewal of the Church and the world and those that oppose us are fighting God.

    Song: *I Have Loved You*

The Assumption

Sing: *Immaculate Mary*

1. **R.** Jesus ascended into heaven and Mary was taken into heaven and we are here this day dwelling in Their Two Hearts. And we live in Their Two Hearts. Jesus is operating in us and soon there will be the Reign of the Sacred Heart and the Triumph of Her Immaculate Heart. And what we do in the Shepherds of Christ Movement will majorly bring this about.

2. **R.** We thank God and we praise Him for giving us especially, this Great Mission and joining us in one mind and one heart with Him and with one another.

3. **R.** My whole life I never knew the things that I know now. But how I know about the Immaculate Heart of Mary and when Fr. Carter used to talk about dwelling in Their Hearts I did not quite understand what he meant. Now I know so much. And we must thank God: the Father, the Son, and the Holy Spirit and thank Mary for her messages. Thank God for teaching us and taking us into the Heart of Jesus and

revealing these things to us.

4. **R.** One of the greatest pleasures that I have, its a pleasure, (I don't know what to call it.) is at the Holy Sacrifice of the Mass when the priest raises the body of Christ and within me I am just overwhelmed with tears and with love of God. This is a great gift that He has given to us. There are so many people in that Church that are not realizing what is going on. But He is giving us this grace that we will spread these messages, that we will talk about the Eucharist, that we will lead the others to the Eucharistic Heart of Jesus.

5. **R.** I want to read a message that I got yesterday. I read it here.

   June 28, 1997 Jesus: I give Myself to you in the Holy Eucharist. In this image (He's talking about the image on the *Apostles Manual* in the prayer book.) My hands are extended in such giving love that I give to you. I extend this invitation to all Shepherds of Christ Associates to live the Blue Book messages and to help to spread the devotion to My Eucharistic Heart throughout this world. It is in the Eucharist I am greatly offended because I give Myself to you. It is through this Movement and the leaders living the Blue Book messages that the devotion will be spread on this earth. I am offended by any conversation before the tabernacle. Discussion of My Eucharistic presence and My love is permitted. Sins are committed, sins of indifference, sins of neglect, disrespect before the Eucharist. That which offends Me greatly is any condemnation of your neighbor in My Divine presence. I beg you to take this Mission with the greatest seriousness. You are Shepherds of Christ members. You are to help spread the devotion of My Eucharistic Heart. I wish this image to be circulated on the material distributed by the Shepherds of Christ. It is the Eucharist that is on the image that will help to lead the people to My Eucharistic Heart. My arms are open and I speak to you. Come to Me My beloved ones, come through the Immaculate Heart of My Mother to My Eucharistic Heart. I am Jesus, Chief Shepherd of the Flock, I give you Myself in the Eucharist. I give you My Mother as your Mother. I give you the Immaculate Heart of the Virgin Mother, My Mother and your Mother. I give you Myself in the Eucharist. I extend My arms to you. I am the bridegroom of your soul.

You come to My altar through the Immaculate Heart of My Mother and I feed you with My Body.

6. **June 28, 1997 continues Jesus:** This is not to indicate that this is the exclusive picture of the Shepherds of Christ Ministries. The picture I request to be blessed by Fr. Carter and placed in All homes of core members, is very important to the devotion to the Sacred Heart and the Movement. I request that the picture be included in front of the Apostles Manual opposite the Prayer for Union with Jesus. I've requested this picture to be placed on the Third Blue Book. This picture is very important to the Shepherds of Christ Movement. It is very important to devotion to My Heart. This was the picture that was on Fr. Carter's ordination card. It will be a picture used to lead many priests and faithful to My Heart. The image on the Apostles Manual is to help increase devotion to the Two Hearts and the Eucharist. The third picture of the Sacred Heart is the picture used in the front of the Blue Book and the candlelight rosaries. Please continue to make available to all members the large picture for candlelight rosaries. The pictures are very important to promote devotion to Our Two Hearts. Please circulate them.

7. **R.** There was another message that I received. This was on June 10th. It was the Feast of the Immaculate Heart of Mary and it has to do about that picture. I got one on the 7th then too. I see this picture of Jesus on the Apostles Manual during Mass and that image makes me cry. It is this Jesus that has swept me away after communion for I see Him as I go to the altar and His arms are open and He gives Himself to me.

   Mary says: Oh, I stood beneath the cross of my Son and I cried!

   R. I have been consumed with the love of these Two Hearts from these pictures. I was overwhelmed with the love of Their Hearts on the Feast of the Immaculate Mary. It is so simple. These Two Hearts are the most perfect Hearts of love and They love us in perfect love. Jesus gives to us this spousal union with Him. Jesus, the most intimate lover, Mary, the all perfect Mother, gives us so much love. The Father picked her, my Mother, His Mother of all of us. It is the Mother of all that leads us to the Heart of Jesus. The gold cross and Eucharist sparkled after communion. (This is how it was yesterday) And their halos glowed. They are alive no matter how we feel inadequate and sinful, the love is there for us despite our ways. It is love He comes for, it is love He gives. It is love. Oh, the child of God the Father, Jesus, the Son of God-made-Man in the womb of the woman clothed with the sun. Mary was visited by the angel, Gabriel and she carried the Light of the world within her very being. This is how she is, clothed as the sun. The chosen Mother, by the Father, the Spouse of the Holy Spirit. The womb in which Mary carried the Light of Life. Thus, she is clothed in Divine grace, a virgin, bearing a child, the Holy One of Israel. And we are the children conceived and brought forth in the spiritual womb of Mary. Mary is our Spiritual Mother. Mary is our Mother. We are the children of light. We are the children of Mary and Mary is from the house of David.

Luke 2:34

Simeon blessed them and said to Mary his mother, 'Look, he is destined for the fall and for the rise of many in Israel, destined to be a sign that is opposed –

8. Song: *Oh Holy Dwelling Place of God*
9. Hail Mary
10. Hail Mary

Mary is Crowned Queen of Heaven and Earth

1. We are being led to be Apostles of the Sacred Heart. But from where we were sitting in the Holy Spirit Center and He was saying, "I'm calling you to be apostles". We have been sent out. The wind is like on us and beating on us, the rain bares down on our face. All kinds of things have happened to us. And we stand strong and it is like Jesus said in this song. This is us. I mean these songs are our songs. We stand on this hill and (here it is)

   Song: *In the deepest recesses of My Heart* (page 10)

   Jesus: I will be with you. The scripture is the truth. I am the way, the truth and the life.

   Song: *In the deepest recesses of My Heart*

   Revelation 12: 1-2

2. **Act of consecration to the Sacred Heart of Jesus and the Immaculate Heart of Mary**

Lord Jesus, Chief Shepherd of the flock, I consecrate myself to Your most Sacred Heart. From Your pierced Heart the Church was born, the Church You have called me, as a member of *Shepherds of Christ Associates*, to serve in a most special way. You reveal Your Heart as a symbol of Your love in all its aspects, including Your most special love for me, whom You have chosen as Your companion in this most important work. Help me to always love You in return. Help me to give myself entirely to You. Help me always to pour out my life in love of God and neighbor! Heart of Jesus, I place my trust in You!

"Dear Blessed Virgin Mary, I consecrate myself to your maternal and Immaculate Heart, this Heart which is symbol of your life of love. You are the Mother of my Savior. You are also my Mother. You love me with a most special love as a member of *Shepherds of Christ Associates*, a movement created by your Son as a powerful instrument for the renewal of the Church and the world. In a return of love, I give myself entirely to your motherly love and protection. You followed Jesus perfectly. You are His first and perfect disciple. Teach me to imitate you in the putting on of Christ. Be my motherly intercessor so that, through your Immaculate Heart, I may be guided to an ever closer union with the pierced Heart of Jesus, Chief Shepherd of the flock.

3. **R.** Do you feel the oneness in your heart when we unite in prayer? That is because it isn't just me and you that are praying here. Jesus is with us and we are united to Him when we pray in an immense union.
4. Song: *A Song from Jesus*
5. **R.** So we should wear our Mission proudly on our chest and thank God continually for the great gifts He has given and that we know Him with this intense sense of knowing that He has given to us. It is a gift. It is a gift to sit in the Church and to want Him so bad that you can't wait to go up to get the Eucharist because you know in your heart that you're going to receive Jesus.
6. **R.** And the time will come and the King will be the King on His throne. And Jesus will Reign in the hearts of men. And men will love Jesus and they will follow the ten commandments. And they will do as the Father intended us

to do, love God and love one another. The commandments were given by God to man. We have disobeyed God. We have not given God the love that is His due. We have not honored and praised Him. We have not respected Him especially in His Eucharistic presence in the tabernacle. And He is calling out to us. That's what this message was yesterday, we cannot speak in front of the tabernacle. We must be very respectful of Jesus there. All of us do it. Somebody comes up and it goes back to what we said at the beginning of the rosary. We cannot worry what people are thinking. The devil talks in our heads. We must focus on Jesus. We must think of Jesus. We must not give in to our wayward thoughts. We must do what He wants us to do. It is to love God and to love one another. We are the leaders of this Movement that is centered in the love of the Two Hearts and we must be lovers.

7. **Jesus:** I am very pleased with each and every person here this day. And I thank you for your love. I am asking you to help to get the mailing to the people in the Movement. I am asking you for fervent prayer every day at the hours specified if possible. I am asking you to use the tape and each and every person to take a tape home this day and to use it all through the day. This tape was given that you will be able to pray the prayers hourly. I am giving to you great grace when you pray these prayers. It is through My Might that the Movement will be spread to the far ends of the earth. Look at yourselves, My beloved apostles, you are walking in My footsteps.

R. I see Peter and I see Paul. Paul was persecuted. Paul persecuted the Church and Peter denied Jesus. We are not perfect. We are human persons and He has given to us great grace. But we must realize that He is pleased with all of our efforts to try to be like Him even though we fall, even though we get tired, even though we do the things that we do, He is with us.

Song: *I Will be With You*

Jesus: Love one another. Be kind to one another. Help one another and realize that I am with you at every second. And that I am guarding you and watching you. Do not be afraid for I am truly with you. This is My Movement for the renewal of the Church and the world and I thank you for answering

My call to come and to help Me spread the fire of My love to this hurting world.

Song: *I Am the Vine, You are the Branches*

R. We really have to pray through the intercession of Peter and Paul because there was something in the scriptures today. It's like I could take his name out and put ours right in there.

Song: *Do You Really love Me?*

8. **R.** Jesus loves us so much.
9. **R.** Jesus calls us to love Him.
10. **R.** Jesus calls us to know His love – Read the Blue Books.

6/29/97

Listen to My Messages

Message from Jesus

Jesus: For they were willful in their ways and they would not listen and I shook the tree and they felt the vibration, but they continued to oppose My Plan, the Plan of the Father. I am telling you to study these messages. You will suffer until you read and study and obey them.

You are so simple in your minds for you see the days events as so important. It is the years, the generations of willfulness that I am acting on.

You, you most sinful race, chosen by God, one after another in the Cincinnati area, have opposed the Father's Plan. One after another have ignored and done their own will. I fight you no longer with My warnings.

I am instructing you to move ahead with the chapel and follow the instructions in the messages I give as warnings and they are ignored. The chapel was not built. I have warned and told you. I am giving messages at this time through Fr. Carter and Rita. Satan will attempt to infiltrate the Movement with false messages that will cause confusion. The messages I have given need to be studied and obeyed. I have given many messages through Rita that have not been obeyed and heeded.

I told you, you would be on the ground suffering, and crying out for relief and the only relief would come in obeying the messages. Your relief will come when you study and read all messages given from December 5, 1996.

As long as you ignore the messages of great importance, you will suffer with great confusion and doubt. If you studied the messages in their entirety you would see what I prophesized has come true.

Be very careful. Satan wants you paralyzed and stopped. He will succeed in great measure and you will suffer further if you do not obey.

I am asking you to move ahead with the chapel and to try to secure the Blessed Sacrament at the Center in Morrow. The opposition has been caused by those who are jealous. The devil has worked in jealousy to stop the Blue Book messages from spreading. I beg you not to give in to the devil.

The plan of the Father is to renew the Church and the world through the Shepherds of Christ Movement.

Now that your Center in Morrow is blossoming, the devil will try to stop your efforts to move ahead by creating doubt and confusion by other visionaries. I have given you a great gift in the Center in Morrow. Since your beginning less than 3/4 of a year ago, you have made a major mark on this world.

Satan will try to stop you. He will use jealousy and doubt. Why do you want to stop that which is working? Why do you listen to those who oppose you and want to cause you harm? The messages are given here. You will have relief when you obey the messages. The devil works through those that will get your attention. He prompts them at the right time. He knows exactly what to say.

I am sorry to see you suffer so much. Your suffering will be alleviated when you pray as instructed and read the messages.

I am Jesus. Only the strong ones will survive. If you give into satan the whole world will suffer. You are an instrument of God's grace.

6/30/97

Introduction to the Shepherds of Christ Prayer Manual

Here are the prayers that so many pray every day at 6:30, especially for the priests. Prayer chapters have helped many priests in parishes and people in these parishes to grow in greater holiness.

Will you form a prayer chapter in your parish and pray with us at 6:30?

One priest praying the prayers can tremendously boost the prayer power.

Shepherds of Christ Prayers

Written by Fr. Edward Carter, S.J.

Father Carter requested that these be prayed in prayer chapters all over the world.

These prayers are available on tapes, discs and the Internet as prayed by Fr. Carter. Fr. Carter prayed them every day at 6:20, the Holy Spirit Novena, Prayer Manual and Rosary

Shepherds of Christ Associates

PRAYER MANUAL

Shepherds of Christ Publications
China, Indiana

Imprimi Potest: Rev. Bradley M. Schaeffer, S.J.
Provincial
Chicago Province, The Society of Jesus

Imprimatur: Most Rev. Carl K. Moeddel
Auxiliary Bishop
Archdiocese of Cincinnati

The Shepherds of Christ Associates Prayer Manual is published by Shepherds of Christ Publications, an arm of Shepherds of Christ Ministries, P.O. Box 627 China, Indiana 47250 USA.

Founder, Shepherds of Christ Ministries:
Father Edward J. Carter, S.J.

For more information contact:
Shepherds of Christ Associates
P.O. Box 627
China, Indiana 47250 - USA

Tel. 812-273-8405
Toll Free: 1-888-211-3041
Fax 812-273-3182

First Printing, September 1994
Second Printing, November 1994
Third Printing, November 1995
Fourth Printing, March 1996

Chapter Meeting Prayer Format

The prayer format below should be followed at chapter meetings of *Shepherds of Christ Associates.* All prayers, not just those said specifically for priests, should include the intention of praying for all the needs of priests the world over.

1. **Hymns.** Hymns may be sung at any point of the prayer part of the meeting.
2. **Holy Spirit Prayer.** Come, Holy Spirit, almighty Sanctifier, God of love, who filled the Virgin Mary with grace, who wonderfully changed the hearts of the apostles, who endowed all Your martyrs with miraculous courage, come and sanctify us. Enlighten our minds, strengthen our wills, purify our consciences, rectify our judgment, set our hearts on fire, and preserve us from the misfortunes of resisting Your inspirations. Amen.
3. **The Rosary.**
4. **Salve Regina.** "Hail Holy Queen, Mother of mercy, our life, our sweetness, and our hope. To you do we cry, poor banished children of Eve. To you do we send up our sighs, our mourning, our weeping in this vale of tears. Turn, then, most gracious advocate, your eyes of mercy toward us and after this, our exile, show unto us the blessed fruit of your womb, Jesus, O clement, O loving, O sweet Virgin Mary. Amen."
5. **The Memorare.** "Remember, O most gracious Virgin Mary, that never was it known that anyone who fled to your protection, implored your help, or sought your intercession was left unaided. Inspired by this confidence, I fly unto you, O Virgin of virgins, my Mother. To you I come, before you I stand, sinful and sorrowful. O Mother of the Word Incarnate, despise not my petitions, but, in your mercy, hear and answer me. Amen."

6. **Seven Hail Marys in honor of the Seven Sorrows of Mary.** Mary has promised very special graces to those who do this on a daily basis. Included in the promises of Our Lady for those who practice this devotion is her pledge to give special assistance at the hour of death, including the sight of her face. The seven sorrows are:

   (1) The first sorrow: the prophecy of Simeon (Hail Mary).

   (2) The second sorrow: the flight into Egypt (Hail Mary).

   (3) The third sorrow: the loss of the Child Jesus in the temple (Hail Mary).

   (4) The fourth sorrow: Jesus and Mary meet on the way to the cross (Hail Mary).

   (5) The fifth sorrow: Jesus dies on the cross (Hail Mary).

   (6) The sixth sorrow: Jesus is taken down from the cross and laid in Mary's arms (Hail Mary).

   (7) The seventh sorrow: the burial of Jesus (Hail Mary).

7. **Litany of the Blessed Virgin Mary.**

   Lord, have mercy on us.
   Christ, have mercy on us.
   Lord, have mercy on us. Christ, hear us.
   Christ, graciously hear us.
   God, the Father of heaven, *have mercy on us.*
   God, the Son, Redeemer of the world,
   have mercy on us.
   God, the Holy Spirit, *have mercy on us.*
   Holy Trinity, one God, *have mercy on us.*
   Holy Mary, *pray for us* (repeat after each invocation).
   Holy Mother of God,
   Holy Virgin of virgins,
   Mother of Christ,
   Mother of the Church,

Mother of divine grace,
Mother most pure,
Mother most chaste,
Mother inviolate,
Mother undefiled,
Mother most amiable,
Mother most admirable,
Mother of good counsel,
Mother of our Creator,
Mother of our Savior,
Virgin most prudent,
Virgin most venerable,
Virgin most renowned,
Virgin most powerful,
Virgin most merciful,
Virgin most faithful,
Mirror of justice,
Seat of wisdom,
Cause of our joy,
Spiritual vessel,
Vessel of honor,
Singular vessel of devotion,
Mystical rose,
Tower of David,
Tower of ivory,
House of gold,
Ark of the Covenant,
Gate of heaven,
Morning star,
Health of the sick,
Refuge of sinners,
Comforter of the afflicted,
Help of Christians,
Queen of angels,
Queen of patriarchs,
Queen of prophets,

Queen of apostles,
Queen of martyrs,
Queen of confessors,
Queen of virgins,
Queen of all saints,
Queen conceived without original sin,
Queen assumed into heaven,
Queen of the most holy rosary,
Queen of families,
Queen of peace,
Lamb of God, who take away the sins of the world,
spare us, O Lord.
Lamb of God, who take away the sins of the world,
graciously hear us, O Lord.
Lamb of God, who take away the sins of the world,
have mercy on us.
Pray for us, O holy Mother of God,
that we may be made worthy of the promises of Christ.

Let us pray: Grant, we beseech You, O Lord God, that we Your servants may enjoy perpetual health of mind and body and, by the glorious intercession of the blessed Mary, ever virgin, be delivered from present sorrow, and obtain eternal joy. Through Christ our Lord. Amen.

We fly to your patronage, O holy Mother of God. Despise not our petitions in our necessities, but deliver us always from all dangers, O glorious and blessed Virgin. Amen.

8. **Prayer to St. Joseph.** St. Joseph, guardian of Jesus and chaste spouse of Mary, you passed your life in perfect fulfillment of duty. You supported the Holy Family of Nazareth with the work of your hands. Kindly protect those who trustingly turn to you. You know their aspirations, their hardships, their hopes; and they turn to you because they know you will understand and protect them. You too have known trial, labor, and weariness. But, even amid the worries of material life, your soul was filled with deep peace and sang out in true joy through

intimacy with the Son of God entrusted to you, and with Mary, His tender Mother. Amen. — (Pope John XXIII)

9. **Litany of the Sacred Heart, promises of the Sacred Heart.**

Lord, have mercy on us.
Christ, have mercy on us.
Lord, have mercy on us. Christ, hear us.
Christ, graciously hear us.
God the Father of heaven,
have mercy on us (repeat after each invocation).
God the Son, Redeemer of the world,
God the Holy Spirit,
Holy Trinity, one God,
Heart of Jesus, Son of the eternal Father,
Heart of Jesus, formed by the Holy Spirit in the womb of the Virgin Mother,
Heart of Jesus, substantially united to the Word of God,
Heart of Jesus, of infinite majesty,
Heart of Jesus, sacred temple of God,
Heart of Jesus, tabernacle of the Most High,
Heart of Jesus, house of God and gate of heaven,
Heart of Jesus, burning furnace of charity,
Heart of Jesus, abode of justice and love,
Heart of Jesus, full of goodness and love,
Heart of Jesus, abyss of all virtues,
Heart of Jesus, most worthy of all praise,
Heart of Jesus, king and center of all hearts,
Heart of Jesus, in whom are all the treasures of wisdom and knowledge,
Heart of Jesus, in whom dwells the fullness of divinity,
Heart of Jesus, in whom the Father is well pleased,
Heart of Jesus, of whose fullness we have all received,
Heart of Jesus, desire of the everlasting hills,
Heart of Jesus, patient and most merciful,
Heart of Jesus, enriching all who invoke You,

Heart of Jesus, fountain of life and holiness,
Heart of Jesus, propitiation for our sins,
Heart of Jesus, loaded down with opprobrium,
Heart of Jesus, bruised for our offenses,
Heart of Jesus, obedient even to death,
Heart of Jesus, pierced with a lance,
Heart of Jesus, source of all consolation,
Heart of Jesus, our life and reconciliation,
Heart of Jesus, victim of sin,
Heart of Jesus, salvation of those who hope in You,
Heart of Jesus, hope of those who die in You,
Heart of Jesus, delight of all the saints,

Lamb of God, Who take away the sins of the world,
spare us, O Lord.
Lamb of God, Who take away the sins of the world,
graciously hear us, O Lord.
Lamb of God, Who take away the sins of the world,
have mercy on us.
Jesus, meek and humble of heart,
make our hearts like unto Yours.

Let us pray: O almighty and eternal God, look upon the Heart of Your dearly beloved Son and upon the praise and satisfaction He offers You in behalf of sinners and, being appeased, grant pardon to those who seek Your mercy, in the name of the same Jesus Christ, Your Son, Who lives and reigns with You, in the unity of the Holy Spirit, world without end. Amen.

Promises of Our Lord to those devoted to His Sacred Heart (these should be read by the prayer leader):

(1) I will give them all the graces necessary in their state of life.

(2) I will establish peace in their homes.

(3) I will comfort them in all their afflictions.

(4) I will be their refuge during life and above all in death.

(5) I will bestow a large blessing on all their undertakings.

(6) Sinners shall find in My Heart the source and the infinite ocean of mercy.

(7) Tepid souls shall grow fervent.

(8) Fervent souls shall quickly mount to high perfection.

(9) I will bless every place where a picture of My Heart shall be set up and honored.

(10) I will give to priests the gift of touching the most hardened hearts.

(11) Those who promote this devotion shall have their names written in My Heart, never to be blotted out.

(12) I promise you in the excessive mercy of My Heart that My all-powerful love will grant to all those who communicate on the first Friday in nine consecutive months the grace of final penitence; they shall not die in My disgrace nor without receiving their sacraments; My divine Heart shall be their safe refuge in this last moment.

10. **Prayer for Priests**. "Lord Jesus, Chief Shepherd of the Flock, we pray that in the great love and mercy of Your Sacred Heart You attend to all the needs of Your priest-shepherds throughout the world. We ask that You draw back to Your Heart all those priests who have seriously strayed from Your path, that You rekindle the desire for holiness in the hearts of those priests who have become lukewarm, and that You continue to give Your fervent priests the desire for the highest holiness. United with Your Heart and Mary's Heart, we ask that You take this petition to Your heavenly Father in the unity of the Holy Spirit. Amen."

11. **Prayer for all members of the Shepherds of Christ Associates.** "Dear Jesus, we ask Your special blessings on all members of Shepherds of Christ Associates. Continue to enlighten them regarding the very special privilege and responsibility you have given them as members of Your movement, Shepherds of Christ Associates. Draw them ever closer to Your Heart and to Your Mother's Heart. Allow them to more and more

realize the great and special love of Your Hearts for each of them as unique individuals. Give them the grace to respond to Your love and Mary's love with an increased love of their own. As they dwell in Your Heart and Mary's Heart, abundantly care for all their needs and those of their loved ones. We make our prayer through You to the Father, in the Holy Spirit, with Mary our Mother at our side. Amen."

12. **Prayer for the spiritual and financial success of the priestly newsletter.** "Father, we ask Your special blessings upon the priestly newsletter, Shepherds of Christ. We ask that You open the priest-readers to the graces You wish to give them through this chosen instrument of Your Son. We also ask that You provide for the financial needs of the newsletter and the Shepherds of Christ Associates. We make our prayer through Jesus, in the Holy Spirit, with Mary at our side. Amen."

13. **Prayer for all members of the human family.** "Heavenly Father, we ask Your blessings on all Your children the world over. Attend to all their needs. We ask Your special assistance for all those marginalized people, all those who are so neglected and forgotten. United with our Mother Mary, we make this petition to You through Jesus and in the Holy Spirit. Amen."

14. **Prayer to St. Michael and our Guardian Angels:**

    "St. Michael the Archangel, defend us in battle. Be our safeguard against the wickedness and snares of the devil. May God rebuke him, we humbly pray, and do thou, O prince of the heavenly hosts, by the power of God, cast into hell Satan and all the other evil spirits who prowl about the world seeking the ruin of souls. Amen."

    "Angel of God, my guardian dear, to whom God's love commits me here, ever this day be at my side, to light and guard, to rule and guide. Amen."

15. **Pause for silent, personal prayer.** This should last at least five minutes.

16. **Act of consecration to the Sacred Heart of Jesus and the Immaculate Heart of Mary.**

"Lord Jesus, Chief Shepherd of the flock, I consecrate myself to Your most Sacred Heart. From Your pierced Heart the Church was born, the Church You have called me, as a member of Shepherds of Christ Associates, to serve in a most special way. You reveal Your Heart as a symbol of Your love in all its aspects, including Your most special love for me, whom You have chosen as Your companion in this most important work. Help me to always love You in return. Help me to give myself entirely to You. Help me always to pour out my life in love of God and neighbor! Heart of Jesus, I place my trust in You!

"Dear Blessed Virgin Mary, I consecrate myself to your maternal and Immaculate Heart, this Heart which is symbol of your life of love. You are the Mother of my Savior. You are also my Mother. You love me with a most special love as a member of Shepherds of Christ Associates, a movement created by your Son as a powerful instrument for the renewal of the Church and the world. In a return of love, I give myself entirely to your motherly love and protection. You followed Jesus perfectly. You are His first and perfect disciple. Teach me to imitate you in the putting on of Christ. Be my motherly intercessor so that, through your Immaculate Heart, I may be guided to an ever closer union with the pierced Heart of Jesus, Chief Shepherd of the flock."

17. **Daily Prayers.** All members should say the Holy Spirit prayer daily and make the act of consecration daily. They should also pray the rosary each day. They are encouraged to use the other above prayers as time allows.

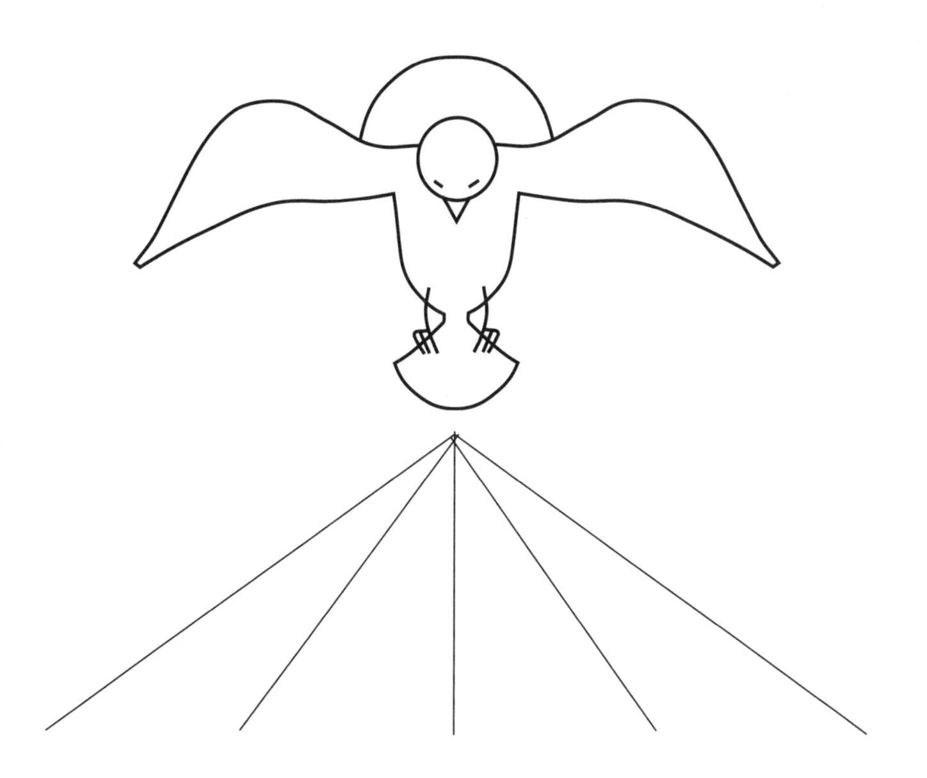

HOLY SPIRIT NOVENA

The Holy Spirit Novnea prayers are also available in Spanish, French, and Portuguese.

Shepherds of Christ Publications
China, Indiana

This book is published by Shepherds of Christ Publications, a subsidiary of Shepherds of Christ Ministries, a tax exempt religious public charitable association organized to foster devotion to the Two Hearts, the Sacred Heart of Jesus and the Immaculate Heart of Mary.

For additional copies, contact us:

Shepherds of Christ Ministries
P.O. Box 627
China, Indiana 47250 USA

(toll free number) 1-888-211-3041

(phone) 1-812-273-8405

(fax) 1-812-273-3182

http://www.SofC.org

Nihil Obstat:
Rev. Daniel J. Mahan, S.T.L.
Censor Librorum
Archdiocese of Indianapolis

Imprimatur:
Archbishop Daniel M. Buechlein, O.S.B.
Archbishop of Indianapolis
Archdiocese of Indianapolis

First Printing: March, 1999
Second Printing: April, 2000

DAILY NOVENA PRAYERS

Opening Prayer

In the name of the Father and of the Son and of the Holy Spirit. Amen.

Dear Father, we come to You in the name of Jesus, in union with Him in the Holy Sacrifice of the Mass, in the Holy Spirit. We come to You united to the Child Jesus of Good Health and the Infant of Prague. We come to You in the perfect, sinless heart of Our Mother Mary, asking her powerful intercession, uniting ourselves to her holy tears. We come to You united to all the angels and saints, and the souls in purgatory.

Prayer for Holy Spirit

We pray for an outpouring of the Holy Spirit on us, to be baptized by the Holy Spirit, that He will descend mightily on us as He did on the Apostles at Pentecost. That the Holy Spirit will transform us from fear to fearlessness and that He will give us courage to do all the Father is asking of us to help bring about the Reign of the Sacred Heart and the triumph of Mary's Immaculate Heart. We pray for the Holy Spirit to descend mightily on the Jesuits and the Poor Clares on the Shepherds of Christ leaders and members and on the whole Body of Christ and the world.

Protection by the Blood of Jesus

We pray that the Blood of Jesus will be spread on us, everyone in our families, and the Shepherds of Christ Movement, that we will be able to move steadfastly ahead and be protected from the evil one.

Healing

We pray for healing in body, mind, and soul and generational healing in ourselves, in all members in our families, and in all members of the Shepherds of Christ

Movement, the Jesuit Community, the Poor Clares, the Body of Christ, and the world.

Prayer for Strength and Light

We adore You, oh Holy Spirit. Give us strength, give us light, console us. We give ourselves entirely to You. Oh Spirit of light and grace, we want to only do the will of the Father. Enlighten us that we may live always in the Father's will.

Eternal Spirit fill us with Your Divine Wisdom that we may comprehend more fully insight into Your Divine Mysteries.

Give us lights, Oh Holy Spirit that we may know God. Work within the heart, the spiritual womb of the Virgin Mary, to form us more and more into the image of Jesus.

Prayer to Be One with God, Father, Son and Holy Spirit

We long for You, Oh Spirit of Light, we long to know God, we want to be one with Him, our Divine God. We want to be one with the Father, know Him as a Person most intimately. We want to know the beloved One, the Sacred Heart of Jesus, and live and dwell in Him at all times, every moment of our lives. We want to be one with You, Oh Spirit of Light, that You move in us in our every breath.

Prayer to Be One in Jesus

Let us experience life in the Sacred Heart of Jesus, so we can say as Saint Paul, "I have been crucified with Christ and yet I am alive; yet it is no longer I, but Christ living in me...." Let us live, united to the Mass, all through the day being one in Him. Let us be able to love and know in this elevated state of oneness with our God. We long for Thee, oh beauteous God, we love You, we love You, we love You. We praise You, worship You, honor You, adore You, and thank You, our beloved God, Father, Son, and Holy Spirit.

Prayer to Dwell in the Hearts of Jesus and Mary

We seek to be one in God, to live and dwell in the Hearts of Jesus and Mary, our little heaven on earth, to experience life in the all perfect, pure, sinless heart of our Mother. We want the Holy Spirit to move in us and to be united to Jesus as the Bridegroom of our souls and be a most perfect sacrifice offered to the Father at every moment as we unite in the Holy Sacrifice of the Mass around the world to help in the salvation of souls.

Prayer for the Holy Spirit and His Gifts

Come Holy Spirit, come, come into our hearts, inflame all people with the fire of Your love.

Leader: Send forth Your Spirit and all will be reborn.

All: And You will renew the face of the earth.

We pray for the seven gifts of the Holy Spirit, we ask for perfection in our souls to make us holy, holy souls likened to God.

Dear Holy Spirit, we give ourselves to You soul and body. We ask You to give us the Spirit of Wisdom, Understanding, Counsel, Fortitude, Knowledge, Piety, and Fear of the Lord.

Prayer for the Word Alive in Our Hearts

We know, dear Holy Spirit, the Word in His human nature was brought forth within the womb of the woman. We pray that His word will be brought forth in our hearts as He lives and dwells in us. We want the incarnation to go on in our lives. Dear Holy Spirit, work in us.

Little Prayers to the Holy Spirit

Dear Holy Spirit, help us not to be ignorant or indifferent or weak, help us to be strong with the love of God.

Dear Holy Spirit, please pray for our needs for us.

Dear Holy Spirit, help us to respect God and to avoid sin. Help us to live in the Father's will.

Dear Holy Spirit, help us to keep Your commandments and to respect authority. Help us to love all things as You will us to love them. Help us to want to pray and always serve God with the greatest love. Help us to know the truth. Help us to have the gift of faith, hope, and love. Help us to know what is right and what is wrong.

A Prayer for Intimacy with the Lamb, the Bridegroom of the Soul

Oh Lamb of God, Who take away the sins of the world, come and act on my soul most intimately. I surrender myself, as I ask for the grace to let go, to just be as I exist in You and You act most intimately on my soul. You are the Initiator. I am the soul waiting Your favors as You act in me. I love You. I adore You. I worship You. Come and possess my soul with Your Divine Grace, as I experience You most intimately.

FIRST WEEK MEDITATIONS NINE DAYS

1. **Romans 8:14-17**

   All who are guided by the Spirit of God are sons of God; for what you received was not the spirit of slavery to bring you back into fear; you received the Spirit of adoption, enabling us to cry out, 'Abba, Father!' The Spirit himself joins with our spirit to bear witness that we are children of God. And if we are children, then we are heirs, heirs of God and joint-heirs with Christ, provided that we share his suffering, so as to share his glory.

2. **Romans 8:5-9**

   Those who are living by their natural inclinations have their minds on the things human nature desires; those who live in the Spirit have their minds on spiritual things. And human nature has nothing to look forward to but death, while the Spirit looks forward to life and peace, because the outlook of disordered human nature is opposed to God, since it does not submit to God's Law, and indeed it cannot, and those who live by their natural inclinations can never be pleasing to God. You, however, live not by your natural inclinations, but by the Spirit, since the Spirit of God has made a home in you. Indeed, anyone who does not have the Spirit of Christ does not belong to him.

3. 1 John 4:12-16

No one has ever seen God, but as long as we love one another God remains in us and his love comes to its perfection in us. This is the proof that we remain in him and he in us, that he has given us a share in his Spirit. We ourselves have seen and testify that the Father sent his Son as Saviour of the world. Anyone who acknowledges that Jesus is the Son of God, God remains in him and he in God. We have recognised for ourselves, and put our faith in, the love God has for us. God is love, and whoever remains in love remains in God and God in him.

4. 1 John 4:17-21

Love comes to its perfection in us when we can face the Day of Judgement fearlessly, because even in this world we have become as he is. In love there is no room for fear, but perfect love drives out fear, because fear implies punishment and no one who is afraid has come to perfection in love. Let us love, then, because he first loved us. Anyone who says 'I love God' and hates his brother, is a liar, since whoever does not love the brother whom he can see cannot love God whom he has not seen. Indeed this is the commandment we have received from him, that whoever loves God, must also love his brother.

5. 1 John 4:7-11

My dear friends, let us love one another, since love is from God and everyone who loves is a child of God and knows God. Whoever fails to love does not know God, because God is love. This is the revelation of God's love for us, that God sent his only Son into the world that we might have life through him. Love consists in this: it is not we who loved God, but God loved us and sent his Son to expiate our sins. My dear friends, if God loved us so much, we too should love one another.

6. Acts of the Apostles 1:1-5

In my earlier work, Theophilus, I dealt with everything Jesus had done and taught from the beginning until the day he gave his instructions to the apostles he had chosen through the Holy Spirit, and was taken up to heaven. He had shown himself alive to them after his Passion by many demonstrations: for forty days he had continued to appear to them and tell them about the kingdom of God. While at table with them, he had told them not to leave Jerusalem, but to wait there for what the Father had promised. 'It is', he had said, 'what you have heard me speak about: John baptised with water but, not many days from now, you are going to be baptised with the Holy Spirit.'

7. Acts of the Apostles 1:6-9

Now having met together, they asked him, 'Lord, has the time come for you to restore the kingdom to Israel?' He replied, 'It is not for you to know times or dates that the Father has decided by his own authority, but you will receive the power of the Holy Spirit which will come on you, and then you will be my witnesses not only in Jerusalem but throughout Judaea and Samaria, and indeed to earth's remotest end.'

As he said this he was lifted up while they looked on, and a cloud took him from their sight.

8. Acts of the Apostles 1:12-14

So from the Mount of Olives, as it is called, they went back to Jerusalem, a short distance away, no more than a Sabbath walk; and when they reached the city they went to the upper room where they were staying; there were

Peter and John, James and Andrew, Philip and Thomas, Bartholomew and Matthew, James son of Alphaeus and Simon the Zealot, and Jude son of James. With one heart all these joined constantly in prayer, together with some women, including Mary the mother of Jesus, and with his brothers.

9. Acts of the Apostles 2:1-4

When Pentecost day came round, they had all met together, when suddenly there came from heaven a sound as of a violent wind which filled the entire house in which they were sitting; and there appeared to them tongues as of fire; these separated and came to rest on the head of each of them. They were all filled with the Holy Spirit and began to speak different languages as the Spirit gave them power to express themselves.

SECOND WEEK MEDITATIONS NINE DAYS

1. John 14:21-31

Whoever holds to my commandments and keeps them is the one who loves me; and whoever loves me will be loved by my Father, and I shall love him and reveal myself to him.'

Judas — not Judas Iscariot — said to him, 'Lord, what has happened, that you intend to show yourself to us and not to the world?' Jesus replied:

'Anyone who loves me will keep my word, and my Father will love him, and we shall come to him and make a home in him. Anyone who does not love me does not keep my words. And the word that you hear is not my own: it is the word of the Father who sent me. I have said these things to you while still with you; but the Paraclete, the Holy Spirit, whom the Father will send in my name, will teach you everything and remind you of all I have said to you. Peace I bequeath to you, my own peace I give you, a peace which the world cannot give, this is my gift to you. Do not let your hearts be troubled or afraid. You heard me say: I am going away and shall return. If you loved me you would be glad that I am going to the Father, for the Father is greater than I. I have told you this now, before it happens, so that when it does happen you may believe.

'I shall not talk to you much longer, because the prince of this world is on his way. He has no power over me, but the world must recognise that I love the Father and that I act just as the Father commanded. Come now, let us go.

2. John 17:11-26

I am no longer in the world, but they are in the world, and I am coming to you. Holy Father, keep those you have given me true to your name, so that they may be one like us. While I was with them, I kept those you had given me true to your name. I have watched over them and not one is lost except one who was destined to be lost, and this was to fulfil the scriptures. But now I am coming to you and I say these things in the world to share my joy with them to the full. I passed your word on to them, and the world hated them, because they belong to the world no more than I belong to the world. I am not asking you to remove them from the world, but to protect them from the Evil One. They do not belong to the world any more than I belong to the world. Consecrate them in the truth; your word is truth. As you sent me into the world, I have sent them into the world, and for their sake I consecrate myself so that they too may be consecrated in truth. I pray not only for these but also for those who through their teaching will come to believe in me. May they all be one, just as, Father, you are in me and I am in you, so that they also may be in us, so that the world may believe it was you who sent me. I have given them the glory you gave to me, that they may be one as we are one. With me in them and you in me, may they be so perfected in unity that the world will recognise that it was you who sent me and that you have loved them as you have loved me.

Father, I want those you have given me to be with me where I am, so that they may always see my glory which you have given me because you loved me before the foundation of the world. Father, Upright One, the world has not known you, but I have known you, and these have known that you have sent me. I have made your name known to them and will continue to make it known, so that the love with which you loved me may be in them, and so that I may be in them.

3. 1 Corinthians 15:20-28

In fact, however, Christ has been raised from the dead, as the first-fruits of all who have fallen asleep. As it was by one man that death came, so through one man has come the resurrection of the dead. Just as all die in Adam, so in Christ all will be brought to life; but all of them in their proper order: Christ the first-fruits, and next, at his coming, those who belong to him. After that will come the end, when he will hand over the kingdom to God the Father, having abolished every principality, every ruling force and power. For he is to be king until he has made his enemies his footstool, and the last of the enemies to be done away with is death, for he has put all things under his feet. But when it is said everything is subjected, this obviously cannot include the One who subjected everything to him. When everything has been subjected to him, then the Son himself will be subjected to the One who has subjected everything to him, so that God may be all in all.

4. Revelation 3:1-3, 12, 16-19

'Write to the angel of the church in Sardis and say, "Here is the message of the one who holds the seven spirits of God and the seven stars: I know about your behaviour: how you are reputed to be alive and yet are dead. Wake up; put some resolve into what little vigour you have left: it is dying fast. So far I have failed to notice anything in your behaviour that my God could possibly call perfect; remember how you first heard the message. Hold on to that. Repent! If you do not wake up, I shall come to you like a thief, and you will have no idea at what hour I shall come upon you.

Anyone who proves victorious I will make into a pillar in the sanctuary of my God, and it will stay there for ever; I will inscribe on it the name of my God and the name of the city of my God, the new Jerusalem which is coming down from my God in heaven, and my own new name as well.

'...but since you are neither hot nor cold, but only lukewarm, I will spit you out of my mouth. You say to yourself: I am rich, I have made a fortune and have everything I want, never realising that you are wretchedly and pitiably poor, and blind and naked too. I warn you, buy from me the gold that has been tested in the fire to make you truly rich, and white robes to clothe you and hide your shameful nakedness, and ointment to put on your eyes to enable you to see. I reprove and train those whom I love: so repent in real earnest.'

5. Revelation 5:9-14

They sang a new hymn: You are worthy to take the scroll and to break its seals, because you were sacrificed, and with your blood you bought people for God of every race, language, people and nation and made them a line of kings and priests for God, to rule the world.

In my vision, I heard the sound of an immense number of angels gathered round the throne and the living creatures and the elders; there were ten thousand times ten thousand of them and thousands upon thousands, loudly chanting:

Worthy is the Lamb that was sacrificed to receive power, riches, wisdom, strength, honour, glory and blessing. Then I heard all the living things in creation—everything that lives in heaven, and on earth, and under the earth, and in the sea, crying:

To the One seated on the throne and to the Lamb, be

all praise, honour, glory and power, for ever and ever.

And the four living creatures said, 'Amen'; and the elders prostrated themselves to worship.

6. Revelation 7:14-17

I answered him, 'You can tell me, sir.' Then he said, 'These are the people who have been through the great trial; they have washed their robes white again in the blood of the Lamb. That is why they are standing in front of God's throne and serving him day and night in his sanctuary; and the One who sits on the throne will spread his tent over them. They will never hunger or thirst again; sun and scorching wind will never plague them, because the Lamb who is at the heart of the throne will be their shepherd and will guide them to springs of living water; and God will wipe away all tears from their eyes.'

7. Revelation 12:1-8

Now a great sign appeared in heaven: a woman, robed with the sun, standing on the moon, and on her head a crown of twelve stars. She was pregnant, and in labour, crying aloud in the pangs of childbirth. Then a second sign appeared in the sky: there was a huge red dragon with seven heads and ten horns, and each of the seven heads crowned with a coronet. Its tail swept a third of the stars from the sky and hurled them to the ground, and the dragon stopped in front of the woman as she was at the point of giving birth, so that it could eat the child as soon as it was born. The woman was delivered of a boy, the son who was to rule all the nations with an iron sceptre, and the child was taken straight up to God and to his throne, while the woman escaped into the desert, where God had prepared a place for her to be looked after for twelve hundred and sixty days.

And now war broke out in heaven, when Michael with his angels attacked the dragon. The dragon fought back with his angels, but they were defeated and driven out of heaven.

8. Revelation 14:1-7

Next in my vision I saw Mount Zion, and standing on it the Lamb who had with him a hundred and forty-four thousand people, all with his name and his Father's name written on their foreheads. I heard a sound coming out of heaven like the sound of the ocean or the roar of thunder; it was like the sound of harpists playing their harps. There before the throne they were singing a new hymn in the presence of the four living creatures and the elders, a hymn that could be learnt only by the hundred and forty-four thousand who had been redeemed from the world. These are the sons who have kept their virginity and not been defiled with women; they follow the Lamb wherever he goes; they, out of all people, have been redeemed to be the first-fruits for God and for the Lamb. No lie was found in their mouths and no fault can be found in them.

Then I saw another angel, flying high overhead, sent to announce the gospel of eternity to all who live on the earth, every nation, race, language and tribe. He was calling, 'Fear God and glorify him, because the time has come for him to sit in judgement; worship the maker of heaven and earth and sea and the springs of water.'

Revelation 19: 7-8

let us be glad and joyful and give glory to God, because this is the time for the marriage of the Lamb. His bride is ready, and she has been able to dress herself in dazzling white linen, because her linen is made of the good deeds of the saints.'

9. Revelation 21:1-10

Then I saw a new heaven and a new earth; the first heaven and the first earth had disappeared now, and there was no longer any sea. I saw the holy city, the new Jerusalem, coming down out of heaven from God, prepared as a bride dressed for her husband. Then I heard a loud voice call from the throne, 'Look, here God lives among human beings. He will make his home among them; they will be his people, and he will be their God, God-with-them. He will wipe away all tears from their eyes; there will be no more death, and no more mourning or sadness or pain. The world of the past has gone.'

Then the One sitting on the throne spoke. 'Look, I am making the whole of creation new. Write this, "What I am saying is trustworthy and will come true." ' Then he said to me, 'It has already happened. I am the Alpha and the Omega, the Beginning and the End. I will give water from the well of life free to anybody who is thirsty; anyone who proves victorious will inherit these things; and I will be his God and he will be my son. But the legacy for cowards, for those who break their word, or worship obscenities, for murderers and the sexually immoral, and for sorcerers, worshippers of false gods or any other sort of liars, is the second death in the burning lake of sulphur.'

One of the seven angels that had the seven bowls full of the seven final plagues came to speak to me and said, 'Come here and I will show you the bride that the Lamb has married.' In the spirit, he carried me to the top of a very high mountain, and showed me Jerusalem, the holy city, coming down out of heaven from God.

Revelation 22:20

The one who attests these things says: I am indeed coming soon.

Amen; come, Lord Jesus.

Scriptural quotations are taken from
The New Jerusalem Bible, Doubleday & Co.
Imprimatur granted by Cardinal Hume.

A Song from Jesus

by Rita Ring

REFRAIN

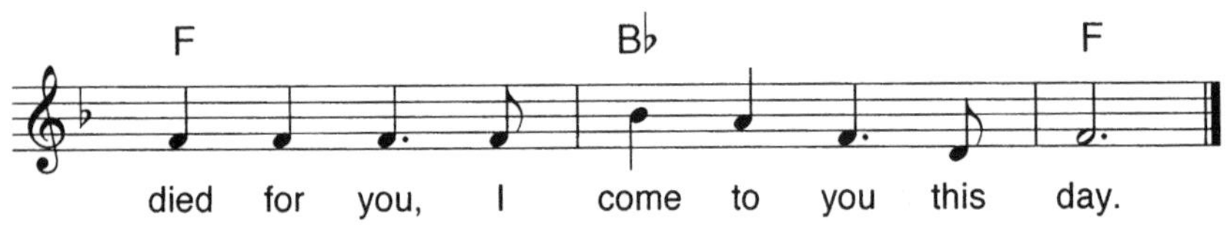

VERSES

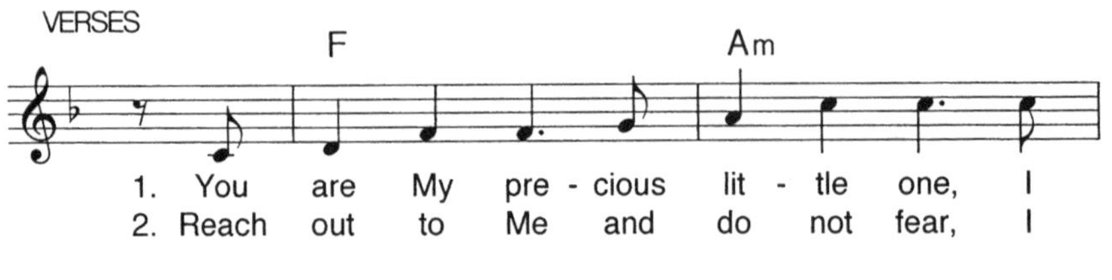

Prayer to the Father
May 16, 1998

My Father,

With my whole heart I desire to consecrate the whole world to the Sacred Heart of Jesus and the Immaculate Heart of Mary. I wish with my whole being for the salvation of souls and that man live according to Thy Holy Will. I pray my Father that we may be one in You and Your Son Jesus and the Holy Spirit that we may intercede to You for this cause.

It is this burning desire within my soul to spread the consecration to the far ends of the earth, that the cries of Your children are cries of glory and honor and adoration, praising God as their God.

My Father, at this moment a soul hangs on the edge of death. For all eternity they will go to a place. It is not the plot of this soul as it trods this barren land to decide on the edge of death. You created us that we would grow in our oneness with God, that we would mature more and more in our image and likeness to God.

And so My Father, I pray with every cell in my body for this earth. In the name of Your Son Jesus I consecrate all the souls of this earth to the Sacred Heart and the Immaculate Heart of Mary in the Holy Spirit in union with the Holy sacrifice of the Mass with all the angels and saints and the souls in Purgatory.

I beg You Father for mercy.

I beg You Father for assistance.

I beg You Father to help us to spread this consecration to the far ends of the earth.

Please help us. We are helpless little ones coming in the heart of our Mother, bleeding from our wounds and our sins.

Your Son, Jesus Christ, shed the last drop of His Blood for the salvation of mankind. We wish to unite in this sacrifice, sacramentally made present in the Mass all over the world at every moment. Help us to make reparation to You for the sins of men.

Please my Father, help us. Held in the heart of Mary and the Heart of Jesus we come as the children of Eve to beg for the Reign of the Sacred Heart and the Triumph of Mary's heart. Look upon our love, Your shepherds in the Shepherds of

Christ, our sacrifices and devotion to You Our Beloved Father. Come by the means of the Holy Spirit and sanctify us and make us whole, that we are one in Your Son Jesus, praying to You, Father, in the name of Your Son Jesus in the Holy Spirit united with all the angels and saints, in the heart of Mary. We beg for help for special intentions concerning the Movement. We beg for help to reach the Churches to give these prayers of Jesus to them, to reach the schools and the family. Help we cry as poor banished children of Eve. Help us Father to do this work the Good Shepherd has entrusted to us. Help us to be one in You that we act as intercessors to help this world to be turned to God as their God, loving, honoring and adoring Him as the Lord of Host is truly present on His throne.

We are Your children Father, we implore You to answer our prayer.

We love You, we worship You, we adore You, we thank you and we sing from the bottom of our hearts, Holy God we Praise Your Name. Alleluia

end of prayer to the Father

A Prayer before the Holy Sacrifice of the Mass

Let me be a holy sacrifice and unite with God in the sacrament of His greatest love.

I want to be one in Him in this act of love, where He gives Himself to me and I give myself as a sacrifice to Him. Let me be a holy sacrifice as I become one with Him in this my act of greatest love to Him.

Let me unite with Him more, that I may more deeply love

Him. May I help make reparation to His adorable Heart and the heart of His Mother, Mary. With greatest love, I offer myself to You and pray that You will accept my sacrifice of greatest love. I give myself to You and unite in Your gift of Yourself to me. Come and possess my soul.

Cleanse me, strengthen me, heal me. Dear Holy Spirit act in the heart of Mary to make me more and more like Jesus.

Father, I offer this my sacrifice, myself united to Jesus in the Holy Spirit to You. Help me to love God more deeply in this act of my greatest love.

Give me the grace to grow in my knowledge, love and service of You and for this to be my greatest participation in the Mass. Give me the greatest graces to love You so deeply in this Mass, You who are so worthy of my love.

- *Mass Book*, December 27, 1995

Prayer for Union with Jesus

Come to me, Lord, and possess my soul. Come into my heart and permeate my soul. Help me to sit in silence with You and let You work in my heart.

I am Yours to possess. I am Yours to use. I want to be selfless and only exist in You. Help me to spoon out all that is me and be an empty vessel ready to be filled by You. Help me to die to myself and live only for You. Use me as You will. Let me never draw my attention back to myself. I only want to operate as You do, dwelling within me.

I am Yours, Lord. I want to have my life in You. I want to do the will of the Father. Give me the strength to put aside the world and let You operate my very being. Help me to act as You desire. Strengthen me against the distractions of the devil to take me from Your work.

When I worry, I have taken my focus off of You and placed it on myself. Help me not to give in to the promptings of others to change what in my heart You are making very clear to me. I worship You, I adore You and I love You. Come and dwell in me now.

- *God's Blue Book,* January 17, 1994

Shepherds of Christ Prayer Cards and Books

Contact us to obtain these for your parish, school, friends, or loved ones.

Consecration to Mary

Dear Mary, my holy mother, I love you so much and I give you my heart. Help me to love God. Help me to love my neighbor as a child of God. Help me to love myself as a child of God.

Amen

Consecration to Jesus

Dear Sacred Heart of Jesus, I love You so much and I give You my heart. Help me to love God. Help me to love my neighbor as a child of God. Help me to love myself as a child of God.

Amen

Rita's Brother, Fr. Joe Robinson's Homily Books

Priestly Newsletter Books

Tell My People

Reponse to God's Love

Response In Christ

Shepherds of Christ Associates Prayer Manuals

English

Spanish

French

Portuguese

Italian

Polish

Holy Spirit Novena

English Spanish French Portuguese Polska

Mass Book

Parents & Children's Rosary Book

Red Rosary Book

Blue Book 12

Blue Book 13

Blue Book 14

All of the books shown here are available from Shepherds of Christ Ministries. Please share these with your friends and family.

We give our hearts to Jesus and Mary with you in love!

- Shepherds of Christ

Open Anywhere

Blue Book 1 Blue Book 2 Blue Book 3 Blue Book 4

Blue Book 5 BB's 6A, 6B, 6C Blue Book 7

Blue Book 8 Blue Book 9 Blue Book 10 Blue Book 11

Shepherds of Christ Ministries Order Form

(You may copy this page to order)

Send Order To:
Shepherds of Christ Ministries
P.O. Box 627 China, Indiana 47250 USA

Fr. Joe Robinson	Qty	Total $
The Word Alive in Our Hearts ($5)	____	______
Focusing on the Word - Cycle B ($10)	____	______
Feed My Soul - Cycle C ($10)	____	______
Steadfast to the Son - Cycle A ($10)	____	______
Reflect on the Word - Cycle B ($10)	____	______
Centered in Christ - Cycle C ($10)	____	______
Inspired To Be Genuine - Cycle A ($10)	____	______
By God Through Me - Cycle B ($10)	____	______
Fr. Carter and Rita Ring		
Shepherds of Christ - Volume 1 ($15)	____	______
Shepherds of Christ - Volume 2 ($10)	____	______
Shepherds of Christ - Volume 3 ($10)	____	______
Tell My People ($10)	____	______
Response to God's Love ($10)	____	______
Response in Christ ($10)	____	______
APOSTLES MANUALS ($15)	____	______
Prayer Manuals ($0.50)	____	______
Holy Spirit Novena ($3)	____	______
Mass Book ($12)	____	______
Parents and Children's Rosary Book ($10)	____	______
Red Rosary Book ($8)	____	______
God's Blue Books: 1 to 15 ($6 each) ______	____	______
Blue Books #'s: ______ ______ ______ ______		______
Totals:	____	______

Name: ____

Address: ____

City: __________________ State: ___________ Zip: __________

To Order or For Information Call Toll free USA: 1-888-211-3041
or on the Internet: www.sofc.org

We pray for you from our Church in China,
24 hours a day before the exposed Eucharist.
We pray eight-day retreats for you every month.